LORD LOTHIAN AND ANGLO-AMERICAN
RELATIONS, 1900-1940

HISTORY OF INTERNATIONAL RELATIONS, DIPLOMACY AND INTELLIGENCE

Series Editor

Katherine A.S. Sibley

St. Joseph's University

VOLUME 13

LORD LOTHIAN AND ANGLO-AMERICAN RELATIONS, 1900-1940

Edited by

Priscilla Roberts

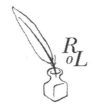

DORDRECHT
2010

This book is printed on acid-free paper.

Library of Congres Cataloging-in-Publication Data

ISSN   1874-0294

ISBN13   978-90-8979-034-7 – hardbound

ISBN13   978-90-8979-033-0 – paperback

CONTENTS

TABLE OF CONTENTS

PREFACE

This volume is the outcome of a shared interest on the part of its various authors in the challenging, chameleonic, and sometimes enigmatic figure of Philip Kerr, the eleventh Marquess of Lothian. Over a period of years, assorted members of the group who sometimes referred to themselves as the 'Lothian Flying Circus' met up in shifting configurations at several conferences in Wales, Scotland, and the United States, to try to elucidate two often elusive questions: what were Lothian's beliefs and views on domestic and international questions; and what impact did he have upon the politics of his time? The chapters included in this book try to provide at least a partial answer to these questions.

Thanks are due to all those who attended presentations of and commented on earlier versions of these chapters, at a colloquium on Lord Lothian held at the Institute for Advanced Studies in the Humanities of Edinburgh University, in May 2001; the annual meetings of the Society for Historians of American Foreign Relations at the University of Georgia at Athens, in June 2002, and George Washington University, Washington, DC, in June 2003; the annual conference of the British Association of American Studies at the University of Aberystwyth, Wales, in April 2003; and the annual conference of the Transatlantic Studies Association at the University of Dundee in June 2008.

The editor's research for this project has been made possible by several generous grants from the University of Hong Kong: a Universitas 21 Fellowship to the University of Edinburgh in 2001; two grants from the Committee on Research and Conference Grants, to attend conferences in the United States and Britain; and a Small Projects Grant, to complete the research and writing on this project. Throughout, Professor Rhodri Jeffreys Jones of Edinburgh University has taken a benign interest in this undertaking, and his introductions have been responsible for the inclusion in this book of chapters by several contributors.

The staff of the historical reading room in the National Archives of Scotland in Edinburgh were immensely helpful in facilitating research in the very extensive papers of the Eleventh Marquess of Lothian. The archivists in the manuscripts reading room at the National Library of Scotland were equally helpful in assisting the editor to navigate through their assorted collections relating to John Buchan (the first Lord Tweedsmuir). Colin Harris and his colleagues at the Bodleian Library, Oxford University, were exceptionally kind in helping the editor to use the papers of the Round Table group and those individuals associated with it. For several years, Mary Bone and her colleagues at the Royal Institute of Affairs at Chatham House have made heroic efforts to guide the editor through that organization's massive archival holdings.

Thanks are due to the Right Honourable Michael Ancram, thirteenth Marquess of Lothian, for permission to quote from the Eleventh Marquess of Lothian's unpublished writings. The twenty-ninth Earl of Crawford and Balcarres very kindly permitted the use of quotations from a letter by the twenty-seventh Earl and letters by Sir Ronald Lindsay. The Harvard Business School allowed the use of excerpts from the unpublished papers of Thomas W. Lamont. The use of quotations from letters by John Buchan, 1st Lord Tweedsmuir, to his brother was permitted by A. P. Watt Ltd. on behalf of Jean, Lady Tweedsmuir, The Lord Tweedsmuir, and Sally, Lady Tweedsmuir, and by the Trustees of the National Library of Scotland. Jane McGowan and the National Library of Australia, Canberra, graciously permitted the use of extracts from the diary of Richard, Lord Casey. The Library and Archives Canada granted permission for the use of material from a letter of Sir Robert Borden.

INFORMATION ON CONTRIBUTORS

Gavin Bailey is a research student at Dundee University, completing a Ph.D. thesis on Anglo-American aviation supply collaboration during the Second World War. He has a particular interest in locating technically-informed military history within the broader context of diplomatic and economic statecraft.

David P. Billington, Jr., received a doctorate in history from the University of Texas at Austin in 1995 and is an independent scholar. His books include *Lothian: Philip Kerr and the Quest for World Order* (2006) and (with David P. Billington, Sr.) *Power, Speed, and Form: Engineers and the Making of the Twentieth Century* (2006).

Greg Kennedy is a Professor of Strategic Foreign Policy at the Defence Studies Department, King's College, London, based at the Joint Services Command and Staff College in Shrivenham. He received his Ph.D. from the University of Alberta in 1998. Before coming to England in 2000 he taught at the Royal Military College of Canada, in Kingston, Ontario, Canada, for both the History Department and the War Studies Department, developing the WS500 Strategic Thought and Thinkers course for the War Studies online M.A. program. He is an adjunct assistant professor of that university. He is the author of an award winning monograph, *Anglo-American Strategic Relations and the Far East, 1933-1939* (2002), and has published widely internationally on strategic foreign policy issues, maritime defense, disarmament, military education, diplomacy, and intelligence. He has published numerous edited books in the Frank Cass/Taylor and Francis series, including (with Keith Neilson) *Far Flung Lines: Studies in Imperial Defence in Honour of Donald Mackenzie Schurman* (1997); *The Merchant Marine in International Affairs, 1850-1950* (2000); (with Keith Neilson) *Incidents and International Relations: People, Personalities and Power* (2002); (with Keith Neilson) *Military Education: Past, Present, and Future* (2006); *Britain's Naval Strategy East of Suez, 1900-2000: Influences and Action* (2007); and *Imperial Defence, 1856-1956: The Old World Order* (2008). His latest book, co-edited with Andrew Dorman, is *War and Diplomacy: From World War I to the War on Terrorism* (2008).

Keith Neilson is a professor in the History Department of the Royal Military College of Canada, Kingston, Ontario, Canada. He has written extensively on British strategic foreign policy, particularly with regard to Russia and the Soviet Union. His most recent books are *Britain, Soviet*

Russia and the Collapse of the Versailles Order, 1919-1939 (2005) and (with T.G. Otte) *The Permanent Under-Secretary for Foreign Affairs, 1854-1946* (2009). At present, Professor Neilson is working on Anglo-American-Canadian relations and the First World War and a study of the inter-war British Foreign Office.

Priscilla Roberts is an associate professor of history at the University of Hong Kong. She is the author or editor of numerous books on diplomatic and international history, including *The Cold War* (2000); *Window on the Forbidden City: The Beijing Diaries of David Bruce, 1973-1974* (2001); *Behind the Bamboo Curtain: China, Vietnam, and the World Beyond Asia* (2006); (with He Peiqun) *Bonds Across Borders: Women, China, and International Relations in the Modern World* (2007); *Bridging the Sino-American Divide: American Studies with Chinese Characteristics* (2007); *Encyclopedia of the Cold War* (2007); and *Encyclopedia of the Arab-Israeli Conflict* (2008). She is currently working on a biography of the banker Frank Altschul, and a study of Anglo-American think tanks and China policy.

Dr. J. Simon Rofe is a lecturer in the Centre for American Studies in the Department of Politics & International Relations at the University of Leicester. His research interests focus on U.S. foreign relations and diplomacy in the twentieth century, with a specific focus on presidential post-war planning. Amongst his most recent publications is *Franklin D. Roosevelt's Foreign Policy and the Welles Mission* (2007).

Melanie Sayers is currently in her fourth year of Ph.D. study at the University of Edinburgh. Her thesis aims to explore the involvement of Philip Kerr in the Irish problem, particularly between the years 1916-1921 when he was private secretary to the British Prime Minister David Lloyd George. She hopes to determine not only the ways in which Kerr was involved but also his influence on the settlement that was finally reached. This forms part of a wider interest in Anglo-Irish politics during this period, including the attempts to solve the Irish problem through self-government and the events that led to the partition of Northern Ireland in 1921.

INTRODUCTION

THE MAKING OF AN ATLANTICIST: PHILIP KERR 1882-1921

PRISCILLA ROBERTS

When Philip Kerr, eleventh Marquess of Lothian and the British ambassador to the United States, died in December 1940, tributes to his work in Washington poured in from both Britain and the United States. Prime Minister Winston Churchill, for most of the 1930s his political opponent over appeasement, gave generous praise in the House of Commons to his accomplishments in winning American support for the Destroyers-for-Bases deal and laying the foundations of what would become Lend-Lease. Lothian's obsequies themselves served to demonstrate Anglo-American solidarity. He received a state funeral in Washington Cathedral, attended by numerous government officials and an impressive array of his many influential American friends and acquaintances; his ashes were temporarily interred at Arlington Cemetery, to be returned to Scotland on an American destroyer when the war ended, and a memorial service was held at Westminster Abbey. Ironically, although John Buchan, the novelist-politician who was then governor general of Canada, had encouraged him to accept the position of ambassador, and Lothian had been personally confident he could handle Anglo-American relations at a highly critical juncture, most Foreign Office functionaries had bitterly opposed his appointment, which went through only on the insistence of Lothian's friend Lord Halifax, the British Foreign Secretary. Within official circles there were pronounced fears that his past support for the appeasement of Germany made him an inappropriate candidate. The tributes to Lothian were not merely an instance of *de mortuis nil nisi bonum*. As some critics, including the youthful John Wheeler-Bennett, whose original horror at the appointment changed dramatically when he worked under Lothian in Washington, had the generosity to admit, well before his death he had triumphantly confounded his critics. Even Sir Robert Vansittart of the Foreign Office, to whom Lothian—who in his view "combined both the looks and the essence of purity"—was for most of the 1930s a *bête noire*, "rarely right by accident in Europe," later wrote that he "spoke with early

P. Roberts (ed.), Lord Lothian and Anglo-American Relations, 1900-1940, 1-43.

authority on the United States, where he became the greatest of all our Ambassadors."[1]

Lothian's success represented a surprisingly triumphant climax to a career that had otherwise failed to fulfil his early promise. It was perhaps revealing that on hearing of Lothian's death his old friend Leo Amery, a former secretary of state for the dominions and colonies, wrote: "He did a wonderful piece of work, though I imagine the most difficult part of it was done. Altogether a very full and valuable life, though somehow not quite all that his sheer intellectual ability might have attained."[2] The eldest—after his brother's wartime death the only—son of adoring parents, with three equally admiring sisters, the strikingly handsome and athletic Philip Kerr bore the burden of his family's and friends' high expectations, privately confessing that "once you have got a reputation ... it is not nice to be beaten, & whether you like it or not you have to keep your shoulder to the wheel."[3] A first in modern history at New College, Oxford, followed by recruitment to Lord Milner's 'Kindergarten' of bright young men who implemented South Africa's post-Boer War reconstruction, won him influential imperialist patrons, including Milner and his successor as governor, Lord Selborne, son-in-law of the British Prime Minister Lord Salisbury. Lady Selborne, conscious that Kerr would eventually inherit a peerage and automatically sit in the House of Lords, recommended he begin a political career by contesting a parliamentary seat, a course Kerr repeatedly rejected, apparently finding partisan rough-and-tumble uncongenial.[4] His preferred *modus operandi* was to influence others, through journalism, as a trusted aide, or by private contacts with elite figures. On leaving South Africa in 1910, he became editor of *The Round Table*, a journal his Kindergarten colleagues established to promote closer

---

[1] Buchan to J. Walter Buchan, 27 April 1939, ACC 11627/83, Tweedsmuir Papers, National Library of Scotland, Edinburgh; David Reynolds, *Lord Lothian and Anglo-American Relations, 1939-1940* (Philadelphia: Transactions of the American Philosophical Society, 1983), 2-8, 58; Alexander Cadogan, *The Diaries of Sir Alexander Cadogan O.M. 1938-1945*, ed. David Dilks (London: Cassell, 1971), 130, 154; Oliver Harvey, *The Diplomatic Diaries of Oliver Harvey 1937-1940*, ed. John Harvey (London: Collins, 1970), 221, 258-259, 274; Sir John Wheeler-Bennett, *Special Relationships: America in Peace and War* (London: Macmillan, 1975), 65-68; Robert Vansittart, *The Mist Procession: The Autobiography of Lord Vansittart* (London: Hutchinson, 1958), 254-255.
[2] Leo Amery, diary entry, 12 December 1940, in *The Empire at Bay: The Leo Amery Diaries 1929-1945*, eds. John Barnes and David Nicholson (London: Hutchinson, 1988), 668.
[3] Kerr to David Kerr, 12 August 1906, GD 40/17/454/39, Papers of the Eleventh Marquess of Lothian [hereafter Lothian Papers], Scottish National Archives, Edinburgh.
[4] Maud Selborne to Lionel Curtis, 6 January 1908, GD 40/17/456/6, Lothian Papers.

integration within the British Empire. Its editors generally took an affirmative view of moderate state intervention to enhance both social justice and national efficiency, urging labor and capital to cooperate in both their own best interests and those of the broader community. Plagued since Oxford by serious religious doubts, Kerr ultimately abandoned his original Roman Catholicism for Christian Science, a faith he adopted in 1914 at the instigation of Nancy Astor, the American-born wife of Waldorf (later Viscount) Astor, a woman who like Kerr had for years succumbed to periodic nervous collapses, and to whom Kerr remained platonically devoted for almost three decades, while becoming her husband's close friend and political associate.[5]

In 1916 Kerr became Liberal Prime Minister David Lloyd George's personal secretary, which he remained until 1921, advising his chief on foreign affairs in particular and wielding substantial influence. This position probably represented the peak of Kerr's pre-ambassadorial power, albeit one observer wryly commented how, on occasion, "Kerr pumps things into [Lloyd George] and he seems to agree and then he goes and does the opposite." Some even suspected the Prime Minister of using association with the highminded Kerr and Astor as "virtuous window dressing," while in practice he followed the counsel of less principled cronies.[6] Lloyd George's secretary and mistress Frances Stevenson, who thought Kerr "the most Christ-like man I have ever known," later recalled that he left Lloyd George "because he felt he was becoming a slave, deprived of freedom both of thought and action. He had a hard struggle to get away, for D. [Lloyd George] fascinated & dominated him."[7]

---

[5] Alice Roosevelt Longworth once quipped of his change of faith that it was "[m]erely a matter of swapping Blessed Virgins in midstream." One of the Astors' sons later suggested that, while his mother claimed "that Philip was indispensable to my father," the latter, "not unreasonably, sometimes found it a bore having Philip Kerr round the house the whole time." Wheeler-Bennett, *Special Relationships*, 48; Michael Astor, *Tribal Feeling* (London: Murray, 1963), 144.

[6] Thomas Jones to Eirene Theodora Jones, 18 April 1917, and Jones, diary entry, 7 December 1917, in Thomas Jones, *Whitehall Diary*, ed. Keith Middlemas, 3 vols. (London: Oxford University Press, 1969-1971), 1:30, 40. In April 1917 C. P. Scott, editor of the *Manchester Guardian*, found Kerr "quite a good ... Scotch Liberal" who was "eager 'to save [Lloyd George's] soul' for Liberalism" by surrounding him with the right "atmosphere." C. P. Scott, *The Political Diaries of C. P. Scott*, ed. Trevor Wilson (Ithaca, NY: Cornell University Press, 1970), 278.

[7] Frances Stevenson, *Lloyd George: A Diary*, ed. A. J. P. Taylor (London: Hutchinson, 1971), 214, 287. As early as April 1917 Kerr told Thomas Jones: "You hate and love [Lloyd George] in turns." Jones to Eirene Jones, 18 April 1917, in Jones, *Whitehall Diary*, 1:30.

Kerr returned only briefly to journalism, but throughout the interwar years wrote and spoke prolifically on those political issues of interest to him, his favorite topics above all international relations, followed by efforts to devise interventionist but non-socialist solutions to Britain's economic and social problems. Kerr did so as one of a "tightly knit group" of individuals within the British polity, described by the biographer of one of them, the economist and editor Walter Layton, as "Liberal radicals who exercised a major influence on public opinion" during the 1920s and 1930s. Most voted Liberal, but they were "apolitical in the sense that they came together to work out practical policies rather than to write party manifestos." They "met each other constantly in Whitehall, in the Westminster lobbies, in clubs, in Fleet Street, the City, and at the ancient universities." Prominent among them were the economists Layton, John Maynard Keynes, Hubert Henderson, and Dennis Robertson; former civil servants, notably Sir Arthur Salter, William Beveridge, and Josiah Stamp; businessmen and bankers with a social conscience, including Ernest Simon, Seebohm Rowntree, and Kerr's close friend, Robert H. Brand; political philosophers, including Gilbert Murray, Graham Wallace, and Ramsay Muir; and Kerr and other idealistic politicians, notably Philip Noel Baker and Charles Masterman. The majority served as civil servants during the First World War, "acquir[ing] in wartime Whitehall a conviction that government could and should intervene to deal with economic crises and to tackle social problems."

> Many had become knowledgeable in how to get things done in Whitehall and Parliament. They had become skilled operators as well as penetrating thinkers. Moreover, they were ready to spend a lot of time on public affairs so as to ensure that their ideas received full publicity and political support. They looked upon themselves as initiators with the advantage of being free of the restraints placed on the higher Civil Service.[8]

Between the wars Kerr, with a background in high-minded journalism, and excellent political connections to both the Liberal Party with which he was formally affiliated and to reformist Conservatives, was very much at home within this group.

From 1925 until he became ambassador in 1939 Kerr was secretary to the Rhodes Trust, a position so congenial to him he retained it even after inheriting his peerage in 1930. Having hitched his wagon to Lloyd George's guttering star just before the Liberal Party entered its interwar

---

[8] David Hubback, *No Ordinary Press Baron: A Life of Walter Layton* (London: Weidenfeld and Nicolson, 1985), 64-65.

decline, Kerr's chances of political advancement were limited, though well into the 1930s he worked diligently drafting various Liberal manifestos and policy statements. After becoming a peer, he served briefly in the National Government as Chancellor of the Duchy of Lancaster and under secretary of state for India, before resigning over the 1932 Ottawa Agreements imposing heavy tariffs on non-empire British imports. For much of the 1930s Lothian attempted to resolve the growing Anglo-German and Anglo-Italian antagonism, efforts that eventually damaged his reputation and compromised his political effectiveness.[9]

According to Churchill, the pre-ambassadorial Lothian conveyed "the impression of high intellectual and aristocratic detachment from vulgar affairs. Airy, viewy, aloof, dignified, censorious," albeit one who "in a light and gay manner" was "always ... good company."[10] (Though Lady Beatrice

---

[9] The major source for Lothian's career is J. R. M. Butler, *Lord Lothian (Philip Kerr) 1882-1940* (London: Macmillan, 1960). A useful memoir by another Kindergarten member is Edward Grigg's introduction to Royal Institute of International Affairs, *The American Speeches of Lord Lothian* (London: Oxford University Press, 1941). The most recent full-length study of Lothian is David P. Billington, Jr., *Lothian: Philip Kerr and the Quest for World Order* (Westport, CT: Praeger, 2006). Two collections of essays focus on him, John Turner, ed., *The Larger Idea: Lord Lothian and the Problem of National Sovereignty* (London: Historians Press, 1988); and Giulio Guderzo, ed., *Lord Lothian: Una vita per la pace* (Pavia, Italy: University of Pavia, 1986). Particular aspects of Lothian's career are covered in Walter Nimocks, *Milner's Young Men: The 'Kindergarten' in Edwardian Imperial Affairs* (London: Hodder and Stoughton, 1970); John Kendle, *The Round Table Movement and Imperial Union* (Toronto: University of Toronto Press, 1975); Alexander C. May, "The Round Table, 1910-66" (D.Phil. thesis, Oxford University, 1995); John Turner, *Lloyd George's Secretariat* (Cambridge: Cambridge University Press, 1980); Reynolds, *Lord Lothian*; Stefan Schieren, *Vom Weltreich zum Weltstaat: Philip Kerrs (Lord Lothian) Weg vom Imperialisten zum Internationalisten, 1905-1925* (London: Lothian Foundation, 1996); Andrea Bosco, *Lord Lothian: Un Pioniere del federalismo, 1882-1940* (Milan, Italy: Jaca Books, 1996); and Kathryn Segal Patterson, "The Decline of Dominance: India and the Careers of Lionel Curtis, Philip Lothian, and Reginald Coupland" (Ph.D. dissertation, Bryn Mawr College, 1989). Recent works in which Lothian is an important protagonist include Nicholas John Cull, *Selling War: The British Propaganda Campaign Against American "Neutrality" in World War II* (New York: Oxford University Press, 1995); James Fox, *The Langhorne Sisters* (London: Granta, 1998); Norman Rose, *The Cliveden Set: Portrait of an Exclusive Fraternity* (London: Jonathan Cape, 2000); and Richard S. Grayson, *Liberals, International Relations and Appeasement* (London: Frank Cass, 2001). An ever-growing number of scholarly articles, some at least generated by the Lothian Foundation's recent revival of interest in his life and legacy, also focus on Lothian.

[10] Winston Churchill, *The Second World War*, 6 vols. (London: Cassell, 1948-1954), 2:490. Robert H. Brand, who knew Lothian well, challenged certain aspects of Churchill's characterization, arguing that Lothian was neither "dignified" nor "censorious," nor did he ever exhibit "aristocratic detachment." In his *Dictionary of National Biography* article on (continued)

Cecil, daughter of the Marquess of Salisbury, who rejected proposals of marriage from both Kerr and his great friend, fellow Kindergarten member and enthusiast for imperial federation Lionel Curtis, was congratulated on thus escaping "two of the greatest bores in the British Empire."[11]) According to A. L. Kennedy of the *Times* newspaper, within a few years of inheriting his peerage Lothian had assumed "quite the appearance of an elder statesman of the Liberal type," and:

> The part of an 18th century nobleman suits him v. well. He has a good presence, tho' a trifle portly, a fine intellect, cultured tastes & an extreme interest in politics. ... [O]ne gets into a keen political discussion within 2 minutes of meeting. He takes a long-term view, & is better at general policy than the next step, but is acute, remarkably well informed, & has met everybody.[12]

The aficionado of detective fiction is tempted to speculate whether Dorothy L. Sayers, like Lothian a graduate of Oxford who retained strong loyalties to that university, and who shared his interest in religious issues and high-minded politics, encountered the fair-haired, classically handsome peer in the first half of the 1930s, when both were active in Oxford affairs. If so, might he have helped to inspire the later metamorphosis of her originally frivolous well-born detective Lord Peter Wimsey into a socially conscious aristocrat with a passion for fast cars and classical music, fully aware that in the modern world he and his class are anachronisms, but nonetheless conscientiously carrying out his responsibilities and undertaking occasional errands for the Foreign Office?

Such unprovable speculations notwithstanding, most of Lothian's peers viewed him less romantically. His shortcomings, notably his tendency to be overcome by passing enthusiasms, his detachment, his failures of judgment, the seeming waste of talents once considered sufficient to make him a serious contender for the next prime minister but three, and his protracted and apparently sincere efforts during the 1930s to reach an understanding with German leader Adolf Hitler, puzzled and exasperated

---

Lothian, however, Brand himself mentioned Lothian's "detachment" from personal ties and party affiliations. Brand, "Philip Kerr: Some Personal Memories," *The Round Table* 50:199 (June 1960), 234-235; Brand, "Kerr, Philip Henry," *Dictionary of National Biography 1931-1940* (London: Oxford University Press, 1949), 509.

[11] Hugh and Mirabel Cecil, *Imperial Marriage: An Edwardian War and Peace* (London: John Murray, 2002), 206.

[12] A. L. Kennedy, *The Times and Appeasement: The Journals of A. L. Kennedy, 1932-1939*, ed. Gordon Martel (Cambridge: Cambridge University Press for the Royal Historical Society, 2000), 82, 147-148.

his contemporaries and subsequent historians alike. This sense of unused ability and unfulfilled promise and his own energetic espousal of his beliefs may, indeed, have helped to make Lothian, whom even his official biographer admitted was "in the front rank of affairs only for a few months," a somewhat disproportionately controversial figure, the target of far fiercer criticism but on occasion also greater adulation than other leading supporters of appeasement.[13] For many, Lothian's undoubted intelligence and well-attested formidable charm seemed only to compound his shortcomings. A. L. Rowse of All Souls College, Oxford, who knew Lothian—"a regular Prince Charming"—well during the 1930s and differed vehemently with him over appeasement, later wrote he "was always glad to see" Lothian, who "was fun to talk to, for he was lively and full of ideas," but nonetheless found in him a "volatile ... element of instability." This, in Rowse's view, led him to become "the outstanding propagandist of 'better understanding' with Hitler, and more dangerous than most, because of his charm, his contacts and friendships at the top of English political society— he belonged to the innermost circle—and because of his ability to write."[14] Michael Astor, who thought him "[a]scetic, unworldly and at the same time somewhat gross," ascribed many of Lothian's shortcomings to his quest for religious truth, arguing:

> The fact that he faltered in his judgement does not detract from the measure of his intellect. He was a highly intelligent man who was also emotionally unbalanced. He was in some way incomplete; and he could not bring all his forces into play. ... Like most people who cannot relinquish their religious doubts he remained concerned essentially with moral standards. As a politician he found himself dealing with people many of whom had little or no moral basis to their actions.[15]

Sir James Butler, Lothian's biographer, who staunchly deplored his stance on appeasement, devoted substantial space to discussing Lothian's errors of judgment and sudden enthusiasms. He quoted—not entirely convincingly— the view of Lord Eustace Percy, a friend of Lothian's for at least three decades, that until he became ambassador in 1939, Lothian never really recovered from his nervous breakdown of 1912, and: "In the interval, he took successively the impress of Lloyd George, of his American friends, of the Cliveden atmosphere and of Liberalism." Brand recalled Lothian's

---

[13] Butler, *Lord Lothian*, v.
[14] A. L. Rowse, *Appeasement: A Study in Political Decline* (New York: Norton, 1963), 31-32.
[15] Astor, *Tribal Feeling*, 139-140.

"extreme open-mindedness" and his "chameleon-like quality" of "[taking] colour from his surroundings," even though "very strong and firm principles ... of liberty, morality, and fair dealing" anchored him and would ultimately "[bring] his mind back to dead centre."[16] Lloyd George more succinctly told an aide that Lothian's "rudder is not equal to his horsepower."[17] In 1932, when British Prime Minister Stanley Baldwin was considering the make-up of his Cabinet, Thomas Jones, deputy secretary to the British cabinet from 1916 to 1930 and another long-time friend of Lothian's, told the premier that he had "ability, unstable judgment; can expound a case very convincingly . . . [and] is apt to be the victim of his most recent experience." Baldwin, in response, described Lothian as a "rum cove" who would "be thoroughly useless *in* the Cabinet but useful outside."[18] Over a decade later, after Lothian's death, Jones wrote:

> When I recall Philip I see him astride a fireplace, with his back to it. The hearthrug became a pulpit. He had an oratorical temperament and delighted in communicating a profusion of opinions and ideals to any casual group of listeners, in elevated abstract diction, dealing only with matters of major importance, and influenced by the country and the company he had most recently visited, America, Germany, leaning now to the Right now to the Left, but returning to a central Liberalism and a theocratic democracy. ... Handsome into middle age, untidy, broad-shouldered, with open gestures, restless arms and hands in and out of his trouser pockets keeping time with his flow of well-turned sentences, positive, assertive, he conveyed a fallacious lucidity of one who had done the thinking and solved the difficulties for you.[19]

Since Lothian's death, historians have differed sharply over his character and historical significance. Butler ranked highly his achievements as ambassador, summarizing them thus: "first, that he made it easier for the United States to co-operate with the British Commonwealth in resistance to totalitarian aggression and, secondly, that when time was vital he speeded up the tendency to co-operate." Butler viewed his major successes as the Destroyers-for-Bases deal and the institution of combined Anglo-American

---

[16] Butler, *Lord Lothian*, 242-243.
[17] Lloyd George to A. J. Sylvester, 1 September 1937, quoted in A. J. Sylvester, *Life with Lloyd George: The Diary of A. J. Sylvester, 1931-45*, ed. Colin Cross (London: Macmillan, 1975), 167.
[18] Thomas Jones, *A Diary with Letters 1931-1950* (London: Oxford University Press, 1954), 44.
[19] *Ibid.*, 514-515.

staff talks shortly after his death.[20] Reynolds concurred, arguing that, despite occasionally demonstrating carelessness, a tendency to speak without due forethought, and over-sensitivity to the American perspective, Lothian "built up a close relationship of mutual trust with American leaders"; made excellent use of the press to mobilize public support; and "provided a clear-cut and plausible argument for Anglo-American cooperation," that American security ultimately depended upon the protection of the British fleet. Reynolds argued that Lothian understood the American political scene far better than most officials in London, and thought his contributions to the Destroyers-for-Bases deal and the origins of Lend-Lease crucial, noting that more than once Lothian's advice prevailed upon an initially reluctant Churchill to make it clear that Britain would fight on, no matter what the circumstances, and to make a frank avowal of Britain's needs to President Franklin D. Roosevelt.[21]

The initially skeptical Wheeler-Bennett, a colleague in Washington, rated especially highly Lothian's efforts to upgrade British public relations in the United States, through his own speeches and addresses throughout the country by other members of his staff; the cultivation of sympathetic contacts among the American press and elites; and the establishment of the British Press Service in New York, which provided high-level officials in London with a broad scrutiny of American press coverage of Britain and the war. Personally, Wheeler-Bennett stated: "The fifteen months during which I enjoyed the honour and pleasure of serving under him are among the most stimulating of my life. I have never known a chief whose inspiration spurred one on to greater heights than one thought it possible to achieve." More broadly, he concluded:

> Throughout the fifteen months of his embassage he never failed to gauge the opinion of America to a nicety. He knew when to cajole and when to shock, when to appeal and when to issue a clarion-call of leadership. His humour was irresistible, his sincerity unquestioned, his statesmanship among the most inspired of our time. His was the hand who laid the foundation of "the Special Relationship."[22]

Nicholas Cull's study of British propaganda in the United States before Pearl Harbor likewise applauded Lothian's skills in managing British public relations, pointing to numerous occasions when he was crucial in

---

[20] Butler, *Lord Lothian*, chs. 14-16, quotation from 318.
[21] Reynolds, *Lord Lothian*, quotations from 58, 59; see also Reynolds, "Lothian, Roosevelt, Churchill and the Origins of Lend-Lease," in Turner, ed., *The Larger Idea*, 93-107.
[22] Wheeler-Bennett, *Special Relationships*, quotations from 115-116.

orchestrating British propaganda strategy, usually in the direction of providing more accurate information and greater access to American journalists, and describing him as "the single most significant figure in the development of British propaganda in the United States."[23] Chapters in this volume by Greg Kennedy, J. Simon Rofe, and Gavin Bailey likewise offer largely favorable assessments of his accomplishments as ambassador, though Bailey does point to some drawbacks in "Lothian's method" of exaggerating, for propaganda purposes, the critical nature of Britain's wartime need for American assistance. D. C. Watt concluded: "Lord Lothian's embassy ... was clearly an enormous success," citing the "covert and effective" liaison work between the New York-based British Information Service (BIS) and the American interventionist organizations, the Committee to Defend America by Aiding the Allies and the Century Club Group, and BIS use of "inter-war inter-university contacts."[24]

By no means all assessments of Lothian as ambassador were so flattering. Rhodri Jeffreys-Jones suggested that, far from being the democratic paragon his admirers proclaimed, he was an elitist and racist whose contacts within the United States were largely limited to likeminded patrician Anglophiles, and whose understanding of that country was narrow; whose performance was flawed by his poor judgment, especially by his continuing willingness to contemplate a negotiated peace with Hitler; and whose contribution to Anglo-American relations was distinctly limited.[25] For Norman Rose, when drawing up the account of Lothian's foreign policy achievements, his protracted support for appeasement and tolerance of Hitler's Germany, together with his elitist outlook, greatly outweighed any positive contributions he might have made as

---

[23] Cull, *Selling War,* quotation from 20.

[24] D. C. Watt, *Succeeding John Bull: America in Britain's Place, 1900-1975* (Cambridge: Cambridge University Press, 1984), 97-98.

[25] Rhodri Jeffreys-Jones, "Lord Lothian and American Democracy: An Illusion in Pursuit of an Illusion," *Canadian Review of American Studies,* 17:4 (Winter 1986), 411-422; Jeffreys-Jones, "The Inestimable Advantage of Not Being English: Lord Lothian's American Ambassadorship, 1939-1940," *Scottish Historical Review,* 63:1 (April 1984), 105-110. In a reworking of these pieces Jeffreys-Jones took a more sympathetic view of Lothian's accomplishments, suggesting that despite his various shortcomings, his "impressive, and perhaps unforeseen diplomatic skill" made him "successful," while as "a political visionary" he was in the longer term "effective." Jeffreys-Jones, "Lord Lothian: 'Ambassador to a People,'" in Turner, ed., *The Larger Idea,* 77-92, quotations from 91 and 92.

ambassador.[26] Reviewing Rose's work, Ian Gilmour concurred that it was hard "to think of an occasion when [Lothian] was right" in foreign policy.[27]

Others took a more detached view of Lothian's support for appeasement. During his lifetime and after, friends and historians alike suggested that Lothian's guilt over his role as Lloyd George's secretary in imposing harsh peace terms upon Germany during the Paris Peace Conference accounted for his readiness to acquiesce in Adolf Hitler's demands during the 1930s.[28] Andrea Bosco depicted Lothian as a "pioneering" figure in the development of closer Anglo-American relations in the Second World War and of appeasement, who from the time he helped to write the March 1919 Fontainebleau memorandum at the Paris Peace Conference favored more lenient treatment of Germany, a man who served as a "focal point" in the circles which supported such policies, and "the first leading politician to meet Hitler personally." Bosco perceived Lothian's actions as motivated at least in part by "expediency," in response to the determination of the United States to remain aloof from Europe. Perceptively, Bosco also drew attention to "an element of ambiguity both in Lothian's personality and in his political action, which aroused some perplexity among his contemporaries, and was to a large extent an important factor in the scant [sic] notice taken of him by historians."[29]

D. C. Watt viewed Lothian as one of a group of "new imperialists," influential "intellectual free-lances" with close ties to leading British politicians and Dominion leaders and "easy access to the quality press," who served on occasion as unofficial diplomatic intermediaries, and who were conscious of the need to retain Dominion support for British foreign policy. "Their attitude to European affairs," he argued, "was guided largely

---

[26] Rose, *Cliveden Set*; cf. Martin Gilbert and Richard Gott, *The Appeasers*, 2nd ed. (London: Weidenfeld and Nicolson, 1967).

[27] Ian Gilmour, "Termagant," *London Review of Books* (19 October 2000), 12.

[28] Wheeler-Bennett, *Special Relationships*, 67; Martel, ed., *The Times and Appeasement*, 247; A. Lentin, *Lloyd George, Woodrow Wilson and the Guilt of Germany: An Essay in the Pre-History of Appeasement* (Baton Rouge: Louisiana State University Press, 1984), 146-150; Rose, *Cliveden Set*, 109-112; Turner, "Lord Lothian and His World," in Turner, ed., *The Larger Idea*, 13-14; Andrea Bosco, "Lord Lothian and Appeasement," in *The Round Table, the Empire/Commonwealth and British Foreign Policy*, eds. Andrea Bosco and Alex May (London: Lothian Foundation Press, 1997), 474, 496. See also Watt's interesting analysis of German efforts to "[predispose] opinion within the British foreign-policy-making elite towards accepting the foreign policy of Nazi Germany." D. C. Watt, *Personalities and Policies: Studies in the Formulation of British Policy in the Twentieth Century* (London: Longmans, 1965), 117-135, quotation from 117.

[29] Bosco, "Lord Lothian and Appeasement," 473-509, quotations from 477, 475, 503.

by a lack of direct experience to set against their first-hand experience of the Dominions." Paradoxically, therefore, while their thinking on Commonwealth affairs was "infinitely more advanced than Churchill's romantic Disraelianism," their European policies "harked back to the isolationism of Lord Salisbury. ... They knew little of central European problems and disliked what they knew," preferring to follow policies of Anglo-German rapprochement. Watt also depicted Lothian as one of a group of convinced Christian Pacifists, Quakers, and Christian Scientists, "governed ... by a basic humanitarian, if not Christian, interest in the avoidance of war," who "made it their business ... to avoid a direct conflict between British and German policy until it was absolutely unavoidable. With the best intentions in the world they thus became the unpaid servants of German and Nazi foreign policy."[30] In his full-length survey of Lothian's entire foreign policy, David P. Billington, Jr., traced many of his subject's attitudes to his Christian Science belief that "false ways of thinking were ultimately at fault for tensions at home and abroad." This was an outlook that "would prove his undoing in relation to Germany." Therefore: "In the support that he gave for appeasing Hitler's demands after 1933, in the belief that doing so was both just and expedient, Lothian gravely undermined the liberal and democratic civilization that he otherwise worked to preserve."[31] Billington devoted substantial attention to Lothian's belief in Anglo-American cooperation, but perceived this as subordinate to his search to overcome the evils of national sovereignty itself through the creation of a world federation of states.

In recent years Lothian's reputation has undergone something of a renascence, as a new generation of historians drew attention to the posthumous impact of his—and other British—calls for world federalism, or at least a federal union of the Western democracies, in inspiring Altiero Spinelli and associated European intellectual federalists into establishing what would eventually become the European Union.[32] Admittedly, John Pinder has drawn attention to the irony that Lothian invariably believed that

---

[30] Watt, *Personalities and Policies*, 160-162, 117-135, quotations from 160, 161-62, 123, 124.

[31] Billington, *Lothian*, quotations from 100 and 112.

[32] See esp. the essays, Andrea Bosco, "National Sovereignty and Peace: Lord Lothian's Federalist Thought"; Ira Straus, "Lothian and the Anglo-American Problematic"; and John Pinder, "Prophet not without Honour: Lothian and the Federal Idea," in Turner, ed., *The Larger Idea*, 108-152; Andrea Bosco, "Lothian, Curtis, Kimber and the Federal Union Movement (1938-40)," *Journal of Contemporary History* 23:3 (July 1988), 462-502; and Grayson, *Liberals, International Relations and Appeasement*.

the closer association of the British Empire or Commonwealth with the United States must be the core and *sine qua non* of any such union of the European democracies, an outlook he believes accounts for Lothian's failure to put forward any concrete proposals for the development of European unity.[33] Turner, too, raised the "irony" that "European federalists" have "honoured [Lothian] as the intellectual ancestor of a concept which he would hardly have recognised and which would have been quite low in his order of priorities."[34] For more than a decade the London-based Lothian Foundation, established during the 1980s but now apparently in hibernation, sought to encourage what it considered to be Lothian's ultimate objective of European unity; it also reprinted two volumes of his speeches and encouraged much of the recent scholarship on his career.[35] Other studies focus primarily upon specific aspects of Lothian's career, especially his longstanding interest in imperial union, his service under Lloyd George, and his part in developing initiatives to give India greater self-rule.[36]

LOTHIAN AS ATLANTICIST

Even though his biographer stated that between the wars Lothian "was above all interested in relations with the United States,"[37] and assessments of his service as ambassador invariably drew attention to Lothian's longstanding commitment to closer Anglo-American relations, Lothian's commitment to what might be described as an Atlanticist perspective has, by contrast, been somewhat neglected, and when mentioned generally subordinated to what were perceived as his broader views on the need to prevent future wars by diluting purely national sovereignty. Turner even suggested that "by the end of his life he had become committed to *Pax*

---

[33] Pinder, "Prophet Not Without Honour," esp. 140-142.

[34] Turner, "Lord Lothian and His World," 19.

[35] Lord Lothian, *Pacifism is not enough: Collected Lectures and Speeches of Lord Lothian (Philip Kerr)*, eds. John Pinder and Andrea Bosco (London: Lothian Foundation, 1990); and *Annals of the Lothian Foundation* 1 (1991). The collections of essays edited by Turner, Bosco, and Guderzo were the end-product of gatherings partly funded by the Lothian Foundation, which likewise financed the reprinting of his *American Speeches*.

[36] See Nimocks, *Milner's Young Men*; Kendle, *Round Table Movement*; Turner, *Lloyd George's Secretariat*; Kenneth Ingham, "Philip Kerr and the Unification of South Africa"; John Turner and Michael Dockrill, "Philip Kerr at 10 Downing Street, 1916-1921"; Gerard Douds, "Lothian and the Indian Federation," all in Turner, ed., *The Larger Idea*, 20-76; and Patterson, "Decline of Dominance."

[37] Butler, *Lord Lothian*, 115.

Anglo-Americana in default of anything else."[38] Several studies of Lothian's activities during the First World War and at the Paris Peace Conference were a partial exception, stressing his eagerness to encourage close cooperation between the United States and the British Empire and his belief that continuing Anglo-American collaboration must form the bedrock of any postwar settlement.[39] These only dealt, however, with one short period of his career. The same is true of Stefan Schieren's article on Kerr's efforts to improve Anglo-American relations between 1918 and 1930, an essay that depicted Kerr as both "an astute visionary" and "a skilled politician," who advocated "an alternative approach to international affairs, anticipating some developments that took place after 1939, culminating in the Atlantic Charter." Schieren suggested that, although Kerr's "vision ... of a future world federation, a common family of man, living in a world ruled by law, not by power, where peace, justice and wealth were immanently present" closely resembled Woodrow Wilson's views on international order, opposition from the British Foreign Office, United States rejection of the League of Nations, American anti-imperialism, and differences over freedom of the seas precluded its practical realization.[40]

Billington's recent and exhaustively researched full-length study of Lothian took this approach even further, arguing that "he struggled throughout his life with a challenge of fundamental importance: how to convert the declining global hegemony of Britain into a more stable and inclusive world order." Nonetheless, Lothian's "life points to the danger of relying on intuition and ideal principle to achieve a better world in the short run." Close association between the United States and the British Empire, perhaps in conjunction with west European powers, was one solution that appealed to him, and that would eventually become a reality with the

---

[38] Turner, "Lord Lothian and His World," 2.

[39] See esp. George Egerton, *Great Britain and the Creation of the League of Nations: Strategy, Politics, and International Organization, 1914-1919* (Chapel Hill: University of North Carolina Press, 1978), 63-109; Egerton, "Conservative Internationalism: British Approaches to International Organization and the Creation of the League of Nations," *Diplomacy and Statecraft* 5:1 (March 1994), 1-20; Egerton, "Imperialism, Atlanticism, and Internationalism: Philip Kerr and the League of Nations Question, 1916-1920," *Annals of the Lothian Foundation* 1 (1991), 95-122; and Michael G. Fry, *Illusions of Security: North Atlantic Diplomacy, 1918-22* (Toronto: University of Toronto Press, 1972), 5-67.

[40] Stefan Schieren, "Philip Kerr and Anglo-American Relations after the Great War," in *The Round Table, the Empire/Commonwealth and British Foreign Policy*, eds. Andrea Bosco and Alex May (London: Lothian Foundation Press, 1997), 450-472, quotations from 452 and 453.

creation of the North Atlantic Treaty Organization (NATO) in 1949.[41] Rose on occasion mentioned, albeit somewhat dismissively, Lothian's belief in Anglo-American cooperation, but his first concern was Lothian's role in appeasement. Predictably, Lothian featured extensively in Carroll S. Quigley's quirky and decidedly conspiratorial account of the Anglo-American "Milner Group"'s influence on international politics from the 1890s to the Second World War. His name also cropped up in Kees van der Pijl's Marxist analysis of the emergence of an Atlantic ruling class, which drew heavily if uncritically upon Quigley's writings.[42] Watt gave the most perceptive characterization of Lothian, regarding him as one of "a numerically very limited but strategically important group of mid-Atlanticist Americophiles" within the interwar British foreign policy elite.[43] In earlier writings Watt also suggested that the Round Table group's objectives gave it "a triple interest in the United States": they viewed it as a country whose success "in the absorption and unification of a great mass of different peoples and traditions" made it a potential model for a united British Empire; they "subscribed largely to the theories that the two countries shared a common culture and a common purpose"; and they considered it a potential ally with whom Britain could establish "an Anglo-American world hegemony" and "dominate the world, widening and strengthening the Pax Britannica, the world order on which they set so much store."[44]

Arguably, Lothian's dedication to Anglo-American cooperation or, more broadly, collaboration between the British Empire and the United States, was the defining theme of his entire career. It is no exaggeration to state that his public service and his multifarious semi-public activities alike in many ways constituted an apprenticeship for both the job and the moment of his ambassadorship, which represented only the pinnacle of three decades of effort to develop closer Anglo-American relations, a preoccupation that underpinned most of his thinking and endeavors. From this perspective, Lothian's public career possessed greater coherence than many have suggested, being dominated by one overall defining theme, a single-minded quest for national advantage and the effort to win the friendship and support of the world's potential great power. This drive

---

[41] Billington, *Lothian*, quotations from 161, 168.
[42] Carroll Quigley, *The Anglo-American Establishment: From Rhodes to Cliveden* (New York: Books in Focus, 1981); and Kees van der Pijl, *The Making of an Atlantic Ruling Class* (London: Verso, 1984).
[43] Watt, *Succeeding John Bull*, 49.
[44] Watt, *Personalities and Policies*, 29-30, quotation from 30.

accounted, moreover, for this erstwhile political lightweight's success in what was, for Britain in 1939-1940, a crucial position. More broadly, his methods and style in pursuing his objectives perhaps go some way toward explaining why, during his lifetime and well beyond, Lothian's character and activities often attracted seemingly—given his fairly secondary political status and influence—excessive condemnation and reproach.

Kerr was by no means unique in his faith, to which portions of the elites of Great Britain, Canada, and the United States, with many of whom Kerr would work closely, also subscribed. From the late 1870s onward the millionaire imperialist Cecil Rhodes, who had close ties with Oxford, resolved to bring about the union of the Anglo-Saxon powers, Britain and its empire, the United States, and Germany, in the hope that together they would permanently dominate the world, an objective for which he initially established an embryonic secret society and later the Rhodes Fellowships. Beginning with British prime minister Lord Salisbury in the late nineteenth century, belief in the desirability of strengthening the Empire's defenses through a *de facto* alliance with the United States was fundamental to the thinking of assorted leading British statesmen, notably the entire Salisbury family, including Lord Robert Cecil and his brothers, his brother-in-law Lord Selborne, and his cousin, Conservative Prime Minister and Foreign Secretary Arthur Balfour; wartime Foreign Secretary Sir Edward Grey; James, Viscount Bryce, British ambassador to the United States in the early twentieth century; the British press magnate Alfred, Lord Northcliffe, proprietor of *The Times*; St. John Loe Strachey, editor of *The Spectator*; and also Lord Milner and various members of The Round Table group, especially the American-born Waldorf and Nancy Astor and Robert Brand, who married Nancy Astor's sister.[45] This was an outlook underpinned by popular social Darwinist ideas of the superiority of the Anglo-Saxon or English-speaking nations current in the late nineteenth and early twentieth centuries, the belief disseminated by numerous influential historians and

---

[45] Egerton, *Great Britain and the Creation of the League of Nations*, 63-109; Fry, *Illusions of Security*, 5-67; Max Beloff, *Imperial Sunset: Britain's Liberal Empire, 1897-1921*, 2nd ed. (London: Macmillan, 1987), 42-46; Bradford Perkins, *The Great Rapprochement: Britain and the United States, 1895-1914* (New York: Atheneum, 1968), 51-53, 65-57; Stuart Anderson, *Race and Rapprochement: Anglo-Saxonism and Anglo-American Relations, 1895-1904* (East Brunswick, NJ: Fairleigh Dickinson University Press, 1981), 86-94, 112-129; David Dimbleby and David Reynolds, *An Ocean Apart: The Relationship Between Britain and America in the Twentieth Century* (New York: Random House, 1988), 25-33; Watt, *Personalities and Policies*, 24-32; Watt, *Succeeding John Bull*, 24-163; and Richard Symonds, *Oxford and Empire: The Last Lost Cause?* (Basingstoke: Macmillan, 1986), 161-165.

political theorists that the Anglo-Saxon race, in effect the British and Americans, was uniquely capable of self-government, had evolved the best and most democratic political institutions to date, and shared a common legal, political, and institutional heritage. Such views were often used to justify imperial rule, which, its supporters argued, provided good government to peoples incapable of running their own affairs themselves in an orderly fashion. Calls for Anglo-American concord and cooperation thus rested on a sense of racial kinship, reinforced by a variety of business, political, intellectual, personal, and familial ties linking British and American elites.[46] They also drew upon the naval writings of the American strategist Alfred T. Mahan, who suggested American national security had throughout the nineteenth century ultimately depended upon the protection of the British fleet, and that in their mutual interests the two countries should therefore harmonize their defense policies.[47]

Kerr was to become one of the greatest British exponents of this outlook, which—perhaps due to his ties with the Americophile Cecil

---

[46] Reginald Horsman, *Race and Manifest Destiny: The Origins of American Racial Anglo-Saxonism* (Cambridge, MA: Harvard University Press, 1981); Anderson, *Race and Rapprochement*; Richard Hofstadter, *Social Darwinism in American Thought*, revised ed. (Boston, MA: Beacon Press, 1955), esp. 170-184; David S. Healy, *US Expansionism: The Imperialist Urge in the 1890s* (Madison: University of Wisconsin Press, 1970), 13-16, 29-33, 38-42, 123-124; Michael H. Hunt, *Ideology and US Foreign Policy* (New Haven, CT: Yale University Press, 1986), 77-79; and Perkins, *Great Rapprochement*, 74-83.

[47] Alfred T. Mahan, *The Interest of America in Sea Power, Present and Future* (Boston: Little, Brown, 1897), esp. 27, 49-51, 55, 107-34, 185-90, 257-59; Mahan, *Lessons of the War with Spain* (Boston: Little, Brown, 1899), 289-298; Mahan, *The Interest of America in International Conditions* (Boston: Little, Brown, 1910), esp. 35-124, 158-185; Philip A. Crowl, "Alfred Thayer Mahan: The Naval Historian," in *Makers of Modern Strategy from Machiavelli to the Nuclear Age*, ed. Peter Paret (Princeton, NJ: Princeton University Press, 1986), 444-477; Kenneth J. Hagan, "Alfred Thayer Mahan: Turning America Back to the Sea," in *Makers of American Diplomacy: From Benjamin Franklin to Henry Kissinger*, eds. Frank J. Merli and Theodore A. Wilson (New York: Scribner, 1974), 279-303; W. D. Puleston, *Mahan: The Life and Works of Captain Alfred Thayer Mahan* (New Haven, CT: Yale University Press, 1939), 9-12, 135-136, 267, 283-289, 304, 324, 327-328; Robert Seager II, *Alfred Thayer Mahan: The Man and His Letters* (Annapolis, MD: Naval Institute Press, 1977), 148-149, 225-226, 348-351, 522-525; William Reitzel, "Mahan on Use of the Sea," in *War, Strategy, and Maritime Power*, ed. B. Mitchell Simpson III (New Brunswick, NJ: Rutgers University Press, 1977), 95-107; Bernard Semmel, *Liberalism & Naval Strategy: Ideology, Interest, and Sea Power during the Pax Britannica* (Boston: Allen and Unwin, 1986), 90-95; Jon Tetsuo Sumida, *Inventing Grand Strategy and Teaching Command: The Classic Works of Alfred Thayer Mahan* (Washington, DC, and Baltimore, MD: Woodrow Wilson Center Press and Johns Hopkins University Press, 1997), esp. 80-92; and Warren Zimmermann, *First Great Triumph: How Five Americans Made Their Country into a World Power* (New York: Farrar, Straus and Giroux, 2002), esp. ch. 3.

family—he apparently imbibed very early in his career. Kerr seems to have shared the racist belief in Anglo-Saxon or Western superiority common to many of his class and background. "I think it true," he lectured in 1923, "that there has never yet been a successful democracy outside the Christian World, and that the most successful ones have been predominantly Protestant."[48] Distinct parallels existed between Kerr's view of his own role in society, as an enlightened aristocrat, and that of Britain and other "civilized" countries in the world. In an essay published in 1916, he described "the human race as one great family, ... divided into a graduated scale varying infinitely from the zenith of civilization to the nadir of barbarism." In his view: "The truth is that the government of backward races by advanced races is ... the result of 'natural laws.'" In character, intelligence, culture, and political development, the white races were, he claimed, innately superior. Kerr further believed that as and when necessary "advanced" races had a positive duty to protect the "backward" from the social disruptions caused by contact between the two by ruling them in their own best interests.[49] Writing to his friend and Round Table associate Lionel Curtis in October 1918, he "expound[ed] our view as to the necessity for some civilised control over politically backward peoples":

> Briefly it is that the inhabitants of Africa and parts of Asia have proved unable to govern themselves, not because they were inherently incapable of maintaining any kind of stable society if left to themselves, but because they were quite unable to withstand the demoralising influences to which they were subjected in some civilised countries, so that intervention of an European power is necessary in order to protect them from those influences and give them time and opportunity in which to establish a form of self-government which is strong enough to withstand these influences.[50]

Moreover: "A nation which has had to assume the responsibility for maintaining good government among a backward people, cannot relinquish that responsibility until the latter have given some clear evidence of their capacity to do so." His experiences in South Africa and also his travels in the United States early convinced him that contact between whites and non-

---

[48] Kerr, "World Problems of Today," in Kerr et al., *Approaches to World Problems* (New Haven, CT: Yale University Press, 1924), 92.

[49] Kerr, "The Political Relations between Advanced and Backward Peoples," in A. J. Grant et al., *An Introduction to the Study of International Relations* (London: Macmillan, 1916), 141-182, quotation from 172.

[50] Kerr to Curtis, 15 October 1918, in *Two Musketeers for the Empire: The Lionel Curtis-Philip Kerr (Lord Lothian) Correspondence 1909-1940*, ed. Andrea Bosco (London: Lothian Foundation Press, 1997), 138.

whites led to racial friction and difficulties, and ideally should therefore be avoided.[51]

Interestingly, however, Kerr was always realist enough to be swayed by personal experience. Even as he publicly urged racial separation in 1910, he also stated "that the Negro race ... has within it the capacity to reach, and will reach, the same stage of development as the average white man."[52] After visiting Japan, he wrote that it was "impossible to regard the Japanese as uncivilized" and that though "Orientals" were "different," it was "pure prejudice" to treat them as "inferior."[53] In India Kerr likewise recognized the presence of a Westernized Indian elite who were unwisely excluded from political participation.[54] Before the First World War, when discussing potential organizations for imperial unity, to the consternation of some of his Round Table colleagues Kerr urged that any imperial council or parliament should include at least some Indian representatives, even if they were denied voting rights, and argued that full dominion status must be the ultimate objective of British rule in India.[55] Likewise, in the 1930s his belief that India would otherwise descend into anarchy led him to support granting voting rights to a far greater proportion of the Indian population than many in the Government of India, the Colonial Office, and Parliament considered feasible. The responsibility of power, he argued, would quickly moderate many of India's more radical firebrand leaders.[56] Africa was another forum where Kerr showed himself relatively liberal on racial issues, at least for his time and class. During the 1920s he opposed

---

[51] Quotation from Kerr, "The Political Relations between Advanced and Backward Peoples," 172; cf. Kerr, "What the British Empire Really Stands For," address to Toronto Round Table Club, 30 July 1912 (Toronto: n.p., 1917), 10-16; Kerr "World Problems of Today," 88-96; Kerr, "World Law and World Peace," in *Approaches to World Problems*, 114-116; Kerr, "The End of War," *The Round Table* 5:20 (September 1915), 786-787; Kerr, "The Harvest of the War," *The Round Table* 6:21 (December 1915), 11-15; Kerr, "The Principle of Peace," *The Round Table* 6:23 (June 1916), 407; Kerr, "The Harvest of Victory," *The Round Table* 9:36 (September 1919), 659-661; Turner, *Lloyd George's Secretariat*, 148-149; Fry, *Illusions of Security*, 18-19, 24-25; Patterson, "Decline of Dominance," 62-64; and Billington, *Lothian*, 13-14, 23-24.

[52] Kerr, article in *The State* 3 (1910), cited in *Billington*, Lothian, 14.

[53] Kerr, "The Anglo-Japanese Alliance," *The Round Table* 1:2 (February 1911), 105-149, quotations from 126-129.

[54] Kerr, "India and the Empire," *The Round Table* 2:8 (September 1912), 587-620.

[55] Patterson, "Decline of Dominance," 63-65, 72-74; Billington, *Lothian*, 23-24; Deborah Lavin, *From Empire to International Commonwealth: A Biography of Lionel Curtis* (Oxford: Clarendon Press, 1995), 115-116; Butler, *Lord Lothian*, 175.

[56] Billington, *Lothian*, 103-112; Patterson, "Decline of Dominance," 254-313; Butler, *Lord Lothian*, 176-89; and Douds, "Lothian and the Indian Federation," 65-76.

legislation in South Africa and East Africa that imposed a color bar in employment, reserving more senior jobs and administrative positions for whites, and also the exclusion of Africans and Asians from political power in those territories. Kerr argued unavailingly that such barriers were not only unjust but would ultimately prove self-defeating, and that educated and able non-whites should have access to political and economic opportunity on equal terms with whites.[57]

Kerr's particular interest in the United States began no later than his early twenties. It was *Alexander Hamilton: An Essay on American Union* (1906), a book by the Scottish businessman F. S. Oliver, that impelled the youthful Kerr and other Kindergarten members to develop their ideas on federalism as an appropriate constitutional arrangement for both South Africa and the British Empire.[58] Kerr met Arthur Balfour, the former Conservative prime minister, in 1908, and in May 1909 he sent that elder statesman a memorandum, written by the French naval attaché in Berlin, recommending that Britain and the United States should join together to form "an Anglo-Saxon Federation" capable of dominating the seas, guaranteeing peace, and checking German imperialism. Kerr suggested Balfour should forward this document to ex-President Theodore Roosevelt, about to embark on a tour of the world, in the hope that Roosevelt would be "inspired to lay the foundation of an Anglo-American alliance," which would, he trusted, also persuade Roosevelt to reject such alternatives as "a German-American alliance."[59] This instructive episode revealed the manner in which, on both the individual and international level, like a moth to a flame Kerr habitually gravitated toward power.

A few months later, in autumn 1909, Kerr and Lionel Curtis embarked on a tour of Canada, intended to lay the groundwork for the establishment of a network of Canadian Round Table groups who would promote closer imperial union. To Curtis' annoyance Kerr, skeptical as to the feasibility of their objective and unable to "see that we [Britain] can offer her [Canada] anything that the United States can't offer just as well," insisted on making an independent trip to the United States, his first visit to

---

[57] Billington, *Lothian*, 85-89.

[58] Butler, *Lord Lothian*, 36; Kendle, *Round Table Movement*, 24; Nimocks, *Milner's Young Men*, 125-29; Lavin, *From Empire to International Commonwealth*, 68, 71; and Billington, *Lothian*, 11.

[59] Kerr to Balfour, 3 May 1909, and enclosure, in Arthur Balfour Papers, British Library, London, cited in Beloff, *Imperial Sunset*, 168 n. 3; and Billington, *Lothian*, 24. There is no evidence in the Theodore Roosevelt Papers to suggest that Balfour forwarded this material to Roosevelt.

that country, supposedly undertaken to study American racial problems in the light of those facing South Africa.[60] He returned in August 1912, when he attended the Progressive Party convention in Detroit and later had lunch with former President Theodore Roosevelt at his Oyster Bay home. On this trip Kerr also visited the 'House of Truth' in Washington, a bachelor establishment at 1727 Nineteenth Street NW, which housed an assortment of rising young American and British diplomats, lawyers, journalists, and businessmen, among them Lord Eustace Percy of the British Embassy; the future Supreme Court justice Felix Frankfurter; the Canadian lawyer Loring Christie, a future aide to Canadian prime minister Robert Borden; Arthur Willert, Washington correspondent for the London *Times*; and the political commentators Walter Lippmann and Herbert Croly, both of whom would soon be employed by a newly established journal, *The New Republic*.[61]

On his first 1909 visit, Kerr's immediate reaction to the United States was straightforward: "I like America."[62] It seems plausible that Kerr was not simply drawn to the United States as a great power, but also found the country personally liberating. Friends would later comment how he seemed almost to assume a different personality when he was in the United States. Kerr quickly imbibed an enthusiastic "affectionate admiration" for the United States, telling a British audience in 1939: "I always feel fifteen years younger when I land in New York."[63] In 1912 he told the architect Sir Herbert Baker how exhilarating he found it to walk through or contemplate the skyscrapers in "the business quarter of S. Francisco, or the water front of Chicago, or the lower end of New York," and that—by contrast to American literature, music, and painting—the country's "architecture has caught the modern American spirit of boundless material enterprise, boundless confidence and boundless energy."[64] One of his major objections to inheriting his title was, it seems, his fear this would "quite spoil the pleasure I used to have in travelling to the New World. One cannot fail to

---

[60] Butler, *Lord Lothian*, 47-51; Billington, *Lothian*, 13-14; Lavin, *From Empire to International Commonwealth*, 109-110; Kendle, *Round Table Movement*, 65-68; Robert Bothwell, *Loring Christie: The Failure of Bureaucratic Imperialism* (New York: Garland, 1988), 33-38; and Nimocks, *Milner's Young Men*, 152-154.

[61] Kerr to Edith C. Roosevelt, 10 August 1912, Reel 151, and Roosevelt's Secretary to Kerr, 13 August 1912, Reel 379, Theodore Roosevelt Papers, Manuscripts Division, Library of Congress, Washington, DC; Butler, *Lord Lothian*, 48; and Billington, *Lothian*, 24-25.

[62] Quoted in Butler, *Lord Lothian*, 40. Somewhat imperceptively, he continued: "It is really extraordinarily like England."

[63] Royal Institute of International Affairs, *The American Speeches of Lord Lothian*, xlii, first quotation from *ibid.*, 1.

[64] Kerr to Sir Herbert Baker, 6 October 1912, cited in Butler, *Lord Lothian*, 253.

be unpleasantly conspicuous."[65] The historian can only speculate on the connection between Kerr's feelings for the United States and the manner in which his comfortable devotion to a firmly married American woman, a relationship which effectively afforded him a virtual second family and the use of several luxurious mansions, together with his conversion to her American faith of Christian Science, not only alleviated his protracted psychosomatic illnesses, but also furnished a convenient escape from both his increasingly irksome Roman Catholicism and family pressures to marry and beget an heir to the title he would eventually inherit.

THE IMPACT OF THE FIRST WORLD WAR

It would, however, take a major international conflict to convert Kerr into a dedicated and lifelong advocate of the cause of Anglo-American cooperation above all else. Shortly before the First World War began Kerr returned to editing *The Round Table*, remaining there until the end of 1916, when he became one of Lloyd George's private secretaries. The journal's quite conscious objective was not to make money—for decades it received substantial subsidies from the Rhodes Trust—but, in Kerr's words, "to propagate our opinions among the best people" and to reach "practically all men of real influence in politics, journalism, business, etc., who are in any way sympathetic."[66] Several hundred free copies of each *Round Table* issue were widely distributed, sent to leading politicians, newspapers, reviews, London hotels and clubs, and the Workers Educational Association.[67]

Before August 1914, although Kerr was concerned by the rising power of Germany, and to some extent Japan, he did not think war necessarily inevitable. "Provided the Empire is able to preserve its territories intact and keep that preponderance at sea which is vital to its existence," he hoped to draw Germany into peaceful collaborative economic development around the world. He nonetheless supported the maintenance of British naval supremacy through increased defense spending, to which he expected the dominions to contribute. Following the late-nineteenth-century Oxford constitutional historian W. H. Stubbs, he did, however, believe that a lengthy historical experience of armed conflict had made Germany—and other continental European states—socially and

---

[65] Quoted in *ibid.*, 144.
[66] Kerr to Robert H. Brand, 28 December 1911, Robert H. Brand Papers, Bodleian Library, Oxford University; and Kerr, memorandum to A. J. Glazebrook, 28 April 1910, cited in Nimocks, *Milner's Young Men*, 180-186.
[67] May, "The Round Table," 81.

politically more authoritarian, with far less of the British liberal commitment to individual rights that underpinned the governments of both Britain and its imperial dominions.[68] Alarmed by conflicting nationalisms and consequent growing tension in the Balkans, in spring 1912 Kerr rather vaguely suggested that nations needed to give up their "worship of their own separate identity, and their objections to its being merged in a large union with other nations," and instead join together and "entrust the control of their destinies to an authority, possessed of the powers to enforce observance of its decrees." A democratic British Empire federation might, he argued, form the core of any such world state.[69]

When war broke out, Kerr continued to sound his earlier themes. He immediately presented the conflict not just in terms of the rival national interests of the Allies and the Central Powers, but as a contest between two ideas of empire, the one liberal and British, "giv[ing] to peoples of the most diverse race, colour and civilization and spread all over the world, peace, unity and freedom," the other authoritarian, intolerant of diversity, and "backed by the sword." Germany, he argued, sought to gain "the hegemony of Europe as the stepping-stone to the hegemony of the world." The war was therefore at heart a battle between liberal democracy and militarist absolutism, which it was to be hoped would end in Germany's conversion to the principles of its enemies. Kerr therefore called for a total national effort in both Britain and the Dominions, to bring about victory whatever the cost. He also viewed the war as an opportunity for national regeneration, a chance to instill virtues of self-sacrifice, unselfishness, and a new sense of service and citizenship in the British people, as they dedicated themselves to the twin objectives of victory and the creation of a more united, just, and democratic society, leaving Britain a revitalized

---

[68] Kerr, "Foreign Affairs: Anglo-German Rivalry," *The Round Table* 1:1 (November 1910), 7-40; Kerr, "The Anglo-Japanese Alliance," *The Round Table* 1:2 (February 1911), 105-149; Kerr, "The New Problem of Imperial Defence," *The Round Table* 1:3 (May 1911), 231-262; Kerr, "The Emigration Question in Japan," 3:3 (May 1911), *The Round Table* 263-269; Kerr, "The Conference and the Empire," *The Round Table* 1:4 (August 1911), 371-425; Kerr, "Britain, France and Germany," *The Round Table* 2:5 (December 1911), 1-57, quotation from 38-39; and Kerr, "The Balkan Danger and Universal Peace," *The Round Table* 2:6 (March 1912), 199-245. On Kerr's early *Round Table* writings, see also Butler, *Lord Lothian*, 44-48; Billington, *Lothian*, 21-24; Turner, *Lloyd George's Secretariat*, 146; and Kendle, *Round Table Movement*, 108-115. All these articles were subjected to intensive editorial discussion by other members of the Round Table group.
[69] Kerr, "The Balkan Danger," quotations from 231, 240.

country that would also be capable of playing a greater and more positive international role in preventing future wars.[70]

Largely for pragmatic reasons, the outbreak of war seems to have intensified Kerr's existing American leanings. One reason he emphasized the idealistic interpretation of the war was undoubtedly his anxiety to win Britain a favorable hearing in the United States, the country whose attitude on such issues as war trade with the Allies, German submarine warfare, and British restrictions on neutral commerce, could vitally affect the chances of Allied success, and whose intervention could potentially bring an Allied victory. *The Round Table*'s editorial committee viewed its wartime role as effectively ancillary and supportive to the official makers of British foreign policy. Indeed, the British Foreign Office reproduced several suitable *Round Table* articles and distributed them for propaganda purposes in neutral countries, most notably the United States.[71]

Kerr's articles repeatedly discussed the future international role of the United States, while for his British and Dominion readers he provided an American perspective. In 1915 he recruited the Canadian-born historian George Louis Beer, of New York's Columbia College, who published a wartime book urging unity and collaboration among the English-speaking peoples, to write regular articles on American issues for the journal. Beer described American public opinion and attitudes toward international organization, while warning his British readers that they should realize that the United States often had its own perspective upon matters relating to the war, which was entitled to respect. In summer 1915 Beer opined that "a daily increasing number [of Americans] perceive that the United States cannot in the future remain aloof from those questions that are determining the course of the world's history." If his country were drawn into the war, he believed: "The existence of common political traditions and ideals will inevitably ... draw the United States more intimately to England than to

---

[70] Kerr, "The War in Europe, *The Round Table* 4:16 (September 1914), 591-615, quotations from 612-613; Kerr, "After Four Months' War," *The Round Table* 5:17 (December 1914), 3-17, quotation from 3; Kerr, "The Schism of Europe," *The Round Table* 5:18 (March 1915), 345-411; Kerr, "The Burden of Victory," *The Round Table* 5:19 (June 1915), 511-520; Kerr, "National Duty in War," *The Round Table* 5:20 (September 1915), 707-723; Kerr, "The Harvest of the War," *The Round Table* 6:21 (December 1915), 1-32; Kerr, "The War for Public Right," *The Round Table* 6:22 (March 1916), 193-231; Kerr, "The Principle of Peace," *The Round Table* 6:23 (June 1916), 391-423; Kerr, "War Aims," *The Round Table* 6:24 (September 1916), 607-613; and Kerr, "The Making of Peace," 7:25 (December 1916), 1-13. On his wartime editorial stance, see also Butler, *Lord Lothian*, 56-60; Billington, *Lothian*, 39-41; and Turner, *Lloyd George's Secretariat*, 146-148.

[71] May, "The Round Table," 172.

any one of the other Powers." When American intervention occurred, Beer welcomed it.[72] He later stated his belief that a "perfect ... identity of purpose" characterized British and American war aims.[73]

In his own articles, Kerr consciously sought to persuade American opinion-makers that their country should follow pro-Allied policies and eventually take a far larger role in world affairs, preferably in collaboration with the British Empire. One tactic Kerr employed was to compare the issues at stake in the Great War and the problems, domestic and international, the conflict generated with those Abraham Lincoln encountered during the American Civil War and "the experience of the great sister-democracy in the United States in its struggle for existence half a century ago."[74] When employing other assorted American analogies, Kerr referred to the early state of lawlessness in the American West, the Monroe Doctrine, and antebellum Americans' disobedience on grounds of conscience to the fugitive slave law.[75]

He also addressed directly particular incidents with potential to disrupt relations between the Allies and the United States. On 6 November 1915, President Woodrow Wilson issued a note championing the cause of neutral rights against all belligerents. Shortly afterwards, Kerr warned that, if the president pushed this policy of neutrality, he would "hinder the triumph of that national liberty of which the American people are themselves among the foremost champions." While not discounting the possibility that the United States might, as Wilson wished, successfully mediate the conflict, Kerr urged that "her Government should no longer

---

[72] G. L. Beer, "American Public Opinion and the War," *The Round Table* 5:20 (September 1915), 797-839, quotations from 837-838; Beer, "America's Reaction to the War," *The Round Table* 6:22 (March 1916), 285-314; Beer, "The United States and the Future Peace," *The Round Table* 7:26 (March 1917), 285-317; Beer, "America's Entrance into the War," *The Round Table* 7:27 (June 1917), 491-514; Beer, *The English-Speaking Peoples, their Future and Joint International Obligations* (New York: Macmillan, 1917); Billington, *Lothian*, 47; Kendle, *Round Table Movement*, 195 n. 44, 252; and Lavin, *From Empire to International Commonwealth*, 160.

[73] Beer, "America's War Aims," *The Round Table* 8:30 (March 1918), 255.

[74] "The Price of War," *The Round Table* 18 (1915), 312-322. quotation from 312. This author of article may well have been F. S. Oliver. Cf. "The End of the War," 779; "The Principle of Peace," 391; "World Law and World Peace," 112, 117-118, 120; and Philip Kerr and Lionel Curtis, *The Prevention of War* (New Haven, CT: Yale University Press, 1923), 44, 70. Kerr lated cited Lincoln as one of the few politicians who "had the religious sense strongly developed." John Grigg, *Lloyd George: War Leader* (London: Allen Lane, 2002), 459.

[75] "The War for Public Right," 217-219, 221-223, 225, 227; "The Principle of Peace," 394, 423; "War Aims," 609; and *Prevention of War*, 16-19, 30-33.

screen itself behind the fiction of neutrality and should declare as the basis of its policy the undoubted determination of the American people to do nothing to help tyranny to vanquish liberty in Europe." Three months later, Kerr again suggested that, given German disregard of the interests of humanity, the United States should not insist on freedom of the seas and neutral rights to trade.[76] In June 1916 he applauded Wilson's "ultimatum to Germany, requiring the abandonment of submarine warfare against merchant shipping on the ground that it was necessarily inconsistent with common humanity," after several American civilians died when a German submarine torpedoed the *Sussex*, an Irish channel steamer. "It means," Kerr stated, "that America has taken a stand for the reign of law as against the reign of force, not on the American continent alone, but throughout the world." With ill-concealed pleasure, he noted that America "may have to go to war to vindicate the principles for which she stands."[77]

In September Kerr sought to allay American fears that Allied plans for future economic cooperation promulgated at the recent Paris Economic Conference did not envisage a trade bloc targeted at the United States. He also emphasized that Germany's conclusive defeat was the essential precondition of any lasting peace settlement.[78] Implicitly responding to Wilson's recent notes to all belligerents demanding that they should state the terms on which they would be prepared to make peace, three months later Kerr reiterated the latter theme.[79] Indeed, Wilson's peace initiative so alarmed Kerr that he sent the Anglo-Irish Liberal Sir Horace Plunkett, who had spent many years in the United States and shared his own hopes that the United States would join the Allies in the war, a letter he hoped would reach Wilson, contending that any American "peace intervention ... would really be on behalf of militarism." He argued against opening any negotiations with Germany until Germany declared her readiness "to restore Belgium, France and Serbia, and to indemnify them."[80]

---

[76] Kerr, "The Harvest of the War," 26-29, quotations from 27, 28; cf. "The War for Public Right," 216-217

[77] Kerr, "The Principle of Peace," 423-424, quotations from 423, 424.

[78] Kerr, "War Aims," 607-612.

[79] Kerr, "The Making of Peace," 1-8.

[80] Thomas Jones to Eirene Theodora Jones, 10 Dec. 1916, in Jones, *Whitehall Diary*, 1:11. Although Kerr's letter is not in the Wilson Papers, in late December Plunkett expressed similar fears both verbally and in writing to Colonel Edward M. House, Wilson's confidential adviser. Plunkett to House, 27 December 1916, *The Papers of Woodrow Wilson*, Vol. 40, ed. Arthur S. Link (Princeton, NJ: Princeton University Press, 1982), 339-342; and Trevor West, *Horace Plunkett: Co-operation and Politics, an Irish Biography* (Washington, DC: Catholic University of America Press, 1986), 143.

Kerr urged that the United States should not simply follow policies of differential neutrality favoring the Allies, but should also participate actively in the postwar settlement. Like his analyses of the causes of the war, at least in part his statements of liberal war aims were almost certainly aimed at the United States, where support for some form of postwar international organization or "League to Enforce Peace" burgeoned after the outbreak of war. As early as December 1914, Kerr argued that, once Germany was defeated, the war's "distant end" would be "that voluntary federation of free civilized nations which will eventually exorcise the spectre of competitive armaments and give everlasting peace to mankind."[81] In mid-1915 Walter Hines Page, the pro-allied United States Ambassador to the Court of St. James, who himself subscribed to the Mahanist thesis that American security depended upon British sea power, reported that Kerr believed that closer Anglo-American relations must form the bedrock of any postwar settlement, and was "red hot for a close and perfect understanding between Great Britain and the United States." Although Page felt that Kerr exaggerated the degree to which the war experience had encouraged democracy in Britain, and believed that Britain should not expect to dominate such an arrangement, he was fundamentally sympathetic to Kerr's thesis.[82] As ambassador, Page effectively endorsed Kerr's reiterated pleas for American acquiescence in British wartime policies and, ultimately, for American support.[83] In June 1915 Kerr stated that "the first and most essential of objects in the war is to compel Germany to admit utter and decisive defeat." He continued, however, that a "vindictive" peace settlement "would only reunite the autocracy and the people in a common hatred, and a common determination to redress the wrong." Moreover, "[u]ntil we reach the stage when the constitution of a

---

[81] Kerr, "After Four Months' War," 9.

[82] Page to Arthur W. Page, 25 July 1915, in Burton J. Hendrick, *The Life and Letters of Walter Hines Page*, 3 vols. (Garden City, NY: Doubleday, Page & Co., 1922), 2:84-87, quotation from 85; and Butler, *Lord Lothian*, 59. Kerr later reviewed Hendrick's life of Page. He may well have drawn on personal experience when stating that "when anyone talked to [Page] about the aloofness or remoteness of America, he used to retort that the real aloofness was in Britain, which still thought itself the centre of gravity in the world, while the centre of progress had really shifted to North America. Britain had to be willing to learn of America before there could be a real 'union of thought.'" Kerr, "Walter Page," *The Round Table* 13:50 (March 1923), 289-299, quotation from 292-293.

[83] On Page's policies, see Ross Gregory, *Walter Hines Page: Ambassador to the Court of St. James's* (Lexington: University of Kentucky Press, 1970); and John Milton Cooper, Jr., *Walter Hines Page: The Southerner as American, 1855-1918* (Chapel Hill: University of North Carolina Press, 1977).

real government of the world has entered the sphere of practical politics, the only security for international peace and liberty will be the determination of the most civilized Powers to uphold the sanctity of international agreements and right, in the first place by all peaceful means, but in the last resort by the sword."[84]

Kerr soon elaborated these themes, charging that one reason for the war was the self-absorption of the "Western Powers," who had thought "only about their own peace and liberty, and ... repudiat[ed], under the plea of avoiding foreign entanglements, any responsibility for maintaining right and justice in international affairs." He charged that: "The inhabitants of the British Commonwealth, like the inhabitants of the United States, have forgotten the true nature of liberty." He called for "the creation of a world state," governed by "a responsible and representative political authority which will consider every problem presented to it from the point of view of humanity and not of a single state or people," and with the power to enforce its decisions. Those nations which were represented in it would need to be democracies, and he suggested that "[t]he British Commonwealth is a perfect example of the eventual world commonwealth." Admitting that "this goal ... [was] out of the range of practical politics," Kerr nonetheless called upon the Great Powers—by implication including the United States—"to create a new and better Concert [of Nations] embracing all people and based upon the reign of liberty and justice between nations." It should, he believed, begin with a "voluntary union of the most liberal states," one which "would not hesitate to maintain the sanctity of international right and liberty, and of international law as defined in agreements, if need be, by force of arms. ... To such a union other Powers might gradually and voluntarily join themselves until it eventually embraced the whole world." Once Germany was defeated, "other nations must admit her to a Concert of civilized Powers on equal terms." Moreover, nations would have to be prepared to discuss with each other "many matters connected with sea-power and land-power, exclusive spheres of influence, and even of economic policy, especially in dependencies, which have hitherto been regarded as the sacred preserves of sovereign states."[85]

From then onward, Kerr argued that international non-involvement was selfish, and that "[t]he problems of humanity will only be solved if all civilized powers co-operate in finding the solution." This, he believed, "involves the establishment of a permanent conference of the great

---

[84] Kerr, "The Foundations of Peace," 589-625, quotations from 612, 613, 617.
[85] Kerr, "The End of War," 772-796, quotations from 773, 790, 783, 787, 792, 793.

powers." In December 1915 he appealed specifically to the United States to be "a member of the Peace Conference, and of the Concert [of Nations] into which it may grow," warning that "on her decision all the hopes of human unity will hang. By breaking with her long-established national tradition and assuming common responsibilities for maintaining right and justice throughout the world she can probably save the world from another Armageddon. By clinging to the policy of isolation she can condemn mankind to another era of estrangement and war."[86] In March 1916 he cautioned that, if Germany won the war, "[t]he most impressive feature in the world will be an aggregation of militarist Powers stretching from the North Sea to the Persian Gulf," controlled by Berlin, and dedicated to the use of force in international affairs. It was essential, therefore, that the Allies "defeat the attempt of Germany to establish the predominance of her own will in the councils of Europe, and to secure a peace which will make it impossible for her, or for anyone else for that matter, to think of making such an attempt again." Once more, he warned: "The really important thing is that the peace, if it is just, should have behind it the guarantee of all the great civilized Powers." Sounding themes which would recur throughout his career, Kerr implicitly suggested that American and British sea power be enhanced and restrictions upon its effectiveness removed, since "sea power is and must be the chief sanction behind international liberty and right."[87]

In June 1916 Kerr suggested that Germany's plans to organize a Mittel Europa bloc, leaving her "dominant over the whole area between the Dwina and the Franco-Belgian frontier, and between the North Sea and the Persian Gulf," would expose that entire region to arbitrary Prussian autocratic rule, and the rest of Europe to "German dictation." "The essential condition of peace," he argued, "is that Germany should be forced to accept such a position that she will no longer be able to dream of dictating successfully to Europe, and so will have no option but to accept the status of equality with her neighbours based upon equal rights for all civilized States." Again, he blamed "the Western democracies" for allowing Germany to reach so powerful a position that only fighting could check it, and in his most forthright statement to date declared: "The creation of a new international order depends mainly upon the Allies and America." While stating that the British Empire would still bear the heaviest burden of all, he continued: "It is essential that America, also, should take part in the

---

[86] Kerr, "The Harvest of the War," 1-32, quotations from 15, 19, 29.
[87] Kerr, "The War for Public Right," 193-231, quotations from 213-215, 226.

work of international reconstruction."[88] In his last, comparatively brief article on the subject, published just before he went to work for Lloyd George, Kerr rather vaguely stated that "if militarism is to be for ever overthrown the neutrals will have to abandon the dream of selfish isolation, and undertake their share of the burdens and obligations of creating an effective security behind public right .... That," he added, "is the goal towards which the nations of the Empire are striving with unfaltering steps. It is for other nations to decide whether it is to be immediately attained."[89]

Kerr's courtship of American opinion habitually enveloped pleas for self-interested national aims in a broad and ample cloak of high-minded, idealistic rhetoric, a tactic that would become his future trademark. It is interesting to speculate what impact his writings had on the influential Americans he sought to reach. As early as summer 1915 Walter Hines Page, the pro-Allied ambassador in London and a former magazine editor, described the periodical as "the best review, I dare say, in the world," and the Round Table group as "perhaps the best group of men here for the real study and free discussion of large political subjects."[90] *The Round Table* sought to increase its circulation and influence in the United States. In April 1916 Curtis discussed the possibility of forming a Round Table branch in the United States to discuss potential cooperation between that country and the British Empire, but Beer persuaded him that "any such connection" would be "fatal," since "[t]he U.S.A. groups would be regarded from the outset as intended to bring the U.S. under the English thumb."[91] In autumn 1917 Kerr's Kindergarten and Round Table colleague Robert H. Brand, now part of the British bureaucracy handling North American munitions purchases, mounted a subscription drive in the United States, advertising in the American journal *The New Republic* and sending mailings to editors, libraries, and academics. *The Round Table* characterized its objectives as "[t]he maintenance of the British Commonwealth of Nations ... [and] the furtherance of close and friendly relations between the Commonwealth and the United States." Although the periodical only increased its American circulation from one to two hundred, mostly in educated northeastern

---

[88] Kerr, "The Principle of Peace," 391-429, quotations from 411, 413, 422, 423.
[89] Kerr, "The Making of Peace," 1-13, quotations from 8.
[90] Page to Arthur W. Page, 25 July 1915, in Hendrick, *Walter Hines Page*, 2:84-85; and Butler, *Lord Lothian*, 59.
[91] Curtis to Kerr, 24 April 1916, GD 40/17/3/250-258, Lothian Papers; Kendle, *Round Table Movement*, 195 n. 44; Billington, *Lothian*, 47; and Bothwell, *Loring Christie*, 92-93.

circles, its editors congratulated themselves on how many of these subscribers were influential members of the American elite.[92]

In the case of the weekly *The New Republic*, founded in 1914 with financial backing from a progressive American businessman and his wife, Willard and Dorothy Straight, Round Table influence may have been substantial. Kerr probably encountered two of its future editors, Walter Lippmann and Herbert Croly, on his 1912 United States trip. Visiting Europe in summer 1914 Lippmann met Geoffrey Dawson, who had been editing *The Round Table* during Kerr's illness, and probably other members of the group. On three trips to Britain during the years of American neutrality the pro-Allied Straight, whose views on the conflict resembled those of Ambassador Page, certainly met several of them when he visited Cliveden. In spring 1916 Curtis visited *The New Republic*'s New York office and, at Kerr's suggestion, tried to reach "some specific agreement with our friends in the U.S.A. as to principles of policy to be adopted." Curtis himself thought the journal's editors exhibited a "repulsive attitude," laying too much emphasis on *realpolitik* and questions of the national interest, and told Kerr he would be "wiser to drop" his original idea.[93]

Kerr himself might, one suspects, have found the journal's personnel far more congenial. From early in the war Straight, a strong supporter of Mahan's theories of sea power, urged *The New Republic*'s editors to follow a pro-Allied line and, albeit too slowly and with overly many qualifications for Straight's liking, essentially they did so. His previous lack of interest in international affairs notwithstanding, Lippmann was largely responsible for developing *The New Republic*'s stance on the war. While less anti-German than Kerr, from early 1915 he called for differential American neutrality policies favoring the Allies, a just peace settlement, and the abandonment of United States isolation. He told a British friend that in spring 1915, at the time when a German submarine sank the British passenger liner the *Lusitania*, drowning many of its American passengers, the journal's editors consciously "decided ... to devote the paper to the creation of an Anglo-American understanding." By January 1916 Lippmann argued that, without "a vision of the Anglo-American future," "crowning disaster" lay in store for American foreign policy. He supported Wilson's spring 1916 endorsement of the League to Enforce Peace program for a postwar international organization, which

---

[92] Billington, *Lothian*, 47.
[93] Curtis to Kerr, 24 April 1916, GD 40/17/3/250-58, Lothian Papers; and Bothwell, *Loring Christie*, 92-93.

he privately hoped would also help to bring the United States into the war. Lippmann also predicted that any such league would rest upon an alliance of American, British, and French sea power. In February 1917, shortly before American intervention, he publicly stated the Mahanist case for his country's participation in the war, that it was an integral part of the "Atlantic community," whose own security had since the early nineteenth century depended upon the implicit protection of the British fleet. For the rest of his career, through the Second World War and into the 1960s, Lippmann was to be one of the foremost American advocates of this perspective, which underpinned the Realist school of internationalist thought. In April 1917, just after the United States finally declared war on Germany, Lippmann again echoed Kerr in stating that the war's objective was "a union of liberal peoples pledged to cooperate in the settlement of all outstanding questions, sworn to turn against the aggressor, determined to erect a larger and more modern system of international law upon a federation of the world." Lippmann was apparently inspired in part by the Russian Revolution of February 1917, an event that likewise briefly impelled Kerr in spring 1917 to urge Lloyd George to present the war as one for "the democratisation of Europe" and a just peace without annexations.[94]

The New Republic furnished only one example of the manner in which the war experience itself contributed substantially to the creation of an Atlanticist tradition of foreign policy among both leading Dominion

---

[94] Lippmann to Graham Wallas, 21 April 1916, in *Public Philosopher: Selected Letters of Walter Lippmann*, ed. John Morton Blum (New York: Ticknor & Fields, 1984), 46; Ronald Steel, *Walter Lippmann and the American Century* (Boston: Little Brown, 1980), esp. 67-73, 88-115; Ross A. Kennedy, *The Will to Believe: Woodrow Wilson, World War I, and America's Strategy for Peace and Security* (Kent, OH: Kent State University Press, 2009), 5-6, 12-14, 27-35, 44-54, 60-64, 104-109, 122-124; David Seidemann, *The New Republic: A Voice of Modern Liberalism* (New York: Praeger, 1986), 1-59; Charles Forcey, *The Crossroads of Liberalism: Croly, Weyl, Lippmann and the Progressive Era, 1900-1925* (New York: Oxford University Press, 1961), esp. ch. 7; David W. Levy, *Herbert Croly of The New Republic: The Life and Thought of an American Progressive* (Princeton, NJ: Princeton University Press, 1985), chs. 7-8; John A. Thompson, *Reformers and War: American progressive publicists and the First World War* (Cambridge: Cambridge University Press, 1987), chs. 4-5; Priscilla Roberts, "Willard D. Straight and the Diplomacy of International Finance During the First World War," *Business History* 40:3 (July 1998), 16-47; and Roberts, "Willard Straight, World War I, and 'Internationalism of All Sorts': The Inconsistencies of an American Liberal Interventionist," *Australian Journal of Politics and History* 44:4 (December 1998), 493-511. On Kerr's views in spring 1917, see Kerr to Lloyd George, n.d. [May 1917], GD 40/929/1, Lothian Papers; and Turner, "Philip Kerr in Downing Street," 39-40.

figures and the politically influential United States patrician elite of the United States East Coast. In the Dominions these included Jan Christiaan Smuts, the highly respected Prime Minister of South Africa, and prominent Canadians, notably Sir Robert Borden, Canada's wartime prime minister, who in 1918 told Leopold Amery, assistant secretary to the British war cabinet, of his hopes that any future world organization would

> unite, by the closest ties of purpose, of interest and of action, the two great English speaking commonwealths which are of themselves sufficiently powerful to dictate the peace of the world if they can subordinate to a common aim the jealousies and divergencies which naturally arise from time to time; and through such an understanding or alliance between Britain and America to have a less active and intimate relationship to the minor complexities and rivalries of European politics.[95]

Assorted influential American Anglophiles likewise believed that Anglo-American collaboration must be central to any lasting international settlement. Theodore Roosevelt was probably the foremost exponent of the Atlanticist outlook, which differed in important respects from the Wilsonian vision of a liberal world order offering most nations at least formal legal equality. American Atlanticists shared the same Anglo-Saxonist beliefs as their British counterparts, heightened, for many patrician Americans, by a desire to maintain social and political dominance over the tide of non-Protestant immigrants from southern and eastern Europe who poured into the United States from the 1880s onward, and to force the newcomers to accept old-stock values and norms.[96] Besides purporting to defend Western civilization, democracy, and Christendom against absolutist Kaiserism, Prussianism, and despotism, American Atlanticists fundamentally emphasized the saliency of military force over liberal principles. They generally advocated intervention in the First World War, the creation of an Anglo-American alliance as the basis of

---

[95] Borden to Amery, 22 August 1918, GD 40/17/1064/2, Lothian Papers; cf. Bothwell, *Loring Christie*, 163-164; and Fry, *Illusions of Security*, 9-11.

[96] On patrician Americans' resentment of the new immigrants, see Anderson, *Race and Rapprochement*, 54-57, 82-82; John Higham, *Strangers in the Land: Patterns of American Nativism 1860-1925*, 2nd ed. (New Brunswick, NJ: Rutgers University Press, 1977), 136-144, 175-182; Richard Hofstadter, *The Age of Reform: From Bryan to F.D.R.* (New York: Vintage, 1956), 176-186; David M. Kennedy, *Over Here: The First World War and American Society* (New York: Oxford University Press, 1980), 63-69; Desmond King, *Making Americans: Immigration, Race, and the Origins of the Diverse Democracy* (Cambridge, MA: Harvard University Press, 2000), esp. chs. 3-7; and Zimmermann, *First Great Triumph*, 455-465.

international security, the maintenance of a favorable international balance of power, Germany's economic reintegration into the European system, and American participation in Europe's economic revival through loans and the cancellation or reduction of war debts and reparations. Besides Theodore Roosevelt, this tradition's adherents included such Republican luminaries as the lawyers Elihu Root, Henry L. Stimson, Frederic R. Coudert, and George W. Wickersham, together with prominent Democrats, among them Wilson's confidential adviser, Colonel Edward M. House, Robert A. Lansing, Wilson's secretary of state, and such mid-level administration figures as Ambassador Page, assistant secretary of the navy Franklin D. Roosevelt, assistant secretary of the treasury Norman H. Davis, assistant secretary of state Frank L. Polk, and John W. Davis, the solicitor general. Significantly for the Allies, among the Atlanticist ranks were the members of the Anglo-American banking house J. P. Morgan and Company, notably J. P. Morgan, Jr., Henry P. Davison, Thomas W. Lamont, and Dwight W. Morrow, together with Morgan employee Willard Straight, assistant treasury secretary Russell C. Leffingwell, a future Morgan partner, and Benjamin Strong, the first governor of the new Federal Reserve Bank of New York, whose crucial assistance enabled the Allies well before American intervention to raise substantial sums of vital war financing in the United States.[97]

Such Americans were generally lukewarm toward President Woodrow Wilson's efforts to create an international organization with broad powers to impose sanctions and enforce world order. Many considered the British Empire and British imperialism admirably benevolent institutions promoting international stability and the ultimate civilization of non-white races. Most thought the creation of a *de facto* permanent Anglo-American or in some cases Allied-American alliance, perhaps reinforced by an Anglo-American guarantee of French security against any potential future German attack, far more central to a lasting

---

[97] On these two traditions, see Priscilla Roberts, "The Anglo-American Theme: American Visions of an Atlantic Alliance, 1914-1933," *Diplomatic History* 21:3 (Summer 1997), 333-364; Nicholas J. Cull, "Selling Peace: The Origins, Promotion and Fate of the Anglo-American New Order During World War II," *Diplomacy and Statecraft* 7:1 (March 1996), 1-15; Thomas J. Knock, *To End All Wars: Woodrow Wilson and the Quest for a New World Order* (New York: Oxford University Press, 1992); and William N. Tilchin, *Theodore Roosevelt and the British Empire: A Study in Presidential Statecraft* (New York: St. Martin's Press, 1997). An extremely interesting and carefully nuanced recent work on Wilson and internationalist forces during the war portrays American thinking on foreign affairs at that time as divided among the forces of 'liberal internationalism,' 'pacifism,' and 'Atlanticism.' Kennedy, *The Will to Believe*.

international settlement than Wilson's broader plans for the League of Nations.[98] Many concurred with Lamont's view, stated in 1918, that:

> For the long future the safety and happiness of both America and Great Britain are dependent upon these two great nations working in accord. The peace of the whole world is dependent upon the same thing. Both nations are, in the last analysis, animated by the same ideals, working for the same ends. Neither desires conquest; each wishes the weaker nations should be able to work out their destinies unmolested; each stands for individual liberty; for a State governed by the people and for the people; each has the same basis of common law, similar language, institutions, similar ideas in education and the civilizing process of liberal education. If it were geographically possible, the two nations ought almost to become one. That being out of the question, still if they work closely together, neither they nor the whole world has anything to fear for the future.[99]

Kerr had frequent wartime contacts with such Americans, some of whom he had known since his pre-war American journeys. Reflecting both the importance to the British war effort almost from the time the conflict began of American loans, munitions and other war supplies, and the significance of U.S. public opinion, with official encouragement influential Americans visiting Britain were invariably cosseted and well entertained. Cliveden, the Astors' Buckinghamshire country mansion, was not only a weekend base for the Round Table group, another of whose key members, Robert Brand, married Nancy Astor's sister Phyllis during the war; then and later it also provided welcome hospitality to numerous well-connected American visitors, among them Morgan partners and employees, such as Davison, Lamont, Morrow, and Straight, and Treasury and State Department officials such as Davis, Polk, and Paul D. Cravath, who took the opportunity to exchange and develop ideas on post-war Anglo-American collaboration. For the most part, Kerr's views accorded closely with those of his American interlocutors, though who influenced whom must be something of a moot question.

---

[98] On these divergences, see Roberts, "Anglo-American Theme," 333-364.

[99] Thomas W. Lamont, "Memorandum for the Lord Reading: Ways to Bring About a Closer Union and to Improve the Relations Between America and Great Britain," November 1917, File 81-12, Thomas W. Lamont Papers, Baker Library, Harvard Business School, Boston, MA. For an account of the genesis of this memorandum, which Lamont spent an Atlantic crossing discussing with Lords Reading and Northcliffe, see Lamont, diary, 3-12 November 1917, File 243-6, Lamont Papers; also Lamont to Reading, 3, 25 October 1917, File 126-16, *ibid.*

Those American Atlanticists who had helped to run the burgeoning inter-Allied wartime bureaucracy often believed, as did their British counterparts, that "the continuation and strengthening of the existing Inter-Allied organizations for economic cooperation" would provide the best basis for postwar international organization. As one wrote to the United States Secretary of the Treasury:

> Indeed, it seems to me that those organizations furnish the nearest approach to an effective League of Nations that the world has ever seen. It may well be that success in continuing the existing Inter-Allied machinery for economic cooperation during the period of the world's convalescence from the economic maladies resulting from the war would lead to the establishment of some permanent international economic machinery which would make for peace and provide an economic weapon with which to discipline any nation which threatened to disturb the peace of the world.[100]

From the viewpoint of British politicians such as Waldorf Astor, such collaboration would also enable the British to retain greater influence over international economic policy.[101]

From December 1916 until early 1921, Kerr was no longer merely a commentator, but one of Liberal Prime Minister David Lloyd George's private secretaries. After the war ended he became the most important of these, and the premier often turned to him for advice. Throughout his years with Lloyd George, one of Kerr's major preoccupations was Anglo-American relations. He dealt closely with visiting American journalists,

---

[100] Paul D. Cravath to William G. McAdoo, 7 November 1918, Box 6, Paul D. Cravath Papers, Record Group 56, General Records of the Department of the Treasury, U.S. National Archives II, College Park, MD.; cf. Memorandum of conclusions reached at conference held at Paris October 17th 1918, *ibid.*; Dwight W. Morrow, "Draft for Armistice not used," February 1918, File Allied Maritime Transport Council-American Supplies Mission-Memoranda and Drafts 1918, Dwight W. Morrow Papers, Amherst College Library, Amherst, MA; Willard D. Straight to Dorothy W. Straight, 12 May 1918, Reel 6, and Straight, diary, 15 May 1918, Reel 12, Willard D. Straight Papers (microfilm ed.), Cornell University Library, Ithaca, NY; and Dean Acheson, *Fragments of my Fleece* (New York: Norton, 1971), 206.
[101] Waldorf Astor to Thomas Jones, 17 November 1918, included in Jones, *Whitehall Diary*, 1:70-72; see also Seth P. Tillman, *Anglo-American Relations at the Paris Peace Conference of 1919* (Princeton, NJ: Princeton University Press, 1961), 260-272; Carl P. Parrini, *Heir to Empire: United States Economic Diplomacy, 1916-1923* (Pittsburgh, PA: Pittsburgh University Press, 1969), 40-54; Burton I. Kaufman, *Efficiency and Expansion: Foreign Trade Organization in the Wilson Administration, 1913-1921* (Westport, CT: Greenwood, 1974), 237-241; and Michael J. Hogan, *Informal Entente: The Private Structure of Cooperation in Anglo-American Diplomacy, 1918-1928* (Columbia: University of Missouri Press, 1977), 20-27.

attempting to persuade them to present the British case on such controversial issues as Ireland, as described by Melanie Sayers elsewhere in this volume. He often advised Lloyd George how to slant his speeches and public pronouncements, especially on such matters as liberal war aims and Irish problems, so as best to accord with American sensibilities.[102] In 1917 he enlisted the prestigious Smuts in efforts to persuade Wilson to allow Great Britain or its dominions to retain many of Germany's colonies, urging that Smuts stress not the communications advantages Britain would gain thereby, but the benefits to the territories themselves from attachment "to a neighbouring free power ... or to a power which has a great colonial experience ... or [from] be[ing] internationalised."[103]

Kerr's most influential contributions to shaping the future international order were his efforts to draw up proposals for the formulation of the new League of Nations that accorded with his own preference for an Anglo-American condominium, initiatives that illuminated the vision of the postwar world at the core of his idealistic earlier pronouncements. Kerr remained eager to draw the United States irrevocably into international involvements, preferably on the Atlanticist model. One of his early tasks for Lloyd George was to help him draft a letter to Wilson, welcoming the American president into the war, and staking a claim to a special relationship of close cooperation between Britain and the United States, the two powers upon whom, the premier argued, the primary responsibility both for winning the war and devising an acceptable postwar settlement would ultimately rest.[104]

In 1918 and 1919 Kerr, together with Maurice Hankey, the long-time secretary to the British cabinet, was a central figure in protracted though ultimately unsuccessful British efforts to modify the League of Nations, attempting to create a body with less extensive powers than President Wilson favored, particularly in terms of enforcing compulsory sanctions against transgressor nations, an organization that would effectively build upon the inter-Allied agencies of economic control and political consultation created in the war's final two years, and be dominated by the United States and Britain. Kerr would have been content with a

---

[102] Numerous examples of Kerr's detailed concern to improve Anglo-American relations are scattered through his voluminous correspondence as secretary to Lloyd George, Files GD 40/17/26-80 and 517-1421, Lothian Papers.
[103] Kerr to Smuts, 14 December 1917, in *Selections from the Smuts Papers*, Vol. III: *June 1910-November 1918*, eds. W. H. Hancock and Jean Van Der Poel (Cambridge: Cambridge University Press, 1966), 576-577.
[104] Grigg, *Lloyd George*, 301-304.

League that functioned only as an annual international consultative conference, essentially the peace conference reconvening once a year to discuss matters of interest to the assembled members, or alternatively, with a body that was constituted as a permanent standing international conference, possessing few real powers and concentrating on such relatively uncontroversial issues as world health. The League of Nations Kerr envisaged, founded upon an implicit or explicit Anglo-American alliance, also accorded closely with the views of many of Kerr's Anglophile American friends, who tended to find Wilson's planned international organization too sweeping and ambitious, and preferred a body that would have effectively been founded upon a more limited U.S. alliance with Britain and perhaps France.[105]

Kerr was particularly uncomfortable with early drafts of the League Covenant that called for the new organization to guarantee the borders of all its member states, provisions that he feared might commit Britain to wars in defense of nations in whose security it had no particular stake. In part at least on his urging, Lloyd George and other British delegates succeeded in diluting this provision.[106] Such reservations may have derived in part from Kerr's fears that the peace terms imposed upon Germany were unduly harsh and likely to provoke radicalism, revanchism, and a quest for revenge in the defeated nation, beliefs which in March 1919 led him, Lloyd George, and others in the British delegation to seek to moderate somewhat the settlement the Germans were compelled to accept at Paris.[107] According to Erik Goldstein, a suggestion Kerr made in March 1919, that the British and Americans should jointly guarantee France's security against future attack, "appears to be the origin" of the treaties for that purpose which those countries negotiated later that year, agreements which were among the casualties of the United States Senate's decision to reject American

---

[105] Kerr, Memorandum on the League of Nations, January 1919, GD 40/54, Lothian Papers [reprinted in Egerton, "Conservative Internationalism," 17-19]; Egerton, "Conservative Internationalism," 1-20; Egerton, "Imperialism, Atlanticism, and Internationalism," 95-122; Fry, *Illusions of Security*, 18-26; Kendle, *Round Table Movement*, 252; Turner, "Philip Kerr in Downing Street," 42-43; and Billington, *Lothian*, 55. Peter J. Yearwood disputes this analysis, but although he brings out Kerr's eagerness to reach a peace settlement acceptable to the United States and to base this upon Anglo-American hegemony, some aspects of his overall interpretation of Kerr's stance as an effective rejection of balance-of-power politics seem less than convincing. Yearwood, "'Real Securities against New Wars': Official British Thinking and the Origins of the League of Nations, 1914-19," *Diplomacy and Statecraft* 9:3 (November 1998), 83-109.

[106] Billington, *Lothian*, 57.

[107] *Ibid.*, 60-62.

membership in the League of Nations.[108] As late as 1937 Kerr still expressed his faith in these agreements, telling A. L. Kennedy of *The Times* "at some length of the importance of the Anglo-Am: guarantee to France in the 1919 Peace Settlement. He [Lothian] made out it was an essential element in it; & the U.S.A.'s failure to uphold it destroyed the whole balance of the Treaty of Versailles."[109] The historian Lloyd Ambrosius has suggested that the proposed Anglo-American security treaty may be considered a forerunner of the post-Second World War North Atlantic Treaty Organization.[110]

Kerr was also eager to moderate American hostility to colonialism by persuading that country to accept quasi-colonial responsibilities, working closely with both Curtis and Beer, who became one of the members of the American Inquiry group established under House's direction to study all questions relating to the peace settlement, in repeated efforts to pressure Wilson into assuming a United States mandate in Armenia or elsewhere.[111] Kerr and his likeminded allies believed that, by tying the United States into the peace settlement, such arrangements would make it impossible for the American government and people to withdraw from greater international involvement in the postwar world. The First World War had, he believed, made active U.S. participation in and support for the settlement that emerged from the peace conference essential to international stability. In the next chapter in this volume, Keith Neilson

---

[108] Erik Goldstein, *Winning the Peace: British Diplomatic Strategy, Peace Planning, and the Paris Peace Conference, 1916-1920* (Oxford: Clarendon Press, 1991), 236; also Turner, "Philip Kerr in Downing Street," 44; and Billington, *Lothian*, 60. On U.S. attitudes toward the French security treaty and the Senate Knox Resolution of 1919, which likewise attempted to provide such an American guarantee, see Ralph Stone, *The Irreconcilables: The Fight Against the League of Nations* (New York: Norton, 1973), 26-27, 41, 44-48, 55, 108; Stone, "The Irreconcilables' Alternatives to the League of Nations," *Mid-America* 49:3 (July 1967), 163-173; Lloyd E. Ambrosius, "Wilson, the Republicans, and French Security after World War I," *Journal of American History* 59:2 (September 1972), 341-352; Keith L. Nelson, *Victors Divided: America and the Allies in Germany, 1918-1923* (Berkeley and Los Angeles: University of California Press, 1975), 79-88; and Walter A. MacDougall, *France's Rhineland Diplomacy, 1914-1924: The Last Bid for a Balance of Power in Europe* (Princeton, NJ: Princeton University Press, 1978), 60-61, 67-68.

[109] Kennedy, diary entry, 18 May 1937, in Martel, ed., *The Times and Appeasement*, 247.

[110] Ambrosius, "Wilson, the Republicans, and French Security after World War I," 341-352.

[111] Kerr to C. J. B. Hurst, 25 November 1919, GD 40/17/211/551-53, Lothian Papers; Kerr, "Harvest of Victory," 668-669; Kerr to Curtis, 15 October 1918, quoted in Butler, *Lord Lothian*, 68-70; *ibid.*, 74-75; Lavin, *From Empire to International Commonwealth*, 160-163; Kendle, *Round Table Movement*, 252-258; Fry, *Illusions of Security*, 24-25; and Billington, *Lothian*, 55-56.

highlights Kerr's distaste for the emergence of a radical Bolshevik regime in Russia, the world's first communist state, pledged to overthrow existing non-communist governments and spread socialism around the globe. Believing that Britain was already over-committed militarily in the Middle East and elsewhere, a victim of imperial overstretch, and that efforts to overthrow the Bolsheviks might well provoke serious leftist unrest at home, Kerr opposed expanding Allied intervention in Russia and hoped that a policy of containment, assistance to non-Bolshevik Russian groups, and ceasefire negotiations for a peace that would reconcile the warring Russian factions, would suffice to deal with the peril the new Leninist ideology posed to liberal values and the existing order.[112]

Such measures were, in Kerr's opinion, likely to prove fruitless without the backing of the United States. Less than a month before the war ended, he warned his friend Lionel Curtis:

> This war has liberated destructive forces infinitely more powerful than any which have hitherto been known. ... You have now got started in the world an active, aggressive religion of social destruction—Bolshevism. It seems pretty clear that the peoples of South America, Africa, China, will be quite incapable of resisting these destructive forces unless the Western Powers help them to do so. ... [T]he Western powers will have definitely to make themselves responsible for seeing that the disorders which are likely to follow this war in these backward lands do not go beyond a certain point.
>
> The extent of this work after the war, sometimes known as the white man's burden, will be so hard that it will never be accomplished at all unless it is shared in proportions equal to their strength by the four allies now united in fighting the Germans. Yet America not only has no conception of this aspect of the problem but has been led by shibboleths and labels to believe that the assumption of this kind of responsibility is iniquitous imperialism ....
>
> You can see what an immense difference it is going to make whether America comes to learn its responsibilities in regard to this matter quickly or slowly. If they are slow in learning we shall be condemned to a period not only of chaos in these backward countries but of strained relations between the various parts of the English-speaking world. On the other hand if only we can get into the heads of Canadians and Americans that the assumption of a share in the burden of world government is just as great and glorious a responsibility as participation in the war, you at once remove the last great barrier to an Anglo-Saxon understanding and give to the whole English-

---

[112] Billington, *Lothian*, 57-59, 71.

speaking world a common task in the execution of which they can show co-operation.[113]

One of the major obstacles Kerr perceived to bringing this scenario into being was the American president. Wilson's support for a League of Nations notwithstanding, Kerr warned Curtis that: "America still has a childlike faith in the virtues of democracy and laisser faire and, unfortunately, Wilson who today is absolute dictator of American public opinion appears to share this view." He described Wilson as "the prophet of Gladstonian liberalism brought up to date. It is admirable as far as it goes, but it also is negative and if it dominates the Peace Conference is bound to produce itself a settlement which will contain within itself the seeds of Gordon disasters and Majubas on a vastly larger scale."[114]

Given the substantial differences between Kerr's preferred form of international organization and the League of Nations that the Paris Peace Conference created at the president's behest, it was perhaps not surprising that, once it ran aground on the shoals of U.S. politics, Kerr demonstrated little commitment to the new institution. For Kerr, as for many in the British government at this time, the highest priority was to ensure American participation in and support for the new postwar world order, a quest in which they were prepared to sacrifice or at least compromise on the League as established by Wilson. As soon as the U.S. Senate rejected the League of Nations in late 1919, Kerr began drafting tentative strategies whereby the Allies might be able to accept United States entry into the League of Nations with such reservations as the Senate might require, schemes that generally involved the weakening or dilution of British commitments under the Treaty of Versailles, especially obligations to the French to uphold a settlement over which Kerr had already demonstrated major misgivings. He also suggested that Britain announce its intention of leaving the League in two years' time unless it modified its Covenant sufficiently to induce the United States to become a member.[115]

Early in 1920 Kerr publicly stated what would be his consistent position on the League for the next two decades, writing in *The Round*

---

[113] Kerr to Curtis, 15 October 1918, in Bosco, ed., *Two Musketeers for the Empire*, 138-139.

[114] *Ibid.*, 138, 140.

[115] Kerr, "Memorandum on American Reservations and British Ratification of the Treaty of Peace," 10 November 1919, GD 40/17/62, Lothian Papers; Kerr to Hurst, 25 November 1919, GD 40/17/211/551-53, Lothian Papers; Kerr to Eric Drummond, 24 December 1919, GD 40/17/56, Lothian Papers; Turner, "Philip Kerr in Downing Street," 52; and Billington, *Lothian*, 64.

Table that "the Treaty and the Covenant, in the desire for ideal solutions, both attempt too much." Some of the Treaty's territorial and reparation provisions he considered unworkable. The American Senate's reservations over the League were, in his opinion, "only a plain statement of views and feelings shared in reality by all the other signatories of the peace." Given the absence of the United States from the League, which made impossible a united Anglo-American front that could dominate the League, he thought Britain should declare similar reservations and seek "the revision of [British] obligations under the League," renouncing especially its pledge to guarantee the territorial and other terms of the Versailles settlement. Britain should state that its action in any given case would be governed solely by its own judgment; should not commit itself to any responsibilities it could not fully discharge; and "must definitely denounce the idea that the League may normally enforce its opinions by military or economic pressure on recalcitrant States." Such modifications, he argued, would mean the League would "sooner or later secure the whole-hearted support of American opinion," and thereby enhance its prospects of success.[116]

From this time onward Kerr's deepest political conviction, its roots dating back at least to the First World War and perhaps even before, remained apparently unchanged: his belief in the desirability of Anglo-American understanding as the foundation for any workable international order. As the United States Senate rejected American membership in the League, Kerr stated he remained "convinced that not only America but the Dominions also will have to take an active share in giving some kind of order and good government to the backward world, which otherwise is going to hopeless chaos."[117] In 1920 he told a clergyman, in words he could easily, *mutatis mutandis*, have written any time in the next twenty years:

> There is no more important work than to establish a good understanding between the American and British democracies. The future largely depends upon the co-operation of all the great Western democracies in the colossal task of rebuilding the world on better lines than those which crashed in ruins during the great war. It is especially on our two countries that the responsibility rests because they have now in especial degree, the wealth, and as I believe, the ideals, necessary to the making of a new and better world. That Great Britain and America will be able, despite all hostile and estranging propaganda, to co-operate in this work, I also believe, because the

---

[116] Kerr, "The British Empire, the League of Nations, and the United States," *The Round Table* 10:38 (March 1920), 221-253, quotations from 228, 244-247; and Butler, *Lord Lothian*, 79.
[117] Kerr to Arthur Glazebrook, 14 November 1919, GD 40/17/209/353, Lothian Papers.

ideals which lie at the bottom of their social, political and religious life are fundamentally the same.[118]

For the next two decades, Kerr became perhaps the most dedicated and eventually the most prominent interwar British advocate of this perspective, engaged in a wide variety of efforts to promote Anglo-American harmony and to entice, allure, alarm, or persuade the United States into close cooperation with the British Empire.

---

[118] Kerr to Rev. J. Morgan Gibbon, 14 June 1920, GD 40 17/209/362-363, Lothian Papers.

CHAPTER ONE

LORD LOTHIAN, RUSSIA, AND IDEAS FOR A NEW INTERNATIONAL ORDER, 1916-1922

KEITH NEILSON

Philip Kerr is best-known for several things: first, as a putative appeaser of Germany in the 1930s, second, as ambassador to the United States from 1939 to 1940, and third, as an advocate of supranational organizations.[1] With respect to the latter, his first vision was imperial federation within the British Empire; his second was a larger, global organization, something he termed "the larger idea." At the core of each of these ideas was Kerr's belief in the supremacy of the Anglo-Saxon world, an outlook that led to his strong advocacy of close Anglo-American relations as a means to achieve a global structure. His attitude to other nations has attracted less comment, however. Here, Russia is a particularly useful state to consider, since in its Tsarist and Soviet manifestations alike it presented a threat both to the wider Anglosphere and to the belief that, in Kerr's own words "law, and not force, must rule the international world."[2]

During the period from 1916 to 1922, when he served as private secretary to the British prime minister, David Lloyd George, Kerr had an opportunity both to develop his ideas and to see how international relations worked in practice. This was a crucial time for his career. He was at the center of affairs, he undertook a number of tasks dealing with international affairs for the prime minister, and he met various people who would play significant roles in the foreign policymaking elites of Britain and other

---

[1] The most comprehensive biography is David P. Billington, Jr., *Lothian: Philip Kerr and the Quest for World Order* (Westport, CT: Praeger, 2006); still of value is J. R. M. Butler, *Lord Lothian (Philip Kerr) 1882-1940* (London: Macmillan, 1960). Also helpful are the essays in John Turner, ed., *The Larger Idea: Lord Lothian and the Problem of National Sovereignty* (London: Historians Press, 1988); and Stefan Schieren, "Between two Extremes: Philip Kerr between Democracy and Empire," in *Chatham House and British Foreign Policy 1919-1945: The Royal Institute of International Affairs during the Inter-War Period*, eds. Andrea Bosco and Cornelia Navari (London: Lothian Foundation Press, 1994), 41-59.

[2] Kerr to Sir Horace Plunkett, 5 December 1916, Arthur James Balfour Papers, Add MSS 49797, British Library, London.

P. Roberts (ed.), Lord Lothian and Anglo-American Relations, 1900-1940, 45-60.

nations. This was particularly so during the Paris Peace Conference. At that gathering, Kerr often served as Lloyd George's alter ego when the prime minister was in London. While it would be an exaggeration to say that Kerr acted in some way akin to a foreign secretary—his primary tasks were to keep Lloyd George informed of events and to ensure that the prime minister's views were known—it is equally clear that he played an important role as an intermediary and that his own opinions at least colored British policy.

At the beginning of the First World War, Tsarist Russia was an awkward ally for British liberals. If the war was being fought to end, among other things, Prussian militarism, then it was difficult to justify achieving this in the company of autocratic Russia.[3] This led to a concerted effort by British commentators, including Kerr, to put the best face on Russia, something that drew the ire of some of Kerr's liberal friends.[4] In 1917, Kerr experienced an evolution with respect to Russia similar to that of many other Allied observers. He began by believing that the February revolution "has given a shock to most accepted institutions, & not least to militarism and the Kaiser."[5] While he did not believe that this would result in 'peace by Easter', he did feel that it might lead to democracy and an improved war effort, but soon realized that the latter was not to occur and that the only beneficiaries of disruption in Russia would be Germany and the Central Powers.[6] And, while initially sympathetic to the Bolshevik ideals of peace without annexation as something that would lead to a democratic peace, by 1918 Kerr realized that Bolshevist principles would undermine the British war effort and lead instead to a compromise peace, something incompatible with his own aspirations. Kerr was, in fact, very much opposed to a negotiated peace. In 1916, for example, he had rejected the idea that the United States might act as a peacemaker, arguing that America "might be driven to suggest peace terms which would in effect involve the partial triumph of the militarist evil, on the humanitarian pleas of saving human life."[7] If American efforts to effect a compromise peace were unacceptable, despite Kerr's belief that "all hopes of a better world

---

[3] The best study of British war aims is V. H. Rothwell, *British War Aims and Peace Diplomacy 1914-1918* (London: Oxford University Press, 1971).
[4] Billington, *Lothian*, 41.
[5] Kerr to Lady Anne Kerr [his mother], 2 April 1917, GD 40/17/466, Papers of the Eleventh Marquess of Lothian [hereafter Lothian Papers], National Archives of Scotland, Edinburgh.
[6] Billington, *Lothian*, 50-51; John Turner and Michael Dockrill, "Philip Kerr at 10 Downing Street," in Turner, ed., *The Larger Idea*, 39-41.
[7] Kerr to Plunkett, 5 December 1916, Balfour Papers, Add MSS 49797.

depend upon the cooperation of the English speaking peoples for human ends," then Bolshevik attempts were doubly repugnant, since they would lead to "class hatred and social strife, inevitably ending in Bolshevist ruin."[8]

Kerr's views and information on Russia were based on his discussions with various well-informed individuals. He carried on an extensive correspondence with two distinguished academic experts on Russia. One was J. Y. Simpson, Professor of Natural Science at Edinburgh University, who had traveled widely in Russia before the war. The second was Bernard Pares, Professor of Russian Language, Literature and History at Liverpool.[9] While these were informal relationships, they ensured that Kerr was at least as aware of events in Russia as anyone in the British government, if not those in the Foreign Office. Kerr also remained in close touch with Simpson after the latter joined the Political Intelligence Department at the Foreign Office, and the two men often discussed Russian affairs during the Paris Peace Conference.

It was, in fact, at the Paris Peace Conference that Kerr's views on Russia both developed and had their greatest influence.[10] One issue that closely involved Kerr was the ultimately abortive attempt to bring the various warring factions in Russia together at Prinkipo in an attempt to resolve their differences. This was a complex matter that played upon concerns important to the British. British troops were in Russia as part of the intervention undertaken to prevent Allied supplies sent to Russia falling into German hands, and whether these forces should remain in Russia was both still undetermined and an issue with important domestic political implications.[11] Nor was this solely a British concern, since over the past

---

[8] First quotation from *ibid.*; the second from Kerr to David Lloyd George, 20 November 1918, as cited in Turner and Dockrill, "Philip Kerr at 10 Downing Street," 41-42.

[9] Lothian's correspondence with Simpson can be found in GD 40/17/26 and GD 40/17/838-864, Lothian Papers; that with Pares is in GD 40/17/28-29, Lothian Papers. For the context of these academic experts and their general impact on Britain's policy toward Russia, see Keith Neilson, *Britain and the Last Tsar: British Policy and Russia, 1894-1917* (Oxford: Clarendon Press, 1995), 106-108.

[10] For the issue of Russia in British policy at the Peace Conference, see Keith Neilson, "'That elusive entity British policy in Russia': The Impact of Russia on British Policy at the Paris Peace Conference," in *The Paris Peace Conference, 1919: Peace without Victory?*, eds. Michael Dockrill and John Fisher (Basingstoke and New York: Palgrave, 2001), 67-102.

[11] In addition to Neilson, "'That elusive entity,'" see Richard H. Ullman, *Anglo-Soviet Relations, 1917-1921*, Vol. II: *Britain and the Russian Civil War* (Princeton, NJ: Princeton University Press, 1968), 99-115.

year the Allies had conducted complicated diplomatic maneuvers over the entire concept of intervention.

In February 1919, the issue of Prinkipo came to a head. Kerr informed Lloyd George, who had returned to Britain to attend to domestic political matters, that an effort was in progress to de-rail the entire Prinkipo concept. Kerr's own views were firm:

> My own view for what it is worth is that we ought to do all that we can to bring the Conference off. It looks pretty certain that we could anyhow get an agreement in regard to peace on the frontiers of Russia and that would be a tremendous gain. The Bolsheviks are careful to say nothing about suspending internal warfare but I think we have got a fairly strong hand to play there too. If neither side is willing to agree voluntarily we can say to [the leader of the White Russian forces in Siberia, Admiral A. V.] Kolchak and his people that we intend to withdraw Allied troops in the Spring, which means that he and his Party will collapse and the Bolsheviks will overrun Siberia. On the other hand we can say to the Bolsheviks that unless they are prepared to make a reasonable settlement with their opponents, we will not send any clothes or boots and that their chief motive in making peace with us, which is the restoration of trade with the outside world, will not be fulfilled.[12]

In Kerr's view, if the Prinkipo proposal were allowed to lapse, the British would soon have to withdraw their troops from Russia. And if Prinkipo were dead, then the British would have to decide whether to support such alternative plans as an "advance on Moscow by Russians or Czechs or whether we are simply going to drift."

Lloyd George concurred with Lothian. "There is nothing worse than indecision," the prime minister asserted; Lloyd George insisted, however, that various issues required agreement before any decision could be made on Prinkipo.[13] The first of these was that no conclusion should be reached in the absence of the American president, Woodrow Wilson, in order to ensure that the latter "face[d] the alternative and share[d] the responsibility." The second was that all of the Russian parties involved had to agree to attend, since to hold a conference with only the Bolsheviks present "would answer no useful purposes."

This entire subject became entangled with domestic politics. Winston Churchill, the secretary of state for war, was the most fervid

---

[12] Kerr to Lloyd George, 11 February 1919, F/89/2/17, David Lloyd George Papers, House of Lords Record Office, London.
[13] Lloyd George to Kerr, 12 February 1919, F/89/2/8, Lloyd George Papers.

advocate of escalating British intervention in Russia.[14] On 12 and 13 February the entire matter was discussed in Cabinet, and despite his averred opposition to "indecision," Lloyd George attempted to sidetrack Churchill by asserting that the issues of cost and the probability of success must be investigated before any decision could be reached.[15] Frustrated, Churchill went to Paris to attempt to push his case for boosting Allied intervention. In Lloyd George's absence, the British delegation was headed by the secretary of state for foreign affairs, Arthur Balfour. Given Balfour's casual approach to bureaucratic details, Lloyd George had instructed Kerr "to extract from him [Balfour] all the information that he can get and write a daily letter to the Prime Minister."[16] This meant that the private secretary was at the center of the dispute between Lloyd George and his rambunctious war minister.

Restraining Churchill was no easy task. On 12 February, Kerr read to Balfour Lloyd George's views about Russia in order to ensure that no doubt existed as to the prime minister's position. This did not deter Churchill. On 15 February, he attended the Supreme War Council in Paris and then informed Lloyd George: "I conceive that we are entitled to count on American participation in any joint measures" in Russia.[17] Kerr's report of the same meeting to Lloyd George was less clear cut: "Mr. Churchill," Kerr wrote, "gathered that the President said that he would agree to this, but the minutes are not so definite."[18] The two men also found themselves differing over the terms of a note to be addressed to the Russians regarding Prinkipo. Churchill wished to make Bolshevik attendance at the conference dependent upon a cessation of hostilities and a withdrawal of troops, while Kerr offered a draft that spoke even-handedly to both sides. Balfour preferred Churchill's version, and Kerr, seeing which way the wind was blowing, quickly changed his own tack, noting: "I am inclined to think that Mr. Churchill's line as regards Prinkipo is the right one." Yet, even if he

---

[14] On Churchill and Russia, see Martin Gilbert, *Winston S. Churchill,* Vol. IV: *The Stricken World 1916-1922* (Boston: Houghton Mifflin, 1975), 219-319.

[15] Minutes, WC 531, 12 February 1919, CAB 23/9; minutes, WC 532A, 13 February 1919, CAB 23/15, The National Archives of the United Kingdom, Kew, London [hereafter TNA].

[16] Hardinge (PUS, FO) to Curzon (acting foreign secretary in London), 11 February 1919, Curzon Papers, MSS Eur F112/212A, Oriental and India Office Collection, British Library, London.

[17] Churchill to Lloyd George, secret and personal tel., 15 February 1919, F[oreign] O[ffice] 371/3956/26048, TNA.

[18] What follows is also based on Kerr to Lloyd George, n.d. [but 16 February 1919], F/89/2/16, Lloyd George Papers, also in GD 40/17/761, Lothian Papers.

was unwilling to oppose Churchill and Balfour directly, Kerr covered himself by warning the prime minister:

> But I cannot conceal from you that in my opinion Mr. Churchill is bent on forcing a campaign against Bolshevik Russia by using Allied volunteers, Polish and Finnish and other conscripts that can be got hold of, financed and equipped by the Allies. He is perfectly logical in his policy, because he declares that the Bolsheviks are the enemies of the human race and must be put down at any cost. Personally as I think you know, I am against such a policy because, to my mind, it must lead to the Peace Conference taking charge of Russian affairs, and if they do that it will end in revolution in the West. ... I think you ought to watch the situation very carefully, if you do not wish to be rushed into the policy of a volunteer war against the Bolsheviks in the near future.

This was not, however, a complete summary of Kerr's own stance on the Russian situation.

Kerr outlined his own views both to Lloyd George and Balfour. To the former, Kerr emphasized that it would be a "fundamental and colossal mistake to be drawn into a war with Soviet Russia."[19] His reasons for this aversion were varied: "I don't see that it is any business of ours how the Russian people govern themselves," he wrote, adding that intervention would "cause grave difficulties at home and would land us with the ultimate responsibility for the government of Russia for a number of years." Kerr's concern over the domestic ramifications of intervention was pronounced. "All that [is] certain," he told his mother at this time, "is that to start in on a new war against Russia is the surest way of producing Bolshevism at home."[20] Kerr did, on the other hand, feel that the British "owe[d] some obligations to Koltchak and other pro-ally Russians .... And I don't think we can honestly clear out and leave them in the lurch." The difficulty with the latter approach was what to do in practice. Here, Lothian advocated giving the White forces "whatever support is necessary to prevent them from being overrun by the Bolsheviks." At the same time, he suggested "get[ting] into relations with the Bolsheviks ... as one belligerent to another" and making it clear that, while Britain had "no intention of attacking Soviet Russia," neither did she have any "intention of deserting our friends."[21] Once this was done, Kerr proposed that the British offer to

---

[19] Kerr to Lloyd George, 16 February 1919, F/89/2/17, Lloyd George Papers; additional details can be found in Kerr's untitled note for Balfour, 16 February 1919, GD 40/17/764, Lothian Papers.
[20] Kerr to Lady Anne Kerr, 18 February 1919, GD 40/17/466, Lothian Papers.
[21] Kerr to Lloyd George, 16 February 1919, F/89/2/17, Lloyd George Papers.

meet with Soviet emissaries in either Helsingfors or Stockholm to discuss a settlement.

This was for the future. More immediately, Lloyd George had to deal with Churchill's belligerent attitude toward the Bolsheviks. While the prime minister favored the secretary of state for war's approach to Prinkipo, he sought to ensure that Churchill did not commit the British to anything more than the sending of 'experts' who would go to Russia as volunteers: "The main idea ought to be to enable Russia to save herself if she desires to do so, and if she does not take advantage of the opportunity then it means either that she does not wish to be saved from Bolshevism or that she is beyond saving."[22] Once Churchill, however, began to discuss "planning War against BOLSHEVIKS," Lloyd George sent his private secretary a copy of a sharp reply designed to curb such initiatives.[23] His reason for doing so was clear. Concerned that Churchill might choose to ignore his wishes, Lloyd George wished to use Kerr as another channel to ensure that the prime ministerial message reached its intended, wider audience, including President Wilson's close confidant, Colonel Edward M. House.

When Kerr followed this course, Churchill was "very indignant." Even though the private secretary had acted in accordance with Lloyd George's instructions, Churchill felt that this "revealed to the Americans the internal disagreement of the British Government and made it seem as if you [Lloyd George] had not confidence that he [Churchill] would represent your views."[24] This latter point was, of course, true. Kerr had to pour soothing words on Churchill's wounded *amour propre*. Suitably mollified, the latter returned to London on 17 February, leaving Kerr to carry on discussions with the Americans on Russia. The following day, Kerr spoke with Colonel House, telling him that the British had "an obligation to defend our friends but that this did not include the obligation to refuse to speak to the Bolsheviks or to conquer Bolshevik Russia on their behalf."[25] Kerr put forward the idea of a policy that would "secure" the White Russian allies and the "small nations on the Western border of Soviet Russia" while simultaneously "allow[ing] Allied agents to penetrate European Russia with full guarantees for life and property." If this were done, Kerr believed that "we should have amply fulfilled our obligations

---

[22] Lloyd George to Kerr, tel. 177, very urgent, 16 February 1919, F/89/2/19, Lloyd George Papers.

[23] Lloyd George to Kerr, tel. 178, 16 February 1919, FO 608/177, TNA.

[24] Kerr to Lloyd George, 17 February 1919, F/89/2/21, Lloyd George Papers.

[25] Kerr to Lloyd George, private & confidential, 18 February 1919, F/89/2/23, Lloyd George Papers; Edward M. House to Lothian, 22 February 1919, GD 40/17/766, Lothian Papers.

and at the same time have struck a deadly blow at the more violent and abominable forms of Bolshevism." If the Bolsheviks were to refuse such terms, Kerr believed that "then we would have a clear case on which to ask Parliament to vote money and individuals to volunteer to help us save non-Bolshevik Russia from Bolshevik aggression." Kerr realized, however, that while he could ventilate his own views on Russia to the Americans, Lloyd George's presence in Paris was required to avoid a policy of "drifting."[26]

Such drift nonetheless continued, as the conference had more pressing issues, including the terms of the proposed German peace treaty, to consider.[27] At the end of May, however, the Allies offered some support to Admiral Kolchak, provided that he adhered to certain conditions. By 12 June, he had agreed to do so, and the stage was set for intervention. This interposition would, however, be limited in nature, and the Allies would not recognize Kolchak's government officially. There were several reasons for this, one of the most significant being the simultaneous desire at the Peace Conference to support the various national movements on the borders of the former Russian Empire. Kerr was firmly in agreement with both non-recognition of Kolchak and support for the national movements. "How can they [the Council of Four]," recognize Kolchak's government, he reportedly said, "when it is only in control of part of the country and there are regions that do not want to have anything to do with him?"[28]

Kerr's views on the scope and scale of intervention reflected the complexities of the situation. On the domestic political front, Kerr was "really alarmed with the trend of opinion at home against the continued presence of our troops in Russia."[29] In terms of the nature of the support to be accorded the White forces, Kerr favored an evacuation of British forces from both the Baltic and Caucasian regions, contending that, because Kolchak had given a guarantee of the future independence of these regions, a British presence was no longer necessary. Kerr's reticence also stemmed from the fact that in such parts of the Empire as Canada support for intervention was limited, while the strain on Imperial defense was immense.[30] "He took the line," one of his interlocutors wrote, "that we were doing as much, if not more, than as an Empire we could safely face." This

---

[26] Kerr to Lloyd George, 19 February 1919, F/89/2/24, Lloyd George Papers.

[27] Neilson, "'That elusive entity,'" 87-92.

[28] J. Y. Simpson to Tyrrell, private & confidential, 13 June 1919, FO 371/4380/PID 461.

[29] Simpson to Tyrrell, 23 June 1919, FO 371/4380/PID 483. The rest of this paragraph is based on this letter.

[30] For these problems, see Keith Jeffery, *The British army and the crisis of empire 1918-22* (Manchester: Manchester University Press, 1984).

concern was also linked to Kerr's long-standing conviction on the need for cooperation between the British Empire and the United States. Kerr felt that the "disgusting thing in the situation to-day was the way in which the Americans, with a population of a hundred millions, and 'stinking with wealth', were withdrawing themselves from their share in the burden of civilization in Europe and Asia."[31] Faced with the realities of the situation in Russia, his dream of an Anglo-Saxon world order seemed to be receding. He also feared that preoccupation with Russia was blinding officials to many other important matters. He was particularly worried that Churchill and others were "so pre-occupied with great schemes in Russia that they are letting the far more important business of getting our own armies into good shape go by the board."[32]

This concern became especially salient for Kerr after the signing of the Treaty of Versailles, when Lloyd George returned to Britain, leaving his private secretary behind with Balfour and some of the staff of the British delegation, entrusted with clearing up the outstanding business of the peace conference. These activities prompted Kerr to develop his own views on the future of international relations and Britain's role therein. Central to his outlook was the role of the United States. Kerr was determined that Britain must not only avoid any friction with the Americans, but also that London had to follow a "positive policy" with respect to Washington. Without this, he averred, the prospect was that the two countries "shall drift into rivalry as being the two great powers of the world." He was, however, optimistic that this scenario would not occur, since "I do think that America and ourselves have fundamentally the same outlook on the world and there is a job which we can do together which neither of us can do alone." This "job" entailed ensuring that disputes were referred to the League of Nations, "which we will mainly control," and "getting a movement on for the education and betterment of the backward races of the world."[33]

The question of the League of Nations had already won Kerr's attention earlier. In April 1918, he had outlined his views on that body. He acknowledged that the "general idea of a League of Nations, in the sense that in future nations must co-operate to promote peace and happiness, and not compete for power and profit among themselves is certainly sound and

---

[31] See also Kerr to Lloyd George, confidential, 18 July 1919, F/89/3/6, Lloyd George Papers.
[32] Kerr to Maurice Hankey, private & personal, 7 July 1919, GD 40/17/1320, Lothian Papers.
[33] Kerr to Hankey, 21 July 1919, GD 40/17/1323, Lothian Papers.

wants propagating as widely as possible."[34] Kerr was also, however, aware of the fact that the very idea of a League of Nations "is also liable to be used as the most insidious form of pacifism." To rely upon the League of Nations to ensure peace, Lothian opined, "would be positively dangerous because it would only lull other nations into a false sense of security during which pacifists would persuade them to reduce their armaments." This would in turn result in "opening the road once more to an attack by Germany or any other ambitious state." As a derivative of such thinking, Kerr maintained that the key prerequisite for a successful League was that "all nations must combine in order to enforce respect for international justice, because in the international sphere as in the national, the enforcement of law and order is the condition of lasting peace." How was this to be done? For Kerr, this required that "all neutrals should join the Allies and develop the Entente into a League of all nations to enforce respect for public right on all who would infringe it." The reason for this was simple: Britain and her allies were the only force in the war that was attempting "to enforce respect for law and justice." Kerr therefore condemned those, "like the Bolsheviks and other pacifists," who wanted "peace at any price," and so were willing to accept a German peace as the price of a League of Nations.

Once the war ended, Kerr's views did not alter. He contended that it was "of the utmost importance that we should keep alive the system of conducting international business which has been evolved during the war and during the Peace Conference."[35] He believed that the principal allies—Britain, France and the United States—should work through the League of Nations to maintain international order. He feared, however, that this new machinery would be opposed by national interests, particularly by those bureaucrats in each country who would jealously guard their own prerogatives. He saw no indication that the embryonic League was coming into existence in any form that could carry out the aims that he envisaged for it. The "League of Nations today," he told the influential Maurice Hankey, secretary to the Cabinet and the Committee of Imperial Defence, "is entirely in the air. Nobody here [Paris] knows anything about it. I don't believe it has any touch whatever with any of the Foreign Offices. It has not got a representative in Paris. It is, in other words, on the highroad to be

---

[34] Kerr to E. Howard (British minister, Stockholm), 22 April 1918, GD 40/17/210, Lothian Papers. The rest of this paragraph and the quotations in it come from this source.

[35] This and the remaining quotations in this paragraph (except where otherwise noted) are from Kerr to Hankey, 21 July 1919, GD 40/17/1323, Lothian Papers.

beaten by the Foreign Offices of the Allies by being side-tracked." To avoid this, Kerr sought to ensure that "men of real political importance" represented their countries on the League.[36] If this were to be the case, he felt it unlikely that the League could have its headquarters in the "oasis" of Geneva, since such men would "want to be in the thick of the political world" in London.

Kerr urged strongly that the pre-war methods of dealing with international relations should not remain unchanged, a position intertwined with his views on the unity of the British Empire. In late 1919, with the question of "whether or not we are going to have a League of Nations ... hanging in the balance," Kerr believed that "our foreign policy and, therefore, the practical form of the Imperial problem" were both in flux.[37] It seemed clear to him that the Dominions and the United States would both "have to take an active share in giving some kind of order and good government to the backward world," but he was uncertain whether America would soon see "that it can't stand out of responsibilities of international government."[38] He also believed that that the Dominions must be consulted on the substance of British foreign policy. Without "continuous consultation and co-operation" between the Dominions and the mother country, "the foreign policy of the British Empire cannot be democratic and representative in any adequate degree."[39]

The question of whether to renew the Anglo-Japanese Alliance juxtaposed the issues of finding a new means of maintaining an international order, the role of the Dominions in British policy, and American participation in world affairs.[40] Kerr felt that defending British interests involved two questions: finding "some way of obtaining security for British possessions in the Far East, and of protecting China against

---

[36] This and the following quotation are from Kerr to Hankey, 24 July 1919, GD 40/17/1324, Lothian Papers.

[37] Kerr to A.J. Glazebrook (Canadian Round Table group), 14 November 1919, GD 40/17/209/353, Lothian Papers.

[38] *Ibid.*; for the context, see also Kerr to Hankey, 11 August 1919, GD 40/17/1334, Lothian Papers; and Loring Christie (Canadian Department of External Affairs) to Kerr, 12 January 1920, GD 40/17/207, Lothian Papers.

[39] Philip Kerr, "The British Empire, the League of Nations, and the United States," *The Round Table* 10:38 (March 1920), 248.

[40] On this issue generally, see Keith Neilson, "'Unbroken Thread': Japan, Maritime power and British Imperial Defence, 1920-32," in *British Naval Strategy East of Suez, 1900-2000*, ed. Greg Kennedy (London and New York: Frank Cass, 2005), 63-72; and Ian H. Nish, *Alliance in Decline: A Study in Anglo-Japanese Relations 1908-23* (London: Athlone Press, 1972), 249-397.

exploitation."[41] Given that the Dominions were "strongly against" renewing the Alliance and that the British could not achieve their aims in the Far East "by our own forces alone," Lothian contended that either the Alliance must be renewed, or a "counterpoise" to Japanese power put in place. For him, the latter could be only the United States. The difficulty was that Washington "would never" enter into an alliance to protect British interests in the Far East. In these circumstances, Kerr felt that the solution was to bring about a "Conference between the United States, Great Britain, Japan and China, with the British Dominions and India represented on the British delegation to discuss the settlement of the Far East." Since a "purely defensive alliance" was not "incompatible with either the text or with the spirit of the Covenant of the League," this would allow all of Lothian's beliefs about how the new international order should function to be reconciled. Underlying this approach, too, were his assumption that such a gathering would discover that the Anglo-Japanese Alliance was no longer necessary, and his more problematic belief that "British, American, Dominion and Chinese interests really run together."

For Kerr this latter conviction, at least with regard to Britain, the United States and the Dominions, was of the essence. Even in 1921, at the height of the '100% American' campaign in the United States, Kerr was convinced that the "issues which divide us [Britain and the United States] are not really fundamental if wisely handled."[42] Although he was aware of the triumphalism then rampant in the United States, a development that led one of Lothian's Canadian friends to remark that the Americans "think they have all the money & power in the world & they're going to do as they damn please, and if the world wants anything of them anytime it can get it on their terms & only their terms & no discussion about it either," he was certain that this could be overcome.[43] One way of doing so was to ensure and encourage the "establishment of relations of real confidence between the British and American Foreign Offices." Should this be accomplished, Kerr believed there would not be "any question outstanding between the two countries which cannot be satisfactorily adjusted[ed]."[44] He viewed Canada as an important mediating factor guaranteeing that such good

---

[41] Kerr to John Dove (a friend from Lothian's time at Oxford and in South Africa), 13 July 1920, GD 40/17/209, Lothian Papers. The rest of this paragraph and the quotations in it are derived from this source.

[42] Kerr to Cunliffe-Owens, 24 March 1924, GD 40/17/208, Lothian Papers.

[43] Loring Christie (Canadian Department of External Affairs) to Kerr, 12 January 1920, GD 40/17/207, Lothian Papers.

[44] Kerr to Cunliffe-Owens, 2 May 1921, GD 40/17/208, Lothian Papers.

relations did develop. "Canada has a vital role to play," he wrote on another occasion, "in interpreting the United States and Great Britain to one another. If it was not for Canada," he concluded, "I should take a much more anxious view of our future relations with the United States than I do."[45]

Kerr did not, however, believe that Britain's ability to deal with all the world's problems was unlimited, especially in the Middle East.[46] He preferred indirect rule to any kind of military administration in the former Ottoman territories that had become British mandates. He felt it "absolutely essential that we should get rid both of the British army and British directive administration as soon as we possibly can." For him, this need derived from another of the forces—nationalism—that the First World War had unleashed in extra-European territories. Kerr felt that Britain needed "to enlist it [nationalism] on our side" in the Middle East, something that could not be done "as long as we keep the ultimate responsibility for law and order and maintain large forces in Mesopotamia." If this were true of the newly-acquired territories, it was doubly so in Egypt. Since Britain had "as large a ham on our forks as we can possibly manage now all over the world," London should "go a long way also in divesting ourselves of the responsibility for the internal government of Egypt." While it was important to "safeguard absolutely our control over the [Suez] canal" and "safeguard equally our position as the sole outside Power entitled to interfere in Egypt, and prevent the French government's interventions" there, the British goal should be to "throw the responsibility of the internal government of that country on its native inhabitants." This was not mere indirect rule. Lothian saw such an approach as part of his greater scheme, mentioned above, of encouraging the "backward world" to achieve higher levels of civilization. "On the other hand," he concluded with an atypical piece of cynicism, "if they [the Egyptians] fail, nothing will do us more good among foreign countries and in India than a practical demonstration that we are still indispensable, and we shall go back into the country with the consent of other nations."

What does an examination of Kerr's experiences during his time as Lloyd George's private secretary demonstrate? In terms of Russia, during this period what developed into his long-standing antipathy toward

---

[45] Kerr to N.W. Rowell (Canadian banker), 3 March 1921, GD 40/17/217, Lothian Papers.
[46] What follows is based on Kerr to Churchill, 28 February 1921, not sent, GD 40/17/207, Lothian Papers. For some background to these problems, see John Fisher, *Curzon and British Imperialism in the Middle East 1916-19* (London and Portland, OR: Frank Cass, 1999).

Bolshevism became established. As an ideology, this radical credo ran directly counter to and imperiled his own beliefs in the primacy of the Anglo-Saxon world. Communism's concept of a new world based on Marxist tenets could not be expected to appeal to Kerr, whose own views rested on completely different principles. In addition to its ideological threat, Soviet Russia also represented a menace to the British Empire, something that Kerr, steeped in the imperialist ideas of Lord Milner's 'Kindergarten', found unacceptable. Some of Kerr's sympathies for German complaints of 'encirclement' in the 1930s can indeed be seen as stemming in part from the fact that he shared the Nazis' distaste for Soviet Russia. The ideological nature of issues relating to the Russian situation was also significant for Kerr, inasmuch as it increased his sensitivity to subjects of a kind that would dominate the interwar period. Although Kerr's observations on Russia and suggestions as to policy toward that country demonstrated no great originality, this reflected the fact that at that time no one could offer much in the way of a constructive British policy toward Russia. And, while Russia never became a central aspect of Kerr's worldview, his dealings with it while he was Lloyd George's private secretary were a material aspect of his development as a statesman.

At a more personal level, dealing with Russia put Kerr at the center of events at the Paris Peace Conference. This was particularly so given Lloyd George's penchant for working through Kerr during his own absences in London. This arrangement placed Kerr in the awkward position of acting as the prime minister's 'minder' over his bumptious secretary of state for war, since Lloyd George wished to ensure both that Churchill kept others informed of the true dimensions of British policy, and that he refrained from committing London to precipitate action on Russia. This situation also gave Kerr an opportunity to ventilate his own views to the prime minister, probably reinforcing the latter's intention to take only limited action. Dealing with the wide-ranging issues related to Russia also clearly broadened Kerr's own horizons. His close contact with various experts on Russia and its 'near abroad'—Simpson, Pares, and the members of the Foreign Office staff in Paris—enhanced his own knowledge of foreign affairs. Dealing with the Foreign Office could, however, be a two-edged sword, since many of its functionaries resented Lloyd George's use of such individuals as Kerr—the Prime Minister's so-called 'garden suburb'—as advisers and agents, who often usurped their own traditional role.[47] As one disgruntled member of the Foreign Office remarked of an embarrassing press campaign concerning the Bullitt mission on Russia: "It's the result of having two Foreign Offices. One directed by the Secretary of State, the other by Mr. Philip Kerr."[48] This meant that Kerr won a reputation among officials as a dangerous amateur, one prone to interfering in matters in which he had no standing, a legacy that gave his views less weight in the 1930s.

This latter point was particularly important in terms of personalities. During Kerr's final years as Lloyd George's private secretary, the prime minister crossed swords incessantly with the secretary of state for foreign affairs, Lord Curzon.[49] At a bureaucratic level the clash between prime minister and foreign secretary was replicated in conflicts between Lloyd George's representatives, such as Kerr, and Foreign Office personnel, including Curzon's private secretary, Robert Vansittart. After Vansittart became Permanent Undersecretary (PUS) at the Foreign Office in 1930, he was a perennial skeptic toward the views of Lord Lothian, as Kerr became in 1930. In 1935, for example, the PUS deprecated Lothian's views on the foreign policy position of U.S. President Franklin D. Roosevelt.[50] He later reiterated this opinion, suggesting that "poor silly Lord Lothian" should be made aware that the British ambassador to the United States thought otherwise.[51] Nor was Vansittart impressed by Lothian's view in 1937 that Britain should help Germany achieve her goals in Eastern Europe, feeling that Lothian had been hoodwinked by the Germans.[52] Indeed, even after Vansittart left office, questions about Lothian's judgment swirled about the Foreign Office. When he visited Roosevelt in 1939, and appeared to argue to the American president that Britain was too weak to resist Hitler without assistance from Washington, this led many in the Foreign Office to believe that Lothian was unfit for any

---

[47] John Grigg, *Lloyd George: From Peace to War 1912-1916* (London: Methuen, 1985), 498-502; and John Turner, *Lloyd George's Secretariat* (Cambridge: Cambridge University Press, 1980).

[48] O'Malley, minute, 23 July 1919, on Kerr to Hardinge, secret, 11 July 1919, FO 371/4002/105169.

[49] For an examination, see G. H. Bennett, *British Foreign Policy during the Curzon Period, 1919-24* (London: St. Martin's Press, 1995).

[50] Vansittart, minute, 27 February 1935, FO 371/19312/F1241/553/10.

[51] Vansittart, minute, 23 March 1935, on Lindsay (British ambassador, Washington) to FO, tel. 71, 21 March 1935, FO 371/18831/C2376/55/18.

[52] Keith Neilson and T. G. Otte, *The Permanent Under-Secretary for Foreign Affairs, 1854-1946* (New York and London: Routledge, 2009), 228-229.

important role dealing with the United States, as such remarks would only strengthen the convictions of those who consider him an appeaser.[53]

The period from 1914 to 1922 was central to Kerr's development as an individual with a role to play in international relations. During this time he was exposed to a wide range of practical issues at a juncture when the verities of the nineteenth century were under fire and new possibilities were emerging. This was particularly evident in dealings with Russia. The switch from autocracy to communism demonstrated both the range of possibilities and the dangers inherent in overthrowing the old order. This helped to solidify Kerr's belief that the future was best guaranteed by the solidarity of those states that shared common values and common goals. For him, this meant Britain, the Empire, and the United States. His vision of the "larger idea" was confirmed. This period also, however, made clearly apparent just how difficult it would be in practice to achieve such a goal. A League of Nations based on an Anglo-American condominium foundered on the shoals of American politics. Expanding the influence of British ideas within the Empire was tempered by the realization that British resources were inadequate to accomplish this unaided, while another aspect of the new world order, growing nationalism in the 'backward' countries, could work counter to Kerr's dream of a world shaped in the Anglo-Saxon image. Kerr's exposure to politics had taught him the difficulties and limitations of what could be done in the official sphere. This was part of the reason why he left the formal structures of international relations in 1922 and instead turned his attention to extra-official means of influencing ideas and events, something that ended only when he became ambassador to the United States in 1939. For Kerr, the legacy of 1916 to 1922 would be an enduring one.

---

[53] See Keith Neilson, "Perception and Posture in Anglo-American Relations: The Legacy of the Simon-Stimson Affair, 1932-1941," *The International History Review* 29:2 (June 2007), 327-328.

CHAPTER TWO

PHILIP KERR, THE IRISH QUESTION, AND ANGLO-AMERICAN RELATIONS, 1916-1921

MELANIE SAYERS

The period between 1916 and 1921 was one of the most turbulent in Anglo-Irish history. During these years the British Government faced rebellion in Ireland and a growing republican threat, while Irish rebels increasingly lobbied for American support of their cause. Britain needed to maintain her own relations with the United States while fighting a world war and dealing with its aftermath. The Irish Question was therefore delicate, and to complicate matters would need to be addressed with consideration for American opinion. As Prime Minister David Lloyd George's personal secretary during this time, Philip Kerr was not only witness to these events, but was involved in the government's handling of them firsthand and behind the scenes.

The main objective of this chapter is relatively straightforward, as the intention is to anchor Kerr within the story of Ireland and Anglo-American relations during this period. Beginning with some contextual exploration of Kerr, Ireland, and the United States, the chapter will highlight and examine Kerr's involvement with and views on the Irish question and its implications for Britain's own relationship with America. Particular reference will be made to Kerr's dealings with and attitude toward Irish-American support of Irish nationalists, and the American government's involvement in the situation, through investigation of specific areas. These include the American Commission on Irish Independence affair, Kerr's handling of the press, the intelligence that he received from American sources on Irish activities, and his negotiations with Colonel Edward M. House, U.S. President Woodrow Wilson's confidential adviser. The aim is to establish Kerr's contribution to this issue during a tense period in transatlantic relations.

Although Kerr's biographers have acknowledged his role in Irish affairs, it is surprising that he has not been more closely connected to American involvement in the Irish question. Kerr's own background and experiences meant that he approached this subject from a particular angle, and in fact possessed certain skills and advantages that would assist him in

P. Roberts (ed.), Lord Lothian and Anglo-American Relations, 1900-1940, 61-78.

dealing with this issue. Since his days in South Africa between 1905 and 1909, Kerr had developed an interest in strengthening the British Empire and her colonies. As a member of the 'Round Table Group,' Kerr was able to take this interest further, and played an active role in promoting imperial federation as a means of strengthening Britain's control over her imperial dependencies. This was also true of Ireland, where the political situation had for decades been a thorn in the British government's side. The Round Table Group actively promoted federation of Ireland as a solution to the problem.

As Lloyd George's personal secretary, Kerr could draw upon this experience. He believed, however, that the United States also had an important role to play alongside Britain in maintaining world order. Kerr therefore envisioned a special relationship between the two powers that he viewed as essential in the long term for a strong international community. To this end, Kerr maintained an impressive range of American contacts, which he developed even in the relatively early stages of his career. Figures such as Horace Plunkett, an Irish landowner who had spent a great deal of time in the United States, could also be very useful to him, since they knew how Irish developments could affect American public opinion. In 1921 Plunkett wrote to Kerr, informing him of Hugh Martin's book *Ireland in Insurrection*, a work he believed would have a profound impact on both British and American opinion.[1] American journalists such as Carl Ackerman and John S. Steele would later assist Kerr in trying to manage American support for the Irish rebels. Kerr's own experiences as a journalist, editing first *The State* in South Africa, and then the journal *The Round Table*, meant that he already had an interest in influencing the press and also in attempting to direct public opinion. As will become apparent in the course of this chapter, these experiences and skills would prove invaluable to him when it came to addressing American involvement in the Irish question.

Some brief contextual exploration of the Irish situation and its connection to the United States is necessary before examining Kerr's role. In more recent decades, especially in the second half of the twentieth century, the connection between the Irish question and the United States took on a different meaning with regards to Irish nationalist aims. A

---

[1] Horace Plunkett to Philip Kerr, 18 April 1921, GD 40/17/80, Papers of the Eleventh Marquess of Lothian [hereafter Lothian Papers], The National Archives of Scotland, Edinburgh; Hugh Martin, *Ireland in Insurrection: An Englishman's Record of Fact* (London: Daniel O'Connor, 1921).

substantial literature already exists on the way in which the years of the Troubles saw Irish nationalists seeking American support in their campaign to reunify Northern Ireland with the south of the country, whether through legitimate means or by terrorist activity.[2] In the last twenty years, indeed, this has become something of a Hollywood theme, with such films as *The Devil's Own* (1997) portraying the efforts of Irish revolutionaries to obtain arms from the United States.[3] At the time of Kerr's earlier career such links on a reasonably large scale were beginning to be significant, although in the early 1900s Irish aims were different. Since the Union of Britain and Ireland in 1800, there had occurred various campaigns to regain a measure of Irish self-government, the most salient examples being the repeal agitation of the 1830s and 1840s, and the Home Rule Movement from 1870 onward. As emigration from Ireland to the United States increased during the nineteenth century, and particularly during the post-famine years, support for Irish nationalism from within America increased, a theme explored by Francis M. Carroll and Alan J. Ward in their works on Ireland and Anglo-American relations during this period.[4]

When Home Rule for Ireland was finally placed on the statute books (though quickly suspended for the duration of the First World War), Kerr was the editor of *The Round Table*. In keeping with the Round Table philosophy of imperial federation, from 1910 his interest in Ireland and the United States had been in relation to American influence on a federal solution for Ireland. At that time Round Table members believed that the Irish cause might prove useful to them in persuading party political leaders that federation of the United Kingdom was a desirable goal. Wider constitutional reconstruction of the United Kingdom would also provide an alternative to Home Rule as a solution to the Irish problem. Although Kerr greatly admired the United States as a political model, where Ireland was concerned his views were very much those of a British imperialist. He believed in self-government as a means of strengthening the British Empire's management of its colonies and dependencies. He was, however,

---

[2] Relevant works include Dennis Clark, *Irish Blood: Northern Ireland and the American Conscience* (Port Washington, NY: Kennikat Press, 1977); Jack Holland, *The American Connection: U.S. Guns, Money, and Influence in Northern Ireland* (Dublin: Poolbeg, 1989); and Andrew J. Wilson, *Irish America and the Ulster Conflict, 1968-1995* (Washington, DC: Catholic University of America Press, 1995).

[3] *The Devil's Own*, directed by Alan J. Pakula (Columbia Pictures Corporation, 1997).

[4] Francis M. Carroll, *American Opinion and the Irish Question, 1910-23: A Study in Opinion and Policy* (Dublin: Gill and Macmillan, 1978); and Alan J. Ward, *Ireland and Anglo-American Relations, 1899-1921* (London: Weidenfeld and Nicolson, 1969).

fully aware that, given the historic connections between Ireland and the United States, American support could assist the Round Table. In a 1910 letter to his friend and fellow Round Table associate Lionel Curtis, Kerr explained how Lord Grey, a supporter of federalism who was at that time serving as Governor General of Canada, had drawn up a scheme in which American financial support would be withdrawn from the Irish parliamentary leader John Redmond and transferred to William O'Brien if the latter would adopt the federal solution.[5] Grey was apparently keen to use the American dimension to the Irish question in order to gain support for his federal vision of the United Kingdom. Indeed, he encouraged Kerr to keep in touch with New York Congressman W. Bourke Cochran, an Irish-American who headed Redmond's committee in the United States. Kerr recognised Cochran's value, as he could draw on his thirty years of experience in the U.S. House to publicize the federal cause. Although Kerr claimed that Cochran was "discredited" and the Round Table could not be openly associated with him, he nonetheless acknowledged Cochran's usefulness in the initial groundwork of "preaching."[6] Kerr was undoubtedly fully aware of just how influential Irish-Americans could be.

By 1916 the political climate had changed dramatically. Britain was engaged in an all-engrossing international conflict, and with the Dublin Easter Rising faced rebellion on home shores. Although Home Rule had been placed on the statute books in 1914, its suspension for the duration of the war had allowed a change of feeling to take place in Ireland, from a desire for limited self-government to complete independence. After 1916, more militant forces opposed to constitutional solutions began to gain strength. Like many involved in British politics at that time, Kerr failed to recognize this shift in Irish feeling. In an article for *The Round Table* in September 1916 Kerr referred to the "continuous financing of Irish politics from America."[7] He was quite aware not only that American money had assisted the rebels, but that the British execution of the rebel leaders had "caused a violent revulsion of feeling, especially in Ireland and America."[8] Besides recognizing American support for and feeling toward Ireland, in this article Kerr took pains to stress Ireland's place within the British Empire, regardless of American opinion. Kerr was highly conscious that, in the existing wartime situation, Britain herself needed American support,

---

[5] Kerr to Lionel Curtis, 10 August 1910, GD 40/17/2/91, Lothian Papers.
[6] *Ibid.*
[7] [Philip Kerr], "Ireland and the Empire," *The Round Table* 6:24 (September 1916), 634.
[8] *Ibid.*, 614.

and therefore the government would need to handle the Irish situation with great care. As Priscilla Roberts argues elsewhere in this volume, one of his main preoccupations as editor during the First World War was undoubtedly a quest to win over elite and public opinion in the United States to support for the Allied cause. Even so, he clearly viewed events in Ireland from a Round Table standpoint.

It was against this backdrop that Kerr joined Lloyd George's wartime secretariat in December 1916. From this vantage point, Kerr could enjoy an even more informed perspective on the difficulties that his government faced in terms of Ireland and Anglo-American relations. Following the 1916 Easter Uprising, in the United States groups such as the Friends of Irish Freedom had grown significantly in membership. Alan J. Ward notes that contemporary reports claimed that the Dublin executions did more than any other event since the beginning of the war to drive Americans back into isolation.[9] The Irish in America certainly strongly opposed American entry into the First World War, and both the U.S. and British governments recognized that Irish agitation would pose a barrier to cooperation between the two nations. President Woodrow Wilson wrote to Lloyd George in April 1917, claiming that the American people would give greater support to the British war effort if an early prospect of substantial self-government for Ireland existed.[10]

Although Kerr worked on Irish affairs between 1917 and 1918, little of this labor was connected to the United States. Some evidence does, however, suggest that he assisted the prime minister in appointing the chairman of the Irish Convention of 1917-1918, a gathering that was held largely to appease American opinion. Following the Convention's failure in 1918, Kerr firmly supported Lloyd George's intention of enforcing conscription in Ireland while simultaneously implementing Home Rule. Although he was fully aware that fierce opposition to the conscription policy for Ireland existed in the United States, Kerr nonetheless supported it unwaveringly, regardless of the repercussions with Irish-Americans, maintaining strongly that Ireland was a part of the Empire and should therefore play her part alongside the rest in fighting the war. In 1918 the newspaper proprietor Alfred, Lord Northcliffe, a man of Anglo-Irish descent who viewed Irish politics within an imperial framework and had headed a six-month British mission to the United States the previous year, wrote to Kerr advising him on the benefits of issuing a statement to the

---

[9] Ward, *Ireland and Anglo-American Relations, 1899-1921*, 127-128.
[10] *Ibid.*, 141.

American press before conscription was enforced. Northcliffe explained to Kerr that "American public opinion is always confused about Ireland." He believed the reason for this was the fragmentary reporting of British speeches in the American press, so that "publicity would be an effective cure for many United States misconceptions on Irish matters."[11] As discussed later in this chapter, Kerr would use this information when working in 1919 and 1920 on the Government of Ireland Bill. Despite the fact that conscription was never enforced in Ireland, Kerr's support for it was significant. Although he believed in maintaining strong Anglo-American relations, in his view the good of the Empire always came first.

Kerr's most extensive dealings with Ireland and Anglo-American relations began in 1919, while he was heavily involved on Lloyd George's behalf in the Paris peace talks. Irish-American support for Irish Nationalists became particularly controversial when the Irish-American Nationalist movement appointed a subcommittee of three to go to Paris, in order to secure safe passage to the peace conference for Irish representatives. The delegates from the movement, three distinguished men, Frank P. Walsh, Michael J. Ryan, and Edward F. Dunne, each of them to some degree involved in politics, assumed the title of the American Commission on Irish Independence. The group travelled to Europe in order to take up the Irish cause, in the process causing much embarrassment to both the British and the American governments and stretching diplomatic niceties to the limit. After President Wilson publicly declared his support for small nations, Irish nationalists latched onto his pronouncement and hoped to bring their case for independence before the peace conference. The objective of the American Commission was to help them to achieve this and, should the Irish nationalists fail to win a hearing, present the Irish case themselves. In their works on the United States and Ireland, both Francis M. Carroll and Alan J. Ward discuss the Commission's activities.[12] Michael Kennedy's study of Ireland's relationship with the League of Nations fails to give any detailed consideration to the American Commission and the support it enjoyed among Irish-Americans.[13] Carroll is the only historian who refers briefly to Kerr, when discussing how he was contacted for the purpose of arranging a meeting between the Commission and Lloyd George, though

---

[11] Northcliffe to Kerr, 30 September 1918, GD 40/17/216, Lothian Papers.

[12] Carroll, *American Opinion and the Irish Question, 1910-23;* Ward, *Ireland and Anglo-American Relations, 1899-1921.*

[13] Michael Kennedy, *Ireland and the League of Nations, 1919-1946: International Relations, Diplomacy and Politics* (Dublin: Irish Academic Press, 1996).

the published papers of the Commission, also edited by Carroll, contain further references to Kerr and his role in this episode.[14]

The diary and correspondence of the Commission reveal that Kerr was contacted by William C. Bullitt, who headed the Intelligence Department for the American section of the Peace Conference, and had offered to assist the commissioners in their efforts to obtain passports to the peace talks for the Irish delegates.[15] Kerr confidentially replied that, while the Irish might possibly be given the passports they wanted, the Americans would surely understand that the British could never allow them to appear before the peace conference. Kerr did, however, agree to meet Walsh and Bullitt to discuss matters further. The commissioners recorded in their diary that Kerr was known to possess very great influence over Lloyd George, especially with regard to the Irish question. The evidence therefore suggests that Americans and Irish-American representatives were aware of Kerr's potential weight and prepared to use it to their own advantage. Since he felt great admiration for the United States as a nation, he was clearly a significant figure in managing Anglo-American relations, and therefore offered great potential as a mediator on the British side. Kerr stated he believed that it would be possible to obtain passports for the Irish delegates, Éamon De Valera, Arthur Griffith, and Count George Plunkett, and agreed to arrange a meeting between the American commissioners and Lloyd George.[16]

Kerr's attitude appeared to represent a great success for the commissioners when they decided to sail for Ireland to meet with the potential conference delegates. In practice, this turned out to be a disastrous move when huge crowds and parades greeted them in Ireland and they made controversial speeches in support of Irish self-government, met with Sinn Féin leaders, and visited prisons where Nationalists were incarcerated to inspect conditions. This proved highly embarrassing to both the Americans and British, as the British press were outraged, according to numerous clippings and reports in Kerr's papers charting the Commission's activities.[17] Lloyd George was no longer prepared to meet the Commission's members or to grant passports to the Irish delegates. The Irish-American agitation also exasperated President Wilson, who refused

---

[14] Carroll, *American Opinion and the Irish Question 1910-23*, 131-132.

[15] F. M. Carroll, ed., *The American Commission on Irish Independence 1919: The Diary, Correspondence and Report* (Dublin: Irish Manuscripts Commission, 1985), 10.

[16] *Ibid.*, 46.

[17] "Papers Relating to the American Commission on Irish Independence," GD 40/17/575-580, Lothian Papers.

any further involvement in the Commission's efforts, given their potential to damage transatlantic relations.[18] The president was relying on British support to establish the League of Nations he envisaged. Even so, on the British side, Kerr had been a key player who had assisted Bullitt, the American official involved, and been instrumental in persuading Lloyd George to hear the Commission's case, endeavors that helped to prepare him for the further difficulties the next two years would bring.

The American Commission on Irish Independence affair may have been one of various factors that contributed to Lloyd George's recognition of the need to address the Irish question immediately. The Commission's activities and their consequences threw into high relief the tensions that the Irish situation inflicted upon the transatlantic relationship, forcing both sides into awkward postures. In October 1919 the British Cabinet appointed an Irish Situation Committee, charged with making proposals to deal with the Irish question. Among the factors that proposals had to take into account was their potential impact upon American opinion. This committee devised the Government of Ireland Bill that partitioned the country and made provisions for self-government. As joint secretary of the committee, Kerr was one of the draftsmen of the Government of Ireland Bill, involved in various ways with its formulation. Although it remains to be determined precisely how much influence Kerr exercised on the architecture of the Bill itself, what is very clear is the extent to which he attempted to manage American opinion while the British tried to devise a solution acceptable to all sides.

Kerr was already fully aware of the damage that had resulted from Irish propaganda in the United States. In a 1919 *Round Table* article, "The Harvest of Victory," he claimed that "America in her self-concentration has allowed herself to be deceived by Irish propagandists," something he hoped would have no further influence upon the proposed Irish settlement.[19] Apparently, therefore, before the Bill was introduced in the British parliament, Kerr assumed the role of attempting to limit any potential damage in the United States by supervising the British government's own propaganda campaign there. As mentioned above, in September 1918 Lord Northcliffe had warned Kerr that the fragmentary nature of press reporting meant American public opinion was always confused about Ireland. An American journalist had advised him that publicity would be an effective

---

[18] John B. Duff, "The Versailles Treaty and the Irish-Americans," *Journal of American History* 55:3 (December 1968), 582-598.
[19] [Philip Kerr], "The Harvest of Victory," *The Round Table* 9:36 (September 1919), 670.

cure for many U.S. misconceptions on Irish matters, information that Kerr apparently remembered, since he kept in regular contact with Britain's official American publicity department during the months when the Government of Ireland Bill was formulated and debated.

Kerr was well aware that the last thing the British government wished to encounter, as it sought to appeal to all parties in the Irish question, was an American backlash. His papers relating to the Government of Ireland Bill include a document from the publicity department outlining the estimated cost of propaganda expenditure in the United States, together with an overview of the scheme.[20] The department drew up a plan for an intensive publicity campaign in the United States over a six-month period, based on the settlement that was reached and the various parties' reaction to it. J. Tilley, one of the architects of this extensive proposal, noted:

> We may look for a plan of some duration, during which every sort of misstatement will be made and every opportunity utilised to prejudice the issue. To counter-act this it will not suffice merely to present the true facts in the form of categorical statements. They will require to be constantly and skilfully reiterated in such a way as to appeal to the interest and sympathy of different classes in America.[21]

The methods contemplated included ordinary news coverage, signed and unsigned articles, interviews, pamphlets, and lectures. The estimated expenditure for the operation and the extra staff involved amounted to £9500 over six months. Everything would, of course, depend upon just how the Irish proposals were received in the United States. The fact that British officials were prepared to implement such a wide-ranging scheme in the United States highlights the importance of American opinion in their eyes, and the extent of their concern over the potential repercussions their proposals might provoke among Irish-Americans.

His papers leave no doubt, therefore, that Kerr was kept constantly updated on American opinion of Irish affairs, as presented in the American press. After the prime minister spoke in parliament in December 1919, introducing the Government of Ireland Bill, Kerr sent him a memorandum stating that his speech and the Irish proposals had received a good press in America. The report Kerr had received from the publicity department highlighted that their reception in the United States had generally gone as the British had hoped, with the Irish proposals not misrepresented; parallels drawn between Ireland and a constituent state in the American federal

---

[20] J. Tilley to Kerr, 7 November 1919, GD 40/17/585, Lothian Papers.
[21] *Ibid.*

union; and the difficulty of the status of Ulster acknowledged.[22] Kerr's influence seems evident here, since at various stages he himself had emphasized all these points. He admitted that there had been some negative press reports, with Irish elements claiming that the true American parallel with Ireland should be the War of Independence, not American efforts to prevent secession during the Civil War. Yet overall the publicity campaign appeared to have been successful, which he considered a positive sign for Anglo-American relations.

Numerous scholars, among them John Wheeler-Bennett, David Reynolds, and Nicholas Cull, as well as J. Simon Rofe and Gavin Bailey in chapters in this volume, have scrutinized Kerr's handling of the press when, as Lord Lothian, he sought to influence British policy between the wars, and especially when he served as British ambassador to the United States in 1939 and 1940.[23] Even though he was involved in some capacity or other with newspapers and journals of opinion for much of his career and had a good working understanding of the press, historians have nonetheless failed to give him credit for his comparable efforts on the Irish question. Kerr clearly sought to limit potential damage and promote good Anglo-American relations through his management of the press and his contacts on the American side. Throughout the 1919-1920 period when the Government of Ireland Bill was developed and introduced, he had regular contacts with John S. Steele, the London correspondent of the *Chicago Tribune*, a relationship that both men undoubtedly found advantageous. Steele knew of Kerr's influence with Lloyd George, stating that if anyone could arrange an interview with the prime minister on Ireland, Kerr was the only man who could do it.[24] In return, Steele provided Kerr with information and advice after making a trip to Ireland, claiming that it was easier for him, as an American journalist, to gain information than would have been the case had he been British. Steele's reports on the Irish question also apparently presented the British favorably, since he sent Kerr cuttings from his newspaper reporting on a Friends of Irish Freedom resolution that condemned the *Chicago Tribune* for its anti-Irish bias. In

---

[22] Kerr to Lloyd George, 2 January 1920, F/90/1/1, David Lloyd George Papers, House of Lords Record Office, London.
[23] See David Reynolds, *Lord Lothian and Anglo-American Relations, 1939-1940* (Philadelphia: Transactions of the American Philosophical Society, 1983); Nicholas John Cull, *Selling War: The British Propaganda Campaign Against American "Neutrality" in World War II* (New York: Oxford University Press, 1995); and Sir John Wheeler-Bennett, *Special Relationships: America in Peace and War* (London: Macmillan, 1975), 65-68.
[24] John S. Steele to Kerr, 19 September 1919, GD 40/17/219/766, Lothian Papers.

letters to Kerr, Steele claimed that he wished to help to maintain and encourage good relations between their two countries, which were jeopardized by what he termed the "wretched Irish mess."[25]

The imperative to manage Irish-American opinion became more apparent following the introduction of the Government of Ireland Bill, as the British government had to deal with the Sinn Féin backlash as Irish nationalists fought for independence rather than dominion Home Rule status. During 1920 and 1921 Kerr became more closely involved with Anglo-American relations and the Irish question, as the republican movement escalated and relied increasingly on American support. Although some literature dealing with Irish intelligence during this period exists, historians have left relatively unexplored the nature of the intelligence Kerr received from American or American-based sources.[26] There has been a lack of focus on informants to whom government aides such as Kerr had access or kept on side. As Lloyd George's private secretary Kerr was not only privy to important firsthand information from a wide range of sources, but could also interview notable Americans who could provide valuable data on the republican movement. In early 1921, the Irish writer George W. Russell (AE) jocularly referred to Kerr as the intelligence officer of the Cabinet's Irish committee.[27] Given existing material in his files and Kerr's contacts with a variety of sources, this description may not have been so very far off the mark.

Letters Kerr received from Louis Tracy, an imperialist British journalist and novelist who headed the New York-based British Bureau of Information, are particularly intriguing. Little has been written on the Bureau of Information itself and its role. Although it closed in January 1919, shortly after the First World War ended, apparently Tracy still gathered valuable intelligence on Sinn Féin operations in the United States, which he sent to Kerr for the prime minister's use. Kerr found it particularly frustrating that Sinn Féin publicity and operations in the United States continued unchecked, with intensifying American support for its

---

[25] Steele to Kerr, 8 January 1920, enclosing undated clipping from *The Chicago Tribune*, GD 40/17/219/782, Lothian Papers.
[26] Christopher Andrew, *Secret Service: The Making of the British Intelligence Community* (London: Heinemann, 1985), 246-258; Rhodri Jeffreys-Jones, *American Espionage: From Secret Service to CIA* (New York: Free Press, 1977), 114-118; and Eunan O'Halpin, "British Intelligence in Ireland, 1914-1921," in *The Missing Dimension: Governments and Intelligence Communities in the Twentieth Century*, eds. Christopher Andrew and David Dilks (London: Macmillan, 1984), 55-77.
[27] George W. Russell to Kerr, 11 January 1921, GD 40/17/78/53, Lothian Papers.

outlook posing a threat to harmonious Anglo-American relations. Kerr may have ensured that an intensive propaganda campaign was launched in the United States, presenting the British side of the case; this could not, however, preclude a rival Sinn Féin campaign and activities in America. Early in 1920 Tracy warned that De Valera and his associates planned a well-organized scheme of American propaganda of a revolutionary nature that might potentially prove more dangerous to Britain than previous attempts, since it sought to manipulate American public opinion in a way that would persuade the U.S. Congress to recognize the Irish Republic. Tracy emphasized that it would be a mistake to treat this threat too lightly, as the movement was widespread and had enthusiastic financial supporters.[28]

Kerr did possess a range of important American contacts who supplied him with valuable reports that might be helpful to the British campaign in Ireland. This fact highlights the existence of Americans who supported Britain and tried to help the situation through negotiations and by providing intelligence. In 1921 Carl Ackerman of the *Philadelphia Public Ledger*, who had recently interviewed the Irish Republican leader Michael Collins at his secret Irish Republican Army (IRA) headquarters in Ireland, passed on information to Kerr on the Republican position. Ackerman told Kerr that a year before, Collins would have been willing to negotiate with the British; by 1921, however, the IRA were confident of victory and were therefore no longer prepared to talk. Ackerman explained that Sinn Féin were prepared to accept nothing less than a republic and would stop at nothing in order to achieve this. He recognized and warned Kerr that the financing of the IRA by American groups represented a danger to Britain, and therefore advised Kerr to try to persuade Lloyd George to give an interview aimed at affecting American public opinion. Writing to the prime minister, Kerr listed the main points Ackerman had made, suggesting that the prime minister should emphasize that there was no distress in Ireland that required White Cross relief; that the government was fighting not the Irish people but extreme fanatics; and that the issue in Ireland was not one of self-government but of Union versus Secession, a point to which the American public could relate.[29] Ackerman's move suggests that Anglo-American relations were not completely strained, merely complicated by the Irish situation and Irish-American support for the nationalist cause. His information must, of course, like all the other evidence involved, be viewed

---

[28] Louis Tracy to Philip Kerr, 24 February 1920, GD 40/17/78/75, Lothian Papers.
[29] Kerr to Lloyd George, 4 April 1921, F/90/1/41, Lloyd George Papers.

with caution and somewhat skeptically. It has yet to be determined just how credible an informant Ackerman was, since Collins had his own motives for speaking to him, and Ackerman himself hoped for an interview with Lloyd George. There is a real possibility that Collins was using Ackerman to convey a propagandist message to the British government by stressing his confident attitude. The episode was, nonetheless, evidence of the extent to which Kerr kept in touch and maintained links with a range of American-based informants, who provided data he could use when advising the prime minister.

When prompting Lloyd George, Kerr did, it seems, recognize the distinction between Irish-American support for Ireland and the American government's own stance. In 1920 Irish-American nationalists had undertaken extensive agitation urging the American government to recognize Ireland's right to independence. After this campaign failed, the U.S. Congress did take unofficial action, dispatching a letter to Lloyd George protesting against the imprisonment of Irishmen without trial.[30] In response, Kerr claimed to his chief that "everybody knows that every politician in America has to play up to the Irish game, and that all this agitation is merely window dressing with a view to meeting the presidential election." He was therefore relatively unconcerned about the impact of this pro-Irish unrest on relations between the British and American governments, although he does seem to have found such congressional interference in British affairs irritating. He advised Lloyd George merely to acknowledge the message from the congressmen, but admitted: "I should rather like to send an insulting reply but I don't think the Prime Minister of Great Britain can do that."[31] Two months later, in July 1920, Kerr even informed Auckland Geddes, the British ambassador, that the Irish situation was beginning to improve, claiming: "Sinn Fein is gradually finding out that it is not all beer and skittles challenging the existence of the British Empire, especially when it finds that the United States has definitely made up its mind not to quarrel with Great Britain for the sake of the Irish politicians."[32] Although Kerr admitted that the actual situation in Ireland was as bad as ever, he seemed confident that the American government was not prepared to damage relations with Great Britain in response to pressure from Irish-American lobbying and Irish activities in the United States.

---

[30] Carroll, *American Opinion and the Irish Question, 1910-23*, 154.
[31] Kerr to Lloyd George, 8 May 1920, GD 40/17/1276, Lothian Papers.
[32] Kerr to Sir Auckland Geddes, 5 July 1920, GD 40/17/1397, Lothian Papers.

Over the long term, Kerr demonstrated far greater concern over the potential damage that Irish-American support for Irish aspirations could inflict on the British Empire. As anti-British activities in the United States escalated, Colonel Edward M. House, one of President Wilson's closest aides, offered to negotiate with Sinn Féin on behalf of the British. In July 1920 Lloyd George sent Kerr to meet him, an interview that historians John Turner and Michael Dockrill have discussed, highlighting the fact that these very delicate negotiations were entrusted to Kerr because Lloyd George and Hamar Greenwood, the British secretary for Ireland, felt they could rely on him implicitly to respond in the right way to points made by the other side. Most importantly for Lloyd George, Kerr would not yield on any important issue merely for the sake of reaching an agreement. It seems, indeed, that Kerr took an extremely uncompromising stance on behalf of British interests, and his own report of this interview was highly illuminating in terms of his attitude toward American involvement in the Irish question.[33] David P. Billington, Jr., claims that Kerr welcomed House's 1920 offer of mediation.[34] Although Kerr recognized that this was a positive development, he also believed that House's good offices had limitations, and held out no great hope that American involvement would serve to avoid the ultimate use of force in Ireland.

Kerr's report of his conversation with House suggests that Kerr left the American in no doubt of the British position, even as he spoke "personally and without authorisation."[35] Kerr made it clear that no room for compromise existed in any settlement involving questions of foreign affairs or defense, because these issues involved Britain and her Empire. He went so far as to say that, although he himself had no authority under any circumstances to speak on behalf of the British government, House's role should be not to negotiate but to make it clear to Sinn Féin what they were up against in terms of the British position. Finally, Kerr noted that he had explained to House that, should war be the only option to prevent Ireland from becoming an independent republic, then Britain would not hesitate, stating: "Anything like independence was utterly out of the question. The effective authority of the United Kingdom Parliament in foreign affairs and

---

[33] John Turner and Michael Dockrill, "Philip Kerr at 10 Downing Street, 1916-1921," in *The Larger Idea: Lord Lothian and the Problem of National Sovereignty*, ed. John Turner (London: Historians Press, 1988), 37.

[34] David P. Billington, Jr., *Lothian: Philip Kerr and the Quest for World Order* (Westport, CT: Praeger, 2006), 68.

[35] Kerr to Lloyd George, 31 July 1920, F/90/1/14, Lloyd George Papers.

defence would be maintained at any cost."[36] The House interview did not simply demonstrate Kerr's position on any possible Irish settlement in 1920, but also highlighted his attitude toward the transatlantic elements affecting this problem. Whilst Kerr admired the United States and encouraged strong relations between that country and Britain, his primary concern was to safeguard the interests of the British Empire. Although he had shown a certain readiness to tolerate American interference in the Irish problem, fundamentally he considered the issue primarily a British affair, which left no room for outside negotiations.

By March 1921, when Kerr resigned as Lloyd George's private secretary, the Irish situation had reached crisis point. Kerr fully recognized the threat posed by American support for the Irish cause. The Government of Ireland Bill had been enacted in December 1920, creating two Home Rule Parliaments, one for the south of the country and one for the six counties of the newly formed Northern Ireland. Irish militants thereupon stepped up their campaign for complete independence, until a truce was called in July 1921 and talks with the British Government began in October. When Kerr left Downing Street he took up the editorship of *The Daily Chronicle*, a Lloyd George-controlled newspaper, and from this new vantage point he continued to communicate with and advise the prime minister. He was apparently particularly alarmed by information he received in September 1921 regarding Sinn Féin's American branch. According to Kerr, there existed a section of Sinn Féin that had no desire to reach a settlement with the British government. His main concern was that the American Sinn Féin supporters of this group were animated not by real love of Ireland, but rather by their hatred for Great Britain, and saw the Irish crisis as an opportunity to smash the British Empire, a cause in which they had joined with foreigners who loathed Britain to establish an international movement led by likeminded Americans. Kerr therefore urged the prime minister to persuade the Irish to accept dominion membership in the British Empire, since otherwise the American Irish would continue to control the situation.[37]

From this time onward, Kerr apparently had little to do with Irish affairs. Once the status of Ireland had been settled in the early 1920s, from then until the time of his death, Kerr's attention turned elsewhere. After leaving *The Daily Chronicle* in 1922, he devoted more time to Christian Science and political journalism, became secretary to the Rhodes Trust in

---

[36] *Ibid.*
[37] Kerr to Lloyd George, September 1921, F/34/2/7, Lloyd George Papers.

1925 and under-secretary of state at the India Office in 1931, and ended his career as British ambassador to the United States in 1939 and 1940. None of these positions apparently gave him any further direct connection to Ireland.

It might be natural to assume that Kerr, by then Lord Lothian, would have had some dealings with Irish matters during his time as ambassador. The Second World War and its implications for the transatlantic relationship naturally dominated Kerr's short tenure as ambassador, and his premature death in December 1940 meant that he did not live to see some of his efforts come to fruition. Given the sizeable Irish-American population of the United States, the international wartime situation, and the Irish Free State's attitude toward the conflict, it seems likely that Kerr, had he lived, would have had to address Irish issues at some stage. The Irish leader Éamon de Valera defended Irish neutrality during the Second World War, using this stance in attempts to establish Ireland as a player on the world stage, and even going so far as to as to offer condolences through the German ambassador on the death of Adolf Hitler in 1945.

Clearly, as demonstrated in this chapter, Kerr was fully aware of American ties to Ireland, and it seems plausible that at some point he would have tried to use his influence to benefit the British war effort. His friend and close associate Waldorf Astor, long-time chairman of the Royal Institute of International Affairs, undoubtedly believed Lothian was in a position to exert some influence upon the Irish situation. In June 1940 Astor wrote to Lothian to request, rather ironically, that he persuade the northern Irish to be more accommodating toward de Valera, asking: "Can you bring any influence to bear on Ulster to come to terms with Dev ... Dev is doing his best but a united Ireland would strengthen his hand and enable him to deal with the IRA ... a few American soldiers or airmen in S. Ireland and in France would have a most steadying effect."[38] Although Astor obviously believed Lothian possessed some power to affect this situation, it remains unclear whether this request had any result or even whether Kerr made any attempt to address it. In 1940 Lothian himself also wrote to Waldorf Astor's wife Nancy, asking if she could arrange a meeting between Winston Churchill, then first lord of the admiralty, and David Gray, the new American minister to Ireland, since Gray was anxious to discuss naval matters.[39]

---

[38] Waldorf Astor to Lothian, 1 June 1940, GD 40/17/398/228, Lothian Papers.
[39] Lothian to Nancy Astor, 20 March 1940, GD 40/17/398/221, Lothian Papers.

These rather inconclusive episodes aside, it is perhaps surprising that—even given his relatively brief span of office—so few archival references to Ireland exist for the time of Lothian's service as ambassador to Washington. Conceivably he might have played a part in yet another possible connection between Irish Americans and British interests. Joseph P. Kennedy, the U.S. ambassador to Britain, was not just an Irish-American but one with close links to the 'Cliveden Set', the group of politicians and journalists, Lothian among them, who congregated at the Astors' Buckinghamshire country house on the Thames. Since Lothian and Kennedy both represented their respective nations to the other at the same time, under normal circumstances regular contacts between them might have been expected. In practice, however, Kennedy's belief that Britain faced almost certain defeat by Germany, at a time when Lothian was pleading the British case with passionate commitment to U.S. President Franklin D. Roosevelt, with whom Kennedy's relationship was increasingly strained, meant that dealings between the two ambassadors were less than straightforward, and their communications limited, though not unfriendly. Had Lothian lived, the two men might have worked together more closely on Ireland. In 1941, when Kennedy was no longer ambassador, it was suggested to Roosevelt that he might be the perfect man to help Britain ease her troubles with neutral Ireland.[40] It was believed that Kennedy might have been able to persuade Éamon de Valera to open Irish ports to British warships.[41] By that date, however, Lothian was already dead, making it impossible to determine what role he might have played in supporting Kennedy as a mediator. Fundamentally, the brevity of Lothian's service as ambassador and his preoccupation with other issues make it extremely difficult to discern whether, at this late stage of his career, he even had any kind of attitude or policy toward Ireland. Given the international situation in 1939 and 1940, Lothian undoubtedly faced more pressing and immediate issues in terms of Anglo-American relations.

It can perhaps be suggested that Kerr's direct involvement in managing Irish affairs and Anglo-American relations provided him with valuable experience upon which he could draw in the latter stage of his career. His knowledge of republican intelligence networks, press management, and Irish-American sentiment could only have strengthened his qualifications as British ambassador to the United States and the skills

---

[40] Michael R. Beschloss, *Kennedy and Roosevelt: The Uneasy Alliance* (New York: Norton, 1980), 235.
[41] *Ibid.*, 235.

he brought to this role, abilities that other contributors to this volume, including J. Simon Rofe and Gavin Bailey, explore at some length. At least once before, when dealing with Colonel House in 1920, Kerr had already sought to negotiate British interests, while trying to appease American opinion. The Irish question was a delicate one, with the potential to set British and Americans at odds, so these experiences may have provided some valuable training for his later assignments.

This chapter has attempted to place Kerr contextually within the story of the Irish Question and Anglo-American relations between 1916 and 1921. His role was varied, since his position as the prime minister's private secretary gave him access to a wide range of correspondence, and he dealt with numerous matters on Lloyd George's behalf. His involvement with such vexed questions as the American Commission on Irish Independence, his management of and relations with the press, his handling of intelligence, and his meeting with Colonel House, all revealed the extent to which Kerr, even if he operated largely behind the scenes, was genuinely at the center of both Anglo-American relations and the Irish situation. His activities focused predominantly upon two main areas: firstly, Irish-American agitation; and secondly, intervention by the American government in the Irish Question. Kerr's concern over Irish-American support for the Irish nationalist cause was consistent. He believed such turmoil posed a substantive threat to the British Empire, and therefore worked to counteract it through propaganda campaigns and his own informants. The second area Kerr handled was the American government's involvement in Irish affairs. Although he apparently found this somewhat irritating, he does not seem to have taken it too seriously, believing that American politicians had to appeal to Irish America. Kerr's ultimate stance on such issues was that, while it was regrettable that these issues should have a negative impact on Anglo-American relations, ultimately the Irish situation was a matter that concerned primarily the British Empire, not the United States. Kerr undoubtedly played a significant role in managing Anglo-American relations with regard to Ireland during the First World War and as Lloyd George's private secretary, and devoted some, albeit limited, attention to the subject even after leaving Downing Street. Managing the Irish question added yet another element to the multi-faceted relationship with the United States he enjoyed over the course of his rather unconventional career.

CHAPTER THREE

THE INTERWAR PHILIP LOTHIAN

PRISCILLA ROBERTS

During the 1920s and 1930s, Philip Kerr—he inherited his long anticipated title in 1930—was active in various capacities. A brief stint as editor on *The Daily Chronicle* in 1921-1922 was followed by lengthy visits to the United States. In 1925 he accepted the office of secretary to the Rhodes Trust, a post he filled until 1939. In the early 1930s, after becoming a peer, Kerr also served briefly in the National Government, first as Chancellor of the Duchy of Lancaster, then as under secretary of state for India. Throughout these decades, he wrote prolifically on domestic and foreign issues, particularly the latter, and sought to play a role, often behind-the-scenes, in the making of foreign policy toward the United States, Europe, India, and Africa.

Apart, perhaps, from his views on Germany, which evolved under the pressure of events, between the wars Kerr's overall outlook on international affairs remained remarkably consistent. "Every day," he proclaimed in autumn 1922, "it is becoming clearer that neither the European nor the world problem can be solved without some form of American co-operation."[1] His other interests notwithstanding, during the 1920s Kerr's greatest preoccupation remained whether and how Britain might persuade the United States to work in cooperation with other nations, rather than following unilateralist policies.[2] "It is not too much to say," he wrote in 1922, "that if the British Commonwealth is to survive, and if the world is to be guided towards unity and peace, it is essential that the United States and the British Commonwealth should act in friendly co-operation."[3]

Fearing that dissension between the United States and Britain might compromise these objectives, after leaving Lloyd George Kerr made

---

[1] Philip Kerr, "America and the International Problem," *The Round Table* 12:48 (September 1922), 711.
[2] J. R. M. Butler, *Lord Lothian (Philip Kerr) 1882-1940* (London: Macmillan, 1960), 102-104, 117-118.
[3] Kerr, "A Programme for the British Commonwealth," *The Round Table* 12:46 (March 1922), 247.

P. Roberts (ed.), Lord Lothian and Anglo-American Relations, 1900-1940, 79-105.

it a self-appointed mission to facilitate the development of that Anglo-American concord he thought so desirable. In spring 1922 he went to the United States for eleven months, in part to pursue studies in Christian Science, returning more briefly in the summer of 1923. On both visits he joined Curtis and several prominent Americans, among them the Anglophile lawyer Paul D. Cravath and General Tasker H. Bliss, former American representative on the Supreme War Council, in two well-publicized lecture series on international problems at Williams College, Williamstown, Massachusetts. Kerr used these to urge the United States to break with isolationism and, in partnership with Britain, take a more active role in running the world. In 1922 he warned Americans that in any international organization force was needed to back up the rule of law; that "the most serious blow" to European peace since the war had been "the withdrawal of [America's] presence and counsel from the consideration of post-war problems"; that nations needed "to recognize that they belong to the larger community of nations"; and that the United States and Britain should "combin[e] with other nations to give some kind of constitutional system to the world."[4] The following summer Kerr stated that "[t]he only way . . . the world will ever get final security for peace and freedom is through the evolution of a world state." Though an ultimate goal, this was not, however, he continued, "within the reach of political action to-day." Force, he contended, was necessary to assure "the reign of law," and it was necessary that there be "some nations sitting around [the League of Nations] table who realize that the League is only a means towards the reign of righteousness, and who have the zeal and the determination to make right prevail." There "has been placed in a special way upon the shoulders of the English-speaking nations in this century," he declared,

> the task of helping mankind to draw up and establish that just world constitution without which it can have neither lasting peace, freedom, nor opportunity. No other peoples seem so well situated to take the lead, though they can and will cooperate; and it seems to me that America, with its high ideals, its great traditions, its immense strength, is inevitably marked out to take a leading part in this work.

Kerr even suggested this was God's particular mission for the United States, the reason it was so wealthy and powerful. In both lecture series, he also invoked the ideals of the Puritan founders of Massachusetts, the

---

[4] Philip Kerr and Lionel Curtis, *The Prevention of War* (New Haven, CT: Yale University Press, 1923), 7-74, quotations from 41, 49, 71.

founding fathers, including George Washington and Thomas Jefferson, and Abraham Lincoln.[5]

Kerr's wide and growing range of likeminded American contacts, familial and otherwise, facilitated his efforts to encourage Anglo-American understanding and cooperation. As an honorary member of the originally American Astor family, he joined an Atlanticist-minded clan whose ramifications by marriage extended widely throughout British and American society.[6] In the mid-1920s Kerr's sister Minna married the son of the president of Case Western Reserve University, in the state of Ohio.[7] Besides those bankers and government officials already mentioned, during the war Kerr worked closely with President Wilson's close adviser Colonel Edward M. House, and on House's staff at the Paris Peace Conference he encountered the former Rhodes scholar Whitney H. Shepardson, a businessman who not only later became an American intelligence operative, Carnegie Corporation executive, and stalwart of the Council on Foreign Relations, but from 1920 to 1934 wrote thirty-one articles on American issues for *The Round Table*.[8] Kerr knew a wide range of influential newspapermen, such as Frank Simonds of the *New York Herald Tribune*, Robert T. McCormick, owner of the *Chicago Tribune*, and Walter Lippmann. His Zionist sympathies also brought him closer to the politically active Harvard law professor and future Supreme Court Justice Felix Frankfurter, who in 1921 told Lothian of the strength of his own "conviction that the peace of the World primarily depends upon the English-speaking people."[9] Kerr carefully nurtured what was from the early 1920s an ever expanding circle of American contacts. Once Kerr became secretary to the Rhodes Trust in 1925, a position he retained until 1939, he visited the United States annually, travelling extensively in almost every

---

[5] Philip Kerr *et al.*, *Approaches to World Problems* (New Haven, CT: Yale University Press, 1924), 75-120, quotations from 110, 111, 118, 117.

[6] See, e.g., Nancy Astor, *My Two Countries* (London: Heinemann, 1923); James Fox, *The Langhorne Sisters* (London: Granta, 1998); and Ronald Tree, *When the Moon Was High: Memoirs of Peace and War, 1897-1942* (London: Macmillan, 1975).

[7] In the 1930s the marriage ended disastrously, when her husband was permanently institutionalized for insanity, but this had no apparent impact upon Kerr's commitment to Anglo-American relations.

[8] See the two volumes of these articles in Whitney H. Shepardson Papers, Franklin D. Roosevelt Presidential Library, Hyde Park, NY.

[9] Felix Frankfurter to Kerr, 7 May 1921, GD 40/17/82/54, Papers of the Eleventh Marquess of Lothian [hereafter Lothian Papers], National Archives of Scotland, Edinburgh; cf. Frankfurter to Kerr, 3 July 1929, File Philip Kerr, Box 72, Felix Frankfurter Papers, Manuscripts Division, Library of Congress, Washington, DC.

continental state and acquiring considerable understanding of the American political system and a near-legendary network of friends spanning the political, academic, journalistic, and Christian Science worlds. In 1939 John Buchan encouraged Lothian "at all costs" to accept the appointment as ambassador, since: "He knows America well, and above all he likes Americans, and there are no people more susceptible to liking."[10]

THE 1920S

By 1930 Kerr felt that his own undertakings to promote Anglo-American relations rivalled the fabled commitment of his friend Lionel Curtis to organic union of the British Empire.[11] They certainly sufficed to prompt Dame Edith Lyttelton to suggest his name in 1928 as a suitable ambassador to the United States.[12] Some such efforts were relatively small scale. In 1921, for example, hoping to moderate American anti-colonial sentiment, he suggested to Sir Edward Grigg, his successor as Lloyd George's private secretary, that every effort be made to assure favorable American newsreel and press coverage of a forthcoming visit to India by the Prince of Wales.[13] He wrote frequently for the *Christian Science Monitor*, from January 1925 to 1931 even producing an unsigned weekly column, "Diary of a Political Pilgrim," summarizing the arguments on political and international subjects he expressed at greater length elsewhere. Kerr justified such writing as "perhaps the best available means of helping the American public to get the news of what is going on in the world, and as the future depends entirely on what they are going to do, it is important that they should understand about the rest of the world better than they do."[14] In 1925 Kerr suggested that the British government send "a first class man" on an informal six-month mission to the United States to obtain international economic information and "ideas as to the best way of developing the resources of the world, and as to the possible modes of co-operation between American capital and British experience in developing the Empire."[15]

---

[10] Buchan to J. Walter Buchan, 27 April 1939, ACC 11627/83, Tweedsmuir Papers, National Library of Scotland, Edinburgh.

[11] Lothian to Curtis, 27 August 1940, GD 40/17/247, Lothian Papers.

[12] Thomas Jones, diary entry, 5 December 1928, in Thomas Jones, *Whitehall Diary*, ed. Keith Middlemas, 3 vols. (London: Oxford University Press, 1969-1971), 2:160.

[13] Kerr to Grigg, 25 August 1921, File GD 40/17/82/60-62, Lothian Papers.

[14] Kerr to Lady Anne Kerr, September 1923, cited in Butler, *Lord Lothian*, 96; and David P. Billington, Jr., *Lothian: Philip Kerr and the Quest for World Order* (Westport, CT: Praeger, 2006), 198 n. 22.

[15] Kerr to Jones, 7 July 1925, in Jones, *Whitehall Diary*, 1:321.

After leaving Lloyd George Kerr declined several invitations to return to *The Round Table*, become foreign editor of *The Times*, or run for parliament, on the grounds that he must devote himself to Christian Science, but in 1925 no such scruples prevented him accepting the position of secretary to the Rhodes Trust. For Kerr, who was habitually skittish about holding public office and preferred to work behind the scenes, this seems to have represented his dream job, allowing him to visit the United States annually and launch a variety of initiatives to enhance relations between that country and his own. His tenure lasted until 1939, far lengthier than any previous secretary's, enabling him to undertake his most sustained work in the Anglo-American sphere. Even when he inherited his title in 1930, Kerr continued as secretary to the Rhodes Trust. Philip Ziegler, in his recent history of that organization, suggests that socially Kerr, as first the heir to and then the incumbent of a major peerage, outranked most of the trustees who were nominally his superiors. He also thought Lothian, as he eventually became, one of the four or five most influential individuals in shaping the Rhodes Trust during its first half-century. Interestingly, his appointment provoked opposition from Rudyard Kipling, who resigned as a trustee over the matter, and Violet, Lady Milner, the widow of Kerr's early patron, both of whom apparently thought Kerr too lukewarm in his support for the British empire, though Leo Amery, a fellow trustee, claimed "Kipling's resignation [was] based on the fact that he does not like Philip Kerr's smile or the fact that he did not serve in the war." (A few years earlier, Kipling had remarked of Kerr that "a Roman-Catholic faith-healer is an unsavoury combination."[16])

As secretary, Kerr used his political influence to push through parliament in 1929 a bill altering the terms of Cecil Rhodes' will so that scholarships need no longer rotate automatically through each American state, but were allocated on merit in larger districts of six states apiece. Kerr and the Rhodes trustees feared smaller states lacked sufficient outstanding candidates with the potential for distinguished elite careers, and their intention was to raise not only the intellectual caliber but also the long-term impact of future Rhodes scholars. As Kerr reported to his trustees in 1926: "Half a dozen men of real influence and ability in public life, in education,

---

[16] Philip Ziegler, *Legacy: Cecil Rhodes, the Rhodes Trust and Rhodes Scholarships* (New Haven, CT: Yale University Press, 2008), 99-102, 197 n; first quotation from Leo Amery, diary entry, 30 June 1925, in *The Leo Amery Diaries*, Vol. I: *1896-1929*, eds. John Barnes and David Nicholson (London: Hutchinson, 1980), second quotation from Rudyard Kipling to John St. Loe Strachey, 22 August 1918, in *The Letters of Rudyard Kipling*, Vol. 4: *1911-19*, ed. Thomas Pinney (Iowa City: University of Iowa Press, 1999), 509.

in journalism, in law or in business can do a thousandfold more than hundreds of average men who never attain to any position of influence outside their own immediate circle of acquaintances."[17]

In another venture to maintain high standards among Rhodes scholars, all of whom already possessed an undergraduate degree, Kerr used Rhodes Trust resources to encourage research and postdoctoral study at Oxford University. In 1936 the Trust donated £100,000 to the university's Appeal Fund to support social studies research on problems of government in the British Commonwealth and the United States. Rhodes House in Oxford collected an outstanding library of books and other materials on the United States. The American presence at Oxford was enhanced in the late 1920s when Frank Aydelotte, the trust's American secretary and president of Swarthmore College, obtained funding from George Eastman, an American millionaire, to provide an annual visiting professorship for a distinguished American academic. During the 1930s its incumbents included John Livingston Lowes of Harvard, Wesley Clair Mitchell of Columbia University, Felix Frankfurter of Harvard Law School, Arthur Holly Compton of the University of Chicago, Herbert Spencer Jennings of Johns Hopkins University, Simon Flexner of New York's Rockefeller Institute, Tenney Frank of Johns Hopkins University, and Joseph Chamberlain of Columbia University's Law School. The 1929 Act also permitted the reinstatement of Rhodes fellowships for German students, a program originally established at Rhodes' behest to fulfil his vision of Anglo-German-American international partnership, but terminated by the Great War. Between 1930 and 1939 eighteen German scholars were selected. After the Nazis came to power in 1933 it became increasingly difficult for the Rhodes Trust to prevent Nazi political influence over the nomination of scholars, but Kerr and the trustees fought strenuously and at first with some success to preserve the independence of the selection process.[18]

---

[17] Kerr, "The Secretary's Report on Visit to Canada and the United States," 6 October 1926, quoted in Billington, *Lothian*, 82.

[18] Butler, *Lord Lothian*, 126-143; Ziegler, *Legacy*, chs. 17-23; Anthony Kenny, "The Rhodes Trust and its Administration," in Kenny, ed., *The History of the Rhodes Trust 1902-1999* (Oxford: Oxford University Press, 2001), 25-39; David Alexander, "The American Scholarships," *ibid.*, 125-142; Richard Sheppard, "The German Rhodes Scholarships," *ibid.*, 371-400; John Darwin, "The Rhodes Trust in the Age of Empire," *ibid.*, 479-516; Frank Aydelotte, *The American Rhodes Scholarships: A Review of the First Forty Years* (Princeton, NJ: Princeton University Press, 1946); Godfrey Elton, ed., *The First Fifty Years of the Rhodes Trust and the Rhodes Scholarships 1903-1953* (Oxford: Basil Blackwell, 1955), 16-32, 157-159, 161-162, 197-201, 209-210; Richard Symonds, *Oxford and Empire:* (continued)

Symbolically and significantly, Kerr suggested that, whereas President Woodrow Wilson's ideas of international organization had been too ambitious, there was much to be said for "the Rhodes thesis that the first step towards stable world peace is the re-construction in some form of the wartime association of the English-speaking nations and also France (in place of Germany) as a genuinely liberal power." He even hoped to stage a public debate on "the question of Wilson vs. Rhodes."[19]

In the public domain Kerr's drive to promote Anglo-American harmony focused particularly upon three often contentious issues: the League of Nations; Anglo-American naval relations; and economic questions. On all of these he wrote and spoke extensively, generally attempting to expound the British position in the United States and the American viewpoint to his own countrymen.[20] Kerr's efforts to accomplish these objectives were conducted principally though by no means entirely within two linked institutions, the Royal Institute of International Affairs or Chatham House, founded at the Paris Peace Conference in 1919, and its American sister organization, the Council on Foreign Relations. With Waldorf Astor, Curtis, Robert Brand, and Kerr prominent in its activities and financial backing from Sir Abe Bailey, a South African millionaire with close ties to Milner, believers in Anglo-American cooperation largely dominated the interwar RIIA, which with Lothian's assistance was able to tap such American funding sources as the Carnegie Corporation and the Rockefeller Foundation.[21]

Although political considerations, financial constraints, and fears of being perceived as a British front finally persuaded the officers of the

---

The Last Lost Cause? (Basingstoke: Macmillan, 1986), 62-79, 161-181; and Billington, *Lothian*, 80-85, 117-118.

[19] Lothian to Frank Aydelotte, 12 May 1933, quoted in Butler, *Lord Lothian*, 135-136.

[20] See Lothian's voluminous speeches and writings file, GD 40/17/411-444, Lothian Papers.

[21] On the RIIA, see esp. Inderjeet Parmar, *Special Interests, the State, and the Anglo-American Alliance, 1939-1945* (London: Frank Cass, 1995), 62-72; Parmar, *Think tanks and power in foreign policy: A comparative study of the role and influence of the Council on Foreign Relations and the Royal Institute of International Affairs, 1939-1945* (Basingstoke: Palgrave Macmillan, 2004), chs. 2-4, 7-8; Parmar, "Chatham House and the Anglo-American Alliance," *Diplomacy and Statecraft* 3:1 (March 1992), 23-47; Parmar, "Anglo-American Elites in the Interwar Years: Idealism and Power in the Intellectual Roots of Chatham House and the Council on Foreign Relations," *International Relations* 16:1 (April 2002), 53-75; Andrea Bosco and Cornelia Navari, eds., *Chatham House and British Foreign Policy 1919-1945: The Royal Institute of International Affairs during the Inter-War Period* (London: Lothian Foundation Press, 1994); and Deborah Lavin, *From Empire to International Commonwealth: A Biography of Lionel Curtis* (Oxford: Clarendon Press, 1995), 165-179.

American institution, originally christened the American Institute of International Affairs, to reorganize itself by merging with an independent organisation, the Council on Foreign Relations, which did not even share the RIIA's name, in practice the two organizations remained rather close. This sprang not solely from their common origins, but also from the commitment to cementing Anglo-American relations which many of the most prominent and active officers in both bodies officers shared. Several of the Council's founders demonstrated pronounced Anglophile sympathies, among them Elihu Root, the Council's first and only honorary president; John W. Davis, a former American ambassador to Britain, and George W. Wickersham, its first two presidents; Cravath, its first vice-president; and several of its founding directors, including Norman H. Davis, the banker Otto H. Kahn of Kuhn, Loeb & Company, and Shepardson, together with one of its greatest benefactors, Thomas W. Lamont of the Morgan investment banking firm, whose views his fellow partners generally endorsed. These individuals were also prominent activists in other transnational organizations designed to promote Anglo-American solidarity, including the Pilgrims Society and the newly-established English-Speaking Union, of which John Davis was the American president and Wickersham the chairman.[22]

As before, Kerr's persistent misgivings over the existing League of Nations gave him a strong predilection to withdraw from European affairs. In 1922 he applauded the British government's refusal to make "an Anglo-French alliance pledging British military support in the event of any infringement of the Treaty of Versailles by Germany." The League, he thought, should restrict itself to considering such issues as "armaments, the use of the high seas, colour problems, the treatment of backward peoples or minorities, all world questions which must all be looked at from a world point of view."[23] Kerr opposed Britain's 1924 adherence to the Geneva Protocol, under which it recognized an obligation to back League decisions with economic or military sanctions, and welcomed the new Baldwin

---

[22] *New York Times*, 4 May 1919; Robert T. Swaine, *The Cravath Firm and Its Predecessors, 1819-1938*, 2 vols. (New York: n.p., 1946-1948), 2:256; William H. Harbaugh, *Lawyer's Lawyer: The Life of John W. Davis* (New York: Oxford University Press, 1973), 424; and Files 27-5 and 27-6, Thomas W. Lamont Papers, Baker Library, Harvard Business School, Boston, MA.

[23] Kerr, "A Programme for the British Commonwealth," *The Round Table* 12:46 (March 1922), 229-252, quotations from 234, 244; and Butler, *Lord Lothian*, 107-110.

government's veto of this move in March 1925.[24] Only reluctantly did he endorse the Locarno agreements of October 1925, whereby Britain, France, Germany, Italy, and Belgium signed security treaties recognizing and guaranteeing each others' frontiers.[25] In 1926 he told a Canadian associate that the League "appears to be falling more and more under the control of Latin Powers & the Continental point of view .... In fact, if the present tendency in Europe is maintained, I fancy Great Britain will increasingly draw out of it in its dealings with local and Eastern European problems just as she drew out of the Holy Alliance in 1822."[26] Soon afterwards he declared that the League "ought to concentrate on one thing and one thing only on developing both public opinion and machinery behind this idea that no alteration of the existing status quo in any part of the world, and that no settlement of an international dispute should be attempted by force, until after the constitutional procedure laid down in the Covenant has been invoked." He continued: "The attempt, made in the [League] Protocol, to link up the League with special problems, such as the stability of the Versailles settlement or the Franco-German problem, is fundamentally unsound and destructive of the central concept of the League." Issues such as the Rhineland problem and international security guarantees should, he argued, be settled by "ordinary diplomatic means apart from the League."[27]

Once the United States signed the Kellogg-Briand Peace Pact in 1928, Kerr launched a protracted and energetic though ultimately abortive campaign to persuade the British League of Nations Union to demand the modification of the League Covenant so as to eliminate provisions for automatic mandatory sanctions, thereby making it consonant with the Pact. His hope was that such action would induce American officials to agree to consultations among Kellogg Pact signatories should a situation likely to lead to war arise, effectively leading the United States to work more closely with the League and perhaps even accept some form of membership. Immediately after the 1922 Washington Conference, at which Britain and the United States agreed to limit their navies, Kerr stated:

---

[24] Kerr, "The British Commonwealth, the Protocol and the League," *The Round Table* 15:57 (December 1924), 1-23; Kerr, "Europe, the Covenant, and the Protocol," *The Round Table* 15:58 (March 1925), 219-241; Butler, *Lord Lothian*, 111-114; and Billington, *Lothian*, 90-91.

[25] Kerr, "The Locarno Treaties," *The Round Table* 16:61 (December 1925), 1-28; Butler, *Lord Lothian*, 115; and Billington, *Lothian*, 91.

[26] Kerr to Loring Christie, 3 March 1926, File GD 40/17/221/95-99, Lothian Papers.

[27] Kerr, Memorandum for Group on Disarmament and Security, 1927, File 4/LOTH, Individual Files, Royal Institute of International Affairs Archives, Chatham House, London.

Sea supremacy is now exercised jointly by the British empire and the United States. . . . [T]he dominion of the sea, with the tremendous issues it carries for the future of mankind, is now vested in the peoples of the English-speaking world. So long as they can co-operate in its exercise and see eye to eye about the purposes for which it is to be used, civilisation and liberty are safe. If they disagree, both are endangered. If they quarrel and fight, both are doomed. What is more, the British Commonwealth itself is doomed, for the United States, with an equal naval power, and infinitely greater resources, would be able to cut Britain's communications with the rest of the Empire.[28]

Shared British and United States naval supremacy was, he believed, the key to the effective imposition of economic sanctions on nations transgressing against the Kellogg-Briand Pact. This strategy would have entailed jettisoning the implied British commitment, through the League, to guarantee and defend the European boundaries set by the Versailles settlement, an undertaking Kerr always considered dubious. For several years Kerr campaigned indefatigably to harmonize the League with the Kellogg-Briand Pact, addressing the RIIA on "The Outlawry of War" in November 1928, pushing his viewpoint in Liberal Party deliberations, and circulating his *Round Table* articles on this topic around his enormous circle of acquaintances in the British Empire and the United States, among them the American Secretary of State Frank B. Kellogg, Alanson B. Houghton, the American ambassador in London, and Salmon B. Levinson, one of the Pact's originators.[29] Indeed, many of those Americans closely associated with the Council on Foreign Relations, including Lamont, Secretary of State Henry L. Stimson, John Davis, and Walter Lippmann, likewise favored developing the Kellogg-Briand Pact into a consultative pact.[30] Kerr only desisted when his endeavors appeared likely to work at

---

[28] Kerr, "A Programme for the British Commonwealth," 247-248.

[29] See Files GD 40/17/117-119, Lothian Papers; correspondence scattered through Files GD 40/17/226-254, Lothian Papers; Kerr, "The Outlawry of War," *International Affairs* 7:5 (November 1928), 361-388; Kerr, "Outlawry of War," *The Round Table* 18:71 (June 1928), 455-476; Kerr, "The Peace Pact," *The Round Table* 18:72 (September 1928), 727-745; Kerr, "A Plea for an Independent Foreign Policy," *The Round Table* 19:73 (December 1928), 1-25; Kerr, "The British Commonwealth, Freedom and the Seas," *The Round Table* 19:74 (March 1929), 229-256; Kerr to Norman H. Davis, 5 June 1928, 20 December 1928, enclosing Kerr to Lippmann, 20 December 1928, Kerr to Davis, 4 March 1929, Box 40, Norman H. Davis Papers, Manuscripts Division, Library of Congress, Washington, DC; Butler, *Lord Lothian*, 118-121; and Billington, *Lothian*, 92-94.

[30] See Priscilla Roberts, "The Anglo-American Theme: American Visions of an Atlantic Alliance, 1914-1933," *Diplomatic History* 21:3 (Summer 1997), 362-363; and Melvyn P. Leffler, *The Elusive Quest: America's Pursuit of European Stability and French Security,* (continued)

cross-purposes with Anglo-American negotiations in preparation for the forthcoming 1930 London Naval Conference.

In the later 1920s Anglo-American naval relations were particularly strained, as the British evaded the ratios imposed under the 1921-1922 Washington Conference treaties by building cruisers, which fell outside these agreements. By 1927 Kerr was corresponding with British Admiralty officials, suggesting potential strategies to allay Anglo-American naval suspicions.[31] He also published several articles on naval policy in *The Round Table*, dispatching numerous copies of each to influential friends in the United States, Britain, and the Dominions, and in March 1928 addressed the National Council for the Prevention of War on the subject in the United States.[32] Kerr publicly deplored an Anglo-French naval compromise negotiated in summer 1928, partly because the United States denounced it, and also because he viewed this as a French attempt "to draw Great Britain into an entente which has an anti-German point."[33] He wrote to Lippmann and Norman H. Davis, an American representative in most of the interwar naval negotiations, welcoming the American passage in late 1928 of a Cruiser Bill which instituted a program of building fifteen new heavy cruisers, a measure they believed would defuse the naval dispute. Kerr hoped the British would tactfully allow their own numbers of heavy cruisers to fall behind the American equivalents, while maintaining superiority in light cruisers.[34] He also suggested to former Secretary of

---

1919-1933 (Chapel Hill: University of North Carolina Press, 1979), 1-14, 161, 227, 285-287.

[31] See Kerr's correspondence with W. C. Bridgeman, 1927, GD 40/17/226/52-58.

[32] Kerr, "The Naval Conference," *The Round Table* 17:68 (September 1927), 659-683; Kerr, "The Naval Problem," *The Round Table* 18:70 (March 1928), 223-255; Kerr, "The British Commonwealth, Freedom and the Seas," *The Round Table* 19:74 (March 1929), 229-256; Kerr, "Naval Disarmament," *The Round Table* 19:75 (June 1929), 447-464; Kerr, "The London Conference," *The Round Table* 20:77 (December 1929), 1-21; Kerr to Davis, 20 March, 5 June, 20 December 1928, enclosing Kerr to Lippmann, 20 December 1928, Kerr to Davis, 24 May 1929, enclosing Kerr, "The Anglo-American Naval Problem," Box 40, Davis Papers; and Billington, *Lothian*, 91-96.

[33] Kerr, "A Plea for an Independent Foreign Policy," *The Round Table* 19:73 (December 1928), 1-25; quotation from Kerr to James Ramsay MacDonald, 16 November 1928, File GD 40/17/243/561-562, Lothian Papers. Davis warned Kerr that in the United States there was an "impression" that the Anglo-French accord represented "a return to the old system of alliances." Davis to Kerr, 27 November 1928, 7 January 1929, quotation from first letter, Box 40, Davis Papers.

[34] Lippmann to Kerr, 4 December 1928, Kerr to Lippmann, 20 December 1928, GD 40/17/242/443-48, Lothian Papers; Kerr to Davis, 20 December 1928, Box 40, Davis Papers. (continued)

State Kellogg that, before beginning formal negotiations, "the British and American governments should satisfy themselves that they are within reach of an agreement."[35] In a memorandum he circulated in 1929, Kerr sounded familiar themes:

> The key to the Anglo-American naval problem, to the disarmament problem, to the problem of making the Kellogg Pact effective is the same. It is that the signatories of the Pact of Paris, and especially the United States and Great Britain should agree, or at least publicly recognise, that they are all vitally interested in any threat to the peace of the world, and, on such threat arising, will take counsel together as to how hostilities can be prevented.[36]

Both Institute and Council also attempted to alleviate the growing tensions dividing the United States and Britain, primarily by establishing coordinated study groups, a transatlantic effort Kerr spearheaded. Indeed, in 1928 he hoped to hold a joint Council-Institute conference on Anglo-American relations to promote his ideas on modifying the Kellogg Pact, a proposal the RIIA ultimately turned down, in part because they feared it might generate "a good deal of propaganda and publicity."[37] In 1928-1929 the RIIA established a 'Special Group on Anglo-American Relations,' chaired by Kerr, whose findings predictably contended that close cooperation between the two powers was in the best interests of both. The group concentrated heavily upon the naval issue, and how to harmonize British naval policies with the demands of the Kellogg Peace Pact; more broadly, its purposes were, as Kerr stated in an early memorandum, "to try to set forth the differences which divide Great Britain and the United States with the object of seeing what can be done to remove them." Kerr argued that, as "manufacturing and exporting countries," Britain and the United States shared common economic interests, and that both alike were "in favour of self-government for all peoples, of individual liberty under the law, of the pacific settlement of international disputes. Neither covets any territory possessed by the other." Even old disputes over imperialism were,

---

For Davis' more cautious reaction to the Cruiser Bill, see Davis to Kerr, 7 January 1929, *ibid.*

[35] Kerr to Frank B. Kellogg, 30 April 1929, Reel 38, Frank B. Kellogg Papers, Manuscripts Division, Library of Congress, Washington, DC.

[36] Kerr, "The Anglo-American Naval Problem," enclosed in Kerr to Davis, 24 May 1929, Box 40, Davis Papers.

[37] Margaret E. Cleeve to Lothian, 1 September 1934, RIIA, "Study Group and Conference on Anglo-American Relations. History of the Proposal," 20 December 1935, File 9/15a, Anglo-American Cooperation-Proposed Study Group, Study Group Files, RIIA Archives. On Kerr's efforts, see also Billington, *Lothian*, 93.

in his view, losing their force. Seeking to avoid fierce naval competition, he recommended that the two countries reach an understanding over mutual interdiction of trade should one or the other be at war, and define limits for cruiser building acceptable to both nations. Going beyond mere conflict avoidance, he concluded by effectively urging Anglo-American international condominium, arguing:

> If the United States and Great Britain really make up their minds not only not to go to war with one another as they have more or less done, but that they will use their whole influence and power to prevent other powers from settling their disputes by war, at any rate on the high seas, the risk of their getting to cross purposes about interference with one another's trade in time of war becomes immensely less. As usual the best safeguard for peace and friendly relations is a common understanding about political questions.[38]

The RIIA also provided a friendly forum where visiting American interlocutors such as Allen W. Dulles, a member of the corresponding Council group, could speak frankly and in confidence on vexed issues in the two countries' relationship, and bring RIIA members up to date with the progress of the group on Anglo-American relations the Council simultaneously established. The first Council study group on Anglo-American relations held its opening meeting in November 1928 and submitted a report in June 1929, a document intended to influence policymakers at the London Naval Conference. In the interim the Council's journal, *Foreign Affairs*, published an article by Dulles suggesting that British and American negotiators should aim at achieving overall parity in combat naval strength, not in specific classes of naval vessels.[39] The American group was chaired by Charles P. Howland, a Boston lawyer, and its membership of seventeen included Davis, Dulles, Wilson's former adviser Colonel Edward M. House, Arthur Bullard of the League of Nations, the international lawyer Philip C. Jessup, Shepardson, the influential columnist Lippmann, and Hamilton Fish Armstrong, editor of the Council's journal, *Foreign Affairs*, together with various academics, New York lawyers, and representatives of other organizations interested in

---

[38] Quotation from Kerr, draft memorandum, 2 November 1928, GD 40/17/97-104, Lothian Papers; see also materials in File 9/9, Anglo-American Relations Study Group, RIIA Archives.
[39] Allen W. Dulles, "The Threat of Anglo-American Naval Rivalry," *Foreign Affairs* 7:2 (January 1929), 173-182; Peter Grose, *Gentleman Spy: The Life of Allen Dulles* (Boston: Houghton Mifflin, 1994), 97, 124; and Parmar, *Special Interests, the State, and the Anglo-American Alliance*, 69-70.

international affairs.[40] The group's objectives were to hammer out a possible American position in the impending London naval disarmament conference; and to devise means of strengthening the recently concluded Kellogg-Briand Pact to outlaw war by considering methods, in collaboration with either or both Britain and the League of Nations, of exerting sanctions, military or otherwise, against nations which resorted to war.[41] The final report stated that the study's objective "was of course to see how the attitudes of the two countries could be harmonized so as to avoid competitive navy building, recriminatory language and ill-will where there should be community of interest."[42]

The Council group made every effort to accommodate the British position. In January 1929 Sir Arthur Salter addressed it over dinner, while in mid-February Dulles and Howland spoke respectively on "technical aspects of the naval situation" and "broader political questions." Three English visitors, Salter, George Young, and Prof. Charles K. Webster of the London School of Economics, were invited to sit at the speakers' table and comment on the addresses for five minutes each "from the British point of view."[43] Even after the group presented its report in mid-1929, its members still reassembled in January 1930 to hear Kerr discuss Anglo-American relations in light of the forthcoming London Naval Conference.[44] *Foreign Affairs* also published related articles by Howland and Kerr, in which each suggested that Anglo-American naval cooperation was the best means of achieving a harmonious conference settlement.[45]

---

[40] The other members were the geographer Isaiah Bowman, of Johns Hopkins University; Raymond L. Buell and James G. McDonald of the Foreign Policy Association; the Boston lawyer, Charles C. Burlingham; Joseph P. Chamberlain of Columbia University's Law School; Walter H. Mallory of the Council on Foreign Relations; Raymond B. Fosdick of the Rockefeller Foundation; and Professor James T. Shotwell of Columbia University and the Carnegie Endowment for International Peace.

[41] Memorandum by Professor Jessup, 16 November 1928, Records of Anglo-American Group 1928-1930, Records of Groups, Council on Foreign Relations Papers, Mudd Manuscripts Library, Princeton University, Princeton, NJ.

[42] Report of Study Group of Members of the Council on Foreign Relations on the Anglo-American Naval Question, 1 June 1929, *ibid.* The hope was that the Council's deliberations would reach the president through what Howland described as Allen Dulles' "private channel to Hoover's ear." Howland to Walter H. Mallory, 18 February 1929, *ibid.*

[43] Mallory to John W. Davis, 13 February 1929, Mallory to Frank L. Polk, 15 February 1929, *ibid.*

[44] List of those attending dinner for Philip Kerr, 23 January 1930, *ibid.*

[45] Kerr, "Navies and Peace: A British View," *Foreign Affairs* 8:1 (October 1929), 20-29; and Howland, "Navies and Peace: An American View," *Foreign Affairs* 8:1 (October 1929), 30-40.

The group's June 1929 report avowedly drew substantially upon recent writings by Kerr in *International Affairs* and *The Round Table*.[46] It argued that war between the United States and Britain should be unthinkable and that, while economic concerns might cause dissension, the only reason such a conflict might arise was potential British interference with American shipping in a war in which the United States remained neutral. Conceding that "public opinion in the United States is determined to have a substantial navy and has a firm intention that it shall be equal to the British," it suggested that the two countries should accept parity of 400,000 tons apiece in cruisers, the major point of contention between the two sides. It also urged that, since it could not be assumed that the Kellogg-Briand Pact alone would prevent future wars, Britain and the United States should coordinate their policies toward subsequent controversies between other nations. Fearing that the Senate would not ratify such a treaty, the group recommended that, following the precedent of the hallowed Monroe Doctrine, it should be implemented by executive action.[47] In effect, such a strategy would have realized the Anglo-American condominium which Kerr, like many leading Council figures, had long envisaged and sought. In practice, even though it did not implement these broader suggestions, the 1930 London Naval Conference drew on Institute and Council recommendations to settle many of the outstanding issues dividing the United States and Britain.

GATHERING STORM CLOUDS: THE 1930S

As the Great Depression took hold in the early 1930s, economic issues, particularly tariffs and war debts, increasingly dominated Anglo-American relations. In 1932 Lothian, always a free-trade Liberal, resigned from the coalition National Government over the protectionist Ottawa tariff agreements. Once Franklin D. Roosevelt, an old friend, became president in 1933, Kerr again attempted to facilitate efforts to reach some settlement of these issues. On a three-week visit to the United States early in 1933 he had

---

[46] Howland, "Outline for the Report of the Anglo-American Group," 17 January 1929, Records of Anglo-American Group, 1928-1930, Council on Foreign Relations Papers; Kerr, "The Outlawry of War," *International Affairs* 7:5 (November 1928), 361-388; Kerr, "The Naval Problem," *The Round Table* 18:70 (March 1928), 223-255; Kerr, "The British Commonwealth, Freedom and the Seas," *The Round Table* 19:74 (March 1929), 229-256; and Kerr, "Naval Disarmament," *The Round Table* 19:75 (June 1929), 447-464.
[47] Report of Study Group of Members of the Council on Foreign Relations on the Anglo-American Naval Question, 1 June 1929, Records of Anglo-American Group 1928-1930, Council on Foreign Relations Papers.

talks with influential Democrats, bankers, and politicians, among them Owen D. Young of General Electric, the retired businessman and long-time Democrat, Bernard M. Baruch, Norman H. Davis, Senators William E. Borah and Bayard Cutting, Thomas W. Lamont, and Prof. Walter Y. Elliott of Harvard. In an attempt to reach an agreement with the incoming Democratic administration on a strategy for joint Anglo-American discussions to tackle the depression and associated economic problems, including war debts, he also met with his long-time associate Colonel House, to whom he later reported on his meetings with British leaders.[48] Before sailing for Britain in February, Lothian publicly suggested that the most vital problem facing both Britain and the United States was to reduce unemployment, a problem to which the payment of the war debts was secondary and should be subordinated.[49] He then circulated to the British Cabinet and, through House, to Roosevelt, a memorandum urging coordinated international action to resolve such issues and bring about economic recovery, unavailingly suggesting that lower-level British and American officials should hold preliminary talks on these matters before their principals met to resolve them. In practice, the president's virtual sabotage of the forthcoming London Economic Conference the following June and his subsequent focus upon United States domestic recovery effectively stymied all such recommendations.[50]

Lothian's commitment to the League of Nations had at best never been more than lukewarm, in part because he feared membership in it might only too easily involve his own country in conflicts in which Britain had no real interests at stake. As the European situation began to deteriorate during the 1930s, Lothian's distrust of the League intensified. As early as 1931 he advised the British government that, should the forthcoming European disarmament conference break down, Britain should withdraw from European affairs and consider as non-binding any obligation to participate in a war in Europe.[51] League of Nations sanctions against nations defined as aggressors were, he feared, virtually bound to prove

---

[48] Lothian, undated handwritten notes, GD 40/17/199/134-141; and Lothian to House, 13 February 1933, Box 72, Edward M. House Papers, Sterling Library, Yale University, New Haven, CT.

[49] *New York Times*, 4 February 1933.

[50] Lothian to House, 24 February 1933, and enclosed memorandum, letters from Neville Chamberlain, H. D. Henderson, John Simon, Robert Vansittart, Stanley Baldwin, and Maurice Hankey to Lothian, February 1933, House to Lothian, 24 February 1933, GD 40/17/199/200-228, 243-244, Lothian Papers.

[51] Butler, *Lord Lothian*, 122.

ineffectual.[52] Lothian fundamentally endorsed the viewpoint of his friend, *The Round Table*'s editor John Dove, that Britain should "avoid committal to any side in Europe," and above all should deliberately "take the line most likely to bring America in in the hour of need, and to enable us even before then to co-operate."[53] Speaking in 1934 at Chatham House, Lothian suggested that Britain restrict its European commitments to a guarantee of French and Belgian security, and otherwise withdraw from the European system, comments he repeated in another address in the same forum in April 1936.[54] In a lengthy personal letter, two months later Lothian proceeded to urge these arguments upon Foreign Secretary Anthony Eden.[55] Again, in 1937 he told the House of Lords that Britain should emulate the United States in adopting a policy of "armed neutrality," and that "the only way in which the world can be guaranteed against another world war and security for democracy ensured" would be "if both the United States and Great Britain stand outside any alliance system either in Europe or in the Far East."[56]

Lothian reached this conclusion only after the repeated rejection of his suggestions that the United States should play a greater world role. Indeed, his initial reaction when Hitler gained power in 1933 was to cite this German development as yet one more argument to entice the United States away from non-involvement in international affairs. Lothian warned American friends such as House that the root cause of "this tragedy was the failure of the United States to accept the League of Nations for the reason that it removed from the Councils of Europe a neutral and moderating influence, it drove France into substituting for the security of Anglo-American-French co-operation in the League [a] system of military alliances with the Little Entente and it made the effective scaling down of reparations such as was contemplated in the original idea of the Reparations Commission impossible until it was too late." He further suggested: "Unless United States comes right forward into international affairs now, you will in the next year or two have a further triumph for reaction, a further war, with the Liberal nations of 1919 not triumphant but confronted with a more formidable combination than that which they had to meet in

---

[52] Lothian, Memorandum on Sanctions, enclosed in Pauline Child to Stephen King-Hall, 12 January 1934, File 9/8c, Sanctions Group, Study Group Files, RIIA Archives.
[53] Dove, "British Foreign Policy," 3 May 1933, GD 40/17/276/575-576, Lothian Papers.
[54] Butler, *Lord Lothian*, 197-200, also 213-217; and Billington, *Lothian*, 123.
[55] Lothian to Eden, 3 June 1936, in Butler, *Lord Lothian*, 354-362.
[56] Lothian, notes for speech in the House of Lords, 2 March 1937, GD 40/17/443/283-285, Lothian Papers.

1914."[57] In 1934 Lothian again suggested to House that the United States, while "declaring that in future under the Kellogg Pact it regarded any definite dispute likely to lead to war as its immediate concern and that it would sit regularly in deliberation about it, in a Pacific Conference, in Geneva, or anywhere else," should "take the leadership for peace" and join the League of Nations with "complete reservations" over those articles of its covenant which committed member states to economic and military sanctions against transgressors. Such a move would, he thought, force Germany, Italy, and Japan to rejoin the League.[58] Shortly afterwards, Lothian suggested that, in any international crisis, Britain and the United States should call a conference to determine the aggressor, impose international economic sanctions upon the nation specified as the aggressor, and employ both countries' naval forces to enforce such an embargo.[59]

As Greg Kennedy describes in detail in the following chapter in this volume, after addressing the Council on Foreign Relations and holding private discussions with various American officials and ex-officials, Lothian also warned the British Foreign Office, which treated his arguments with some skepticism, that in the interests of maintaining Anglo-American concord, Britain must coordinate its Far Eastern policies with those of the United States, and if necessary adopt a firmly anti-Japanese line and support Chinese independence to that end.[60] Over a decade earlier, in mid-1920, when he was still British Prime Minister David Lloyd George's private secretary, Lothian had called for greater U.S. involvement in the Pacific as a "counterpoise" to growing Japanese power, a solution he

---

[57] Lothian to House, 11 April 1933, GD 40/17/200/250-256, Lothian Papers; and Butler, *Lord Lothian*, 191-194.

[58] Lothian to House, 20 November 1934, File GD 40/17/200/268-272, Lothian Papers.

[59] Lothian, "The Anglo-American Naval Problems," 24 August 1934, GD 40/17/280/1-8, Lothian Papers.

[60] "Isolation, Alliance, or Kellogg Pact," *The Round Table* 24:95 (June 1934), 469-489; Lothian, "Navies and the Pacific," *The Round Table* 24:96 (September 1934), 693-716; Lothian, "Power Politics in the Pacific," *The Round Table* 25:97 (December 1934), 1-20; see also Lothian to Sir Reginald Haskins, 23 May 1935, GD 40/17/289/31, Lothian Papers; Henry L. Stimson, diary, 5, 8, 22, 30 October 1934, 20 March 1935, Diary of Henry L. Stimson (microfilm ed.), Sterling Library, Yale University, New Haven, CT; Lothian to the Editor, *The Times*, 18 February 1935, enclosed in Lothian to Stimson, 22 February 1935, Reel 88, Henry L. Stimson Papers (microfilm ed.), Sterling Library, Yale University, New Haven, CT; Billington, *Lothian*, 115-117; D. C. Watt, *Personalities and Policies: Studies in the Formulation of British Policy in the Twentieth Century* (London: Longmans, 1965), 95-99; Norman Rose, *The Cliveden Set: Portrait of an Exclusive Fraternity* (London: Jonathan Cape, 2000), 140-143; and Parmar, *Special Interests, the State and the Anglo-American Alliance*, 70.

hoped would provide "security for British possessions in the Far East" while "protecting China against exploitation." He had believed that the best way to bring this about was to call a "Conference between the United States, Great Britain, Japan and China, with the British Dominions and India," to reach an international agreement that would enable Britain to jettison the Anglo-Japanese Alliance of 1902, a treaty that was unpopular with both the United States and the Dominions and was coming up for renewal in 1922. Lothian's hopes became reality in 1921-1922, when the United States government convened a conference at Washington that concluded the Five -Power and Nine-Power Treaties, setting limits on naval armaments among the signatory powers and accepting the *status quo* in the Pacific.[61] Billington claims that Lothian's efforts to influence public opinion on Pacific policy during late 1934 and 1935, especially his somewhat indiscreet public speeches and writings raising the possibility that Britain might reach an understanding with Japan in the Far East, effectively renewing the Anglo-Japanese alliance that had been allowed to lapse in 1922, represented a deliberate campaign on his part to prevent the British Foreign Office adopting any such Pacific policies of concessions to Japan, since these might well have had a detrimental impact on Britain's relations with the United States. As ever, his greatest concern was to preserve good Anglo-American relations at almost any cost.[62]

Lothian was not the mere apologist for Hitler that later allegations suggested; he had no great love for what he termed "dictatorship and racialism."[63] Through his Christian Science and Rhodes associates in Germany and other sources, he was unpleasantly familiar with many of the repressive features of Nazi rule, even though he chose to blame these upon the treatment defeated Germany had endured.[64] Even in 1925, he had written: "Germany will never submit to her present position of subordination forever. She would not be the great nation she is if she did. Eventually she will demand the right to the free control of all her own territory, and to deal with her neighbours on equal terms. ... And if these demands are ... denied her, she will begin to prepare to recover her equality

---

[61] Kerr to John Dove, 13 July 1920, GD 40/17/209, Lothian Papers.

[62] Billington, *Lothian*, 115-117.

[63] Lothian to J. W. Dafoe, 3 January 1934, GD 40/17/273/255, Lothian Papers; Lothian, "The Recoil from Freedom," *The Round Table* 23:91 (June 1933), 4; cf. A. L. Rowse, *Appeasement: A Study in Political Decline* (New York: Norton, 1963), 31.

[64] Butler, *Lord Lothian*, 197, 205-207; Billington, *Lothian*, 117-122; and Ziegler, *Legacy*, 162-165.

and independence by force of arms."[65] While he supported British rearmament, until the late 1930s Lothian hoped to reach a lasting settlement with the Nazis, one whose concessions would, he argued, eventually moderate the nature of the regime. He urged upon Hitler and other German leaders that Germany should rejoin the League in exchange for the convening of a conference to consider its grievances and other international questions.[66] In 1936 he told British Foreign Secretary Anthony Eden of his confidence that, if appropriate concessions were made to Germany, there was "a good chance of the 25 years peace of which Hitler spoke."[67]

In May 1937 Lothian sent Neville Chamberlain, the British Prime Minister, Eden, various other British leaders, Smuts of South Africa and the other Dominion prime ministers, and Roosevelt accounts of his conversations with Hitler, Field Marshal Hermann Goering, and Reichsbank president Hjalmar Schacht, suggesting that, although the situation was "dangerous," German demands for union with Austria and a free hand in Eastern Europe were not unreasonable. In articles in *The Round Table*, letters to *The Times*, and parliamentary speeches he also propounded these views.[68] In early 1938, Lothian accepted the *Anschluss*, when Germany formally took over Austria. Although he felt some initial misgivings, he eventually supported the Munich agreement of September 1938, whereby Germany annexed much of Czechoslovakia.[69] Only the late 1938 *Kristallnacht* anti-Jewish pogrom in Germany, followed in March 1939 by the German occupation of Prague and the rest of Czechoslovakia, convinced Lothian that compromise with Hitler was impossible, leading him to call publicly, in parliament and in writing, for a "Grand Alliance" of Britain, France, and the Soviet Union against the fascist powers, a coalition

---

[65] Kerr, "Europe, the Covenant and the Protocol," 231.

[66] Lothian, memorandum, 17 February 1935, GD 40/17/202/121-122, Lothian Papers; Lothian to Joachim von Ribbentrop, 20 March, 11 April 1935, GD 40/17/202/149-156, 164-166; Butler, *Lord Lothian*, 202-204; and Billington, *Lothian*, 118-121.

[67] Lothian to Eden, 3 June 1936, in Butler, *Lord Lothian*, 354-362, quotation from 355.

[68] Butler, *Lord Lothian*, 217-129; the full text of these interviews is given in Butler, 337-353; and Billington, *Lothian*, 127-128. As requested, Davis passed on his copies of these interviews to Roosevelt. Lothian to Davis, 7 May 1937, enclosing memorandum, "Interview with Hitler, May 4th, 1937," "Interview with General Goering, May 4th, 1937," "Dr. Schacht, May 5th 1937," File Germany 1933-1938, Box 31, President's Secretary's File, Franklin D. Roosevelt Papers, Franklin D. Roosevelt Presidential Library, Hyde Park, NY; and Lothian, "The Problem of Germany," *The Round Table* 27:107 (June 1937), 485-532.

[69] Butler, *Lord Lothian*, 225-226; and Billington, *Lothian*, 133-134.

that might, if sufficiently determined and resolute, be able to convince the wavering United States as well as the British dominions to join them.[70]

One guiding principle of Lothian's interwar diplomacy was the effort to avoid British entanglements in conflicts his country might not be able to win without outside assistance. While some historians have cited Lothian's guilt over his part in imposing harsh peace terms on Germany or his religious and moral principles to account for his attitude towards Hitler's regime, he made no real move to address German grievances until Germany became strong enough to pose a major challenge to British power. Lothian's rather desperate efforts to avert war by reaching some kind of understanding with Hitler, by offering Germany colonies in Africa, for instance, arguably arose not primarily from his belief that the postwar settlement had unfairly disadvantaged Germany, but from a cold-blooded calculation that, without American support and assistance, Britain was too weak to oppose Germany alone, and should therefore acquiesce in German ambitions. At the RIIA's annual garden party in 1937, he

> told [Leo Amery] all about recent interviews with Hitler and Goring, describing the former as essentially a prophet and the latter as a genial buccaneer of the F. E. [Smith] type. He says the Germans are very anxious to be friends with us if they can but that if we allow things to drift and don't help the solution of the Central European question they will solve it by force, in which case we are likely to climb down ignominiously. The colonies, he agreed, are a pure question of prestige, and if the other issue is solved might be met by some token restitution like the Cameroons.[71]

While Lothian undoubtedly tried, albeit with little success, to persuade German officials to moderate the more unpleasant aspects of their regime, he demonstrated few if any qualms at the prospect of abandoning to rule by a brutal and racist government either central Europeans or the indigenous inhabitants of African colonies where, he had always claimed, the West had a duty to act as a civilizing and moderating influence. Underlying Lothian's rhetorical idealism was a profound respect for raw power, of whatever kind it might be.

Paradoxically, he was less conciliatory toward Italy, and after the government of Benito Mussolini invaded Ethiopia in 1935, urged that Britain, which had recently affirmed its support for the League of Nations,

---

[70] Butler, *Lord Lothian*, 227-228; Billington, *Lothian*, 134-136; and Lothian, "The Grand Alliance Against Aggression," *The Round Table* 29:115 (June 1939), 441-456.
[71] Leo Amery, diary entry, 25 May 1937, in *The Empire at Bay: The Leo Amery Diaries 1929-1945*, eds. John Barnes and David Nicholson (London: Hutchinson, 1988), 441.

impose full-scale economic sanctions on Italy and, if necessary, close the Suez Canal to vessels bound for Italy.[72] This may well have reflected Lothian's judgment that Italy represented a less serious threat than Germany. Writing to Eden in 1936 urging British rapprochement with Germany, Lothian also contended that such an understanding would enable Britain to deal effectively with any Italian threat.[73] In the mid-1930s Lothian's readiness to abandon Eastern Europe to Germany, even with or perhaps because of the prospect this would lead Germany into war with the Soviet Union, shocked both William Dodd, the American ambassador to France, and William Bullitt, the first American ambassador to the Soviet Union. Dodd wrote of receiving a letter from Lothian in which the marquess

> indicated clearly that he favors a coalition of the democracies to block any German move in their direction and to turn Germany's course eastwards. That this might lead to a war between Russia and Germany does not seem to disturb him seriously. In fact he seems to feel this would be a good solution of the difficulties imposed on Germany by the Versailles Treaty. The problem of the democracies, as he sees it, is to find for Japan and Germany a stronger place in world affairs to which, in his opinion, they are entitled because of their power and tradition. He hopes this can be accomplished without any sacrifice to the British Empire …[74]

Urging a policy of British detachment from most continental commitments upon Foreign Secretary Eden, Lothian argued that:

> provided our complete disinterestedness in Eastern Europe is combined with the Locarno guarantee against unprovoked aggression against the frontiers and soil of France and Belgium, the German General Staff, in the event of another European war, will probably … reverse the Schlieffen plan and strike Eastwards first while remaining on the defensive in the West.

A definite British commitment against Germany, by contrast, would mean that Germany "must … attempt to strike at us first from the air in the hope

---

[72] Butler, *Lord Lothian*, 210-211; Rose, *Cliveden Set*, 146-147; and Billington, *Lothian*, 122.
[73] Lothian to Eden, 3 June 1936, in Butler, *Lord Lothian*, 358-359.
[74] William E. Dodd, diary entry, 6 May 1935, in William E. Dodd, Jr., and Martha Dodd, *Ambassador Dodd's Diary 1933-1938* (London: Victor Gollancz, 1941), 241; cf. William C. Bullitt to Roosevelt, 10 January 1937, in Orville H. Bullitt, ed., *For the President Personal and Secret: Correspondence between Franklin D. Roosevelt and William C. Bullitt* (Boston: Houghton Mifflin, 1972), 204; and Billington, *Lothian*, 129-130.

of weakening the most powerful of her enemies."[75] In Lothian's view, one final advantage of such a policy was that

> detachment is the only basis upon which we shall be able to find a common policy towards Europe with the Dominions and move towards that informal naval co-operation with the United States ... which is the best way of preventing the dictatorships from establishing themselves on the oceanic highways and therefore the best security for free institutions over half the world.[76]

While he dabbled in European diplomacy and eventually won notoriety as a supporter of appeasement and a member of the 'Cliveden Set,' Britain's relations with the United States remained Lothian's greatest preoccupation. From 1934 onward Lothian again insistently urged the holding of a joint Council-Institute conference on Anglo-American relations, which took place in 1936, and the establishment of a collaborative study group in this area. Although other commitments prevented his attendance, he was heavily involved in the project to which this meeting gave rise, a two-year joint study group on Anglo-American relations, mandated to consider those questions of war debts, currency stabilization, and reciprocal tariff reduction which the conference had pinpointed as particular sources of Anglo-American friction.[77] In early 1937 the Council and the RIIA each established sub-groups on War Debts and Trade Practices, who exchanged highly confidential memoranda and other documents across the Atlantic and commented on their proposals and analyses. The deliberations of the Trade Practices group, to which government officials in both countries were privy, contributed to the successful negotiation in November 1938 of a reciprocal trade agreement between Britain, the United States, and Canada.[78] Lothian himself joined the War Debts sub-group, which

---

[75] Lothian to Eden, 3 June 1936, in Butler, *Lord Lothian*, 360; cf. Billington, *Lothian*, 123.

[76] Lothian to Eden, 3 June 1936, in Butler, *Lord Lothian*, 360.

[77] On Lothian's part in the genesis of both conference and study group, see RIIA, "Proposal for a Conference on Anglo-American Relations," 22 July 1936, File 9/15a, American Cooperation Group-Proposed Study Group Correspondence, RIIA Archives, and other materials in this file. For a description of the conference, see Priscilla Roberts, "Underpinning the Anglo-American Alliance: The Council on Foreign Relations and Britain between the Wars," in *Twentieth-Century Anglo-American Relations*, ed. Jonathan Hollowell (London: Palgrave, 2001), 32-33.

[78] See materials in File 9/15a, Group-Anglo-American Cooperation All Correspondence, RIIA Archives; Robert D. Schulzinger, *The Wise Men of Foreign Affairs: The History of the Council on Foreign Relations* (New York: Columbia University Press, 1984), 35-38; Roberts, "Underpinning the Anglo-American Alliance," 33-34; and Richard N. Kottman, (continued)

attempted to devise a settlement of the war debts to the United States on which Britain had defaulted in 1933 that the British could afford and the Americans would accept. For over eighteen months British and American sub-groups exchanged memoranda; each commented on the other's suggestions, and on occasion visitors from one country, such as the American diplomat Norman H. Davis, attended a group meeting in the other. The British proposals were largely drafted by Lothian's banker friend Robert H. Brand and the economists Geoffrey Crowther and Hubert Henderson, but Lothian commented extensively on them, especially from the perspective of making them politically acceptable in both the United States and Britain. He suggested that, in the interests of improving Anglo-American relations, Britain resume at least token payments on its debt.[79] Eager to address all outstanding issues disturbing Anglo-American relations, in spring 1938 he also sought to expand the Anglo-American Group's scope to include Far Eastern questions.[80]

Lothian concurrently continued his self-appointed mission to explain British policies to influential Americans. In the early to mid-1930s Lothian addressed the Council on Foreign Relations at least four times, on diverse topics including British policies in India, "The Future Government of Asia," naval policies in the Pacific, and, in 1936, "The Present World Crisis."[81] On the latter occasion he warned that collective security had broken down and that, although Britain had finally embarked on rearmament, war either between Russia and Germany or between Germany and the Western powers might well occur before this program was complete, in which case a knockout blow was possible. He apparently stated that all the work of the League had been excellent, with the exception of its efforts to prevent war. He also took the opportunity to mention again his conviction, expressed in his Burge Lecture the previous year, that a European federation involving "some kind of a federal government and a federal army" was essential to the maintenance of European and possibly

---

Reciprocity and the North Atlantic Triangle, 1932-1938 (Ithaca, NY: Cornell University Press, 1968), ch. 7.

[79] See, e.g., Lothian to F. T. Prince, 28 August 1937, File 9/15c, Group Anglo-American Cooperation-War Debts Committee Correspondence, Study Group Files, RIIA Archives. Further information on the War Debts group is to be found in this file and File 9/15d, War Debts Committee Correspondence Memorandum, Study Group Files, RIIA Archives; File Anglo-American Relations Group 1937-38, Records of Groups, Council on Foreign Relations Papers; and Roberts, "Underpinning the American Alliance," 34-35.

[80] Cleeve to Mr. Hubbard, 24 August 1938, File 9/15a, Anglo-American Cooperation Group-Proposed Study Group, RIIA Archives.

[81] Meetings Files, Council on Foreign Relations Papers.

world peace, an interesting proposal but one whose implementation at that time would have been virtually unattainable.[82] This was one of three talks Lothian gave in New York during that visit, including one to the Bond Club and one at a dinner at Lamont's house.[83]

Lothian's advocacy of federalism as a solution to international problems was a continuation of the tactics he had used ever since the First World War, of effectively bridging the admittedly sometimes less-than-clearcut division between Wilsonian universalists and Rooseveltian Atlanticists and shrouding a limited and specific national goal, the creation of an Anglo-American alliance, in an expansive cloak of idealistic rhetoric. In his 1922 and 1923 Williamstown lectures Kerr had advocated federalism, urging that, to solve the continuing problem of war, nations should relinquish their sovereign powers relating to the making of war to a higher federal authority.[84] Lothian repeated these views to an RIIA study group on International Sanctions, set up in the early 1930s in response to the Japanese invasion of Manchuria, rather verbosely contending

that sooner or later the more advanced of the nations will be compelled to recognize that if they are to have peace they must be willing to surrender some part of their sovereignty to a common authority which will command the allegiance of all individual citizens within its boundaries and that they will then devise a method of pooling what might be called sovereignty in the international sphere while leaving intact sovereignty in the national sphere which will be a discovery in political machinery as far in advance of the federal system as the federal system was in advance of the parliamentary system and the parliamentary system of the city states system of Greece.[85]

Lothian viewed such arrangements as a potential alternative to the League of Nations, and specifically stated that they were based upon the late eighteenth-century federal structure devised by Alexander Hamilton for the United States. In 1935 he stipulated that only democratic nations could or should enter into such a compact, possibly initially through a European federation and an Anglo-American federation, thus neatly squaring the

---

[82] Digest of dinner discussion, 20 October 1936, Meetings File, Council on Foreign Relations Papers.
[83] Lamont to Nancy Astor, 23 October 1936, File 82-5, Lamont Papers.
[84] Lothian, "The Prevention of War," Williamstown lectures, 1922, in Lord Lothian, *Pacifism is not enough: Collected Lectures and Speeches of Lord Lothian (Philip Kerr)*, eds. John Pinder and Andrea Bosco (London: Lothian Foundation Press, 1990), 39-85; Kerr and Curtis, *The Prevention of War*; Kerr *et al.*, *Approaches to World Problems*.
[85] Quotation from Lothian, Memorandum on Sanctions, enclosed in Clarke to King-Hall, 12 January 1934, File 9/8c, Sanctions Group, Study Group Files, RIIA Archives;

circle to reconcile his universalist and Atlanticist predilections. Anglo-American unity was his immediate objective, even though world federation remained the putative, but very distant, ultimate goal. Finally abandoning his quest to modify the League of Nations, Lothian argued that organization had effectively failed because it lacked the capability to address the problems generated by nationalism.[86]

Lothian gave more concrete evidence of his inclinations in his proposal early in 1937 to former Secretary of State Henry L. Stimson that the best means of avoiding war was for

> Pan-America and the British Commonwealth to re-create the situation created earlier by Great Britain alone which prevented world war between 1815 and 1914—that is to say to create a group of peace loving and democratic nations sufficiently strong that nobody will think of attacking them and sufficiently self-contained to avoid being dragged into the whirlpool of a local European or Far Eastern War.

Such a combination would, he believed, be able to prevent or at least localize and contain wars and "to bring about a just instead of an unjust peace."[87] In 1938 and 1939 Lothian became an enthusiastic supporter of the scheme for 'Federal Union' or 'Union Now,' a strongly Atlanticist compact between the Western democracies, the British Dominions, and the United States, advocated then and for a subsequent twenty years by Clarence Streit, a *New York Times* journalist and former Rhodes scholar. Even though he apparently believed the plan as promulgated was unfeasible, Lothian thought its wide discussion would generate more practicable schemes with better chances of implementation, and perhaps an effective Anglo-American alliance.[88]

---

[86] Lothian, "Pacifism Is Not Enough Nor Patriotism Either," Burge lecture, 1935, "The Demonic Influence of National Sovereignty," 1937, "National Sovereignty and Peace," 1938, all in Lothian, *Pacifism is not enough*, 179-263; Lothian, "New League or No League," *International Conciliation* 325 (December 1936), 589-604; Bosco, "National Sovereignty and Peace: Lord Lothian's Federalist Thought," in *The Larger Idea: Lord Lothian and the Problem of National Sovereignty*, ed. John Turner (London: Historians Press, 1988), 108-123; Ira Straus, "Lothian and the Anglo-American Problematic," *ibid.*, 124-136; and John Pinder, "Prophet Not Without Honour: Lothian and the Federal Idea," *ibid.*, 137-152.

[87] Lothian to Stimson, 11 February 1937, Reel 92, Stimson Papers; cf. Thomas Jones to Lady Grigg, 25 February 1936, in Thomas Jones, *A Diary with Letters 1931-1950* (London: Oxford University Press, 1954), 176-177.

[88] See essays by Straus and Pinder cited in note 86; also Andrea Bosco, "Lothian, Curtis, Kimber and the Federal Union Movement (1938-40)," *Journal of Contemporary History* 23:3 (July 1988), 462-502; Lothian, *Pacifism is not enough*, 21-22; correspondence with (continued)

Soon, however, Lothian would have an opportunity to make his own contribution to the creation of an Anglo-American alliance, when his friend Lord Halifax, who became foreign secretary after Anthony Eden's resignation in early 1938, decided to appoint him as British ambassador to the United States. At a time of international crisis for his own country, as it stood beleaguered against powerful enemies, the man who had most often sought to influence policy from the sidelines, through his writings and by advising senior government officials at home and abroad, would now be entrusted with an executive position, handling vital negotiations with top American leaders. Finally, he would have the opportunity to attempt to make his fundamental diplomatic beliefs a reality.

Clarence Streit and others on Federal Union, 1938-39, Files GD 40/17/369-397, Lothian Papers; Lothian, "Democracy and World Order," *The Observer* (5 March 1939); Butler, *Lord Lothian*, 243; and Billington, *Lothian*, 137-138.

CHAPTER FOUR

LORD LOTHIAN, THE FAR EAST, AND ANGLO-AMERICAN STRATEGIC RELATIONS, 1934-1941

GREG KENNEDY

When considering how strategic foreign policy is made, the manner in which individual policy makers develop, evolve and act on their mental maps is important for a number of reasons.[1] In the first place, the *way* in which that map is created can reveal what sorts of values are placed on certain relationships. Second, it is useful to know whether that view is a construct based primarily on intellectual or learned knowledge, or gained through actual contact with the people, geography and society of the area. Considerations of race, culture, economics, morals, ethics, geography, and so on are all important when deciding the way in which various sorts of power can be utilized in international relations. The weight of value placed on these elements varies according to the manner in which that information was obtained.

This chapter will analyze the nature of the strategic mental map Philip Kerr, Lord Lothian, created over the period of 1934-1940. This periodization represents the last six years of his life. As such, and with his final post being that of British ambassador to the United States, this time is arguably the most definitive for gauging not only what was his mental map of Anglo-American strategic relations in the Far East, but also what he thought that informal relationship could do to provide stability and security in the region against an aggressive and expansionist Japan. After a long career as a supporter of closer Anglo-American relations, of a strong League of Nations, and of a world in which a federal union of the democracies was necessary to maintain peace, Lothian was bent on making an impression in the United States. The issue is, was his attempt to make an impression also in step with the requirements of being a good diplomat during a time of acute crisis for Great Britain's very survival?

---

[1] For best concepts of mental maps, see Keith Neilson, *Britain, Soviet Russia and the Collapse of the Versailles Order, 1919-1939* (Cambridge: Cambridge University Press, 2005); and Zara Steiner, *The Lights that Failed: European International History, 1919-1933* (Oxford: Oxford University Press, 2005).

P. Roberts (ed.), Lord Lothian and Anglo-American Relations, 1900-1940, 107-132.

Philip Kerr's opinions regarding Anglo-American cooperation in the Far East were formulated shortly after the First World War. As Lloyd George's private secretary, Kerr had access to an enormous amount of information on the various plans for the reconstruction of war-torn Europe. As part of that reconstruction, the United States and Japan, each with their own individual views of how the new international system should work, had to be factored into the British attempt to establish a workable new world order. For Kerr, the imperative was not just the reconstruction of a functioning Europe, but also the re-establishment of Greater Britain's place as the head of the English-speaking world. And, in order for that role to be secured, a sound, accommodating and accepting relationship had to be established with the United States.[2] Moreover, it was in the Far East and with Far Eastern security matters that such a relationship needed to begin. In line with this, in July 1920, Kerr asked the British ambassador to the United States, Auckland Geddes, to consider how the United States could be brought into some sort of four-cornered agreement in the Far East.[3] Kerr was concerned that the forthcoming need to renew the Anglo-Japanese Alliance in 1921 might potentially both create deep divisions between the Dominions (who opposed the renewal) and Britain, and also give rise to tensions between the United States and the British Empire, given the possible threat that Japan's Twenty-One Demands posed to American interests and the Open Door in China.[4] He asked Geddes for any information the Ambassador could provide on the American position:

---

[2] Philip Kerr to Maurice Hankey, 21 July 1919, GD 40/17/1323, Papers of the Eleventh Marquess of Lothian, National Archives of Scotland, Edinburgh [hereafter Lothian Papers]; Kerr to John Dove, 13 July 1920, GD 40/17/209, Lothian Papers. For a full statement of this outlook, see Kerr to David Lloyd George, 2 February 1921, GD 40/17/1412, Lothian Papers:"I am more and more impressed by the fact that the greatest problem which confronts us now is not Europe but our relations with the English-speaking world. Our own future and the future of history depends [sic] upon the way in which we handle these young vigorous democracies in the next year or two. If we handle them rightly I think we can make a combination which will really be able to clean up old Mother Earth, more or less under our influence and direction. If we handle them wrongly, the Empire as we know it will disappear and the centre of gravity of the English-speaking world will definitely pass to the United States."

[3] Kerr to Auckland Geddes, 5 July 1920, GD 40/17/1397, Lothian Papers.

[4] Ian H. Nish, *Japanese Foreign Policy in the Interwar Period* (Westport, CT: Praeger, 2002); P. Duus; R. H. Myers; and M. R. Peattie, eds., *The Japanese Informal Empire in China, 1895-1937* (Princeton, NJ: Princeton University Press, 1991); and Michael A. Barnhart, *Japan Prepares for Total War: The Search for Economic Security, 1919-1941* (Ithaca, NY: Cornell University Press, 1987).

To my mind the issue fundamentally is this. We must find some way of obtaining security for British possessions in the Far East, and of protecting China from exploitation. We cannot do it by our own forces alone. Therefore, we must either continue the policy of the Alliance which gives us both security and influence over Japan or we must find some counterpoise. I see no other counterpoise than the United States. By this I do not mean that we should enter into an Alliance with the United States because I am sure that they would never do this. But it means that the United States must interest itself formally in the Far Eastern situation in such a way that Japan will realize that if she takes action either against us or against China she will find the United States against her, and that we have some real security that if we drop the Alliance we shall not be left in the lurch if we get into trouble with Japan....What I am afraid of is, that the United States will wobble, shilly shally, and refuse to commit itself to such an extent that we shall be driven to renew the Japanese Alliance. Personally I would prefer to come to some four-cornered arrangement between ourselves, Japan and the United States which would secure the stability of the Far East. But I don't quite see on what basis it would be proposed which would be effective and which the United States would accept.[5]

Lothian's wish was granted by the conclusion of the Nine and Four-Power Treaties, which were a part of the Washington Naval Treaty of 1921-1922.[6] The only successful collective security agreement to involve Great Britain and the United States, the Washington Treaty provided the linkage that he desired to see, in terms of American and British cooperation on

---

[5] Kerr to Geddes, 5 July 1920, GD 40/17/1397, Lothian Papers.

[6] Emily O. Goldman, *Sunken Treaties: Naval Arms Control between the Wars* (University Park: Pennsylvania State University Press, 1994); Christopher Hall, *Britain, America, and Arms Control, 1921-37* (New York: St. Martin's Press, 1987); Malcolm H. Murfett, "Look Back in Anger: The Western Powers and the Washington Conference of 1921-1922," in *Arms Limitation and Disarmament: Restraints on War, 1899-1939*, ed. B. J. C. McKercher (Westport, CT: Praeger, 1992), 83-104; Stephen W. Roskill, *Naval Policy Between the Wars*, vol.1, *The period of Anglo-American antagonism, 1919-1929* (London: Collins, 1968), 70-75; J. Kenneth McDonald, "The Washington Conference and the Naval Balance of Power, 1921-22," in *Maritime Strategy and the Balance of Power: Britain and America in the Twentieth Century*, eds. John B. Hattendorf and Robert S. Jordan (Basingstoke: Macmillan, 1989), 189-213; Ian H. Nish, *Alliance in Decline: A Study in Anglo-Japanese Relations, 1908-23* (London: Athlone, 1972); Erik Goldstein and John Maurer, eds., *The Washington Conference, 1921-22: Naval Rivalry, East Asian Stability and the Road to Pearl Harbor* (New York: Routledge, 1993); Roger Dingman, *Power in the Pacific: The Origins of Naval Arms Limitation, 1914-1922* (Chicago: University of Chicago Press, 1976); and William R. Braisted, *The United States Navy in the Pacific, 1909-1922* (Austin: University of Texas Press, 1971).

international matters in the post-war world.[7] After 1932, however, as Japanese aggression in China, as well as naval expansion, put ever greater pressure on the treaty signatories, Lothian returned to the theme of the need for a united Anglo-American front to provide stability and security in the region.

From the British Foreign Office's viewpoint, Lothian's initial foray into interwar diplomacy in North America on the Far Eastern issue was not a resounding success. In September 1934, in an attempt to revive the idea of an Anglo-American alliance to provide security in the Far East, he produced a substantial memorandum for the Foreign Office, entitled "The Anglo-American Naval Problem." He also wrote an article for the September issue of *The Round Table* dealing with the London Naval Treaty

---

[7] Steiner, *The Lights that Failed*. By 1928, Lothian's overall view of America's position in international relations had become: "Great Britain, too, can fully sympathise with the American desire to extricate herself from European complications as soon as possible, for she herself adopted the policy of 'magnificent isolation' after the Napoleonic wars. But still, in Britain, US withdrawal and demands for debt repayment have created a deep rooted doubt in Great Britain as to whether the United States as a nation is a good citizen in the world sense, and therefore whether it is possible to come to any firm understanding or basis of cooperation with her for the maintenance of peace or justice in the world. The feeling that the United States, as a nation, though idealistic in her abstract professions, is selfish when it comes to her own interests and will in practice refuse to take her share of responsibility for world peace but will seek to 'dictate' her solutions concerned in her own interests now goes deep in the attitude of Great Britain to the United States. ... On political policy there is no disagreement whatever between the United States and the British Commonwealth. They are both against political autocracy of the Napoleonic type, against revolution of the Bolshevik type, against 'militarism' and conscription and diplomacy of threat and force. They are in favour of self-government for all people, of individual liberty under the law, of the pacific settlement of international disputes. ... The question is at bottom a political question and requires a political solution. The real issues are these.
(a) Can any special arrangement be come to between the United States and Great Britain which will sufficiently assure each that its trade will not be interfered with by the other, except with its consent or under conditions of which it would approve.
(b) Can any general agreement on the lines of the Covenant or the Peace Pact be arrived at which similarly will assure each side that its trade will not be interfered with by the other except under conditions which have some recognised international sanction ....
(c) How would such arrangements be affected by the policies of Japan, France, Italy, or other naval powers? ... But speaking broadly the most hopeful line of advance is that provided by the Peace Pact. If the United States and Great Britain really made up their minds not only not to go to war with one another as they have more or less done, but that they will use their whole influence and power to prevent other powers from settling their disputes by war, at any rate on the high seas, the risk of their getting to cross purposes about interference with one another's trade in time of war becomes immensely less." Lothian, undated 16-page memorandum, "Anglo-American Relations" (c. 1928), GD 40/17/97, Lothian Papers.

system and, in particular, the upcoming round of talks due to take place in 1935.[8] Lothian called upon Great Britain to decide on the best path forward for the provision of security in the Far East, which in his view was a closer relationship with the United States. He felt that the latter should include a declaration by both nations to out-build the Japanese if the Asiatic power did not continue to accept the ship ratios established at the 1930 London Naval Conference. Further, Lothian highlighted the American and British tensions over the concept of "freedom of the seas" and how each nation viewed in very different lights the ability to interfere with commerce at a time of war. His solution was to persuade the Atlantic nations to agree to two principles: firstly, that if war threatened or broke out both nations would immediately call a conference of non-belligerents to set up a scheme of embargo and sanction against an agreed upon aggressor; and secondly, except in so far as such an embargo or blockade had been imposed against the declared belligerent/aggressor, the seas would remain open to the trade of all other nations and the U.S. Navy and Royal Navy would work to ensure those waters were kept open.[9]

Sir Robert Craigie, the chief naval negotiator for the Foreign Office, and Sir Robert Vansittart, the Permanent Under Secretary, were the chief critics of Lothian's views. Vansittart saw Lothian's desire for an open and formal Anglo-American system of cooperation and arbitration for dealing with sanction and blockade issues as a flight of fancy.[10] When considering either taking a hard line against Japanese threats to escalate naval building, or making overtures to the Americans about such overt security cooperation, Vansittart and Craigie were both cautious. Each wondered just how far the Americans would be willing to collaborate with such a British proposal. Neither official, moreover, thought Lothian was particularly well-informed or knowledgeable about Japan's internal attitudes and intentions on naval issues.[11] Both admitted that they themselves believed such a new cohesion of Anglo-American interests would be desirable, and agreed the suggested alliance would be appropriate,

---

[8] Lothian, memorandum, "The Anglo-American Naval Problems," September 1934, F(oreign) O(ffice) 371/17599/A7185/1938/45, The National Archive (TNA), Kew, London; FO minutes regarding Lothian memo in A7185, 7-10 September 1934, FO 371/17599/A7186/1938/45; Lothian, "Navies and the Pacific," *The Round Table* 24:96 (September 1934), 693-716.

[9] Lothian, memorandum, September 1934, FO 371/17599/A7185/1938/45.

[10] *Ibid.*, Vansittart marginalia pages five and six.

[11] Craigie, minute, 7 September 1934, also Vansittart, minute, 13 September 1934, FO 371/17599/A7186/1938/45.

sentiments very much in line with those expressed by Lothian. Neither, however, thought many of his "concrete suggestions" were genuinely practical in the current international situation.[12] Craigie believed that the suggestion advanced in this memorandum that Japan would be willing to accept the necessary conditions regarding the maintenance of the Open Door was "unduly optimistic." As for the idea of the United States and Great Britain building two vessels for every Japanese ship constructed in violation of the 1930 London Naval Treaty ratios, both Vansittart and Craigie were skeptical that either the political or economic will to do so existed in the democracies. They took a similar view of Lothian's proposed pre-war or wartime conference on blockade or sanction designed to allow the U.S. Navy and Royal Navy to oversee all global maritime trade.[13] Both men, however, were also willing to admit that Lothian's writings dealt with an important question: what was Britain's policy in the Far East? Should Britain pursue a closer Anglo-American relationship or capitulate to Japan's ever-growing expansion? They felt, moreover, that the mere asking of such questions was a valuable educational process for both the general public and politicians alike, on both sides of the Atlantic, and thus a potential catalyst to the taking of political action:

> This paper of Lord Lothian's and his article in "The Round Table" bring out the urgency of formulating a definite answer to the following question: are we going to steer for the kind of Anglo-American co-operation which Lord Lothian outlines, or are we going to line up with Japan (in other words "throw up the sponge" in the Far East) and so make further Anglo-American co-operation impossible? Unless a much clearer policy is formulated by the Cabinet before we meet the Japanese and have further talks with the Americans, it seems pretty clear we shall fall between two stools. This is an undignified position and exposes any Foreign Office to far more devastating criticism than would a firm seat even on the wrong stool.... I venture therefore with all deference to recommend that there should be further meetings of the Cabinet Committee at least a fortnight before the Japanese are due to arrive and that the Treasury policy of aiding and abetting Japan against the United States should then be firmly dealt with and the issue brought to a head.[14]

While Lothian had not offered realistic or concrete solutions to many of the problems facing British policymakers struggling with the Far Eastern issue and Anglo-American relations, his attempts to highlight the issues and

---

[12] Craigie, minute, 7 September 1934, FO 371/17599/A7186/1938/45.
[13] *Ibid.*
[14] *Ibid.*

choices facing decisionmakers were helpful to the Foreign Office's needs. That appreciation on the part of the professional diplomatists would be either strengthened or weakened depending on how well Lothian put forward the British position on the matter during his upcoming interview with President Franklin D. Roosevelt the following month.

Lothian had his audience with the American president on 10 October 1934. During the interview, the two men discussed British politics, particularly personalities and party agendas on foreign affairs, as well as some economic issues. The bulk of their conversation, however, dealt with how to handle the growing tensions in the Far East.[15] Lothian told Roosevelt that the context of the Washington Naval Treaty had now changed in two critical ways. The first was the alteration in the willingness Japan had demonstrated in 1922 to accept the restrictions imposed on its expansion in the Far East. Now, he argued, Japan was an expansionist power set on disrupting the status quo established by the Washington system. Britain, in addition, now faced a two-front threat from disruptive powers, for, besides Japan in the Far East, Britain had to face the prospect of a hostile and disruptive Germany and perhaps even Italy in Europe. Therefore, given the need to maintain a powerful naval presence in two places, when the reality of its naval situation made it impossible to sustain such a posture, Great Britain was faced with three strategic alternatives: either, firstly, to build a large naval force that could be stationed permanently in Singapore; or, secondly, to have a definite understanding with the United States as to how the two powers would police the Far East; or, thirdly, to re-establish some sort of new Anglo-Japanese Alliance that would safeguard British interests again as it had in the pre-World War One period.[16]

Roosevelt listened with interest to these options. He told Lothian flatly, supporting the suspicions Craigie and Vansittart had expressed earlier, that the United States could not make an open, overt commitment to any bilateral collaborative security arrangement, even if he himself wanted such an alliance. Therefore, even an informal understanding was of limited value, as the next president could ignore such a gentlemen's agreement. Anglo-American co-operation would have to remain based on the similar identity of the fundamental interests and ideals that bound the two nations together. When pushed on the topic of Japanese parity, however, the

---

[15] Letter from Lindsay and attached record of interview by Lothian, 12 October 1934, FO 371/18184/F6784/591/23.
[16] *Ibid.*

president assured Lothian that America would not accept it. If Japanese actions ended the London Naval Agreement terms and unilaterally began a naval arms building program, he would immediately ask Congress for 500 million dollars to strengthen the U.S. Navy. He also emphasized that under such circumstances he would have no trouble in obtaining such funding. Roosevelt described the Japanese long-term plan as expansionist and imperialist and agreed with Lothian that current Japanese actions were based on the desire to expel the two English-speaking nations permanently from the region. The president also thought that eventually Britain and her Dominions would have to build more naval power than they then possessed, because it would not be possible for Great Britain to come to terms with Japan in its present temper.[17] Lothian ended the meeting by appealing to Roosevelt to do all he could to ensure that America was actively seen to be engaged in the "front lines" of deterring Japan's expansion, an appeal to which "[t]he President did not demur ... though he expressed no consent."[18]

The Foreign Office itself remained unmoved by this exchange of opinions. Most of the president's comments merely confirmed the line that senior Foreign Office functionaries already held: the Americans would not and could not commit to anything formal and overt, and therefore would not guarantee to assist in safeguarding British interests in the Far East.[19] Craigie summed up the outcome of the interview, expressing the standard resignation and frustration that generally accompanied all Foreign Office attempts to entice the Americans into a bigger international role: "It is obvious that now, as always hitherto, it is quite futile to expect United States co-operation with the United Kingdom on specific points, in specific ways, and in specific places.... If we expect nothing definite we are not disappointed and therefore not irritated. This does not mean that we must not on our side aim at co-operation in a large way or at a harmony of general aims. This we must do, always remembering at the same time that the benefits we can get from this are likely to be negative rather than positive."[20] Lothian's ideas on how to achieve security in the Far East had again proven to be out of step with the political realities of both the British and American positions, to say nothing of the Japanese aspirations. As a

---

[17] *Ibid.*

[18] *Ibid.*

[19] See Greg Kennedy, "1935: A Snapshot of British Imperial Defence in the Far East," in *Far Flung Lines: Studies in Imperial Defence in Honour of Donald Mackenzie Schurman,* eds. Greg Kennedy and Keith Neilson (London: Frank Cass, 1997), 190-216.

[20] Craigie, minute, 19 November 1934, FO 371/18184/F6784/591/23.

confirmatory exercise his efforts were welcome, as were his attempts to educate President Roosevelt about Great Britain's strategic dilemma. But little of practical value had come out of the process, either positively or negatively. That situation, however, was soon to change.

On 17 October, 1934, at a private luncheon speech to some thirty Canadian members of the Ottawa branch of the Canadian Institute of International Affairs, attended by various important political figures (but no sitting minister), Lothian gave what was regarded as a very frank speech on the options facing Britain with regard to the Far East.[21] He told his audience that there were only three courses open to the British Empire: those he had put forward to Roosevelt earlier in the week. The Foreign Office was unhappy that Lothian had included the idea of reviving the Anglo-Japanese Alliance as one possible option open to policymakers. Overall, they felt annoyance with Lothian, considering his speech to be an indiscreet and untimely public announcement of such matters. Any statements, even by non-government officials, that seemed to carry any suggestion that British policymakers might take such an option seriously, were seen as a factor that would precipitate increased tension not just in Imperial relations, but most certainly in Anglo-American relations.[22] The last thing the Foreign Office desired during the period leading up to the next series of naval talks in 1935 was that the U.S. delegates should suspect that Great Britain might broker a preferential arrangement with Japan at the expense of the other Washington Treaty powers. Throughout the autumn of 1934, however, as preliminary talks for the 1935 London Naval Conference were held in London, Lothian insisted on continuing to air in public the difficulties of achieving a trustworthy Anglo-American alliance, as well as the obstacles Great Britain faced in returning to a cooperative Anglo-Japanese situation.[23] The Foreign Office did not appreciate such an open and complete analysis of the weakness of the British naval position in the Far East.

The final straw for Vansittart and the Foreign Office came in early 1935, as Lothian continued to write articles in such newspapers as *The Times*. From the perspective of experts on Japanese foreign policy, such as the British ambassador to Japan, Sir Robert Clive, the main weakness of Lothian's assessment of the dynamics at work in the naval problem was his

---

[21] Secret and personal telegram, 18 October 1934, FO 371/18184/F6297/591/23.

[22] *Ibid.*, Orde and Wellesley, minutes, 26 and 27 October 1934; Secret and personal telegram from Mr. Archer to Sir H. Batterbee, Dominions Office, 19 October 1934, FO 371/18184/F6686/591/23.

[23] Copy of Lothian, "Crisis in the Pacific," article published in *The Observer*, 18 November 1934, FO 371/17600/A9128/1938/45.

insistence that there existed a moderate Japanese party whose appeals to the Japanese people would be aided by a strong Anglo-American front. Clive and the Foreign Office, by contrast, feared that any such overt and open encirclement of or obstacle to Japan's expansionist stance would instead reinforce the entrenched sense of grievance and mistreatment that the Japanese people held against the two Western powers.[24] Vansittart thought Lothian's uninformed public pronouncements were doubly damaging. Not only were his continued calls for closer Anglo-American strategic relations arousing bitter resentment among the Japanese Government and people, but the continued inferences of incompetence or lack of resolve he leveled at the professional Foreign Office personnel were also affecting British public opinion and politicians.[25] Vansittart called for information provided by Clive to be circulated to the Cabinet as a counter-measure to Lothian's public utterances.[26] The Marquess had gone beyond the level of the acceptable, according to the Permanent Under Secretary, and his amateurish and dangerous pontifications required immediate and powerful correction before the carefully considered no bloc policy being conducted by the Foreign Office[27] was gravely jeopardized:

> We are all clearly concerned to keep on good terms with Japan. We have no illusions whatever about her; she means to dominate the East as Germany means to dominate Europe. We have to play for time and to avoid clashes, in our own interests. After very careful examination we are united in finding that there is no golden road in this policy. We have to feel our way carefully from day to day and year to year. The ideas, and expressions of Lord Lothian … cut definitely across this policy. For the present we need only concern ourselves with Lord Lothian's last letter to The Times (Feb.18th) which has given such comprehensible offence to Japan. That none of these gentlemen have any real knowledge of their subject is well illustrated by the fact brought out so conclusively in this dispatch [Clive's of 7 January]. That the whole of Lord Lothian's reasoning reposes on complete ignorance of a fundamental fact. (The same is true of his European publications.) He postulates the existence of something that, of course, does not exist …. We have not at best, much material wherewith to pursue our safety first policy toward Japan. Such

---

[24] Confidential despatch (which became Secret Cabinet Paper C.P.80(35)) from Clive to Sir John Simon (Secretary of State for Foreign Affairs), 7 January 1935, FO 371/19359/F1090/483/23,.

[25] For such materials as were produced by General Smuts, Lord Lothian and others, see extracts, 13 November 1934 to 18 February 1935, FO 371/19359/F2518/483/23.

[26] Vansittart, minute, 2 March 1935, FO 371/19359/F1090/483/23.

[27] For 'no bloc policy' see Kennedy, "1935: A Snapshot of British Imperial Defence in the Far East."

as it is, it is still further impaired by such outpourings as this last letter of Lord Lothian, which is a culmination. It is impossible or almost impossible, to get it out of the head of foreigners—particularly distant foreigners—that when letters are written to The Times by people of importance they do not somehow reflect the views of HMG [Her Majesty's Government].[28]

At the Cabinet level, among a vast part of the British public, as well as in the Dominions, the Foreign Office's views concerning the best way forward on the matter held sway. Lothian's objective of closer Anglo-American strategic relations in the Far East was, nonetheless, to a large extent achieved in 1935, but with one crucial difference: that relationship was neither overt nor open.[29] Instead, while an enhanced sense of trust and understanding, as well as mutual interest in ongoing closer naval and political cooperation, had grown out of the Anglo-American naval negotiations, the need for that closer relationship to remain informal and unexpressed remained unchanged from when President Roosevelt explained that circumstance back in October, 1934.

By the early months of 1939, however, the international situation had altered greatly. Japan had revealed just how aggressive it would be in China, with an attack on that nation in July 1937. The September 1938 Munich agreement had also clarified the situation in Europe, highlighting German aggression and Anglo-French military-political weaknesses. As Britain looked to replace its long-standing ambassador to the United States, Sir Ronald Lindsay, Lothian's affinity for that country and his close ties to various political and public figures, as well as his belief that the Anglo-American axis was the best provider of global security, made him a potential candidate for the job. But he was not the only option. In January 1939, Oliver Stanley, President of the Board of Trade, was thought to be the early favorite to replace Lindsay.[30] Despite continued public and private discussion over his suitability for the post, however, by early March Lothian's ascent to the Embassy in Washington was a reality.[31] Lindsay

---

[28] *Ibid.* See also Telegram from Clive to Foreign Office, 26 February 1935, and associated minutes, FO 371/19359/F1292/483/23.

[29] Greg Kennedy, *Anglo-American Strategic Relations, 1933-1939: Imperial Crossroads* (London: Frank Cass, 2002).

[30] Lord Crawford to Buchan (Governor General to Canada), 24 January 1939, ACC 9769, 97/9, Crawford Papers, National Library of Scotland. I would like to thank the present Lord Crawford and Balcarres for permission to use these papers.

[31] Crawford to Buchan, 2 March 1939, ACC 9769, 97/9. Lothian annoyed President Roosevelt during another private conversation on Anglo-American relations in mid-February. See Roosevelt to Roger B. Merriman, 15 February 1939, FDR-PSF, Franklin D. Roosevelt Papers, Franklin D. Roosevelt Presidential Library, Hyde Park, New York, in (continued)

himself was tired of the United States and feared having to be ambassador to that nation if war broke out in Europe. Lindsay was well aware of the improvements he himself had contributed to the Anglo-American strategic relationship, but he had no desire to oversee the operation of those hard-won bonds in wartime, especially if that role now meant attempting to entice America into a European war:

> I have been Ambassador here for 9 years & during that time this country has come to a point of friendliness towards us that is beyond anything we could have dreamed of. But if we are in a war, I'm definitely not the man to try to topple the U.S. into it also. There's something of conscience in this, & something too of a conviction that this kind of grim work needs a man with more energy drive & "chin" than I possess. And to be honest about myself, there are moments when I feel that I can't stand this country for another week, with its sloppy uneducated thinking, & its systematic intellectual dishonesty. This old dog has been through the hoop so often that he can hardly bring himself to rise to it again.

Most importantly, however, he had pressing family business concerning his wife's mother and her estates that he wished to attend to back in England.[32]

Lothian's appointment to the post elicited few suggestions that he was poorly prepared to take on the task before him. There were, however, concerns that at times his judgment of when and on what topic to speak was

---

which Roosevelt wrote to a friend: "I wish the British would stop this 'We who are about to die, salute thee' attitude. Lord Lothian was here the other day, ... and went on to say that the British for a thousand years had been the guardians of Anglo-Saxon civilization, that the scepter or the sword or something like that had dropped from their palsied fingers, that the U.S.A. must snatch it up, that F.D.R. alone could save the world, etc., etc. I got mad clear through and told him that just so long as he or Britishers like him took that attitude of complete despair, the British would not be worth saving anyway. What the British need today is a good stiff grog, inducing not only the desire to save civilization but the continued belief that they can do it. In such an event they will have a lot more support from their American cousins, don't you think so?" There were also worries over questionable speeches Lothian was making describing the United States as the home of Liberalism, and also on prohibition in the British Army. See Crawford to Lindsay, 6 July 1939, ACC 9769 97/10. It was indeed Lothian's love of speech making that alarmed many in the British policymaking elite, including Lord Crawford, who wrote to Buchan: "People here are very sceptical about his [Lindsay's] successor, as they are very much afraid that Lothian will cultivate his favourite occupation of speech-making; in fact he has been talking a good deal about America ever since the appointment was announced, to which I should say, being one of those who think that the Diplomatic Service in the United States should be very reserved, nothing can be more dangerous than British propaganda." Buchan, the Governor General of Canada, shared these fears. Crawford to Buchan, 27 July 1939, Buchan to Crawford, 31 August 1939, ACC 9769, 97/9.
[32] Lindsay to Crawford, 27 June 1939, ACC 9769, 97/10.

not always diplomatically astute. Some critics also thought Lothian too Continental in his strategic focus, and lacking in detailed imperial knowledge, particularly with regard to special requirements that he be prepared to deal with Far Eastern questions. In March 1939, the Secretary of State for Foreign Affairs, Lord Halifax, asked Lindsay to comment on Lothian's suitability for the job should war break out. Lindsay was highly complimentary in his critique of his replacement's abilities:

> I have been conscious that in the limited Foreign Office circle which knows of his selection, there are misgivings of a more or less pronounced nature, which go beyond the Foreign Office natural preference for a career man speaking the Foreign Office jargon and knowing all the ropes. For my part I have never shared these misgivings and my conviction that he will make a good Ambassador is strengthened since my return. Lothian has been a lot in America in the last four or five years. He likes meeting people, he has seen a tremendous number, and they like him. Withal he has the knack of moving about a great deal in an unobtrusive (not a secret or surreptitious) manner. This is a valuable quality for a British Ambassador in America, whose power to influence the United States Government will be impaired if he is presented by the press to the public as an influential man. He has antennae and understands this. If he has to follow a bolder and more forward line of policy than I have, he will be wary enough to begin cautiously and sensitive enough to become aware of possible danger.[33]

In May Lindsay wrote to Lothian to ask him to be more cautious where and when he spoke once he took over the role of ambassador. Lindsay's advice was that Lothian should not become branded as a propagandist in the eyes of the American policymaking elite. Lothian's open and public calls for Anglo-American unity on security matters could no longer form part of his official persona. The Americans, said Lindsay, had to be allowed to reach that conclusion themselves. If the American people and their leaders did not believe that the choice of closer and more overt relations was their own act, but was instead a response to a manipulative campaign by the British, only suspicion and greater tensions between the two nations would result.[34]

Lothian agreed with Lindsay's advice that he speak less publicly or openly than in the past. He assured the outgoing ambassador that he was doing all he could to distance himself from various works that either he himself had produced earlier, or that used his own writings to promote the idea of the Anglo-American policeman of the world. He hoped thereby to

---

[33] Lindsay to Halifax, 10 March 1939, FO 800/324, Halifax MSS, TNA, Kew, London.
[34] Lindsay to Lothian, 16 May 1939, GD 40/17/392, Lothian Papers.

limit just how much criticism the various isolationist groups in the United States could heap upon him:

> I can only trust that if I hold my tongue now and follow your admirable example after I get to the United States that my past may be forgotten so that I can be judged on my actual conduct as an Ambassador. Anyhow, except for the inevitable Pilgrims dinner, I do not propose to say anything which can have any bearing on Anglo-American relations or on international organization until I reach the United States.[35]

Lothian's arrival at the Washington Embassy, however, was postponed from June 1939 to August of that year. While that delay was in part due to the Foreign Office's wish that Sir Ronald Lindsay see the royal visit to North America through to its conclusion, there was another reason.[36] Lothian and Foreign Secretary Lord Halifax both believed that Lothian could not leave until the possible summer crisis with Germany was played out.[37] Although the Tientsin Crisis still gave the British cause for concern in the Far East, all eyes were now firmly fixed on Europe. If a European war were to break out in July or early August, Lothian would be able to enter into his new job fully aware of the views of Prime Minister Neville Chamberlain and Lord Halifax on the situation, ensuring that he could undertake discussions with President Franklin D. Roosevelt and Secretary of State Cordell Hull with a complete knowledge of Britain's position.[38]

Even so, while the British were becoming more fixated on the European problem, the Americans were taking a more aggressive stance against the Japanese in the Far East by denouncing the 1911 Commercial Treaty with Japan. With British interests in the Far East dependent on the United States for their protection, especially given the deteriorating situation in Europe, Britain needed to ensure that it maintained a parallel strategic position with the Americans. While Lord Lothian undoubtedly placed the European imperative foremost in his new role, the reality of the informal Anglo-American parallel deterrence strategy toward Japan was an issue that could not be mishandled.[39] One of Lindsay's last acts as ambassador to the United States was indeed to point out to the Foreign

---

[35] Lothian to Lindsay, May 25, 1939, GD 40/17/392, Lothian Papers.

[36] Benjamin D. Rhodes, "The British Royal Visit of 1939 and the 'Psychological Approach' to the United States," *Diplomatic History* 2:2 (Spring 1978), 197-211.

[37] Harvey to Lindsay, 11 July 1939, FO 794/17, Harvey MSS, TNA, Kew, London; Lothian to Norman H. Davis, 11 July 1939, GD 40/17/389, Lothian Papers.

[38] Lindsay to Harvey, 27 June 1939, Cadogan, minute, 6 July 1939, FO 794/17.

[39] Ashley Clarke, minute, 1 August 1939, FO 371/23528/F8151/6457/10.

Office how profoundly disturbed the United States was becoming over the shifts and possible changes to the balance of power in the Far East.[40] In particular, if President Roosevelt or Secretary of State Cordell Hull became convinced that for whatever reason Britain was not willing to stay the course in the Far East, leaving America to carry the bulk of the burden in deterring Japan or in supporting the Chinese war effort, American willingness to safeguard the British position in that region would be greatly diminished. Ashley Clarke, one of the senior clerks in the Foreign Office's American Department, nicely summed up that reality when he pointed out that:

> [T]he rules of American conduct of foreign policy are fairly well known to us now; and our need of American support is such that we are bound to shape our own action according to those rules. One of the rules is that when America takes any definite action in relation to the Far East, e.g. denunciation of the Japanese Treaty, she does not expect to be asked "Would you like us to do the same?" or "Would you support us if we did the same?" She expects us to fall into line without our offering or soliciting any embarrassing confidences. When we do fall into line, the Administration likes to be able to say to the public that as far as they are concerned our action was just another coincidence. This procedure is apt to involve us in risks ... but that is the side our bread is buttered.[41]

No other voice in the Foreign Office dissented from that analysis, nor could anyone make a logical and factual argument to refute it. Such was the strategic reality of Britain's Far Eastern situation in the summer of 1939.[42] Lothian, therefore, entered into a position that had two major fronts that required attention in equal measure (Europe and the Far East), if he were to continue successfully the impressive work done by Lindsay over the previous nine years in making Anglo-American strategic relations as unified as they were.[43]

Since he firmly believed in the moral and cultural need for the two English-speaking powers to work in a united fashion for the betterment of the entire world, it was not difficult for Lothian to appreciate the centrality of a joint Anglo-American strategic security relationship.[44] One of the

---

[40] J. Balfour, minute, 6 August 1939, FO 371/23528/F8245/6457/10.

[41] Clarke, minute, 18 August 1939, FO 371/23530/F8930/6457/10.

[42] Keith Neilson, "Defence and Diplomacy: The British Foreign Office and Singapore, 1939-1940," *Twentieth Century British History* 14:2 (June 2003), 138-164.

[43] Kennedy, *Anglo-American Strategic Relations, 1933-1939.*

[44] Lothian was a supporter of the work of American author and former Rhodes scholar Clarence K. Streit, whose book, *Union Now*, called for the democratic nations of the world (continued)

major reasons that Lothian's understanding of the nature of the ties between the British Empire and the United States was on solid ground had nothing to do with racial affinity, cultural similarity, or shared Christian moral values. It was instead his own *realpolitik* understanding that sea power was fundamental to each nation's strategic position and the way in which that common need brought the two nations together militarily. What was more problematic was to ensure that Lothian's own views on this issue did not embarrass or hamper the American administration's ability to work in that informal and plausibly-deniable fashion they had developed with the British over the previous nine years. If Lothian were too open, too aggressive, or too insistent, particularly with the volatile American press, his attempt to establish a closer, more open, formal strategic alliance might have the opposite effect, creating greater tensions between the two nations. That, in turn, would impair their ability to deter Japan, particularly navally.

On 30 August 1939, Ambassador Lord Lothian presented his credentials to President Roosevelt. The occasion gave the two men an opportunity for initial discussions of the strategic situation facing both the British Empire and the United States. Lothian was struck by the personal lack of neutrality that Roosevelt displayed toward the dictator powers. Japan and the Far Eastern situation occupied a good deal of the conversation.[45] The President told Lothian that he thought that the Russo-German agreement of that year would cause Japan to seek some sort of negotiated agreement with China, to be brought about with British and American assistance. If such were the case, Roosevelt said, the two Western powers should be friendly toward the suggestion but show no eagerness. If, however, Japan turned more hostile in the future, he would apply further military pressure on that nation by the deployment of aircraft carriers and bombers to the Aleutians, threatening the Japanese mainland, as well as by moving the American main fleet to Hawaii.[46] Roosevelt's views coincided with Lothian's own priorities as ambassador, to ensure the smooth and continued progress of the solid relations Lindsay had constructed over Far Eastern security matters. It was also clear, however, that in the near future Lothian would have to make his own

---

to create a U.S.-style federal union in order to maintain world peace. See Lothian to Streit, 25 May 1939, GD 40/17/395, Lothian Papers. Lothian asked Streit to cease using his name in further publicity releases for the book, as such an association might now damage his ability to be viewed impartially by other American political commentators.

[45] Lothian, telegram to Foreign Office, 31 August 1939, FO 371/22815/A5899/98/45.

[46] *Ibid.*

pronouncements on that strategic relationship and that he would have to be wary of how he portrayed the issue to the American people.

In preparation for the latter one of the first things Lord Lothian did after this conversation with President Roosevelt was to write to the former First Sea Lord and Minister for Co-ordination of Defence, Admiral Lord Chatfield. Lothian outlined his views of the British strategic situation and asked Chatfield to comment on his own interpretation, since: "If I am to have any real effect here it is essential that I should understand thoroughly the British view of the future of the war."[47] The strategic position, as Lothian saw it, consisted of five key elements. Russia's defection to Germany had eliminated the possibility of a two-front war. This lack of a second front meant that in all likelihood Britain had to be prepared for a long, drawn-out war, much like the First World War. This meant the main strategic weapon for the British, as in the previous conflict, would be a long-distance blockade. As for the other main powers in the equation, no one knew what Italy was likely to do, nor could Japan's actions be predicted. With regard to the latter, however, Lothian was sure that the Asian power would be certain to exploit British and French difficulties in Europe to its own ends in the Far East. Finally, Americans were obsessed with trying to ensure that they did not become embroiled in the war in Europe.[48] All of this, Lothian told Chatfield, meant that Britain needed to win at sea and in the industrial arena, the two being inextricably linked. Moreover:

> In the long run the United States of America holds the decisive cards in both respects. Her fleet can make the Pacific, Australia, and Singapore secure, as against Japan. And her machine industry can produce a volume of munitions, especially bombers from a base which cannot be attacked, which will eventually be decisive both against Germany and Italy.[49]

Chatfield replied to Lothian eleven days later, agreeing with most of the points the ambassador had made. In contrast to Lothian, Chatfield was very positive about the situation in the Far East, advising Lothian that he [Chatfield] did not anticipate any big developments in that region in the near future. That stability in the Far East, said Chatfield, was due almost entirely to the restraining influence of the United States, particularly its potential ability to deploy massive power at sea. He trusted in the American

---

[47] Secret, private and personal letter, Lothian to Chatfield, 15 September 1939, CHT/6/2, Chatfield Papers, Royal Maritime Museum Library, Greenwich, London.
[48] *Ibid.*
[49] *Ibid.*

willingness to help safeguard British interests in the Far East, telling Lothian:

> It always seems to me that is our safest quarter in which to enlist the help of the United States, should it ever be necessary. In fact, I always feel she will volunteer help there <u>before</u> we ask for it whenever she thinks the situation is too dangerous, and that I have no doubt you agree with.[50]

Lord Halifax reinforced Chatfield's views on the Far Eastern aspect of Lothian's mission. The foreign secretary was confident that Lothian entered into his new job fully aware of the true nature of Anglo-Japanese relations, particularly that the Foreign Office did not believe that any general agreement would either eliminate the Japanese threat or arrive any time in the near future. Halifax reinforced the point that Lothian would continue to make, as Ronald Lindsay had time and again, that the British Empire would not make a separate deal with Japan over the balance of power in the Far East. As for Anglo-American relations and the China question, Halifax told Lothian that it was of the greatest importance to the British war effort that the United States not be allowed to reproach Britain in any way over such Far Eastern issues.[51] Lothian was therefore aware of the need to tread carefully where Anglo-American relations and the Far Eastern question were concerned. He was determined not to allow perceptions that Britain might leave the United States to hold the ring alone in the Far East, a belief created by the Simon-Stimson controversy of 1932, to be rekindled or enhanced.[52] As 1939 came to a close, Lothian told Geoffrey Dawson, editor of *The Times*, that the United States was prepared to stand up for its rights in the Far East, and that meant that indirectly it was protecting British interests as well. The United States would continue to maintain economic pressure on Japan, such as embargoing war materials, as well as providing financial support for the Chinese war effort. Most importantly, Lothian did not believe that U.S. actions were a danger to Britain's global position. He doubted very much that such actions would immediately cause Japan to

---

[50] Chatfield to Lothian, 26 September 1939, CHT/6/2, Chatfield Papers.
[51] Halifax to Lothian, 27 September 1939, FO 800/397.
[52] Lothian to William Allen White, 6 April 1939, GD 40/17/387, Lothian Papers; F. W. Alexander to Lothian, 5 May 1940, GD 40/17/398, Lothian Papers. For the full context of this issue that Lothian had to deal with, see Keith Neilson, "Perception and Posture in Anglo-American Relations: The Legacy of the Simon-Stimson Affair, 1932-1941," *The International History Review* 29:2 (June 2007), 313-337.

look southward toward British and Dutch possessions, thereby taxing already stretched British military assets.[53]

Still, while the new British ambassador to the United States was himself confident of American willingness to aid Britain's position in the Far East, American policymakers, by contrast, were still uncertain of the ambassador's place in the policymaking network. The Secretary of State, Cordell Hull, was wary of the new ambassador's ability to transmit an accurate appreciation of the American strategic view back to London. Through the American ambassador to Japan, Joseph C. Grew, who enjoyed close relations with the British ambassador to the same country, Sir Robert Craigie, Hull developed a sense of mistrust over how Lothian was interpreting the U.S. attitude toward the Far Eastern situation. Craigie had informed Grew of various interpretations Lothian had placed upon Hull's policy toward the region.[54] Craigie and Grew viewed Lothian's reporting to London as being too aggressive in its demands for transparent and open Anglo-American actions to thwart Japan, given the secretary of state's own views. Craigie opposed Lothian's desire to create a more formal and open alliance aimed at deterring Japanese expansion, highlighting the fact that, with the war in Europe now a reality, any premature attempts to contain Japan through more overt Anglo-American actions would only undermine any moderating influences within Japan's own policymaking elite. In contrast to Lothian, and in accordance with Hull's own tendencies, Craigie did not support taking any rigid Anglo-American stance toward Japan. The British ambassador to Japan told Grew that, unlike Lothian, he believed that moderate economic pressures and some gestures of accommodation toward Japan's resource and prestige aims in the area, excluding China, were a better course of action.[55]

Hull informed Grew that discussions in Washington he himself and other members of the State Department had held with Lothian had not been

---

[53] Lothian to Dawson, 18 December 1939, GD 40/17/400, Lothian Papers; see also Lothian to William Waldorf Astor, December 18, 1939, GD 40/17/398, Lothian Papers.

[54] Grew to Hull, 5 January 1940, U.S. Department of State, *Foreign Relations of the United States [FRUS]1940*, Vol. IV, *The Far East* (Washington, DC: Government Printing Office, 1955), 252.

[55] *Ibid.* For further evidence on those within the Washington policymaking process see entry of 16 June 1940, The Washington Diaries of R.G. Casey, 1940-42 [hereafter Casey Diaries], National Library of Australia, RGC.1 CONFIDENTIAL, where he claims: "Lothian appeared to have wholly misinterpreted what I said—so I sent out another cable this evening expanding on my talk to Welles, in case others besides Lothian might have similarly misread it." This was in regard to Lothian wanting to arrange a conference in London with Anglo-American Far Eastern strategic cooperation as its main theme.

of any significance, in terms of indicating any marked shift in America's policy toward Japan.[56] The Secretary of State assured Grew that the "slant" Lothian was giving on the U.S. attitude toward moderate elements in Japan was not being accurately reported. Specifically Hull told Grew:

> We find no recollection anywhere of any statement comparing or contrasting forces of moderation in Japan with moderate elements in Germany. There was made a statement comparing the controlling elements. What one of our officers said with regard to the possibility of a Japanese drive southward was that he saw no reason for being immediately alarmed over that possibility while the Japanese continue to be heavily involved in China, while they possess substantial reserves of petroleum, while they have reason to desire to keep open their sources of supply from the United States, and while they have reason to believe that such a drive would involve them sooner or later in hostilities with one or more of the great powers. By no one was there made the statement which appears as point 4: question was raised whether the Japanese authorities were not calculating that by a settlement of the minor disputes they would be able to avoid necessity of meeting the desires of occidental governments with regard to matters of greater importance—a calculation which, if made, would be unfortunate in its effects and consequences.[57]

Hull's confidence in Lothian's aims in reporting American attitudes on the matter was, therefore, diminished. That faith was further reduced by conversations between Lothian and the State Department's Far Eastern adviser, Stanley K. Hornbeck. In June Lothian expanded on his idea that Britain and the United States should take a stronger stand against Japan, particularly over demands to close the Burma Road, a key link in the supply of war matériel to China. Should Britain fall to a German invasion, moreover, then Lothian advocated moving the Royal Navy to Singapore, leaving the American fleet to guard the North American continent from any further German attack.[58] Such actions were in stark contrast to the assumption in London and Washington that the Royal Navy would maintain itself in Canada and continue to prosecute a full-scale war against the German invaders.[59]

---

[56] Hull to Grew, 6 January 1940, *FRUS 1940*, Vol. IV, *The Far East*, 253.

[57] *Ibid.*

[58] Memorandum of conversation between Stanley K. Hornbeck and Lothian, 20 June 1940, *ibid.*, 361.

[59] Alex Danchev and Daniel Todman, eds., *War Diaries, 1939-1945: Field Marshal Lord Alanbrooke* (Berkeley: University of California Press), 2001; and Roskill, *Naval Policy Between the Wars*, Vol. I; and Vol. II: *The Period of Reluctant Rearmament, 1930-1939* (London: Collins, 1976).

Such suspicion of the credibility of the new actor within the Anglo-American Far Eastern policy making network was unfortunate at this particularly delicate period in the relationship between the two countries. If Lothian's aim were to push America further, to promise more than it was currently prepared or able to deliver, the only outcome would be to create resistance among the American policymakers. Never seeking to be pushed into the lead on Far Eastern matters, a point made by Lindsay to the Foreign Office many times during his tenure, the United States government had to be allowed to arrive at its own conclusions of when and how to take precisely what action.

Lothian remained undeterred, however, as to the willingness, and the reality, of the United States holding the ring for the British Empire in the Pacific. In November 1940, he wrote to his friend Victor Cazalet, a Conservative member of parliament, who had mentioned in an earlier letter that anti-American sentiment was circulating throughout England. Remembering the sequence of events in the First World War, certain British circles were angered that once again America seemed reluctant to carry out what they considered its proper duty to stand beside England quickly and, instead, seemed to want to wait to obtain greater advantage at Britain's expense.[60] Lothian's reply in early November reflected his interpretation of American actions to date:

> The best answer to the criticism which is being made in England of the United States today is, that the United States is really holding the baby for us in the Pacific. There she has moved into the front line, and so long as she maintains her present policy the British and French interests in the Pacific are secure.[61]

Lothian's desires conflicted with the realities of the true nature of the Anglo-American relationship in terms of cooperation in the Far East in the summer of 1940. After the fall of France in June 1940, Japanese pressure mounted on Britain to close the Burma Road, the main artery of war matériel to China. Lothian's advice to the Foreign Office was to ask Tokyo if there was any possibility of a comprehensive agreement. His main suggestions for a settlement centered around the idea that the European powers should grant Japan access to oil and rubber concessions in return for a generous settlement with Chiang Kai-shek and a non-fortification

---

[60] Victor Cazalet to Lothian, 2 October 1940, GD 40/17/399, Lothian Papers.
[61] Lothian to Percival Witherby, 30 April 1940, GD 40/17/406/204-206, Lothian Papers; Lothian to Sir Alan Lascelles, 2 April 1940, GD 40/17/514, Lothian Papers; and Lothian to Cazalet, 3 November 1940, GD 40/17/339, Lothian Papers.

agreement which would keep Japan out of the European war and Germany out of the Pacific Ocean.[62] Lothian's views were naïve. While he realized that the United States was watching the Burma Road issue carefully, in order to ascertain if a now isolated Britain would perhaps concede key aspects of support for China under greater Japanese pressure, the ambassador did not grasp the difficulties any sort of settlement with Japan would entail for the Anglo-American relationship. Nor, according to the Foreign Office, did he appreciate that there was little incentive for the Japanese to be willing to "play the game" now that Britain was so vulnerable.[63] If Britain acquiesced rapidly, or indeed tried now to negotiate some type of overall settlement with the Japanese, American propaganda, particularly the China Lobby, would cry appeasement and betrayal, making even more difficult any sort of progress in creating a workable Anglo-American deterrence strategy toward Japan.[64] Given the delicacy of the Anglo-American relationship at that point, Lothian's handling of the Burma Road issue, therefore, is an instructive example of his strengths and weaknesses as ambassador to Britain's most important ally.

Lothian believed that the American policymaking elite had more influence on American actions in the Far East than did public opinion. In early July he informed the Foreign Office that, while American public opinion might indeed take Britain to task for closing the Burma Road temporarily, he believed that U.S. financial and economic pressures on Japan would continue.[65] This view put him squarely in disagreement with Sir Robert Craigie and many of the Foreign Office officials tasked with overseeing Britain's Far Eastern policy. Much of the Foreign Office's concern was over whether or not Lothian had accurately assessed what the Americans would infer from both any closure or, after such an event, the reopening of the Burma Road. Here, a lack of clarity in the ambassador's aims and direction clouded the decision-making process.[66] While still arguing that Britain should not voluntarily close the Road, he had to acknowledge that without a guarantee by the United States that it was willing to commit military forces alongside British personnel in an effort to

---

[62] Lothian, telegram to Foreign Office, 5 July 1940, FO 371/24666/F3544/43/10.
[63] Dening, minute, 7 July 1940, and Brenan, minute, 8 July 1940, FO 371/24666/F3544/43/10.
[64] Gage, minute, 9 July 1940, FO 371/24666/F3544/43/10.
[65] Lothian, telegram to Foreign Office, 9 July 1940, FO 371/24666/F3544/43/10.
[66] Craigie, telegram to Foreign Office, 11 July 1940, FO 371/24667/F3568/43/10; and Sterndale Bennett, memorandum, "The Burma Road," 1 October 1940, FO 371/2470/F4489/43/10.

confront Japan over the issue, Britain might have little alternative to shutting down the route. He also discerned the connections to the European situation. Lothian believed that a now more educated and aware America would not welcome the closure, but also could not argue against the realities of the British strategic position due to events in Europe. Overstretched, alone and without the military resources needed to contemplate a two-front conflict, Britain's temporary buying of time while it took stock of its situation was a pragmatic act that the majority of the American public and policymaking elite would understand, if not like. Lothian believed that the United States, now educated to a level of understanding of the strategic difficulties facing Britain, would sympathize with that plight and appreciate the closure as an unavoidable necessity. Others, such as the Foreign Office, were reluctant to make this leap of faith.[67]

Given the predominance of Europe in Anglo-American affairs, Lothian followed the only option available to him. He continued to impress upon the Americans the need for their continued hard economic stance on Japan, as well as increased military aid to Britain. The latter, he argued, would allow Britain to regain its military strength more speedily, a recovery that was not only important for the welfare of the British situation in Europe, but a vital necessity if London was to have any continued effective ability to deter increasing Japanese aggression. He also called for joint Anglo-American conferences and planning sessions on the Far East, with the intention of sending a strong message of solidarity to Japan.[68] In addition, he kept Hull and Roosevelt informed of the progress of Anglo-Dutch discussions on pooling military resources, so that American policymakers could enjoy as accurate as possible a picture of the true state of the military situation in the Far East.[69] In particular, having come to accept the limits on U.S. ability to move overtly, Lothian emphasized to Hull the particular importance of sustained economic pressure on Japan.

The ambassador continued throughout October to try and entice the Americans into taking a more open part in Anglo-Dutch naval and defense talks, but to no avail. Still, the very act of continuing to share the most up-to-date information on such activities was important, as by doing so the ambassador continued to create bonds of trust and confidence with

---

[67] *Ibid.*

[68] Memorandum of conversation between Hull, Lothian, and Casey, 16 September 1940, *FRUS 1940*, Vol. IV, *The Far East*, 120.

[69] Memorandum of conversation between Hull and Lothian, 30 September 1940, *ibid.*, 159.

American policymakers.[70] By mid-October, as the need to make a decision as to whether to keep the Road closed, or reopen it and risk the ire of Japan, drew near, Lothian's interpretation of the importance of reopening the Road for Anglo-American relations in the Far East had won the day.[71] As the year wore on, Lothian's ability to interpret the American strategic position toward the Far East to London, and vice versa, improved, gaining him the much needed credibility he had lacked in his early days as ambassador.

In November, Lothian traveled back to London to obtain the most confidential and informed perspective he could on the British strategic position so as to enhance that credibility. While in London he impressed upon members of the British policymaking elite the need for continued wooing of the American public and policymakers. On Far Eastern issues, the required message was that Britain would follow where America led.[72] In particular, the Ambassador told former Foreign Secretary Sir John Simon how he had been pouring oil on the troubled waters of the Simon-Stimson controversy, something that had plagued American confidence in any Anglo-American Far Eastern relationship since 1933.[73] Upon his return to Washington later that month, Lothian updated Hull on the most current British strategic thinking. Lothian's opening points concerned the position of Singapore and the Far East. He informed the Secretary of State that both he [Lothian] and London were very concerned that Japan might attempt to assault the outpost. As part of a campaign to dissuade the Japanese from such an act, Lothian returned to his call for Hull to acquiesce in open, formal joint Anglo-American defense talks and to consider allowing U.S. naval units to operate from the British base at Singapore, as a signal of solidarity.[74] Hull was reluctant, but he did reassure the ambassador that "there should undoubtedly be collaboration with the view of making known to each other any and all information practical in regard to what both might have in mind to do, and when and where, in case of a military movement by Japan in the South or in some other direction."[75] Lothian's personal campaign to educate Hull and other members of the American policymaking elite, as well as the more general propaganda drive aimed at informing the American people of Britain's needs, were becoming

---

[70] Memorandum of conversation between Hull and Lothian, 5 October 1940, *ibid.*,167.

[71] Halifax to Churchill, 25 September 1940, FO 371/24670/F4646/43/10.

[72] Simon to Cadogan, 19 November 1940, FO 371/24693/F5239/261/10.

[73] Neilson, "Perception and Posture in Anglo-American Relations," 313-338.

[74] Memorandum of conversation between Hull and Lothian, 25 November 1940, *FRUS 1940*, Vol. IV, *The Far East*, 220.

[75] *Ibid.*

successful, building confidence and overcoming the initial suspicion of his abilities. Unfortunately, in early December 1940, just as he was coming into his own as a valued and trusted interpreter of Anglo-American relations in the Far East, Lothian died suddenly.

His close colleague during his time in Washington, the Australian Ambassador Richard G. Casey, best summed up Lothian's style and impact on the Anglo-American Far Eastern policy making process:

> I'm going to miss Lothian greatly. He was so easy to work with. In the peculiar relationship between the British Embassy and this Legation, you need an easy-going flexible minded man as British Ambassador. My mind works best when I have some individual with whom I can argue out a problem—someone against whom one can fling one's arguments—and they come back at you—and vice versa. This is the way Lothian and I worked. Neither of us necessarily accepted the other's arguments but we bounced them backwards and forwards and continued to do so until we came to some agreed solution. It so happened, by good chance, that we both liked that sort of thing—and so we worked well together, although anyone coming into the room while the process was on would get the impression that we were in violent discord but it was only the process working itself out.[76]

Lothian's tenure as Ambassador was not that of a great man coming in to save the day for Anglo-American strategic relations. He inherited a viable, proven and efficient system of information sharing from Ronald Lindsay. Lothian's initial forays into Far Eastern policymaking caused questions to be raised over his vision of the nature of the Anglo-American relationship, the extent of Britain's willingness to confront Japan openly, and his ability to subordinate his own desires to the realities of the situation. Nonetheless, he grew rapidly into his role as one of the key players in that policymaking process. His belief in the need for an Anglo-American condominium to safeguard the world's stability made him a wise selection as ambassador, even if his attempts to press for the acknowledgment of such an open alliance were at times detrimental to the achievement of that goal. His belief in the use of maritime power by the two nations, while at times unsophisticated and unappreciative of the political difficulties involved, was by instinct correct. He recognized, first, the global power that such an alignment could bring to bear on those powers that wished to use force to change the international order. Second, he knew that, from a base of industrial, fiscal, and maritime strength, Anglo-American power could be the stabilizing force he sought. Despite his initial trials and problems in

---

[76] Casey, Diaries, 22 December 1940.

grasping the delicate political and military nature of the informal Anglo-American relationship in the Far East, Lothian's efforts contributed positively to the eventual creation of a strong Anglo-American coalition in that region. By the time of his death, Lothian had developed a precise and accurate mental map of Anglo-American strategic relations in the Far East.

CHAPTER FIVE

LORD LOTHIAN'S AMBASSADORSHIP IN WASHINGTON

AUGUST 1939-DECEMBER 1940[1]

J. SIMON ROFE

This chapter covers the ambassadorial career of Philip Kerr, the eleventh Marquess of Lothian (1882-1940), who arrived in Washington on the eve of the Second World War in Europe and held the post of British ambassador until his death in December 1940. Lothian's ambassadorship set in motion aspects of the role of the British ambassador and the embassy in Washington that would transcend the rest of the twentieth century. Lothian was a vital conduit for transatlantic relations and for the British embassy becoming a 'central institution' in relations between the United States and Great Britain.

Throughout the period of his ambassadorship the United States held to a neutral position, as prescribed by the legislation of that name. The interpretation of American neutrality was, however, to change so as to allow increased assistance to be provided to the Allies and the United Kingdom particularly: from the revision of the Neutrality laws to allow for Cash and Carry purchases, through the Destroyers-Bases deal signed at the beginning of September 1940, and the ground work for the Lend-Lease Act passed after Lothian's death in March 1941. Increasingly important to the assistance this brought Britain was Lord Lothian, who believed firmly in an understanding between Washington and London. This Atlanticist school of thought, with its antecedents in 'Mahanist' strategy married to Lothian's heritage as part of 'Milner's Kindergarten', meant for Lothian a deliberate understanding between the English-speaking peoples based on compatible national interests that, crucially, would facilitate American material aid and

---

[1] An earlier version of this chapter appeared in Michael F. Hopkins; Saul Kelly; and John W. Young, eds., *The Washington Embassy: British Ambassadors to the United States, 1939-77* (Houndsmills, Basingstoke, and New York: Palgrave Macmillan, 2009), 14-32.

P. Roberts (ed.), Lord Lothian and Anglo-American Relations, 1900-1940, 133-165.

psychological support while endeavoring to secure British interests on a world stage.[2]

The chapter will begin by examining the circumstances of Lothian's appointment to Washington and his background and character, before addressing Lothian's approach to his ambassadorship and the substantive issues involved. The latter were plentiful, as would be expected for an ambassador whose country was at war for all but the first few days of his time in Washington. With the conflict against the Axis providing an omnipresent influence, this section will analyze Lothian's approach in relation to the revision of the Neutrality Act (November 1939); issues of American neutral rights and a 'minor crisis' in Anglo-American relations (January 1940); Germany's spring advances and Churchill's accession to the office of prime minister (April-May 1940); the Fall of France (June 1940); the Destroyers-Bases deal (August 1940); and finally then the preparations for what would become Lend-Lease Aid later in 1941. In all of these Lothian's influence would be critical to furthering British interests. That Lothian can be considered one of the architects of the Lend-Lease Act, a program passed four months after his demise that enabled the United Kingdom to finance a total war effort to overcome the Axis, serves to illustrate the influence of the eleventh British ambassador to Washington. In exploring these issues the nature of Lothian's relationships with both his own government and the Roosevelt administration will become evident.

Lothian's position as head of the British permanent mission to the United States was intimately intertwined with his own approach to the ambassadorship. The technological circumstances of his times (that is, before the era of mass communication), the need to react to events in Europe and manage crises during his time in Washington, and the brevity

---

[2] Lothian's belief in Atlanticist thinking was deeply held. It had a strong Mahanist heritage, as was clear in a letter Lothian wrote to Lord Halifax, the British foreign secretary, in March 1940. Lothian stated: "The real reason for its [the United States'] 150 years of tranquillity and freedom from international complications has been because all the entries from Europe in the Atlantic have been controlled by the British Navy." Lothian to Halifax, 11 March 1940, CHAR 20/15, Churchill Papers, Churchill Archive Centre, Churchill College, Cambridge. Such views were increasingly widely held amongst the political classes in the United States after the publication of Mahan's book *The Influence of Sea Power on History 1660-1783* in 1890 and the presidency of Theodore Roosevelt in the early twentieth century. Historian David Billington surmises Lothian's understanding of Atlanticism as follows: "Lothian wanted the United States and the United Kingdom to anchor a world order in which the civilisation of the advanced English-speaking nations could secure itself and spread." David P. Billington, Jr., *Lothian: Philip Kerr and the Quest for World Order* (Westport, CT: Praeger, 2006), 4.

of his appointment, meant he was not able to address every aspect of an ambassadorial post. Thus, as will become evident in the coverage of events during the course of the chapter, Lothian's ambassadorship *majored* in "promoting friendly relations." Further, lobbying was a particularly delicate task during an era when "propagandising" was actively avoided, with one Foreign Office official explaining "the reason we do not attempt propaganda in the USA is the firm and invincible opposition of the embassy."[3] Although directly referring to Lothian's predecessor, this policy would continue to apply during his term, given the need to be sensitive to American opinion. Nonetheless, in all of these diplomatic tasks Lothian's appreciation of the American public as a key constituency that he needed to address was crucial in enlightening the American people and their elected representatives as to the predicament that Britain found herself in during his ambassadorship. As David Reynolds has written, the "ability to appreciate the American point of view was one of his distinctive characteristics."[4] Allied to this was Lothian's appreciation that he needed to translate to a skeptical audience in London the value of recognizing the influence of American opinion upon the Roosevelt administration in order to achieve British ends. He clearly understood that he had to play to two constituencies on either side of the Atlantic. Lothian explained to Halifax in March 1940 that "one of the difficulties of a British Ambassador in the United States is that he has to talk at the same time to two democratic audiences 3,000 miles away from one another and each with entirely different backgrounds."[5] Collectively, this approach I have termed elsewhere Lothian's ambassadorial "prescription for Anglo-American

---

[3] The Head of the General Department of the Foreign Office, Sir Neville Ronald, continued: "This is an old bone of contention between us at the FO and Sir R. Lindsay and his predecessors." Comments by Ronald, 16 February 1939, attached to a telegram entitled "The United States attitude towards Britain" by Mallet to Scott, 26 January 1939, A1143/1143/45 FO 371/22827, The National Archives of the United Kingdom (TNA), Kew, London. The Foreign Office, in light of the missive over propaganda, were equally keen to know what prominent British individuals were saying in the United States. As an example Halifax wrote to Lothian to enquire about the activities of Duff Cooper, who resigned from the Cabinet over Munich and would become Minister of Information in May 1940: "I should be grateful if you will warn Duff Cooper on his arrival not to say anything suggestive of the United States coming into the war, and not to enter into any old and, I hope, effete controversies about Munich. I should be very glad if you would report to me in due course what he is saying." Halifax to Lothian, 13 October 1939, Viscount Halifax Miscellaneous Correspondence, FO 800/324, TNA.
[4] David Reynolds, *Lord Lothian and Anglo-American Relations, 1939-1940* (Philadelphia: Transactions of the American Philosophical Society, 1983), 5.
[5] Lothian to Halifax, 11 March 1940, CHAR 20/15, Churchill Papers.

understanding."[6] That it succeeded in establishing Lothian in both camps is seen by the influence the ambassador wielded in the latter portion of his ambassadorship in addressing the Destroyers-Bases deal and the origins of Lend-Lease, as discussed below.

The method of Lothian's communication with London was primarily via telegram, and he used it plentifully, hence the preponderance of these records used here. Lothian augmented the telegram and use of the telephone by revisiting the United Kingdom in the autumn of 1940 (he left Washington on 15 October, returning on 23 November). Most significantly for the way Lothian would operate, he devoted considerable effort to writing pleas to friends and associates in the United Kingdom to send firsthand accounts of Britain's predicament that he could relay to individuals in the United States. Besides corresponding officially with Lord Halifax and other members of the Cabinet, Lothian encouraged other persons to send him information.[7] Writing to the Minister for Co-ordination of Defence, Lord Chatfield, only three weeks into his post, Lothian requested "any facts and figures which I can use to bring home the real issues and the real facts to Roosevelt and other leaders here." Lothian continued his plea to Chatfield: "Believe me there is nothing more important you can do than to equip me with the facts and the arguments which will bring home to the United States the real situation which confronts us."[8] In this letter Lothian's belief that information was influence is clear. It would be accurate to say that Lothian's approach to his ambassadorship was nonconformist; but that reflected the conformity of his predecessor, which will be addressed forthwith. In Washington Lothian believed in face-to-face contact with a range of administration figures and those on Capitol Hill (he had seen the president and the secretary of state, Cordell Hull, within the first few days of his appointment and nearly all of the leading State Department figures within the first week); in open and friendly relations with the Washington press corps, many of whom he

---

[6] J. Simon Rofe, "Prescription and Remedy: Lothian's influence upon Anglo-American relations during the Phony War," *The Round Table* 96:389 (April 2007), 158.

[7] Lothian wrote to Robert Boothby, the Conservative member of parliament, in November 1939 thanking him for an initial despatch before going on to say: "I hope you will send me any more memoranda of that kind which you may circulate to others. They are most useful to me." Lothian to Boothby, 3 November 1939, GD 40/17/399/138, Papers of the Eleventh Marquess of Lothian [hereafter Lothian Papers], The National Archives of Scotland, Edinburgh.

[8] Lothian to Chatfield, 15 September 1939, CHT/6/2 Papers relating to Anglo-American Relations 1939-40 Correspondence with the Marquis of Lothian, Lord Chatfield Papers, National Maritime Museum, Greenwich.

already knew from his days in journalism; and frank and earnest assessments of Britain's predicament to, his most crucial audience, the American people.

By the time of his death Lothian had become a valued intermediary for promulgating the British position to those in Washington, while also earning the respect of the Foreign Office because of his devotion to furthering the British position. In facilitating discussion of detailed and emotive issues, Lothian laid notable foundations for the intimate—often termed 'special'—transatlantic relationship that grew once the United States became a belligerent in the war. Throughout Lothian's ambassadorship his open approach to the purposes of his mission, though not without noteworthy contretemps, served to further the strategic relationship between Washington and Britain that would prove so important during the Second World War.[9]

---

[9] While Lothian was ambassador for just fifteen months, the significance of this period and the extent of his career prior to arriving in Washington has ensured that the literature on him is plentiful. Sir James R. M. Butler wrote an authorized biography of Lothian, published in 1960, but did not have complete access to Lothian's papers. See J. R. M. Butler, *Lord Lothian (Philip Kerr) 1882-1940* (London: Macmillan, 1960). This text was supplemented in 1983 by David Reynolds' extensive account of Lothian's time as ambassador. Reynolds, *Lord Lothian*, 1-65. While Reynolds presented Lothian's time in Washington in a largely positive light, subsequent articles by Rhodri Jeffreys-Jones took a more critical view. Rhodri Jeffreys-Jones, "The Inestimable Advantage of not being English: Lord Lothian's American Ambassadorship 1939-1940," *The Scottish Historical Review*, 63:1 (April 1984), 105-110; and "Lord Lothian and American Democracy: An Illusion in Pursuit of an Illusion," *Canadian Review of American Studies* 17:4 (Winter 1986), 411-422. Further work on Lothian was undertaken by Andrea Bosco, who discussed Lothian's attitude toward appeasement as a means of securing the continent. Bosco, "Lord Lothian and Appeasement," in *The Round Table, The Empire/Commonwealth, and British Foreign Policy*, eds. Andrea Bosco and Alex May (London: Lothian Foundation Press, 1997), 473-510. This work also contains another useful chapter by Stefan Schieren, "Philip Kerr and Anglo-American Relations after the Great War," *ibid.*, 451-472. More recently, Priscilla Roberts has written on Lothian and others in the Anglosphere of the early twentieth century, in light of Atlanticist thinking. Priscilla Roberts, "Lord Lothian and the Atlantic World," *The Historian* 66:1 (March 2004), 97-127; and "World War I and Anglo-American Relations: The Role of Philip Lothian and *The Round Table*," *The Round Table* 95:383 (January 2006), 113-139. David P. Billington, Jr., took up elements of this approach in his recent biography, which addressed Lothian's influence on international affairs and his efforts to forge a New World Order throughout his entire lifetime. Billington, *Lothian*. The most recently published writing on Lothian was my own article examining his role in resolving the 'minor crisis' in Anglo-American relations in early 1940. Rofe, "Prescription and Remedy," 151-171.

LOTHIAN'S APPOINTMENT

Lord Halifax, Lothian's successor, was to have a masterful influence on Anglo-American relations before arriving in Washington himself, due to his role as foreign secretary in appointing his fellow nobleman to the position of ambassador to Washington. The appointment of Lothian, announced in the spring of 1939 some six months after he had agreed to accept the role, was not, however, free from contention and concern. Almost as soon as Halifax began to contemplate the appointment in the spring of 1938, his suggestion of Lothian as ambassador drew criticism from individuals within the Foreign Office, the institution charged with conducting British diplomacy, and was also the reason why considerable soundings were taken from the most important constituency in the appointment of an ambassador to Washington, the Roosevelt administration itself.[10] That these misgivings were overcome testifies to the experience and conviction Lothian brought to furthering Anglo-American understanding and, importantly, Halifax's personal appreciation of this.

The Foreign Office's concerns over Lothian, led by Sir Alexander Cadogan as permanent under secretary, were deeply felt and would only be overcome once Lothian proved himself in the post. They centered on the question of whether Lothian was "the right man" and reflected a dual appreciation of a preference that the next ambassador should come from within the Foreign Office, and the role played by the serving ambassador, Sir Ronald Lindsay. On the first strand, Cadogan's biographer writes that he "did not want the post to go to an outsider," and historian David Reynolds agrees that senior Foreign Office officials "wished to keep the job within the diplomatic service."[11] Further questions were raised by some who pondered whether it was really wise to consider Lothian, given that he had previously contemplated accommodating Hitler's demands and his lengthy association with Nancy, Lady Astor and her by then notorious 'Cliveden Set'.[12] It was alleged at the time, and especially in the aftermath

---

[10] By summer 1938, however, Halifax, foreign secretary only since the beginning of February, had come to believe that an appointment in the mould of James Bryce, the historian and politician who had been ambassador from 1907 to 1913, would best serve British interests. For an account of Bryce's career, see John T. Seaman, Jr., *A Citizen of the World: The Life of James Bryce* (London & New York: I. B. Tauris, 2006).

[11] Alexander Cadogan, *The Diaries of Sir Alexander Cadogan O.M. 1938-1945*, ed. David Dilks (London: Cassell, 1971), 82-83; Reynolds, *Lord Lothian*, 8.

[12] On the former point, by the mid-1930s Lothian, along with many others, was ready to sanction changes to the Versailles Treaty. Lothian told a Council on Foreign Relations Study Group meeting in New York in October 1936: "Speaking for myself, I do not believe that
(continued)

of Munich, that this group exerted a "pro-Fascist influence on His Majesty's Government."[13] The reality was far from a fascist conspiracy, and Lothian's association with Astor rested on a shared spirituality centered on Christian Science, although one historian characterized this attachment as "politically maladroit loyalty."[14] Yet in the United States the idea that such a 'Set' existed, amplified no doubt by Astor's American heritage and her place in British society, became a "prevalent myth," to the extent that reaction to it was covered in the Embassy's annual report to London.[15] Following his time in South Africa, Lothian became editor of *The Round Table*, a journal that sought to promote transatlantic understanding as part of its commitment to the British Empire. Lothian joined David Lloyd George's personal staff when the Welshman became prime minister in 1916 and accompanied him to Versailles as his private secretary at the war's end. Being in Paris gave Lothian exposure to many influential Americans, including a young assistant secretary of the navy, Franklin D. Roosevelt, but also to the difficulties of the post-war world. Resigning from public life in 1921, Lothian served briefly as editor of *The Daily Chronicle* and wrote—often from the United States—for a number of newspapers,

---

Hitler wants to fight the West. He does desire or thinks he will have to fight Russia." M204 Study Group Reports, "The Present World Crisis," Digest of Dinner Discussion with Lord Lothian as guest, 20 October 1936, Records of the Council on Foreign Relations 1921-1951, microfilm ed. (Bethesda MD: University Publications of America, 1996). Further, in a personal meeting with Hitler in the spring of 1937, Lothian was open to changes to the Versailles regime. The Canadian Prime Minister met Lothian in May 1937 and recorded that he [Lothian] felt that the situation was "very critical," and that the "bad peace" of Versailles had to be "made over in a fair way rather quickly if trouble is to be averted." Diary entry, 10May 1937, Diary of William Lyon Mackenzie King, National Archives of Canada, Ottawa. Lothian's reading of Hitler changed after Munich, as events convinced him that Germany posed a threat to mutual transatlantic understanding and interests. He wrote to the American banker Thomas W. Lamont in March 1939: "The last attack of Hitler's on Czechoslovakia seems to me very serious. Up till then it was possible to believe that Germany was only concerned with recovery of what might be called the normal rights of a great power, but it now seems clear that Hitler is in effect a fanatical gangster who will stop at nothing in order to beat down all possibility of resistance anywhere to his will." Lothian to Lamont, 19 April 1939, GD 40/17/383/416, Lothian Papers. The often critical Jeffreys-Jones eventually concluded that "there can be no doubt about the intensity of his ultimate opposition to Hitler." Jeffreys-Jones, "Lord Lothian and American Democracy," 418.

[13] Annual Report on the United States for 1938, from Mr Mallet, Chargé d'Affaires, 17 February 1939, A1882/1882/45 FO 371/22832.

[14] Jeffreys-Jones, "Lord Lothian and American Democracy," 418.

[15] David Scott, minute dated 7 March 1939, FO 794/18; Annual Report on the United States for 1938, from Mr Mallet, Chargé d'Affaires, 17 February 1939, A1882/1882/45 FO 371/22832, TNA.

including *The Times* and *The Observer*, before taking the post of secretary of the Rhodes Trust in 1925, which he remained until 1939. His principal role was to administer the international scholarship program, and through this he sought to encourage liberal-democratic values. With his extensive experience of the United States, by the late 1930s Lothian could be charged as having already gone 'native', but given the lack of appreciation in London of how best to facilitate the promotion of British interests, his firsthand knowledge of America and Americans proved vital to his time as ambassador.[16] Indeed these experiences, allied to his belief in Anglo-American relations, meant he was the outstanding candidate in Halifax's mind and explain why the foreign secretary pressed Lothian's appointment in the face of Foreign Office skepticism.

The ire of Foreign Office functionaries over Lothian's appointment was exacerbated by their appreciation of the incumbent ambassador. While it is often said that papal succession depends on the waist size of the man being replaced, elements of this 'Yin' and 'Yang' are as evident in the appointment of ambassadors to Washington. It is therefore worth dwelling momentarily on Lindsay's attributes, as they contrast in a number of areas to those Lothian would exhibit. Lindsay was an archetypal Foreign Office diplomat who had been in Washington since 1930. Described by Reynolds as "tall, moustachioed, distinguished," Lindsay oversaw relations with the administration away from public attention. In actual fact Lindsay's approach betrayed a diffidence that would never be part of Lothian's method as ambassador: the former, although resident in Washington since 1930, did not give a press conference until the eve of the royal visit in the summer of 1939.[17] The visit of the king and queen—the first time British monarchs came to the United States—had already had a delaying impact upon the announcement of Lothian's appointment as ambassador and his taking up his post. Halifax had initially wanted to install Lothian in office in the autumn of 1938, but the impending royal visit meant Lindsay

---

[16] Berridge explains that 'going native' or 'localitis' is an "occupational hazard" for the professional diplomat. Geoff Berridge, *Diplomacy: Theory and Practice*, 3rd ed. (Basingstoke: Palgrave, 2005), 112.

[17] Reynolds, *Lord Lothian*, 2. Lindsay had served in Washington previously: he was second secretary between 1905 and 1907 and first secretary from 1919 to 1920. Lindsay successively married two Americans, firstly the daughter of Senator J. Donald Cameron of Pennsylvania, and following her death, Elizabeth Sherman Hoyt of New York, "the cousin of his first wife and a long time friend of Eleanor Roosevelt." Benjamin D. Rhodes, "The British Royal Visit of 1939 and the 'Psychological Approach' to the United States," *Diplomatic History* 2:2 (Spring 1978), 199.

remained until after the king and queen had been and gone in the summer of 1939. Lindsay, a model of discretion and well versed in diplomatic custom, ensured that the Washington embassy ran without incident, thus making Whitehall's job all the more straightforward.

Lothian, by contrast, would circumvent convention and leave London seeking to rein him in on occasion. The most prominent such episode was Lothian's indiscreet remarks over the state of British finances in November 1940, which will be considered later in this chapter. Yet while Lindsay would oversee orderly diplomatic conduct, his lack of profile outside Washington came to injure Anglo-American relations, to the point that *Time* wrote in the summer of 1940 that Lothian's predecessor had administered an embassy with a reputation for "unapproachability, swank, [and] disregard for US ways."[18] As will be seen, Lothian did seek to take on the role of promoting British interests beyond the diplomatic coterie in Washington, and to the American people. Although historian Rhodri Jeffreys-Jones questions just how effective this strategy was in the American heartlands, the change of approach was clear.[19] That Lothian was able to observe his predecessor's lengthy stint in Washington from various quarters provided him with an opportunity to redefine the parameters of the ambassadorship. From the outset Lothian sought to be more proactive than Lindsay in making British representations, in clarifying British intentions, and in outlining the British predicament. Given the calamitous events that were to unfold during Lothian's tenure, this approach would be vital in upgrading his position and making it the pre-eminent channel in Anglo-American relations.

In looking at the appointment from beyond Whitehall, David Reynolds deftly explains the transatlantic soundings that were exchanged during 1938 and 1939 over Lindsay's successor. Such individuals as Norman H. Davis, a Roosevelt confidant in foreign affairs, Lord Tweedsmuir (John Buchan), Canada's governor general and a fellow member of 'Milner's Kindergarten', and Roger Merriman, Roosevelt's

---

[18] "Lord Lothian's Job," *Time*, 8 July 1940, accessed 12 October 2007.

[19] Debate exists over the extent to which Lothian engaged with the wider United States public. Jeffreys-Jones has contributed to this by citing the less than complimentary obituary of Lothian by William Allen White, the Republican editor of the Kansas *Emporia Gazette* who subsequently chaired the influential 'Committee to Defend America by Aiding the Allies'. This view, however, overlooks Lothian's recognition that he needed to focus his attention as ambassador upon key opinion-formers, most of whom were to be found within the East Coast establishment. Jeffreys-Jones, "The Inestimable Advantage of Not Being English," 416.

Harvard professor, were the parties to communications that made their way between the president and the Foreign Office. These messages suggested a non-career diplomat would be welcomed in Washington, but further questions over Lothian's suitability were raised after he received something of a dressing down from Roosevelt in January 1939. At a time when Lothian had accepted the ambassadorship but Roosevelt did not know of his guest's imminent appointment the pair clashed, not for the last time, over Lothian's pleas for American assistance. To use Reynolds' phrase, Roosevelt was "trying to stiffen British resolve" in rebuffing Lothian and thereby encourage levels of British self-reliance that would mean the president could avoid ever sending American forces into battle on foreign fields. This trait of Rooseveltian thinking was something that would return to the pair's conversations after September 1939. Even with Roosevelt's stiff words to Lothian, in conversation with Canadian Prime Minister Mackenzie King at the end of January 1939, Lothian still felt able to describe the President as "very much with Britain."[20] So despite differences of opinion, the president and the ambassador would enjoy each other's company, as their meetings lacked formality, were often conducted over and during dinner, and extended into the evening. The Foreign Office's concerns nonetheless lingered, and after Roosevelt's strong rebuke became known in Whitehall, Lindsay raised with him the possibility of Lothian being put forward as ambassador. Harking back to their earlier meeting at Versailles, Roosevelt referred to Lothian "as a very clever Private Secretary" before stating: "Look here, there can be no possible difficulty about his *agrement* or any thing of that sort."[21] Maintaining this emphasis, Halifax wrote to Lothian telling him that "the President has given his agrement in respect of your appointment."[22] This endorsement, allied to his experience and faith in mutual interests in Anglo-American relations, reassured Halifax that his choice of Lothian was sound. He was announced as the next ambassador later in April 1939, and took up the post at the end of August, as the German military crushed Polish resistance.

---

[20] Diary entry, 30 January 1939, Diary of William Lyon Mackenzie King.

[21] Lindsay to Foreign Office, 29 March 1939, FO 794/18. Referenced in David Reynolds, "FDR on the British: A Postscript," *Massachusetts Historical Society Proceedings* 90 (1978), 106-110.

[22] The full text of the letter was: "As I mentioned on the telephone yesterday we have just had a telegram from Sir Ronald Lindsay in Washington announcing that the President has given his agreement in respect of your appointment as Ambassador." Halifax to Lothian, 19 April 1939, GD 40/17/379/91, Lothian Papers.

FURTHERING BRITISH INTERESTS AND FRIENDLY RELATIONS: LOTHIAN AND AMERICAN OPINION

Lothian's appreciation of the influence of American public opinion was made starkly apparent to him in his first meeting as ambassador with the president, in the autumn of 1939. The encounter made clear to him the importance of establishing the profile of the ambassador to an American audience, while also relaying their influence to those back in London. At this first meeting on 1 September Roosevelt told Lothian that, despite "every fibre" sympathizing with Britain and France, he was duty bound to enforce the Neutrality laws, so as to head off any opposition that might accuse him of involving the United States in the European conflict. The enactment of the Neutrality laws prevented further purchases of American war materials by the United Kingdom. The President countered "that the best way of getting the Act repealed was to bring home to public opinion what its enforcement meant in denying needed supplies to Britain and France."[23] Unsurprisingly, a revision of the Neutrality laws to permit 'cash and carry' purchases, of which the British could take advantage, was to the fore for Lothian during the autumn of 1939.

Lothian's method to address this and further British interests in both Washington and more widely in the United States reflected the broader approach he sought for his ambassadorship. In essence it was to establish himself within and without Washington as a plain-speaking representative of the British position. Beyond that, as he would openly state to his American audiences, he would not plead for assistance nor seek to suggest courses of action for the United States. Thus Lothian would not directly address revision of the Neutrality laws in any substance, but began to promote British interests through a series of addresses approximately every four to six weeks during his appointment. These served related public and private purposes. Firstly, these speeches provided the opportunity to spread his message through the syndicated press to the American people, beyond their immediate audience, which was often small numerically and select in social terms.[24] In January 1940 Lothian wrote to Sir Abe Bailey, a

---

[23] Lothian to Halifax, 5 September 1939, Halifax MSS FO 800/324. With a Jeffersonian heritage this opposition is commonly referred to as Isolationist, although its adherents varied in their opinion of the literal meaning of the word, and their desire for 'non-entanglement' is perhaps a more helpful descriptor. Wayne S. Cole, *Roosevelt and the Isolationists 1932-1945* (Lincoln: University of Nebraska Press, 1983), remains the leading discussion of the influence of the Isolationist school.

[24] Reynolds put this succinctly as "allowing the natural mechanism of the US media to do Britain's publicity for her." Reynolds, *Lord Lothian*, 34. That Lothian's speeches were read (continued)

South African financier and statesman, that he was "glad to say" that a speech to the Chicago Council on Foreign Relations at the beginning of the year "got very wide publicity and also had an excellent reception from the press."[25] A related and more private purpose was to stimulate debate in opinion-making circles and provide Lothian with the opportunity to develop his views. To do this he sent copies of his speeches to leading journalists, opinion-formers, and members of the administration in Washington, as well as colleagues in the United Kingdom.[26] By way of example, Adolf A. Berle, the dedicated Anglophobe assistant secretary of state, responded positively to receiving a copy of a speech Lothian made in St. Louis in the early spring of 1940, writing to Lothian that he had "read the press accounts of it [the speech] with a great deal of pleasure: and I should like nothing better than to have a chance to chat with you about it."[27] Lothian's approach therefore helped to facilitate an ongoing dialogue on the British position with the administration.

In terms of providing substance to his pronouncements, his speech to the American branch of the Pilgrims Society on 25 October 1939 is typical in revealing Lothian's approach to the ambassadorship. The speech was framed in language familiar to Americans. Lothian stated:

> As a fellow democracy, therefore, we feel we have the right, indeed the duty, to tell you our story, to explain to you and all other democracies what we are doing and why we are doing it. But having done that we feel that it is for you and you alone to form your own judgement about ourselves and about the war. That, of course, is your inalienable right.

Lothian continued in the same candid fashion: "We want to tell you the facts as we know them, and our point of view about them, from London. But having done so, by our own democratic principles we are bound to

---

rather than listened to was helpful to Britain's cause. Sir Godfrey Haggard, then British Consul-General in New York, recalled after the ambassador's death: "His addresses read much better than they sounded, as his delivery tended to be uninspired and professorial. Extempore or in conversation he was more at his ease." Comments by Sir Godfrey Haggard, GD 40/17/514/37, Lothian Papers.

[25] Lothian to Sir Abe Bailey, 17 January 1940, GD 40/17/398/462, Lothian Papers.

[26] Examples of other individuals to whom Lothian sent copies of his speeches are James M. Witherow, a Minnesota attorney, and Percival Witherby of the Canadian Bank of Commerce. Correspondence with James M. Witherow, GD 40/17/406/276-360, and Percival Witherby, GD 40/17/406/361-406, Lothian Papers.

[27] Adolf A. Berle to Lothian, 26 April 1940, GD 40/17/399/28-32, Lothian Papers.

leave you perfectly free to form your own judgements."[28] This point was crucial to Lothian's conception of the role the ambassador should play, namely, not to be seen to be driving events but to ensure a British account of them was presented. Reynolds neatly expresses this as Lothian appreciating "the value of a well-timed, well-publicised utterance. Like a pebble thrown into a pool, it set in motion ripples of discussion among opinion-leaders and the foreign-policy public."[29] Writing to Halifax only days into the job, Lothian spoke of how it would take "a long time to reeducate 130 million people into a truer perspective," whilst recognizing that "such reeducation can only be done by the Americans themselves." This appreciation acknowledges that as ambassador at this time he was to promote British interests by actively doing little. He went on, "with the pace of modern events it will not be reeducation at all but the sudden realisation that their own vital interests are in danger which will drive American public opinion to action."[30]

Such a clear assessment of events would be a hallmark of his ambassadorship. It also ties to the qualifications for the post with which his predecessor credited Lothian in March 1939, when he endorsed the appointment, telling Halifax that Lothian "has the knack of moving about a great deal in an unobtrusive (not a secret or surreptitious) manner."[31] Lindsay proceeded to highlight Lothian's ability to operate away from the limelight, "a valuable quality for a British Ambassador in America, whose power to influence the United States Government will be impaired if he is presented by the press to the public as an influential man. He has antennae and understands this."[32] In stating the British case in his speeches Lothian was carefully promoting British interests while studiously avoiding what might be construed as lobbying for political purposes. David Billington concludes that Lothian "reached out to the American people in a way that no regular diplomat could have done."[33]

Lothian explained his understanding of the parameters he had to operate within late in the autumn of 1939. When asked by J. P. Morgan banker Thomas W. Lamont to speak at a luncheon at the University Club, he explained that he was "quite clear that the number of public speeches a

---

[28] Lothian's speech at the Pilgrims Society Dinner, New York, 25 October 1939, sent to Chatfield, CHT/6/2 Chatfield Papers.

[29] Reynolds, *Lord Lothian*, 33-34.

[30] Lothian to Halifax, 5 September 1939, Halifax MSS FO 800/324.

[31] Lindsay to Halifax, 10 March 1939, Halifax MSS FO 800/324.

[32] Lindsay to Halifax, 10 March 1939, Halifax MSS FO 800/324.

[33] Billington, *Lothian*, 141.

British Ambassador should make should be strictly limited, but informal talks 'off the record' are a different matter."[34] Here again, as 1939 drew to a close, Lothian was articulating the boundaries he had to operate within as British ambassador to Washington. These were appreciated in Washington. Moffat in early December recorded that Lothian "seems to have made a good start."[35] It is important to recognize that Lothian's work in establishing friendly relations with those in London, the administration, and indirectly with the American people, was not simply an end in itself. Rather, it was a means to engender meaningful and practical understanding in Washington when the United Kingdom found itself in dire straits later in the year.

Lothian's execution of this strategy was not, however, without risks. He recognized that his approach could have potential repercussions, since once his words were in the public domain there was little scope to clarify them further to the American people. This was clearly a concern for those in London, leading Halifax to write at the end of January 1940 with, in the ambassador's words, "warning considerations" and "very mild criticism" over Lothian's speech in Chicago to the Council on Foreign Relations.[36] Lothian had suggested that "democratic control of the seas" meant the United States assuming "responsibility for a Monroe Doctrine of the seas," which had prompted Halifax's rebuke.[37] The ambassador's response was to point to the success of his speeches amongst the American people and claim that "they have been a success here precisely because I have felt that I knew the American mind well enough to be quite frank and to deal frankly with controversial issues." Lothian could make such assertions with some confidence.[38] *Time* magazine wrote that his "speech was one of the most effective, skilful briefs yet delivered for the Allied cause. It was the sort of talk which earns Britain a reputation for fair

---

[34] Lothian to Lamont, 27 November 1939, GD 40/17/402/195, Lothian Papers.

[35] Moffat, Diplomatic Diary entry, following conversation with Joseph P. Kennedy, 8 December 1939, Vol. 44 Diplomatic Correspondence 1940, The Jay Pierrepont Moffat Papers, Houghton Library, Harvard University, Cambridge, MA.

[36] Lothian, speech to Chicago Council on Foreign Relations, 4 January 1940, GD 40/17/408/15, Lothian Papers.

[37] Lothian to Halifax, 11 March 1940, CHAR 20/15, Churchill Papers.

[38] C. K. Allen, the Warden of Rhodes House, Oxford, wrote to Lothian in February 1940, enclosing the opinion of a Canadian colleague who had been in the United States at the time of Lothian's Chicago speech: "The American press and radio announcers have given it a wonderful approval." Allen to Lothian, 14 February 1940, GD 40/17/398/158-160, Lothian Papers.

dealing and open-minded thinking."[39] This clearly aligned with Lothian's approach. Lothian was aware that his appreciation of the reaction of the American people on the ground and the perceptions of those in London differed, and he remarked to Halifax: "I can imagine what my speeches would have been like if they had first been minuted by all veterans of the Foreign Office at home!"[40]

While his utterances in January 1940 had few ramifications, Reynolds' analysis of Lothian's speech of 19 June at Yale University suggests that later he overstepped the mark. The ambassador's address was a frank account of the importance of the Royal Navy to American security, as he told his audience: "The outcome of the grim struggle will affect you almost as much as it will affect us. For if Hitler gets our fleet, or destroys it, the whole foundation on which the security of both our countries has rested for 120 years will have disappeared."[41] While reflecting his Atlanticist outlook and consonant with Lothian's previous utterances, this speech caused bleak assessments of Britain's position in some quarters of the American press, who questioned whether it was worth assisting the United Kingdom if their cause was already doomed. This also unnerved American public opinion as to their country's ability to remain wholly aloof from the conflict, though once the initial reaction had passed the speech did serve to heighten appreciation of Britain's predicament. The net effect was to bring American opinion around and provide impetus for Roosevelt to act. *Time* wrote some three weeks after the speech that "U.S. public opinion, which last year was unwilling to face the savage reality of war, last week was prepared to admit that it had a decisive, selfish, personal interest in what happened to the British Fleet."[42] Even when Lothian appeared to injure the British cause by sharing his desperate view of events after the fall of

---

[39] "The Noblest of Englishmen," *Time*, 15 January 1940, http://www.time.com/time/magazine/article/0,9171,772318,00.html, accessed 12 October 2007.

[40] Lothian to Halifax, 11 March 1940, CHAR 20/15, Churchill Papers.

[41] Lothian, speech at Yale University Alumni Luncheon, University Hall, Yale, 19 June 1940, GD 40/17/406/490, Lothian Papers. Lothian had learnt from Secretary of State Cordell Hull the week before this speech that the "navy friend of Great Britain [Roosevelt] like myself would expect her to fight to the last dollar, to the last man and to the last ship, if necessary; ... that, of course, Great Britain would not think of turning the fleet over to Germany." Memorandum of conversation between Hull and Lothian, 11 June 1940, Cordell Hull Papers, Manuscripts Division, Library of Congress, Washington, DC.

[42] "Lord Lothian's Job," *Time*, 8 July 1940, http://www.time.com/time/magazine/article/0,9171,772318,00.html, accessed 12 October 2007.

France, the unintended consequence of his candid utterances therefore brought matters to a head as Britain's situation deteriorated over the summer.

CLARIFYING INTENT: MINOR AND MAJOR CRISIS RESOLUTION

While this scenario replicated itself somewhat in the final weeks of his life, after press reports of Lothian's remarks on Britain's straitened financial position, at the beginning of 1940 it would instead be his mollifying attributes that would be to the fore. As 1940 began Lothian was to use his pacifying skills to good effect in clarifying British intentions and promoting friendly relations with Washington. In so doing his relaying of American concerns to London mitigated a 'minor crisis' in Anglo-American relations, as well as availing Whitehall of advanced knowledge of the presidential mission of Under Secretary of State Sumner Welles to Europe in February-March 1940.[43]

The specter of a crisis in Anglo-American relations arose in January 1940 as disagreements over the wartime rights of neutrals came to a head. Crucially, Lothian was in place to ensure the crisis *only* earned the adjective 'minor'. The phrase was coined by President Roosevelt himself in conversation with Lothian, as he spoke of the State Department's disquiet over a "perceived lack of respect for American neutral rights and the worry amongst the American people that Britain was seeking to drag the United States into the war."[44] From the outset of the war the British, through the Royal Navy, adopted a policy of blockade in their economic warfare campaign. This posed serious problems to U.S. trade with Europe, and put London firmly in the State Department's sights, to the extent that Secretary of State Cordell Hull admonished Lothian on 22 January 1940. Hull explained that there was "a steadily increasing feeling in this country that American commercial and other interests are being severely injured by discriminations and unnecessary restrictions, ... to the detriment of American interests."[45] Jay Pierrepont Moffat, chief of the Division of European Affairs at the State Department, added in conversation with

---

[43] The substantive issues of this section are dealt with in greater depth in Rofe, "Prescription and Remedy," 151-171.

[44] *Ibid.*, 155.

[45] Hull continued that things "will soon reach a stage where the advantages of these discriminations and restrictions will be decidedly less than the bad reactionary effects in this country." Memorandum of conversation between Hull and Lothian, 22 January 1940, Hull Papers.

Lothian that "there was a general feeling that the United States had been particularly friendly to Great Britain, had even gone out of its way to give special forms of help, but that Great Britain had taken this friendship so much for granted."[46] Still worse for Lothian, the Department's alarm was made public over the weekend of 21-23 January 1940 when the *New York Times* published a departmental *aide mémoire* stating its "serious concern" over British conduct.[47] Such sentiments were deeply troubling to Lothian, given his desire to convey a clear account of the United Kingdom's position to the American public.

Lothian's ability to protect British interests while mollifying the State Department's concerns provided a test of his approach to the ambassadorship. Lothian intensified his efforts to explain himself to the Roosevelt administration in Washington. After a second meeting with Hull, Lothian sought out other prominent State Department officials, including Moffat and Assistant Secretary of State Breckinridge Long. The ambassador listened patiently as both told him how British conduct in the Atlantic was turning American opinion against the United Kingdom. Long explained that "the sooner the British realise the effect their actions were having on the American people the sooner they could expect better relations with the American Government and better support from the American people."[48] Lothian's next move illustrates succinctly the manner in which he sought to exert his influence for the British cause. He drew upon the experienced diplomat Norman H. Davis, a longtime presidential sounding board, for help. The latter complied with Lothian's request, spending "the better part of the day on the telephone urging an easing off of the pressure on the British." This Moffat learnt when he was a recipient of a call from Davis that afternoon.[49] That call indicated to Moffat that Lothian was "very much worried."[50] This also served to show just how deeply in earnest Lothian was, and when Moffat met Lothian the next day the

---

[46] Moffat, Diplomatic Diary entry following conversation with Lothian, 25 January 1940, Vol. 44 Diplomatic Correspondence 1940, Moffat Papers.

[47] The *aide mémoire* was published in the *New York Times* on 23 January 1940, and followed a number of articles criticizing Great Britain. On 21 January 1940, for example, the newspaper published a piece by Edwin L. James entitled "Britain's Mail Search Annoys United States: Extension of Hunt for Contraband to Postal Shipments of This Country Raises a Thorny Issues and Recalls World War Friction."

[48] Breckinridge Long, *The War Diary of Breckinridge Long: Selections from the Years 1939-44*, ed. Fred L. Israel (Lincoln: University of Nebraska Press, 1966), 59.

[49] Moffat, Diplomatic Diary entry following conversation with Lothian, 25 January 1940, Vol. 44 Diplomatic Correspondence 1940, Moffat Papers.

[50] *Ibid.*

ambassador made every effort to overcome the Department's concern. The ambassador "said that he wanted to be of help" and pledged that he would "keep in close touch with the Department," Moffat recorded. With a view to furthering an open relationship between the embassy and the Department, Lothian continued that he "hoped that we [the Department] would feel free to call on him whenever desired," while also suggesting that his staff at the embassy "make a practice of dropping down from time to time to talk things over informally with members of the Department, rather than of waiting until a specific case had arisen." Lothian's sentiment illustrates that the ambassador was mindful of the value to the British cause of the appearance of the ambassador and the embassy availing themselves to the American government, both to placate the immediate issue and to pre-empt any future disagreements.

In conjunction with Lothian's pacifying role in Washington in overcoming the minor crisis in transatlantic relations, he also understood the importance of informing the Foreign Office in London of how British policies appeared in the United States. At the end of January and beginning of February, Lothian boosted his efforts to convey the state of affairs in the United States to officials back in the United Kingdom. As American disquiet reached its height, Lothian wrote to London that it was "of the utmost importance that we should in the next few weeks do everything we can to meet the State Department's view."[51] Lothian supplemented this with further correspondence to Halifax explaining American irritation and, importantly, suggesting a British course of action that addressed both the American people and the country's government. Lothian wrote that "the essence of the case" was that "we have to prove to the USA, which includes public opinion as well as the Administration, that any action we take affecting them is really necessary for the winning of the war."[52] To illustrate the importance of the link between British actions, the administration, *and* the American people, Lothian wrote a lengthy paper entitled simply "US Foreign Policy and Public Opinion," which he sent directly to Halifax and others in Britain.[53] In it Lothian explained the state of American opinion and why it was important for the British to take notice of it. In language akin to that which Lothian used in his public speeches he warned: "The one fatal thing is for us to offer the United States advice as to

---

[51] Lothian, Telegram No. 83 to the Foreign Office, 21 January 1940, A1084/434/45 FO 371/24248.

[52] Lothian to Halifax, 27 January 1940, Halifax MSS FO 800/324.

[53] Lothian to Halifax, Despatch No. 119, "United States Foreign Policy and Public Opinion," 1 February 1940, Halifax MSS FO 800/324.

what she ought to do. We have never listened to the advice of foreigners. Nor will the Americans." He went on to explain the public's appetite for information and the dangers of propaganda:

> She is glad of information. She is quite ready to listen—indeed is anxious to listen—to our views, provided they are expressed as our own opinions and do not include any expression of opinion as to what the United States should do. But just because the British have a power of emotional appeal, due to common ancestry, common language, common ideals, anything which looks like British propaganda designed to influence American policy creates a cold fury in the American mind.[54]

Such assessments were having an effect in London. At the individual level, Halifax annotated after reading Lothian's account: "A very good despatch." Reflecting later in February, he wrote:

> I read with great interest your despatch of February 1 of which you sent me a special copy. You have succeeded in giving me so clear a picture of the state of feeling in America, and of the kind of problems with which that feeling confronts us, that I am all the more anxious to respond to your request for a similar picture of the position here.[55]

Clearly Lothian's reporting to London was instigating the response he desired, one that would mitigate American ire in Washington. More broadly, when the Ministry of Economic Warfare's Frank Ashton-Gwatkin arrived in Washington in February 1940, he was charged with paying "particular emphasis [to] the possibility of meeting the various protests and complaints which have recently been received from the State Department," indicating that a once skeptical Foreign Office was warming to Lothian's mantra.[56]

As Lothian drew the 'minor crisis' to an end, another issue arose that illustrated how the ambassador was facilitating Anglo-American relations through his embassy and how he was able to negotiate with President Roosevelt directly in line with British interests. Lothian learned on 1 February 1940 that the president intended to send Sumner Welles, his

---

[54] The case against propaganda was made to Lothian on a number of occasions. The banker Thomas Lamont, for example, wrote to him: "[I]f some of your compatriots get up a propaganda machine, the workings of which are always only too manifest, the effect would greatly prejudice the British cause in this country. Therefore, I venture very respectfully to hope that you and all your associates will discourage any set effort along these elaborate lines." Lamont to Lothian, 15 December 1939, GD 40/17/402/198, Lothian Papers.
[55] Halifax to Lothian, 29 February 1940, Halifax MSS FO 800/324.
[56] Foreign Office minute, 9 February 1940, W2390/79/49 FO 371/25137.

under secretary of state, to Europe on a multifaceted mission. Over the course of the following week Lothian was able to present the British position and, alongside concerns expressed by Secretary of State Cordell Hull, materially influence the shape of the mission. When they met at the beginning of February, Lothian learned that the president was sending his close confidant Welles to Europe "solely to advise the President and the Secretary of State whether there was any possibility of ending the war in the near future."[57] Although the mission reflected a raft of thought-processes in Washington in dealing with the European conflict, Lothian immediately realized the potential uproar it might cause in London. Lothian reported his conversation to London in terms which sought to soothe any unrest, emphasizing that the president's "ideas about peace [are] practically the same as ours," and explaining further that Roosevelt's vision "must include restoration of freedom to Czechoslovakia and [the] Poles in some real form and guarantees that there would be no renewal of aggression during any of our life-times."[58] Lothian's hopes to pre-empt London's objections proved fruitless, as opinion in Whitehall was scathing toward the president's intentions to initiate a peace move. Cadogan called it an "awful, half-baked idea" and saw the mission as Welles arriving "over here with a flourish of trumpets to collect data on which Roosevelt is to proclaim [the] basis of peace!"[59] The response from Prime Minister Neville Chamberlain was no less forceful: a four-page, seventeen-point refutation of the president's proposal.[60] In the aftermath of the minor crisis and in light of the efforts he had made to establish warm relations with those in Washington, Lothian faced a test in representing his government.

The ambassador's approach was to play to the intimacy of his relationship with Roosevelt and share with the president the information he had received from London. What made this significant was that Lothian let Roosevelt have both Chamberlain's detailed telegram and, crucially, a private document for Lothian from Chamberlain explaining further his

---

[57] Lothian, Telegram No. 142 to Halifax, 1 February 1940 (sent 1:37 am 2 February received 10:35 am 2 February [all times are local]), Halifax MSS FO 800/324.

[58] *Ibid.*

[59] Cadogan, *The Diaries of Sir Alexander Cadogan*, 253.

[60] Neville Chamberlain, Telegram No. 172 to Lothian, 3 February 1940, Halifax MSS FO 800/324/165. Also filed as Telegram from Chamberlain to Lothian 121.840 Welles, Sumner/69½, U.S. Department of State, *Foreign Relations of the United States 1940*, Vol. 1, *General* (Washington, DC: Government Printing Office, 1959), 1.

objections to the president's plan.[61] Roosevelt acknowledged the force of London's objections to the intention to make public the Welles mission's goals as being to investigate peace and agreed to remove this from its public remit. The ambassador reported "that in any published instructions to Welles [Roosevelt] would probably avoid use of the word 'peace' and simply send him on a tour of enquiry."[62] Lothian again relayed this to London, where Roosevelt's intentions raised additional objections. In a further meeting with the president, the ambassador disclosed both a point by point response and a private memorandum in presenting the British position. Ultimately the wider motivations for the Welles mission outweighed the objections London raised, and on 9 February 1940 Roosevelt announced that Welles would be traveling to Europe "solely for the purpose of advising the President and the Secretary of State as to present conditions in Europe."[63] It is worth noting that Roosevelt still despatched Welles to a warring Europe in mid-February, and even though he had removed mention of this motivation from his mission's publicly announced goals, this would not stop speculation over presidential peace moves, but Lothian's conveying of British doubts was nonetheless significant. The objections he relayed from London resonated with those Secretary of State Hull had also expressed to Roosevelt and the president, in many respects an ever malleable policymaker, eventually changed the mission's public objectives to remove any direct mention that Welles intended to explore the possibilities of peace. This episode provides an example of how, by investing in his personal relationships with the president and other American officials, Lothian was able to impart unfavorable news without injuring Anglo-American relations.

NEW DIMENSIONS TO ANGLO-AMERICAN RELATIONS

Assessments of the Washington embassy in the spring of 1940 cannot avoid being viewed in the light of the cataclysmic changes to Europe's geopolitical landscape.[64] At the end of March the Phony War was still in

---

[61] Chamberlain, Telegram No. 173 to Lothian, 3 February 1940 (despatched 1.45 am 4 February), Halifax MSS FO 800/324.

[62] Lothian, Telegram No. 160 to Chamberlain, 6 February 1940, Halifax MSS FO 800/324.

[63] Transcript of White House Press Release of 9 February 1940, Box 76, President's Secretary"s File, Franklin D. Roosevelt Papers, Franklin D. Roosevelt Presidential Library, Hyde Park, NY. For further discussion of the Welles mission, see J. Simon Rofe, *Franklin D. Roosevelt's Foreign Policy and the Welles Mission* (New York: Palgrave, 2007).

[64] In explaining further the importance of the British embassy in Washington to Anglo-American relations it is worth considering the position of the American embassy in London. (continued)

play, but just three months later France had fallen and the United Kingdom stood alone off a continent dominated by Nazi Germany. Throughout this period Lothian sought to maintain his intimacy with the administration, while also reporting home on the machinations of the United States.

In writing to Halifax in late April after the invasion of Denmark and Norway, Lothian acknowledged the prevailing flux in American opinion. "The state of opinion in the United States of America is difficult to crystallise in a despatch because things are so fluid here and so constantly changing." Despite this Lothian stuck to the tenets of his previous counsel: "Speaking generally, however, the appreciation set forth in my despatch of February 1st still holds."[65] Clearly in Lothian's estimation the changing situation in Europe had not permeated the American populace to the point of inspiring a change of attitude in the administration, but it was having *an* effect. He concluded: "I do not think I can be more explicit. The United States is still dominated by fear of involvement and incapable of positive action. On the other hand the war is steadily drifting nearer to them and they know it." Cultivating this latter understanding would again carry some risks for Lothian in terms of overexposing the British position, but these were challenges that as events transpired he was more than prepared to tackle.

While the events of April meant the Phony War had ceased, two events on 10 May would materially influence Lothian's ambassadorship. The first was Operation Weserübung, the German attack on the Low Countries; the second, the appointment as British prime minister of Winston S. Churchill. These events propelled the ambassador to the forefront, and at least in Reynolds' view meant that for the rest of his life Lothian would play "a major role in Anglo-American relations"[66]. The importance of Churchill to Anglo-American relations in subsequent years is something that numerous volumes have addressed; suffice it to say that, in contrast to his predecessor Neville Chamberlain, he greatly valued relations

---

Since the war had begun the previous autumn Joseph P. Kennedy, the American ambassador, had urged Roosevelt to make peace. As Lothian befriended the president during the Phony War, his American counterpart was increasingly marginalized by those in London, the president, and the rest of the State Department. Moffat succinctly expressed this situation by stating: "If Kennedy says something is black and Lothian says it is white, we believe Lord Lothian." Nancy Harvison Hooker, ed., *The Moffat Papers: Selections from the Diplomatic Journals of Jay Pierrepont Moffat, 1919-1943* (Cambridge, MA: Harvard University Press, 1956), 5.

[65] Lothian to Halifax, 29 April 1940, Halifax MSS FO 800/324.
[66] Reynolds, *Lord Lothian*, 14.

with Washington. Lothian aired his views on Churchill to Moffat in the fall of 1939. "He [Lothian] said that nine days out of ten Churchill was magnificent," the American recorded, "but the tenth day during a crisis he was apt to lose his head, close his ears, and refuse to listen to reason." Yet Lothian was clear as to Churchill's attributes. "Despite this weakness, Lothian felt he had the exuberance, drive and leadership which England craved."[67] The reservations in Lothian's words were an acknowledgment that, while Lothian and Churchill had known each other for several decades, the beginning of the war had left them rather at cross purposes. As is well known, as soon as Churchill returned to the Admiralty at the beginning of the war, he began a correspondence with Roosevelt that would ultimately include many thousands of memoranda, telegrams, notes, and letters.[68] During the Phony War the correspondence was limited in scope, with the vast majority of communications emanating from the First Sea Lord. Churchill's use of this channel during the war's early months irked Lothian. The former's correspondence had not been disclosed to the ambassador even though members of the State Department had learnt about it.[69] A solution was found in Churchill's agreement to send copies of the letters to Lothian, "thus keeping Lothian fully informed," Halifax, who had mediated between the two, explained, "while giving the President the feeling that he has a special line of information."[70] This satisfied Lothian for a few months, until the Tyler Kent espionage affair of mid-May 1940 cast into question the security of using the American embassy in London.[71]

---

[67] Moffat also noted that: "Lloyd George had discovered during the Great War that the way to get him [Churchill] out of such moods was to send him to the front for a day or two when he immediately recovered a sense of proportion." Diplomatic Diary entry following conversation with Lothian, 26 September 1939, Vol. 44 Diplomatic Correspondence 1940, Moffat Papers.

[68] For details of the correspondence, see Warren F. Kimball, ed., *Churchill & Roosevelt: The Complete Correspondence*, Vol. I, *Alliance Emerging October 1933–November 1942* (Princeton, NJ: Princeton University Press, 1984). For further analysis of this relationship, see, e.g., Joseph P. Lash, *Roosevelt and Churchill 1939–1941: The Partnership That Saved the West* (London: Andre Deutsch, 1977).

[69] Undoubtedly reflecting Roosevelt's interest in the naval engagement, it was Churchill's extensive account of the Battle of the River Plate that was evidently circulated to the State Department, as the British account was mentioned by Berle and Moffat in conversation with Lothian. Diplomatic Diary entry following conversation with Lothian, 26 December 1939, Vol. 44 Diplomatic Correspondence 1940, Moffat Papers.

[70] Halifax to Churchill, 19 January 1940, ADM 199/1928.

[71] The arrest of Kent, a cipher clerk at the embassy in London, the seizure of almost two thousand documents at his flat, and the overriding of his diplomatic immunity, which meant he spent the rest of the war in prison, have given rise to much speculation, particularly (continued)

The importance Churchill attached to his relationship with Roosevelt, as the gravity of his position as prime minister of a beleaguered Britain became starkly apparent to him, meant he reverted to using the American embassy but also to keeping Lothian fully informed. Richard Casey, the Australian minister in Washington once that country established its own legation in March 1940, confided to his diary in mid-June that Lothian shared with him "the cables that are passing direct (or through Lothian, or through Kennedy) between Winston and the President." The Australian added: "These are clearly dictated by Winston himself as they are in his unmistakeable style— and are very good."[72] Reynolds adroitly explains the importance of the clash between Churchill and Lothian over correspondence with the president, stating: "The significance of the controversy was that the correspondence threatened to undermine Lothian's position as trusted intermediary between London and Washington."[73] Lothian's key role in Anglo-American relations depended upon his access to transatlantic communications. "Information is influence," Reynolds continues, "and Lothian fought tenaciously and successfully to maintain his status as the major channel between the two leaders." This instance illustrates clearly what Lothian had been positioning himself for since his arrival: to become the pre-eminent conduit in transatlantic relations.

THE DESTROYERS-BASES DEAL: THE ACME OF LOTHIAN'S AMBASSADORSHIP?

The transfer of fifty aged American destroyers to the United Kingdom at the same time as ninety-nine year leases for bases in British possessions in the Western Hemisphere were granted to Washington was by any measure a remarkable international agreement. Given the relative positions of the

---

amongst those who argue that there was some arrangement between the president and the new prime minister over American involvement in the war. For further information, see Warren F. Kimball and Bruce Bartlett, "Roosevelt and Prewar Commitments to Churchill: The Tyler Kent Affair," *Diplomatic History* 5:4 (Fall 1981), 291-312.

[72] Diary entry, 15 June 1940, GD 40/17/517 Diary of Richard Casey, Lothian Papers. Carl Bridge has done considerable work on Casey's time in Washington, and recently published Carl Bridge, ed., *A Delicate Mission: The Washington Diaries of R. G. Casey, 1940-1942* (Canberra: Australian National Library, 2008). See also Bridge, "Casey and the Americans: Australian War Propaganda in the United States 1940-1941," *Working Papers in Australian Studies,* Working Paper 30 (London: Australian Studies Centre, Institute of Commonwealth Studies, 1988), 1-17. Other sources include Christopher Water, "Casey: Four Decades in the Making of Australian Foreign Policy," *Australian Journal of Politics and History* 51:3 (September 2005), 380-388.

[73] Reynolds, *Lord Lothian,* 17.

two nations, with the United States still neutral and Great Britain a warring country standing alone, it was all the more notable. Lothian was prominent in bringing this deal to conclusion and vital to the diplomatic correspondence that facilitated the agreement between Washington and London. Though the negotiations were testing, with the British embassy's legal adviser John Foster taking a prominent part, they were in turn facilitated by the groundwork Lothian had laid with both the administration and the American public during the previous months of his ambassadorship.

The ambassador approached the prospect of transferring bases to Washington with his Atlanticist views in mind. If British and American sovereignty were conjoined in defending territory in the Western Hemisphere, this would signal the close alignment of interests between the two nations. To bring this about, Lothian recommended, beginning in "the latter half of May 1940," that the United Kingdom "should spontaneously offer the United States facilities for defence in British West Indian Islands."[74] Just a week before the final agreement was reached, Lothian was arguing "that there should not be cold commercial bargaining but a friendly sentimental interest between the two Governments, which would offer a basis for gifts back and forth, but which would be voluntary and apparently without definite understanding in advance."[75] Those in London, however, saw things differently. From early summer many in Whitehall were more concerned with what tangible benefits could be obtained from the United States. In conversation with Sir John Balfour of the Foreign Office, Churchill voiced this sentiment, explaining: "It doesn't do to give way like this to the Americans. One must strike a balance with them" before intimating that "you are ready to meet reasonable requests from them." This would have the important ancillary effect of proving "you are alive and in fighting form."[76] Lothian was prepared to overlook this last element, favoring instead the potential benefits of Anglo-American understanding.

That he was nonetheless able to reconcile London's desire for tangible reward with Washington's approach, governed as it was by considerations of American opinion, facilitated this remarkable agreement, a reflection of Lothian's skill and dedication as ambassador. In an interview

---

[74] Draft, "The Bases for Destroyers Negotiations," Papers of Sir John Balfour, FO 800/433, TNA.
[75] Memorandum of conversation between Hull, Roosevelt, and Lothian, 25 August 1940, Hull Papers.
[76] Draft, "The Bases for Destroyers Negotiations," Balfour MSS, FO 800/433.

for the *Washington Merry-Go-Round* in mid-July, he explained to Drew Pearson that the "resolution of our people is very high," before outlining the twin elements underpinning the eventual deal. Lothian said of Britain's West Indian possessions that "she would make some arrangement with the United States regarding them if there was danger of their falling into enemy hands," while adding that it is "far easier to defend the United States and Canada by controlling the mouth of the Straits of Gibraltar, the English Channel, and Cape Town." "If these exits are held by a hostile force," Lothian warned, "they can raid you anywhere."[77] This pronouncement, following his Yale speech the previous month, effectively set out once again the British situation and its implications for the American people. While any attempt to manipulate reaction to these broadcasts might be counterproductive, their overall impact was to give Britain's position greater prominence.

Yet the craft that Lothian applied earlier in his ambassadorship can be questioned when one investigates the finer points of these delicate diplomatic negotiations. The initial British request had included appeals for twenty torpedo boats, Flying Fortress bombers, flying boats, and 250,000 rifles, requirements that were overlooked in the final agreement on the deal. In explaining this omission, it is vital to appreciate that Lothian was keen to conclude the transfer primarily for its symbolic benefit, rather than for any tangible payback it might bring. Responsibility for the exclusion of these items can also be laid at the Roosevelt administration's door, given the president's capacity for opaqueness in addressing detail, compounded by the switch in mid-August from Welles to Hull as the chief American point of contact in negotiations, when the secretary of state returned to Washington.

In assessing Lothian and the Destroyers-Bases Deal of 2 September 1940 it is vital to recognize the anxiety, brought on by the prospect of British defeat in the summer of 1940, that enshrouded his thinking. Lothian's desperation was caused, not simply by the possibility of a German invasion of Britain but by his fear that any such event would jeopardize his Atlanticist conception of the world. This makes it possible to explain, if not to excuse, his neglect of the details.[78] That the Destroyers-

---

[77] Transcript of interview by Pearson with Lothian, 22 July 1940, GD40/17/406/81, Lothian Papers.

[78] It is in this light that one can reach some resolution of the debate between historians David Reynolds and Rhodri Jeffreys-Jones. Reynolds suggests: "Although somewhat careless in finalising the diplomatic negotiations, Lothian played an invaluable part during August in helping 'sell' the deal to the American public." Reynolds, *Lord Lothian*, 31. Jeffreys-Jones, (continued)

Bases Deal was successfully presented to the American people as assisting hemispheric defense, with Roosevelt's message to Congress terming it an "epochal and far-reaching act of preparation for continental defense in the face of grave danger," over and above the practical value of the destroyers (which would take varying degrees of time to be serviceable), is one of its most noteworthy features.[79] Lothian deserved considerable credit for both this approach and for the entire conclusion of this agreement, since his ambassadorship had created an amenable environment in which such sensitive diplomatic discussions could take place, while also stimulating debate among the American people. Most importantly for Lothian, at this critical time for Britain, the Destroyers-Bases deal symbolized the increasing alignment of British and American interests.

THE FINAL ACT: LOTHIAN'S MOMENTUM FOR LEND LEASE

In the weeks before his death, Lothian sought once more to bring Britain's plight before the American people and the Roosevelt administration. In the fall of 1940 the ambassador's focus was Britain's financial extremis, and it was on this issue that the legacy of Lothian's ambassadorship was felt most keenly. Yet this was another area where Lothian would need to balance the challenges of revealing London's predicament, while eliciting assistance from the administration and presenting a link between Britain's situation and the American public. "Lothian's appreciation of the techniques of publicity and the importance of information," Reynolds writes, "were to be displayed most outstandingly in his handling of Britain's dollar crisis in the final month of his life."[80]

Beginning in the summer of 1940, with the Battle of Britain still raging and the Destroyers-Bases deal far from being finalized, Lothian was charged with presenting to the administration an account of the British position. On 5 July he met with Secretary Hull to discuss a British *aide*

---

however, argues that while Lothian, through his Yale speech and by his raising of the British profile, was certainly important in making the American public aware of the straits facing the United Kingdom, one must recognize that many other individuals played a role in this, so that: "The vitally important Destroyers-Bases deal cannot be said to have been chiefly Lothian's work, even if he did contribute to it." Jeffreys-Jones, "The Inestimable Advantage of Not Being English," 419.

[79] Roosevelt, message to the Congress informing them of the exchange of certain over-age destroyers for British naval and air bases, 3 September 1940, *Congressional Record*, 3 September 1940.

[80] Reynolds, *Lord Lothian*, 34.

mémoire on this subject. Its forecast was gloomy. Having addressed the urgent requirement for war materials, the document went on:

> So long as gold and other foreign assets at their disposal permit, His Majesty's Government will of course continue to pay cash for essential armaments, raw materials and food stuffs. They feel however that they should in all frankness inform the United States Government that it will be utterly impossible for them to continue to do this for any indefinite period in view of the scale on which they will need to obtain such resources from the United States.[81]

This assessment put Britain's financial status firmly on the U.S. agenda. While the prospect of invasion existed the issue was subsumed, but once the worst of that danger had passed, Lothian took up this cause. When he returned to the United Kingdom, he took the opportunity to probe officials in London for more information he could use to outline the British case. Much to his frustration, he found policymakers in London in a state of abeyance, awaiting the outcome of the presidential election on 5 November and fixated on the details of the shipping crisis. While Lothian's counsel on how to handle the Americans was much in evidence once he returned to Washington, at the time his interlocutors in London saw the outcome of the election as pivotal, not merely just another opportunity for Roosevelt to maneuver the United States into assisting Britain. Lothian therefore began his return journey to Washington shortly after Roosevelt's electoral victory somewhat disappointed, and with no indication, moreover, of the discernible change in the administration's attitude those he left behind in Britain had anticipated.

Upon docking in New York Lothian made some remarks to the assembled pressmen, which when reported caused a considerable storm, sending shock waves through transatlantic relations. The press reported Lothian as saying: "Well boys, Britain's broke; it's your money we want." Some debate exists as to whether these represented Lothian's exact words or were rather creative reporting of what he said, but the ramifications of these news stories were clear. Initial reaction in the American press, which ran the story en masse, was shock at this candid admission. Nor was the Roosevelt administration impressed. Treasury Secretary Henry Morgenthau, Jr., told Canadian Prime Minister Mackenzie King that, since Lothian's "remark about British financial resources being well nigh

---

[81] Memorandum of conversation between Hull and Lothian, 5 July 1940, Hull Papers.

exhausted, he ... had had a very difficult time dealing with the situation."[82] Perhaps the most fervently upset were British officials back in London, since Lothian had "stepped out" so far in front of Whitehall in disclosing such a sensitive opinion. Churchill himself chided Lothian in a telegram, yet it seems clear that, in his desire to initiate debate over British finances, Lothian was taking a calculated risk with the American public and the Roosevelt administration. Casey, who spoke to Lothian on an almost daily basis, recorded a week after his disclosure that the ambassador had been "mildly reproved by FO, for having spoken publicly about financial needs on arrival in NY." Casey went on to suggest that the overall outcome might well be beneficial, since the issue was now being discussed: "So that Lothian's 'gaffe' may well be a blessing in disguise."[83] Reynolds agrees, stating: "Roosevelt was beginning to face up to this problem, but Lothian's remarks, or rather the press reports of them, sparked off a major press and political debate which obliged him to act."[84]

Lothian's counsel to Churchill to disclose to the president further details of Britain's predicament, which the prime minister followed in a letter on 8 December, was integral to building momentum toward the Lend-Lease legislation of March 1941. Like Lothian's Yale speech in mid-June, therefore, the reports of Britain's financial plight illustrated the risk in inducing discussion amongst the American public for fear that they would question whether Britain was in any position to be helped effectively. These questions clearly pervaded administration thinking during the summer, as assurances were sought over the future of the British fleet, and continued later in the year as American officials contemplated whether the United Kingdom would be able to keep on fighting. While Lothian's comments on both occasions were rather blunt instruments, he used them fully cognizant of their impact. Given his previous posture, many in London and elsewhere appreciated this. Mackenzie King, Canada's prime minister, considered Lothian's New York press statement "indiscreet" only "in the manner in which it was expressed."[85]

---

[82] Diary entry, 5 December 1940, Diary of William Lyon Mackenzie King.
[83] Diary entry, 30 November 1940, GD 40/17/517 Diary of Richard Casey, Lothian Papers.
[84] Reynolds, *Lord Lothian*, 56.
[85] Diary entry, 12 December 1940, Diary of William Lyon Mackenzie King.

THE AMBASSADORSHIP OF LORD LOTHIAN: AN EVALUATION

When Lothian arrived as ambassador in Washington the United Kingdom was embarking upon a war against Nazi Germany that would stretch every sinew of its national assets. In securing ultimate victory some six years later Great Britain would find itself allied to the United States in a Grand Alliance that bore hope for a new world order founded on mutual transatlantic understanding. By the time such a peace emerged, Lothian would have been dead for over four years, but he was definitely conscious of the gravity of his times. In the fall of 1940 he told a correspondent: "In many ways we are living in the greatest period in human history, when the choice lies before us between a disastrous regression and a great new advance."[86] These words reflect that it was with such weighty dilemmas that Lothian, a man not given to melodrama, grappled throughout his life and during the course of his appointment as ambassador to Washington.

As ambassador, Lothian was a crucial conduit in Anglo-American relations. To this task he brought a conviction in Atlanticism, believing it his duty to pursue understanding in transatlantic relations based on mutual recognition of shared national interests. In Reynolds' view, Lothian "appealed to America's interests rather than to sentiment" in outlining common cause.[87] Given Britain's perilous predicament during the summer of 1940 the role of Lothian, together with others, in conceiving and implementing measures that were vital to British security, in the form of the Destroyers-Bases deal and the Lend-Lease program, should not be underestimated. That he was able to exert such influence as the preferred channel of communication reflected the groundwork he had put in during his opening months as ambassador. When doing so, Lothian presented himself as the public face of his Washington mission. While still wary of appearing—especially in contrast to his predecessor—to indulge in propaganda, Lothian described Britain's predicament without offering suggestions as to how American opinion should react, and became a trusted interface with the administration in promoting the understanding needed between the United States and the United Kingdom. Overall he succeeded with both the administration and the wider American populace. Before the conclusion of the Destroyers-Bases deal and with Britain's future in the balance, *Time* wrote: "Last week even professional Anglophobes," of whom Washington possessed a sizeable minority, "were compelled to admit that if the U. S. had not understood the British case—and its meaning

---

[86] Lothian to J. G. Latham, 9 October 1940, GD 40/17/402/234, Lothian Papers.
[87] Reynolds, *Lord Lothian*, 58.

to the U.S.—it had not been because Lord Lothian had fallen down as an Ambassador."[88] Besides undertaking this task in Washington, Lothian had to translate to a skeptical audience in London the value of understanding American opinion in order to achieve British ends. This twin endeavor represented the nub of the approach Lothian applied to his ambassadorship.

His task would not prove easy. At the beginning of November 1939 Sir Alexander Cadogan, perhaps the most skeptical of Lothian's Foreign Office critics, showed no greater appreciation of his ambassador than previously. After reading a Lothian despatch explaining American opinion in the aftermath of revision of the Neutrality Act, he characterized Lothian as a "phrase-monger" who had composed a "meaningless letter."[89] Crucially, however, as Greg Kennedy's chapter also demonstrates, over time the prevalent opinions of Lothian widely shared by Cadogan and others in the Foreign Office changed. When resolving the minor crisis, Cadogan's analysis concisely reflected Lothian's maxim: "[We] must certainly do all that we can to keep the United States govt informed. I hope the American dept will keep an eye out for anything that might be going on that may affect the United States, and inform Lord Lothian accordingly."[90] Under Lothian's direction, his outlook became the predominant view in London.

This chapter has focused self-consciously on Lothian and his ambassadorship. Despite the subsequent importance of practical issues, such as purchasing, which would be run through the embassy, during his time as ambassador Lothian, as Gavin Bailey's chapter also demonstrates, subordinated these to what he saw as his main objective, to foster closer ties between the English-speaking nations.[91] Here, the public proclamations

---

[88] "Lord Lothian's Job," *Time*, 8 July 1940, http://www.time.com/time/magazine/article/0,9171,772318,00.html, accessed 12 October 2007.

[89] Cadogan, *Diaries of Sir Alexander Cadogan*, 324.

[90] David Scott, the American Desk's departmental under secretary, wrote of the need to keep Lothian "more fully posted" as "regards explaining our policy to the United States Govt." Comments by Scott, 31 January 1940, and Cadogan, 1 February 1940, attached to Foreign Office minute by J. V. T. Perowne, 29 January 1940, A825/434/45 FO 371/24248.

[91] As ambassador, Lothian would operate at his own behest and be the public face of British representation. His alterations to the embassy in Washington were of marginal substance. He did increase the physical size of the grounds, purchasing an area of public park land below the rose gardens up to Massachusetts Avenue and donating it to the embassy. He also left two Chippendale mirrors in the embassy's drawing room. See the British Embassy website, http://www.britainusa.com/, accessed 10 October 2007. The embassy staff, including (continued)

made during his ambassadorship were key in stimulating support from the American people. Most importantly, Lothian had a firm grasp of American public opinion and its vagaries. He spoke decisively and with "increasing authority," but without rhetorical flair, meaning that American audiences received his utterances "much less critically than they usually do."[92] He himself described the American populace as watching events in Europe "with all the keenness and intimate knowledge of the personalities and the moves in the diplomatic game characteristic of spectators at a football match." Lothian was to provide the American people and the Roosevelt administration with expert commentary and analysis of the events of his time, while also offering his British audience scrutiny of the "crowd." In doing so he understood from the outset that the self-publicist role carried with it the risk of misinterpretation, and would no doubt have welcomed *Time*'s assessment in July 1940 that he had "not been criticized as a propagandist." Indeed, the only mild cavil that was expressed, "that he had spent too much time at the State Department," was one that would have been equally welcome to Lothian.[93]

The final words of this chapter were prepared by Lothian for a speech on 11 December 1940, delivered in his absence by John Butler, the embassy's counsel, because the ambassador was on his deathbed. Once again, he resorted to a bare statement of the British position and, in light of the debate over his remarks upon his return to the United States, or perhaps mindful of his own mortality, he professed a conundrum for the American people:

> I have endeavoured to give you some idea of our present position, of the dangers and problems of 1941, of our hopes for the future. It is for you to decide whether you share our hopes and what support you will give us in realising them. We are, I believe, doing all we can. Since May there is no challenge we have evaded, no challenge refused. If you back us you will not be backing a quitter. The issue now depends largely on what you decide to do. Nobody can share that responsibility with you. It is the great strength of democracy that it brings responsibility down squarely to every citizen and

---

Lothian, numbered just twenty-two at the beginning of 1940, including the commercial counselor and secretary, plus naval, military, and air attachés. Britain also had consuls in a number of prominent cities across the United States.

[92] Sir Godfrey Haggard, comments, GD 40/17/514 37, Lothian Papers.

[93] "Lord Lothian's Job," *Time*, 8 July 1940, http://www.time.com/time/magazine/article/0,9171,772318,00.html, accessed 12 October 2007.

every nation. And before the Judgement Seat of God each must answer for his own actions.[94]

Lothian passed away during the night of 11-12 December, 1940.[95]

---

[94] Lothian, speech to be delivered at the American Farm Bureau Association dinner, Lord Baltimore Hotel, Baltimore, MD, 11 December 1940, GD40/17/398/541, Lothian Papers.

[95] Mackenzie King was given a copy of Lothian's address, which he lauded in his diary, stating: "It is the best thing I have read on the war—a model in every particular; comprehensive, concise, sound of real historical and spiritual worth. A true analysis of causes, of conditions and objectives. The speech of a real scholar; a brave man and a true Christian. It seemed to sum up his life's work in an inspired fashion." Diary entry, 21 December 1940, Diary of William Lyon Mackenzie King.

CHAPTER SIX

CREATING A SENSE OF CRITICALITY:

'LOTHIAN'S METHOD' AND THE EVOLUTION OF U.S. WARTIME AID TO BRITAIN

GAVIN BAILEY

A British wartime ambassador to a neutral Washington once characterized his role in the following terms: "[I]t would be necessary to act on three main fronts: the Administration, the Congress and the media. . ."[1] Although the ambassador in question was Sir Nicholas Henderson, and the war at hand was the 1982 Falklands Conflict, this encapsulates much of Lord Lothian's role in similar circumstances in 1940. Indeed, when it came to shaping opinion within the administration, legislature, and media, Lothian pioneered the concept of a British ambassador bridging the gaps between these audiences and Whitehall. Lothian's success in this was acknowledged by his successor, Lord Halifax, when he contemplated the difficulties of following "Philip Lothian's method" of handling "tedious senators and inquisitive pressmen."[2] Lothian himself had no doubt about the decisive factor behind Henderson's three fronts; as he put it, "what ultimately counts here is public opinion."[3]

Arriving in Washington on the outbreak of war in September 1939, Lothian had to contend with the hostile influence of American public opinion toward the evolution of a closer Anglo-American relationship. The policy of U.S. neutrality was based on deep-seated popular values of American exceptionalism, isolationism, anti-colonialism, and Anglophobia. It had been reinforced by the rejection of the ambitions of Wilsonian internationalism immediately after the First World War. The constraints public opinion placed on the help that Franklin D. Roosevelt's

---

[1] Sir Nicholas Henderson, "The Washington Embassy: Navigating the Waters of the Potomac," *Diplomacy and Statecraft* 1:1 (March 1990), 45.
[2] Conversation between Halifax and Leo Amery, 18 December 1940, in *The Empire at Bay: The Leo Amery Diaries 1929-1945*, eds. John Barnes and David Nicholson (London: Hutchinson, 1988), 669.
[3] J. R. M. Butler, *Lord Lothian (Philip Kerr) 1882-1940* (London: Macmillan, 1960), 270.

P. Roberts (ed.), Lord Lothian and Anglo-American Relations, 1900-1940, 167-199.
© *2010 Republic of Letters Publishing. All rights reserved.*

administration could provide to the Allies had been made clear to Lothian, notably by the U.S. under secretary of state, Sumner Welles, and by the president himself.[4] In his official and private correspondence, Lothian accurately reported the administration's inability to enter the war until the Axis powers directly threatened American interests, and admitted the limited nature of the supplies available to aid the Allies.[5]

"Lothian's method" shaped American public opinion by using the informal, journalistic style of his personal diplomacy to engender a sense of critical involvement in British fortunes amongst his American audiences. Central to Lothian's strategy to involve his American audience was a thesis of criticality expressed through the diplomacy involved in securing military supplies from the United States. This thesis of criticality operated in two directions; firstly, it asserted the vital importance of Britain to American interests in a manner that transcended the constraints of isolationism which had hindered attempts to develop a closer Anglo-American strategic relationship before the outbreak of war. Secondly, it exaggerated the importance that the contribution of immediate American supply aid could make to continuing British resistance. Lothian defined this thesis when recommending the best approach for eliciting American support after the evacuation of the British Expeditionary Force from Dunkirk in early June 1940:

> The only effective argument is that we are fighting for civilisation with our backs to the wall, that if we go, future prospects of democracy will be very poor and that any assistance we can get immediately may make the difference between success and failure.[6]

The impact of his approach was clearly effective on the U.S. public, its primary target. As the American press observed after his early death in December 1940: "We cannot recall that an ambassador from a great power

---

[4] "Commitment to action was one thing the administration could not undertake unless public opinion was ready to support it." Lothian to Foreign Office, Telegram No. 506, 16 September 1939, ADM 116/4103, The National Archives of the United Kingdom (TNA), Kew, London. In conversation with Lothian, Roosevelt defined the limitations upon his action as being the legal restrictions of the Neutrality Act and public opinion. Lothian to Foreign Office, Telegram No. 718, 13 May 1940, F[oreign] O[ffice] 371/24192, TNA, Kew, London.

[5] Lothian to Foreign Office, Telegram No. 718, 13 May 1940, FO 371/24192; Lothian to J. M. MacDonnell, 8 May 1940, GD 40/17/402/477, Papers of the Eleventh Marquess of Lothian [hereafter Lothian Papers], The National Archives of Scotland, Edinburgh.

[6] Lothian to Churchill, Telegram No. 931, 8 June 1940, FO 371/24239.

has ever before addressed the American people directly, saying in effect, 'If you help us we shall win; if not we shall lose.'"[7]

Lothian's characterization of the critical importance of American supply aid to Britain operated in consonance with the primary British strategic desire for an American alliance after the catastrophic events of 1940 that culminated in the fall of France that June. It also reflected the rhetoric British Prime Minister Winston Churchill used in his public statements and correspondence with Roosevelt. This can, however, obscure the fact that the representation of criticality was a tactic which exaggerated the value of the immediately available American military supplies for larger diplomatic purposes.

The thesis of criticality which Lothian used was born of a pre-war strategic appreciation drawn up by one of his influential contacts in Whitehall long before the crisis caused by the German victories of 1940. This appreciation was designed to help overcome political and legislative obstacles to the development of a closer strategic alliance between the United States and Britain by defining a strategic relationship between the two countries that would appeal to the American public's perception of their own national interests. This allowed the supply measures involved in Lothian's diplomacy to become stepping-stones toward achievement of the larger objective of full Anglo-American strategic collaboration, which was the primary goal of British statecraft.

Understanding the significance of Lothian's influence on supply diplomacy demands an appreciation of the distinction involved between the military value of the 1940 supply measures and their diplomatic importance in shaping American public opinion. This in turn requires a detailed exploration of the specific supply measures involved, such as the destroyers-bases deal and the supply of American fighter aircraft, and Lothian's role in their development. This analysis will reveal the existence of an expectational gap between the rhetoric employed to secure those supply measures, and their military value as this was understood by contemporaries at the time. Examination of this expectational gap reveals how it was created by rhetoric designed to secure larger diplomatic objectives that went beyond military aid, and how it was then managed in order to avoid prejudicing those objectives. This process illustrates the extent to which diplomatic strategy, as defined by Lothian's method, informed procurement diplomacy.

---

[7] Butler, *Lord Lothian*, 315.

The success of Lothian's method in engaging his American audience with the thesis of criticality involved in the 1940 supply measures established the tone and character of the ensuing Anglo-American wartime relationship and much of its subsequent historiography.[8] A re-examination of the role of Lothian's method in British supply diplomacy with the United States therefore has great significance to the understanding of the evolution of the Anglo-American strategic relationship.

Lothian's method was well-established before he assumed his appointment in Washington in September 1939. Andrew Roberts has characterized him as having "non-parliamentary political influence of a type seldom seen in today's politics," on the basis of how Lothian acted as an intermediary to float Foreign Office positions in *The Times* during the Munich crisis of 1938.[9] The foreign secretary, Lord Halifax, and the editor of *The Times*, Geoffrey Dawson, were old friends of Lothian's who had listed Lothian as their top choice for the job of ambassador to Washington to the Foreign Office in July 1938.[10] Lothian's early attempts to expand his circle of acquaintances beyond this pre-war establishment elite may have occasionally attracted scorn thanks to his social class, but there can be no doubt of his position within it, or that he had established the fundamentals of his informal method of communicating the views of this elite to the press well before he became an ambassador.[11]

When it came to communicating the message of these politicians and officials, Lothian was more than a simple mouthpiece. His personal diplomacy involved shaping the message that he communicated to his audience, much like a journalist writing an editorial. As his biographer observed: "He wrote articles rather than books, and their purpose was to

---

[8] David Reynolds, "Lothian, Roosevelt, Churchill and the Origins of Lend-Lease," in *The Larger Idea: Lord Lothian and the Problem of National Sovereignty*, ed. John Turner (London: Historians Press, 1988), 94; Alan P. Dobson, *US Wartime Aid to Britain, 1940-1946* (London: Croom, Helm, 1986), 2; Randall Bennett Woods, *A Changing of the Guard: Anglo-American Relations, 1941-1946* (Chapel Hill: University of North Carolina Press, 1990), 7-10; and Christopher Thorne, *Allies of a Kind: The United States, Britain, and the War Against Japan, 1941-1945* (Oxford: Oxford University Press, 1979), 279-280.

[9] Andrew Roberts, *"The Holy Fox": The Life of Lord Halifax* (London: Weidenfeld and Nicolson, 1991), 109.

[10] Alexander Cadogan, *The Diaries of Sir Alexander Cadogan O.M. 1938-1945*, ed. David Dilks (London: Cassell, 1971), 90.

[11] "Philip Kerr has left and gone on a tour to the North Country to make his first acquaintance with 'the lower orders.'" Thomas Jones to Bonar Law, 19 May 1921, in Thomas Jones, *Whitehall Diary*, Vol. I: *1916-1925*, ed. Keith Middlemas (Oxford: Oxford University Press, 1969), 158.

present in clear language a summary of facts and considerations leading up to a conclusion."[12]

Lothian's experience as a journalist was oriented toward shaping opinion. Before the First World War, as a member of Lord Milner's 'Kindergarten' in South Africa Kerr briefly edited a pro-imperialist journal, *The State*, and then became founding editor of *The Round Table*, established by the Round Table group (several of whose members were, like Lothian himself, key figures in the subsequent establishment of the Royal Institute for International Affairs) to bolster and strengthen the British Empire. As Prime Minister David Lloyd George's private secretary during and after the First World War, Lothian put much effort into handling the press. In the early 1920s he had a short stint as editor of *The Daily Chronicle* newspaper, and thereafter was a frequent author of articles and letters, pamphleteering for his favored causes in *The Round Table* and other influential journals and newspapers. Lothian absorbed some of the skills of a journalist and editor, and described one particular tactic of his professional experience which was to become one of the prominent features of his method as ambassador: "It is impossible in a paper the size of *The Chronicle* to discuss political questions. The utmost that can be done is a short leaderette with a snap to it."[13] The operation of Lothian's leading analysis within a populist, journalistic approach in 1940 was probably best observed by Harold Nicolson, who commented on the "consummate ease" with which Lothian managed a press conference in October 1940, and the strategic message he got across in the process: "[The] US came to understand that our interests and the strategic points of the Commonwealth were essential to themselves. It was a fine talk and it went well. Our press were delighted."[14]

Ironically, Lothian's reputation as an amateur diplomatist, originally gained during the period spent as David Lloyd George's private secretary and member of his 'Garden Suburb', had initially prompted Foreign Office doubts over his suitability as ambassador.[15] Lothian's proficiency with the press, his reputation as an idealistic and meddling

---

[12] Butler, *Lord Lothian*, 240.

[13] Jones, diary entry, 23 November 1921, *Whitehall Diary*, 1:180.

[14] Nicolson, diary entry, 22 October 1940, in *Harold Nicolson: Diaries and Letters 1939-1945*, ed. Nigel Nicolson (London: Collins, 1967), 122.

[15] Alan J. Sharp, "The Foreign Office in Eclipse 1919-22," *History* 61:202 (June 1976), 206; and John Turner and Michael Dockrill, "Philip Kerr at 10 Downing Street, 1916-1921," in *The Larger Idea: Lord Lothian and the Problem of National Sovereignty*, ed. John Turner (London: Historians Press, 1988), 55-56.

amateur from his period with Lloyd George, and his subsequent interventions in diplomatic issues in person and through the press during the 1930s—some of which are described in Greg Kennedy's chapter earlier in this volume—left suspicions amongst some of the Whitehall elite. Alexander Cadogan, the Permanent Secretary at the Foreign Office, dismissed Lothian as "a phrasemonger" on those grounds.[16] Lothian was aware of these reservations, but he did not fundamentally modify his style in consequence. Instead he turned his propensity for making selectively indiscreet comments to the press from a vice into a virtue.

His early speeches as ambassador aroused Foreign Office concern by touching upon sensitive issues such as democratic control of the seas, and hinting at a need for future international organization and European federalism. In March 1940 he acknowledged to Halifax that his speeches were "somewhat indiscreet," but argued they were nonetheless successful "precisely because I have felt that I knew the American mind well enough to be quite frank and to deal frankly with controversial issues."[17]

Lothian's "indiscreet" comments on controversial issues, calculated to exceed his brief from Whitehall in order to achieve a greater impact on the American public mind, would come to the fore in the evolution of Lend-Lease later in 1940. There can be little doubt, however, that his earlier statements indicate that his adoption of them as a diplomatic tactic was deliberate and was to be understood as such in the Foreign Office. Calculated indiscretion was therefore one aspect of Lothian's method; facilitating discreet and even secret contact between influential individuals behind the scenes to achieve diplomatic ends was another. This was clearly evident in his encouragement of the exchange of scientific information with the United States.

In June 1940 Lothian provided the impetus behind the exchange of British scientific information with the United States, propelling the Cabinet toward agreement over Churchill's initial resistance. He was originally contacted by A. V. Hill, a scientific advisor to the British embassy in Washington, who passed on a query from Frank Aydelotte, director of the Institute of Advanced Studies at Princeton University, regarding the sharing of cutting-edge military scientific information such as radar direction used

---

[16] Cadogan, diary entry, 27 November 1939, *Diaries of Sir Alexander Cadogan*, 234.

[17] Lothian to Halifax, 11 March 1940, Winston S. Churchill Papers [hereafter Churchill Papers], CHAR 20/15, Churchill College Archives Centre. The criticism refers to Lothian's speech to the Chicago Council of Foreign Relations, 4 January 1940, in Royal Institute of International Affairs, *The American Speeches of Lord Lothian: July 1939 to December 1940* (London: Oxford University Press, 1941), 47-63.

for anti-aircraft guns. It is perhaps significant that Aydelotte was also American secretary to the Rhodes Trust, of which Lothian had served as the secretary between 1925 and 1939.[18] When arguing in favor of the proposal to the War Cabinet, Lothian's old colleague Maurice Hankey was astutely able to perceive Lothian's objective beyond the military and technical considerations ostensibly involved:

> What one wants to do is to get as many people as possible in the U.S.A. favourable to our cause, especially in the influential strata of society. Both the scientists and the military authorities fall into that category in present circumstances.[19]

Lothian went further. He urged the acceptance of the small numbers of individual American idealists and adventurers who wanted to enlist in the British forces. He even advocated the removal of the oath of attestation to the British monarch made during enlistment to the British Commonwealth armed forces, which might prejudice the U.S. citizenship of such volunteers. When the War Office expressed no interest in such individuals for supplementing British military manpower, Lothian was quick to focus on their diplomatic significance, stating: "I think the proposal should be encouraged for political reasons as every American who joins the British forces becomes a propagandist."[20]

While Lothian publicly rejected engaging in propaganda himself, it is clear that his method involved facilitating pro-British propaganda to influence U.S. public opinion from diverse American sources. These went beyond Hankey's appreciation of "the influential strata of society" and Lothian's innovation in requesting that a press attaché be added to the Washington embassy staff.[21] The over-riding of the War Office's disinterest in the militarily insignificant number of American volunteers for the British forces indicates how policy could be modified at Lothian's behest to take into account larger diplomatic objectives beyond the immediate scope of the measures concerned. This applied to the strategic "generosity" involved in the exchange of secret technical information that Lothian encouraged, where the British had less to gain than did the U.S. services from such British advances as the cavity magnetron used in radar development. It also applied to the public relations benefits to be gained by accepting the enlistment of ordinary American individuals in the British armed forces.

---

[18] Ronald W. Clark, *Tizard* (London: Methuen, 1965), 249-255.
[19] Hankey, memorandum, 23 July 1940, FO 371/24256.
[20] Lothian to Foreign Office, Telegram No. 1092, 23 June 1940, FO 371/24256.
[21] Butler, *Lord Lothian*, 257.

This was an example of a response by Lothian to opportunities which arose in the summer of 1940. But his use of personal contacts to further diplomatic ends was exercised in a far more systematic manner in the origin of the thesis of criticality which he preached. This sprang from a strategic appreciation which was to provide the framework for his approach as ambassador and in consequence dominate Anglo-American supply diplomacy.

Lothian prepared for his ambassadorship in 1938 by contacting Hankey, the recently retired chairman of the Committee of Imperial Defence, and asking for a strategic appreciation of the effect on the United States of a collapse of the British Empire.[22] Lothian had been a close contemporary of Hankey's since his days as Lloyd George's private secretary, when Hankey had run the Cabinet Office and War Cabinet secretariat.[23] Hankey had remained at the epicenter of Whitehall's strategic and defense bureaucracy until his retirement in July 1938.[24] Hankey's memorandum was specifically designed to be used to influence American audiences, leaving Lothian "adequately armed to talk to some of my American friends."[25] The Hankey memorandum provided Lothian with the rationale of 'criticality' to demonstrate the strategic value of Britain to the United States, and it did so in terms of critical outcomes that transcended the traditional ideological and Anglophobic suspicions that informed American isolationism. This was an argument for American entanglement with Britain sold on the basis of pulling American—not British—chestnuts out of the fire.

But if Hankey demonstrated the 'criticality' of Britain to the United States by raising the specter of a British defeat by the fascist powers, encouraging American support to avoid that defeat required the identification of specific measures which could be demonstrated as 'critical' to the U.S. public. In January 1940, after a dispute with the U.S. authorities over neutral shipping rights through the British naval blockade of Germany, Lothian identified the material required: "The United States will stand anything that we can prove to be really necessary for winning the war, but in future we shall have to prove it."[26] The supply of such 'proof' in

---

[22] Typescript copy of Hankey's memorandum, "The Value of the British Empire to the United States," 16 December 1938, GD 40/17/444, Lothian Papers; see also Stephen Roskill, *Hankey: Man of Secrets*, Vol. III: *1931-1963* (London: Collins, 1974), 371.

[23] Peter Rowland, *Lloyd George* (London: Barrie and Jenkins, 1975), 418.

[24] Lord Ismay, *The Memoirs of General the Lord Ismay* (London: Heinemann, 1960), 89.

[25] Lothian to Hankey, 12 December 1938, GD 40/17/372/344, Lothian Papers.

[26] Lothian to Colonel Charles Kerr, 29 January 1940, GD 40/17/402, Lothian Papers.

the form of naval, military, scientific and even financial information to meet American requirements became a feature of Lothian's advice to Whitehall for the rest of that year.

Lothian's initial period as ambassador from his arrival in the United States in August 1939 until the following spring followed the familiar pattern for a wartime British diplomat resident in Washington. The issues that arose, such as neutral trading rights against the enforcement of a British naval blockade, might just as well have come up in 1914 or even 1812. The crucial period in Lothian's career when he departed from this conventional template followed the trajectory of crisis that culminated in the fall of France in May-June 1940. This period of crisis provided the fullest scope for Lothian's pre-existing conceptions of 'criticality' and 'proof' to dominate Anglo-American diplomacy.

The sense of criticality evident in British supply diplomacy with the United States is usually assumed to have been derived directly from the strategic requirements of the desperate situation the British found themselves in during this period. When considering the course of future strategy after the anticipated fall of France in May 1940, the British Chiefs of Staff made it clear that they were counting upon "the full economic and financial support" of the United States, and listed measures such as the supply of American destroyers and fighter aircraft as necessary for defending Britain in the critical next few months.[27] Thus 'criticality' had been explicitly associated with American supply by the British military planners, and diplomatic policy could be expected to conform to this appreciation. But this is not the whole story. Full economic and financial support was not forthcoming from the United States until Lend-Lease was enacted in 1941, while the American ability to fulfil the critical military needs identified—such as fighter aircraft and destroyers—was to prove limited, as Lothian already knew.

The conventional understanding of British efforts to secure aid from the United States in this period follows the lead established by Churchill's own account, which places his secret correspondence with Roosevelt at the heart of Anglo-American supply diplomacy.[28] Roosevelt had initiated this correspondence after Churchill returned to office as the First Lord of the Admiralty in September 1939, and it burgeoned after

---

[27] "British Strategy in a Certain Eventuality," WP (40) 168/CoS (40) 390, CAB 66/7.

[28] Joseph P. Lash, *Roosevelt and Churchill 1939-1941: The Partnership That Saved the West* (New York: Norton, 1976). Reynolds challenges this, in the process emphasizing Lothian's role in 1940. David Reynolds, *In Command of History: Churchill Fighting and Writing the Second World War* (New York: Random House, 2005), 199-203.

Churchill replaced Neville Chamberlain as prime minister in May 1940.[29] At that point it became a central feature of British supply diplomacy, containing numerous appeals for munitions and supplies to bolster the Allied war effort as France collapsed under German attack.[30] Lothian was initially placed outside the loop on this channel of communication, but successfully gained access to it in January 1940, and was subsequently used by Churchill to deliver select messages in July, thus obtaining admittance to Roosevelt.[31] Lothian then influenced the content and timing of these telegrams, and did so according to his pre-existing strategy of asserting 'criticality' through the media and supplying 'proof' of British needs.

This pattern can be clearly seen in the evolution of the Destroyers-Bases deal between May and August 1940. The supply of destroyers was central to Allied supply requests from the United States. These dated from the first appeal made by Churchill as prime minister to Roosevelt on 15 May 1940, when he asked for "forty or fifty of your older destroyers to bridge the gap between what we have now and the large new construction we have put in hand at the beginning of the war."[32] At this point destroyers held in storage since the end of the First World War were being reconditioned by the U.S. Navy for service in patrolling the Neutrality Zone announced at the Panama conference in October 1939.[33] These destroyers appeared to have the potential to supplement Allied naval power at a time when the Italians, with a navy equivalent in size to the French, threatened to enter the war against the Allies. Roosevelt's initial response ruled out the supply of the destroyers on the grounds that it would have required the approval of an isolationist-dominated Congress.[34] Churchill repeatedly returned to the issue in June following considerable destroyer losses during

---

[29] Winston S. Churchill, *The Second World War*, Vol. I: *The Gathering Storm* (London: Cassell, 1948), 345.

[30] Winston S. Churchill, *The Second World War*, Vol. II: *Their Finest Hour* (London: Cassell, 1949), 21-24; and Warren F. Kimball, ed., *Churchill and Roosevelt: The Complete Correspondence*, Vol. I: *Alliance Emerging, October 1933-November 1942* (Princeton, NJ: Princeton University Press, 1984).

[31] David Reynolds, *The Creation of the Anglo-American Alliance, 1937-41: A Study in Competitive Co-operation* (Chapel Hill: University of North Carolina Press, 1982), 87; and note from John Peck, Churchill's Private Secretary, 3 July 1940, in response to Lothian's requests in telegrams 994, 14 June 1940, and 1110, 24 June 1940, FO 371/24192.

[32] Churchill to Roosevelt, C-9x, 15 May 1940, Kimball, ed., *Complete Correspondence*, 1:37.

[33] Wayne S. Cole, *Roosevelt and the Isolationists, 1932-45* (Lincoln: University of Nebraska Press, 1983), 361.

[34] Roosevelt to Churchill, R-4x, 16 May 1940, Kimball, ed., *Complete Correspondence*, 1:38.

the Dunkirk evacuation and after Italy's entry into the war confirmed the fears outlined in May.[35]

The supply of destroyers fitted within the strategic context that Lothian had already selected to legitimize British power to American perspectives. In March 1940 he had expounded his theory of "democratic control of the seas" to Halifax.[36] This was a straightforward interpretation of Mahanist naval strategy that advocated Anglo-American naval collaboration to secure American defense. Speaking to Roosevelt on 17 May, Lothian threatened the keystone of Mahanist naval strategy by raising the specter of the loss of the Royal Navy in the Atlantic.[37] This was characterized by the Foreign Office as justifiable "blackmail," but linked the fate of the British fleet—and continuing British resistance—to the supply of the destroyers. Lothian went on to bring this scenario to the attention of the American public in speeches to Columbia University Alumni on 4 June and in public at Yale University on 19 June.[38] These pronouncements had understandable resonance at a time when the British were preoccupied with the fate of the French fleet under the control of the Vichy government after the Franco-German armistice. Roosevelt's fears about the British capacity for resistance and Churchill's unwillingness to bargain over the future of the fleet in anticipation of a British defeat meant that no progress toward an agreement on the provision of destroyers was made throughout June and July. Lothian was certainly aware that there was no intention in London of transferring the fleet across the Atlantic, after being rebuffed when he asked Churchill if designs, spares, and supplies for maintaining the fleet were required in Ottawa.[39] By the end of June, Churchill had made it clear that there was no further benefit in discussing the destroyers until the success of British resistance without them over the next three months had made British prospects of survival more credible.[40]

The resulting hiatus was eventually broken after Lothian pressured Churchill to return to the issue at the end of July, and the basis of a deal

---

[35] Churchill to Roosevelt, C-13x, 11 June 1940, Kimball, ed., *Complete Correspondence*, 1: 43; Churchill to Lothian, Telegram No. 1156, 17 June 1940, FO 371/24240.
[36] Lothian to Halifax, 11 March 1940, Churchill Papers, CHAR 20/15; and Lash, *Roosevelt and Churchill*, 34-35.
[37] Lothian to Churchill, Telegram No. 759, 18 May 1940, FO 371/24192.
[38] Royal Institute of International Affairs, *The American Speeches of Lord Lothian*, 100-101; and Reynolds, *The Creation of the Anglo-American Alliance*, 115.
[39] Lothian to Churchill, Telegram No. 1032, 18 June 1940, Churchill to Lothian, 22 June 1940, PREM 3/476/10.
[40] Churchill to Lothian, Telegram No. 1304, 28 June 1940, PREM 3/476/10.

was agreed in August. Factors behind the progression of the deal were the growing realization of its long-term political importance, as argued by Lothian and the Foreign Office on the British side, and a growing American perception of the capacity of the British to survive during the Battle of Britain, distilled in part from the reports of U.S. military observers who were encouraged by Lothian. Lothian had also been in contact with pro-Allied pressure groups, who had produced an influential press statement supporting the legality of transferring the destroyers through the executive authority of the President rather than with congressional approval. Finally, the interest of Frank Knox, Roosevelt's new secretary of the navy, in securing U.S. bases in the Caribbean provided the "molasses" Roosevelt believed would be required to overcome potential opposition.[41] Lothian had vainly attempted to encourage a British offer of base facilities to forestall demands for them as a *quid pro quo* for the destroyers. The Cabinet had finally agreed to Lothian's suggestion at the same time as the administration linked the issue of the bases to the supply of the destroyers, but the transfer of sovereignty involved in West Indian sites affected by the bases deal was subsequently to cause considerable friction in Whitehall.

Throughout this period, Lothian had been responsible for persuading administration officials such as Knox of the British need for destroyers by linking them with British survival and the fate of the British fleet.[42] This had progressively influenced administration officials in favor of the deal. By early August Knox had become the primary agent acting to conclude the deal in the Roosevelt cabinet, despite describing Lothian's approach at the time as a "pitiful story."[43] In June Henry Morgenthau, Jr., the U.S. Treasury Secretary, whom Roosevelt had appointed to coordinate Allied supplies, was certainly convinced by the Churchill/Lothian argument: "After reading this, unless we do something to give the English additional destroyers, it seems to me it is absolutely hopeless to expect them to keep going."[44]

The 'criticality' thesis was clearly in evidence. So was the 'proof' fed to sympathetic media representatives. At Lothian's behest the U.S. media had been provided with increasingly detailed secret information on the British destroyer position and losses. In response to U.S. press coverage

---

[41] Reynolds, *The Creation of the Anglo-American Alliance*, 124.

[42] Lash, *Roosevelt and Churchill*, 207.

[43] John Blum, ed., *From the Morgenthau Diaries: Years of Urgency 1938-1941* (Boston: Houghton Mifflin, 1965), 176.

[44] Kimball, ed., *Complete Correspondence*, 1:49; Blum, ed., *From the Morgenthau Diaries*, 162.

of the issue, and after consultation with sympathetic American opinion makers, Lothian had advised Churchill on the tone, content, and timing of his appeals to Roosevelt and in public for American aid. On 24 May, he advised the War Cabinet of the specific tactics to adopt in British appeals for the destroyers after meeting William Allen White, chairman of the influential pressure group, the Committee to Defend America by Aiding the Allies.[45] In June, when the deal's prospects had dimmed and Whitehall's interest had apparently waned, Lothian indicated the significance of the American press in driving his campaign: "I presume if there were any chance of getting destroyers, etc., you would have no objection to public campaign in this country describing Britain's vital need for them."[46]

From May to July requests for the destroyers were often triggered by Lothian returning once more to the subject after Whitehall or the White House had reached an impasse. Lothian's method was thus responsible for 'pulling' British supply requests, quite separately from the 'push' of strategic requirements originating from the military and naval authorities in London. Lothian was also responsible for selling the concept of an exchange of bases for the destroyers to Whitehall. This fitted within American strategic concerns with hemispheric defense, but it triggered opposition in Whitehall from the Colonial Office and even Robert Vansittart, the diehard anti-Nazi permanent under secretary at the Foreign Office until 1938.[47] Lothian was then responsible for initiating the second phase of the démarche, beginning at the end of July, when he overcame Churchill's reluctance to conclude the deal in terms of a *quid pro quo* for bases. The conduct of Lothian's diplomacy reveals the influence that U.S. public opinion exerted upon British strategic appeals through that diplomacy. This is particularly significant when considering the military value of the destroyers, as the tardy conclusion of the deal directly undercut the chronological requirements emphasized by Churchill when he originally requested them from Roosevelt.

Churchill had stepped back from the prospective deal in June, just as a German invasion of Britain appeared imminent following the loss of France. This implicitly undermined any causal link between the supply of the destroyers and continued British resistance. Even when the deal returned to the top of the agenda in August, the Colonial Office and the Admiralty—in theory the service department most concerned with

---

[45] Lothian to War Cabinet, Telegram No. 817, 24 May 1940, FO 371/24239.
[46] Lothian to Churchill, Telegram No. 1492, 24 July 1940, FO 371/24240.
[47] Reynolds, *The Creation of the Anglo-American Alliance*, 122-123.

obtaining the destroyers for vital operational needs—formed the mainstay of resistance to the American terms.[48] Churchill was prompted by Admiralty concerns to describe the destroyers privately as "not vital," in complete contradiction to the rhetoric Lothian had encouraged.[49] Even a pragmatist like Cadogan, resistant to the periodic fits of Churchillian pique, agreed with Churchill when he claimed the destroyers were not worth the exchange demanded for them.[50]

Lothian's argument prevailed in the end, with the Admiralty accepting the offer of the bases being made "as a gesture of good propaganda value" and the Foreign Office emphasizing the "wider political consideration" served by such practical evidence of the unity of interests involved.[51] The change in emphasis evident between the May and August phases of the negotiations—from assertions of immediate military criticality to acceptance on political grounds—was attributable to the chronology of the deal, and the manner in which it operated within British naval rearmament policy. This is a facet of the developing Anglo-American supply relationship which has traditionally received little attention, but which emphasizes the longer-term political value of the deal at the expense of assertions of immediate criticality.

Churchill had repeatedly stressed the need for the destroyers to meet operational needs in the period before the output of British construction programs became available.[52] Royal Navy construction programs during the rearmament period of 1936-1939 had concentrated on building the variety of larger vessels required to field a "balanced fleet" by the chosen target date of 1942.[53] The speed with which the German threat had escalated in 1938-1940 had left the naval construction program lagging in the areas required to counter the German submarine threat to British maritime importation, which had previously reached crisis proportions during the First World War.[54] Churchill, who had been concerned by the shortage of destroyers for anti-submarine escort duty on his return to the

---

[48] Roberts, *"The Holy Fox,"* 256-257.

[49] Reynolds, *The Creation of the Anglo-American Alliance*, 127.

[50] Cadogan, diary entry, 23 August 1940, *Diaries of Sir Alexander Cadogan*, 323.

[51] Director of Plans, Admiralty, 30 June 1940, and Halifax to Lord Lloyd, 19 July 1940, ADM 116/4409.

[52] Churchill to Roosevelt, 25 August 1940, in Churchill, *Their Finest Hour*, 364.

[53] Joseph A. Maiolo, *The Royal Navy and Nazi Germany, 1933-39: A Study in Appeasement and the Origins of the Second World War* (London: Macmillan, 2002), 153.

[54] Peter Padfield, *War Beneath the Sea: Submarine Conflict 1939-1945* (London: John Wiley, 1995), 25.

Admiralty in September 1939, blamed the loss of the aircraft carrier *Courageous* to U-boat attack on this, and suggested purchasing destroyers from the United States to alleviate it.[55] In November 1939 the head of the Foreign Office American desk identified the supply of surplus destroyers as one of the possible steps short of belligerency which an American policy of "highly benevolent neutrality" might permit.[56]

While this was not taken up at the time, it indicates that the destroyer shortage was a pre-existing problem, identified as a potential area where Britain might benefit from the display of the benevolent neutrality policy expected from the Roosevelt administration, and was not specifically driven by the destroyer losses in the first half of 1940 in isolation. This begs a re-examination, from a naval rather than diplomatic perspective, of the nature of the British destroyer shortage that drove the appeals for the U.S. ships in the summer of 1940.

The existing destroyer shortage was compounded by the entry of Italy into the war in June, with a submarine fleet twice the size of the German fleet, the loss of the French navy to the Allies, and the subsequent closure of the Mediterranean to Allied shipping. This imposed additional commitments on the remaining British destroyer strength.[57] The need to concentrate up to forty destroyers on anti-invasion duties further denuded British convoys of escort protection until the immediate danger of seaborne landings passed with the arrival of autumn weather.[58] This left British shipping poorly protected, resulting in several months of high losses to submarine attack, that German U-boat crews in consequence christened 'the Happy Time'.[59] The need for reinforcement was therefore pressing, but the U.S. destroyers were not the only available source of supply.

The Royal Navy were well aware of the need to expand the production of escort vessels to meet the German submarine threat. In the 1939 Naval Estimates the Admiralty had had already adopted a program of building smaller and simplified anti-submarine destroyers, the *Hunt* class,

---

[55] Martin Gilbert, *Finest Hour: Winston S. Churchill 1939-1941* (London: Heinemann, 1991), 33.

[56] Minute by David Scott, 28 February 1940, FO 371/24239.

[57] 32 destroyers had been lost since the outbreak of war, with half of the remaining total destroyer strength being out of action due to damage. Churchill to Roosevelt, C-17x, 15 June 1940, Kimball, ed., *Complete Correspondence*, 1:49-50. The Italian navy had 115 submarines in June 1940. Clay Blair, *Hitler's U-Boat War: The Hunters 1939-1942* (London: Weidenfeld and Nicolson, 2000), 164.

[58] Churchill to Ismay, 1 July 1940, Churchill Papers, CHAR 20/13.

[59] Stephen Roskill, *The War At Sea 1939-45*, Vol. I: *The Defensive* (London: Her Majesty's Stationery Office, 1976), 348.

specifically to supplement the existing program of expensive, larger, and more capable fleet destroyers.[60] In addition, the Admiralty had added a crash production program of an even smaller and more basic escort vessel, the corvette. The anticipated output of this construction program lay behind Churchill's assertion of the temporary shortage in escort vessels until February 1941 which the American destroyers were required to meet.[61]

After the conclusion of the bases deal in early September, fifty American destroyers were commissioned into the Royal Navy as the *Town* class; only forty of them, however, had completed the transit to Britain by the end of 1940, and only nine were in operational service by then, long after the immediate threat of invasion had passed and the anti-invasion destroyer flotillas dispersed once again to escort duties.[62] The *Towns* arrived too late to meet the original need specified for them, and required extensive repair and refitting before they could become effective escort vessels.[63] Disconcerted by the problems and delays encountered with them, Churchill had the Admiralty compile a report on them at the end of December. For diplomatic reasons, this was excluded from his correspondence with Roosevelt at the sensitive juncture when Lend-Lease was about to go before Congress.[64] The *Towns* were unpopular ships and the class was, overall, a marginal contribution to the British anti-submarine campaign.[65]

---

[60] Viscount Cunningham of Hyndhope, *A Sailor's Odyssey: The Autobiography of Viscount Cunningham of Hyndhope* (London: Hutchinson, 1951), 193-194; and Stephen W. Roskill, *Naval Policy Between the Wars*, Vol. II: *The Period of Reluctant Rearmament 1930-39* (London: Collins, 1976), 450.

[61] In total, the British pre-war and wartime building programs produced seventeen fleet destroyers, twenty-five escort destroyers (including *Hunts*), two sloops and fifty-one corvettes, with a further thirty anti-submarine trawlers by the end of 1940, with similar numbers to follow in 1941. Appendix I, "New Construction Programmes 1939-1940," Churchill, *The Gathering Storm*, 555; and Churchill, *Their Finest Hour*, 364.

[62] J. R. M. Butler, *Grand Strategy*, Vol. II: *September 1939-June 1941* (London: Her Majesty's Stationery Office, 1957), 245.

[63] Arnold Hague, *Destroyers for Great Britain: A History of the 50 Town Class Ships Transferred from the United States to Great Britain in 1940*, 2nd rev. ed. (London: Greenhill Books, 1990), 17. One of these, *HMS Buxton*, only arrived in Britain a year later, in November 1941, after extensive maintenance problems which had prompted the Admiralty to request a replacement. Churchill to First Lord of the Admiralty, M.413, 12 December 1940, Churchill Papers, CHAR 20/13.

[64] Churchill to Roosevelt, Telegram No. 3795, 31 December 1940, PREM 3/422/1. The report was sent via the U.S. naval attaché in London instead.

[65] One commander claimed that the use of one of them as a bomb ship on a one-way mission to destroy the St. Nazaire drydock in 1942 was "the best thing that could have happened to the Town Class destroyers." Martin Middlebrook, *Convoy: The Battle of Convoys SC122* (continued)

The problems with the operational utility of the *Town* class were recognized in April 1941. That month the prospect of supplying a further thirty destroyers to meet the continuing British need for escort vessels in the Battle of the Atlantic was raised by Cordell Hull, the U.S. secretary of state. In his draft response Churchill emphasized his preference for "new destroyers which could come into action forthwith and stand up to the severe service," in clear contrast to the *Towns*.[66] In the event, instead of supplying further destroyers, Roosevelt extended the neutrality zone further into the Atlantic, redeployed units of the Pacific Fleet to the Atlantic, and established U.S. bases in Greenland and then Iceland.[67] At this point the negotiations over the base leases involved in the destroyer deal had encountered serious difficulties when the price being exacted exceeded the apparent value of the American supplies involved.[68] Opposition within Whitehall had by then grown to include a Foreign Office retreating from Lothianesque concepts of generosity when dealing with the Americans. In the end this opposition was over-ruled by Churchill, who was mindful of the potential political difficulties it might cause during passage of Lend-Lease. Again, larger diplomatic imperatives dominated supply issues that were supposedly dictated solely by military needs.

Although the events of spring 1941 transpired after Lothian's death, they indicate that the outlines established by Lothian remained in force up to a year later. Concepts of strengthening naval collaboration in sympathy with Mahanist theory remained at the center of Anglo-American diplomacy, but the evidence used to further this aim, such as the management of the serviceability reports on the *Towns* or the supply of secret naval information on the British destroyer position, was selectively

---

and HX229 (London: Allen Lane, 1976), 32. The *Towns* claimed eight U-boat kills during the war, compared to twenty-six claimed by their equivalent British First World War-vintage destroyers reconditioned as escorts, or the thirty-nine claimed by the pre-war fleet destroyers. Table 18, "U-boat sinkings by Class," David K. Brown, "Atlantic Escorts 1939-45," in *The Battle of the Atlantic 1939-1945: The 50th Anniversary International Naval Conference*, eds. Stephen Howarth and Derek Law (London: Greenhill, 1994), 470.

[66] Churchill to Halifax, Telegram no. 2411, 5 May 1941, Churchill Papers, CHAR 20/38.

[67] Robert Dallek, *Franklin Roosevelt and American Foreign Policy, 1932-1945* (New York: Oxford University Press, 1995), 260-265. The British did receive ten *Lake* class U.S. Coast Guard cutters, which were to prove effective escort vessels. Blair, *Hitler's U-Boat War: The Hunters*, 229-230.

[68] "[T]he British diplomatic performance during the lease negotiations revealed the determination of leading policy makers—including Churchill—to resist American claims in spite of the expressed and deeply held wish to obtain critical aid from the US." Charlie Whitham, "On Dealing with Gangsters: The Limits of British 'Generosity' in the Leasing of Bases to the United States, 1940-41," *Diplomacy and Statecraft* 7:3 (November 1996), 620.

employed under the influence of political considerations. This indicates how the nature of the 'proof' of British military needs was informed by the political considerations required to convince U.S. audiences. The chronology of the deal and specifically the hiatus of June-July 1940 indicated how, paradoxically, British appeals for critical American aid were ineffective until they were reinforced by practical demonstration of their ability to resist without that aid. It can also be seen that the content, tone, and timing of British appeals for the destroyers were driven as much by the requirements of Lothian's method as they were by strategic needs in Whitehall.

A reconsideration of the dynamic changes in the context of inter-allied diplomacy involved in the evolution of the Destroyers-Bases deal brings the concept of their criticality to the British further into question. The period of the negotiations when the destroyers were most associated with strategic criticality were the original requests in May-June 1940. British appeals in this phase were driven by the requirements of Franco-British diplomacy, or at least a triangular Anglo-French-American diplomacy, which have been customarily ignored by Anglophone historiography when examining Anglo-American supply diplomacy in 1940. This has left unexplored a vital dimension to understanding the political importance of American aid.

The British began looking for ways to bolster the French will to resist as soon as the magnitude of the crisis created by the German offensive of 10 May became manifest. Securing obvious gestures of U.S. support appeared to be the most decisive way to keep France in the war. The first direct appeal for American aid sprang from the French premier's approach to William C. Bullitt, the U.S. ambassador to Paris, on 14 May 1940. This preceded Churchill's first appeal to Roosevelt and covered the same supply needs—notably aircraft and destroyers to counter the threat of Italian belligerency.[69] In the period before the French collapse on 22 June, the British themselves were faced with a series of desperate appeals for fighter aircraft to reinforce the French. These originated in parallel with French demands for visible signs of American assistance which the British Foreign Office encouraged, urging the British ambassador to France:[70]

---

[69] Bullitt to Secretary of State, Telegram No. 659 section three, *For the President, Personal and Secret: Correspondence Between Franklin D. Roosevelt and William C. Bullitt*, ed. Orville H. Bullitt (London: Andre Deutsch, 1973), 416-417.
[70] Butler, *Grand Strategy*, 2:183-185, 197-201.

Please suggest to the French Government that they should make urgent and repeated appeals to the United States for assistance and support material and moral which may help to turn the scale at this highly critical moment.[71]

Thus the first phase of Anglo-American supply diplomacy in May-June 1940 was implicitly connected to the necessity of implementing diplomatic gestures which could sustain the French political will to continue fighting. These paralleled but also preceded the British efforts to secure American aid for themselves which were couched in the same terms, although British willingness to continue the struggle without American support was to prove a distinct and separate issue. Lothian was instructed that the British intended to carry on fighting after the French collapsed, even if ultimate victory required full American economic collaboration which was not evident by that stage.[72] But the rhetoric associated with American supply after June retained the message of criticality which sprang from the failed attempt to keep France in the war.

The real significance of the destroyers deal was political and diplomatic, not military, and this was understood at the time. Lothian himself acknowledged that "the long distance implications of the agreement are likely to be very important."[73] The exceptionalism involved was admitted by the Foreign Office, when it downgraded further specific procurement negotiations associated with the destroyers deal from the ambassadorial level at the end of 1940: "The 'Destroyers-Bases' deal was, of course, an exception, but then that was clearly a diplomatic and political question of the first importance and went far beyond the sphere of pure supplies."[74]

This was true not just of the destroyers deal, but also of the whole issue of American supply. This can be understood by examining the other primary military need expressed in the Lothian-Churchill diplomatic strategy: aircraft supply. Fighter aircraft were a constant feature of British appeals for American aid in 1940, paralleling the requests for destroyers, and similar dynamics become apparent when their military value is assessed. On 22 May Lothian instructed Churchill on how to pitch the tone

---

[71] Foreign Office memorandum to Sir Ronald Campbell, British ambassador to France, Telegram No. 154, 16 May 1940, FO 371/24192.

[72] Chiefs of Staff memorandum Cos (40) 455, "Plans to Meet A Certain Eventuality: Aide Memoire for H.M.'s Ambassador at Washington," 13 June 1940, FO 371/24311

[73] Lothian to John Bassett, editor of *The Montreal Gazette*, 9 September 1940, GD 40/17/398/594, Lothian Papers.

[74] Draft letter from Foreign Secretary to First Lord of the Admiralty, 12 December 1940, CAB 115/83.

and content of his correspondence with Roosevelt in a manner best calculated to secure American assistance. In a direct parallel with his role in precipitating British strategic requests over the destroyers, he advised Churchill to make a statement specifying that the British intended to continue their resistance but that British capacity to do so would be "greatly increased" by supply of "the latest type of fighting aeroplanes."[75] Two days later Lothian followed this up with advice from pro-Allied pressure groups when urging Churchill to make a statement on supply needs before a press conference including American journalists.[76]

Lothian's method was therefore operating on British aircraft procurement policy. A detailed exploration of American aircraft supply in 1940 reveals, however, a more complex picture, with political and diplomatic factors arising from Lothian's method influencing military supply issues. Just as in the case of the destroyers, the criticality associated with American aircraft supply sprang from diplomatic requirements during the fall of France. The subsequent demonstration of the marginal operational value of the supplies involved contradicts the attribution of military criticality made in their favor.[77]

While the British had restricted their pre-war purchases of American aircraft to maritime patrol aircraft and trainers, the French had relied upon American aircraft such as the Curtis P-36 fighter as a decisive supplement to their front-line strength.[78] In April 1940, the British had joined in a substantial Anglo-French aircraft purchase program in the United States, which included orders for the P-40, a P-36 equipped with a more powerful engine. The rationale for this was largely political, to establish an American financial and industrial stake in the Allied cause.[79] The British had little interest in the type after rejecting existing U.S. combat aircraft on qualitative grounds at the beginning of 1940. They

---

[75] Lothian to War Cabinet, Telegram No. 793, 22 May 1940, FO 371/24239.

[76] Lothian to War Cabinet, Telegram No. 817, 24 May 1940, FO 371/24239.

[77] Gavin Bailey, "The Narrow Margin of Criticality: The Question of the Supply of 100-Octane Fuel in the Battle of Britain," *English Historical Review* 123:501 (April 2008), 394-411.

[78] Robert J. Young, *In Command of France: French Policy and Military Planning, 1933-1940* (Cambridge, MA: Harvard University Press, 1978), 210; and Bullitt to Secretary of State, 13 February, 23 November 1939, *Foreign Relations of the United States 1939*, Vol. II: *General, the British Commonwealth and Europe* (Washington, DC: Government Printing Office, 1956), 501, 520.

[79] H. Duncan Hall, *North American Supply* (London: Her Majesty's Stationery Office, 1955), 120-121.

anticipated that French orders would take up all the P-40s produced for export until 1941, at which point they were expected to be obsolete.[80]

Accelerated deliveries of American aircraft then became of crucial importance in the effort to keep the French in the war, as the loss of air superiority to the German Luftwaffe became a principal explanation for the unfolding French defeat. Despite the indifference of the Royal Air Force (RAF) toward it, the P-40 was the only American fighter believed to be competitive with the primary single-engined fighters of the day, and featured several times in British appeals for American supply alongside the destroyers. On 20 May Churchill described the delivery of U.S. Army Air Corps (USAAC) P-40s as "[o]ur most vital need," and the Allies requested releases of the first production batch about to be delivered to the USAAC.[81] Lothian reiterated the immediate importance of the demands, notably on 23 May to the State Department, although without immediate success.[82]

By August the resistance to the diversion of aircraft from initial U.S. service deliveries had subsided, and the British were offered 200 of the USAAC contract in addition to the output of the French contract which the British had by then taken over. By this point the RAF still had little interest in current production of the P-40, preferring later production variants designed with modifications to incorporate combat experience, such as self-sealing fuel tanks. This left the Air Ministry in August tactfully rejecting the offer of the USAAC P-40s for which Churchill and Lothian had appealed in May and June.[83]

Even as ex-French P-40s began to arrive in Britain in the autumn of 1940, the British were left with a continuing problem of reconciling the expectational gap between the operational use of these fighters and the supply diplomacy conducted to secure them in the first place. The operational use of the P-40 was not governed by the statement of immediate needs for defense against invasion which lay behind the appeals of May-June 1940. By July 1940, as the Battle of Britain began, the RAF had

---

[80] Assistant Chief of the Air Staff to the Permanent Under-Secretary at the Air Ministry, 15 January 1940, AIR 8/293; Arthur Purvis to Jean Monnet, Purco 118, 15 May 1940, CAB 85/14.

[81] Churchill to Roosevelt, C-11x, 20 May 1940, Kimball, ed., *Complete Correspondence*, 1: 40.

[82] Sumner Welles, memorandum of conversation with Lothian, 23 May 1940, U.S. Department of State, *Foreign Relations of the United State 1940*, Vol. III: *The British Commonwealth, the Soviet Union, the Near East, and Africa* (Washington, DC: Government Printing Office, 1958), 3.

[83] Air Commodore Slessor, Director of Plans, Air Ministry, to Sir Arthur Salter, 17 August 1940, AIR 19/173.

confirmed their rejection of the P-40 for service as an interceptor and relegated the ex-French P-40s to secondary duties in Army Co-operation Command. Later production P-40s, improved by British-inspired modifications, were to be sent to the Middle East. But even in that theater, the contemporary variant of the P-40 was not regarded as an adequate substitute for British fighters. Pending the delivery of the improved P-40s in 1941, the RAF began exporting Hawker Hurricane fighters to the Middle East to meet the need for modern fighters there. This decision was made several months before the first shipments of ex-French P-40's even arrived in Britain.[84] This indicates a substantive divergence between the rhetoric employed to secure the P-40s, and their actual value to British strategy. The P-40 was never regarded as an adequate substitute for British fighters, even in the overseas theater selected as the main focus of American aircraft supply, and even when fighter aircraft were the most critical British strategic need as the Battle of Britain raged.

The British were aware of the expectational gap that arose as a consequence of their limited employment of such high-profile supplies. In January 1941, as public debate over Lend-Lease began in America, they deployed a temporary detachment of P-40s in a Fighter Command Spitfire squadron to undercut the possible diplomatic criticisms that might result from their apparent neglect of the aircraft.[85] Just as Churchill backed away from critical reports on the *Town* class destroyers, or over-rode objections in the destroyers-bases lease negotiations when these threatened to cause political problems during the passage of Lend-Lease, the RAF's token use of the P-40 in Britain indicates the degree to which political considerations could determine decisions on the operational deployment of American supplies. As a consequence, the supply of American fighter aircraft to Britain in 1940 reveals dynamics of diplomatic—rather than military—importance.

The destroyers and P-40s initially entered transatlantic supply diplomacy because of their political importance to the French. After the fall

---

[84] Churchill to First Lord of the Admiralty, 12 July 1940, Churchill Papers, CHAR 20/13; Memorandum to Deputy Director War Operations, "Re-equipment of Forces in the Far and Middle East," and Memorandum to Deputy Director Plans (Operations), Air Ministry, 30 July 1940, AIR 20/5552.

[85] Air Member for Supply and Organisation (AMSO), "Equipment of a Fighter Squadron with Tomahawks," 90th ERP committee meeting, 19 January 1941, AIR 20/5777. The Tomahawks were attached to 234 Squadron, who continued their existing operational duties with their Spitfires, while the Tomahawks saw no action. 234 Squadron Operations Record Book, January-February 1941, AIR 27/1439.

of France they represented potentially valuable additions to British military capacity when the British were confronted by the loss of continental Europe to the Germans, the entry of the Italians into the war, and the increasing threat of Japanese attack in Asia—the nightmare scenario for pre-war British strategy. But their value was overstated, primarily because their military worth was eclipsed by their diplomatic potential as stepping-stones toward the larger collaboration with the United States that British strategic needs demanded. This was explicitly acknowledged in the destroyers deal, and was evident in aircraft supply. Lothian himself knew that American aircraft production in any strategically meaningful sense remained up to two years away:

> The Americans are sending over all they can in the way of airplanes and equipment. But, as you know, it normally seems to take about two years from the time you begin to lay down an airplane factory to the time when it comes into full production.[86]

This left British strategy for confronting the anticipated German invasion in the summer of 1940 and continuing their resistance entirely contingent upon their own resources, rather than dependent upon American aid. At the beginning of July it was clear that Lothian himself shared the confidence evident in Whitehall that Britain would successfully resist the expected German assault.[87] He stated: "My own impression is that Hitler is going to find England a far tougher nut to crack than he realises and that we shall come through all right ...."[88]

This can be contrasted with his demarche of October-November 1940, when he described a new raft of financial assistance to Britain in the starkest terms as essential for British survival. David Reynolds has identified Lothian's critical role in shaping this initiative which led to Lend-Lease, both by priming London to make a new appeal for more substantial and comprehensive aid, and by directly influencing American public opinion himself, in the most significant example of Lothian's method.

---

[86] Lothian to Aikman, 1 July 1940, GD 40/17/398/121, Lothian Papers.

[87] Harold Nicolson may not have agreed with this, but—pace Andrew Roberts's treatment of Halifax's position over Munich and Dunkirk—Lothian's interest in German terms should not be misrepresented. Nicolson, diary entry, 22 July 1940, *Harold Nicolson: Diaries and Letters 1939-1945*, 104.

[88] Lothian to Victor Cazalet, 1 July 1940, GD 40/17/378/508, Lothian Papers. It is perhaps significant, too, that on the same date Lothian instructed his bankers to make no change to his financial arrangements for 1941. "Unless Mr. Hitler begins to succeed...," Lothian to A. G. Watson, 1 July 1940, GD 40/17/372/588, Lothian Papers.

Lothian returned to Britain in October-November 1940, in part to lay the groundwork for a new British approach for American supply to follow the conclusion of the presidential election in November. As he stated in his request to return:

> Public opinion here has not yet grasped that it will have to make far reaching decisions to finance and supply us and possibly still graver ones next spring or summer unless it is to take the responsibility of forcing us to make a compromised peace.[89]

To compel America to confront these decisions and resolve them in Britain's favor, Lothian suggested a "ruthless expose of the strategic dangers" to disperse "a fog of complacency" in a country "saturated with illusions" about the British position.[90] The new departure from Lothian's preceding diplomacy was the extension of criticality to the larger and longer-term issue of finance. But the attribution of a critical responsibility for British resistance to U.S. support remained. As John Colville, Churchill's assistant private secretary, commented on Lothian's draft for Churchill's letter to Roosevelt: "It is intended to make R. [Roosevelt] feel that if we go down, the responsibility will be America's."[91]

Lothian's alleged comments designed to prepare American public opinion and made at the landing stage on his return to New York on 22 November quickly became notorious. Sir John Wheeler-Bennett, one of his staff at the time, claimed that Lothian had baldly announced to the assembled press: "'Well boys, Britain's broke, it's your money we want.'"[92] As David Reynolds has observed, there is no conclusive evidence to show that Lothian used these precise words.[93] But they certainly met the criteria of "a short leaderette with a snap to it." *The New York Times* got the point, stating that:

> Putting England's case directly to the American public, the Marquess of Lothian, British Ambassador to the United States, said on arriving yesterday

---

[89] Lothian to Churchill, Telegram No. 2063, 20 September 1940, FO 371/24246.

[90] Reynolds, "Lothian, Roosevelt, Churchill and the Origins of Lend-Lease," 97; and Butler, *Lord Lothian*, 264.

[91] Diary entry, 12 November 1940, John Colville, *The Fringes of Power: Downing Street Diaries*, Vol. I: *September 1939-October 1941* (London: Sceptre, 1986), 344.

[92] John W. Wheeler-Bennett, *King George VI: His Life and Reign* (London: Macmillan, 1958), 521.

[93] Reynolds, "Lothian, Roosevelt, Churchill and the Origins of Lend-Lease," 98-100.

at La Guardia Field aboard the Atlantic Clipper that England was near the end of its fiscal resources and would need financial aid in 1941.[94]

There can be little doubt that his actual remarks did engender a new sense of impending crisis amongst the American press, who proceeded to ring up British officials in Whitehall for comment on wild rumors inspired by his statements.[95] Lothian was compelled to defend his utterances to Churchill, but unrepentantly maintained that it was necessary to combat the illusions of American public opinion, which remained "the ultimate determinant."[96]

This was the archetypal example of Lothian's personal diplomacy reaching out to shape American public opinion directly via the press, at the cost of some discomfort in Whitehall and the administration as his "indiscretion" moved in advance of British and U.S. government policy. The end result of Churchill's Lothian-inspired 8 December letter was Roosevelt's evolution of the policy of Lend-Lease, which envisaged funding British supply in the United States through an administration-controlled and congressionally-approved procurement process. Unlike the destroyers deal, which had been resolved by executive action to avoid legislative opposition, Lend-Lease confronted Congress with administration policy to finance aid for the allies on a major scale. That the administration could contemplate this step in early 1941 was due in part to Lothian's assertions of criticality not only taking hold in the administration, but winning credibility with the American public.

Lothian's approach ran the risk of overstatement, however. Morgenthau, probably the most dedicated supporter of American aid to the allies in Roosevelt's cabinet, indicated the danger that Lothian's thesis of criticality posed toward the complementary policy of generating confidence in British ability to survive: "It is not difficult to understand why the impression had gotten around in Washington that things are going badly with England after one listens to Lothian."[97] This apparent pessimism conferred tactical advantages, not least in selling the concept of aiding Britain to the American public on the grounds of urgent necessity. During the Lend-Lease hearings, administration officials such as Morgenthau and

---

[94] "Envoy Flies Here!," *The New York Times*, 24 November 1940.

[95] Nicolson was called by the New York press at 3 a.m. on 26 November and asked if Lothian had requested two battleships from Roosevelt. *Harold Nicolson: Diaries and Letters 1939-1945*, 129. The Treasury were contacted by American journalists on 22 November. FO 371/24249.

[96] Lothian to Churchill, Telegram No. 2793, 23 November 1940, FO 371/24249; and Reynolds, "Lothian, Roosevelt, Churchill and the Origins of Lend-Lease," 100.

[97] Blum, ed., *From the Morgenthau Diaries*, 199.

Henry Stimson, the secretary of war, testified on the criticality of continuing American supply for continuing British resistance against the Axis powers. Morgenthau stated that, lacking American financial aid, there was "nothing for Great Britain to do but stop fighting."[98]

Lothian's method influenced Lend-Lease in several significant ways. The sense of immediate criticality engendered over the issue was successful in winning public support. This undercut legislative opposition and compelled isolationists to agree with the need for the measure. 'America First' delegates who were called to testify during the debate expressed sympathy for Britain and supported other forms of aid. Even the alternative bill put forward by isolationists Arthur H. Vandenberg and Robert A. Taft in the Senate extended dollar credits to the British. This implicitly abandoned the provisions of the Johnson Act (which denied the British access to U.S. loans as a consequence of defaulting on their First World War debt), one of the key achievements of pre-war isolationism. Anti-interventionist opposition had therefore been forced to concede the policy of aid to Britain.[99] Much of the responsibility for the administration's successful tactics can be attributed to Lothian, who played a direct role in shaping and facilitating those tactics—establishing the survival of Britain as falling within the American national interest, and then asserting the criticality of American aid by employing various forms of military and financial data to serve as 'proof'.

The success of the critical dependence thesis had drawbacks, however. In terms of Lend-Lease it sponsored a perception that economic and military supply aid could only be utilized to meet deficiencies. The British had laid themselves open to this danger by their approach toward securing American supply in 1940. The statistical basis for British production planning in the United States, such as that used by the Layton mission in September 1940, had deliberately stressed deficiencies between required targets in munitions production and the projected ability of British domestic production to meet them. This colored the thinking of U.S. service departments toward British requests for aid; Lend-Lease shipments could only be envisioned once British supplies could be demonstrated to

---

[98] Warren F. Kimball, *The Most Unsordid Act: Lend-Lease, 1939-41* (Baltimore: Johns Hopkins Press, 1969), 189; and Harold B. Hinton, "No Dollars Left," *The New York Times*, 29 January 1941.

[99] Cole, *Roosevelt and the Isolationists*, 415; and Arthur H. Vandenberg, *The Private Papers of Senator Vandenberg*, eds. Arthur H. Vandenberg, Jr., with Joe Alex Morris (Boston: Houghton Mifflin, 1953), 9-10.

American satisfaction to be exhausted or inadequate, and not just when the British requested them.

This was paralleled by the equivalent perception in the area of finance. Convincing the legislative opposition of British financial exhaustion required proof that Britain was, in Roosevelt's phrase, "scraping the marrow."[100] This lay behind Morgenthau's pressure to sell off British holdings, such as the American Viscose firm, which was sold at a loss during the Lend-Lease hearings. It also led to substantial friction in the later war period, as the United States attempted arbitrarily to limit British dollar reserves and restrict British competitive exports to adhere to the accepted basis of Lend-Lease aid.[101]

By establishing Lend-Lease as a measure necessitated by British financial exhaustion, Lothian grossly simplified the complex economic issues involved in the international British economy across the British Commonwealth and Sterling Area. The nub of the problem was identified by Churchill when he rebuked Lothian's indiscretion with the press on finances: "While it is generally understood that you were referring wholly to dollar credits, actual words attributed to you give only too much foundation to German propaganda to broadcast that we are coming to the end of our resources."[102] Warren F. Kimball has noted how this deliberate misunderstanding prospered, as the perception of "bankruptcy" penetrated the thinking of administration officials favoring further aid to Britain: "Many Americans, including Cordell Hull and Frank Knox, never really grasped the fact that Britain could run out of dollars without being bankrupt…"[103]

The 'bankruptcy' characterization has retained a lasting impact on historiography, with historians such as Correlli Barnett and Paul M. Kennedy adopting it to embody their economically determinant thesis of absolute and abject British dependence upon the United States.[104] Yet the United States only supplied 17.3% of British Commonwealth munitions by

---

[100] Warren F. Kimball, "'Beggar My Neighbour': America and the British Interim Finance Crisis, 1940-41," *Journal of Economic History* 29:4 (December 1969), 770.

[101] Dobson, *US Wartime Aid to Britain*, 126-184; and Woods, *Changing of the Guard*, 87-93.

[102] Churchill to Lothian, Telegram No. 3233, 27 November 1940, FO 371/24249.

[103] Kimball, *The Most Unsordid Act*, 237.

[104] Correlli Barnett, *The Audit of War: The Illusion and Reality of Britain as a Great Nation* (London: Macmillan, 1986); and Paul M. Kennedy, *The Rise and Fall of the Great Powers: Economic Change and Military Conflict from 1500 to 2000* (London: Fontana, 1989), 113, 473.

value throughout the war years, and the 5.6% of British munitions supplied from the United States in the first eighteen months of the war were realized by the expenditure of British financial resources.[105] Lend-Lease was of considerable significance to the British war effort, but that significance has been exaggerated at the time and subsequently. Any evaluation of it, or of American supply to Britain during the war in its totality, cannot be determined by the assertions of British diplomacy of 1940-1941 in isolation.

Lothian's assertions of criticality within that diplomacy were contradicted by the immediate value of American aid to the British war effort. As Warren Kimball observed: "As much as the leaders in Washington publicly talked about the Lend-Lease plan as a means of keeping England in the war, they knew full well that meaningful aid was a year or more away."[106] This was apparent at the time when the rhetoric deployed to secure American supplies was contrasted with their actual military value. After Lothian's death, Churchill irritably responded to a Lothianesque statement by the British Consul-General in New York on the vital importance of American aid to Britain in 1940: "We have not had anything from the United States that we have not paid for, and what we have had has not played an essential part in our resistance."[107]

The existence of this expectational gap illustrates the tensions that could arise when military supply policy was dictated by diplomatic strategy as a consequence of Lothian's method. The subordination of supply policy to diplomatic strategy inherent in Lothian's method was even evident within his contacts in the Allied procurement bureaucracy. On supply issues Lothian worked in close consultation with Arthur Purvis and Jean Monnet of the British Purchasing Commission in New York. Purvis and Monnet were apostles of the need to achieve full mobilization of American economic potential behind the Allies, and perceived Allied procurement requests as the mechanism to achieve this. Purvis himself played a dominant role, influencing Lothian's tactics and even drafting some of Lothian's telegrams to the cabinet.[108]

Purvis himself admitted the cyclical and dynamic approach Lothian recommended to British appeals for American aid, born of his appreciation

---

[105] Hall, *North American Supply*, 3.
[106] Kimball, *The Most Unsordid Act*, 147.
[107] Churchill to Foreign Secretary, 20 December 1940, Churchill Papers, CHAR 20/13.
[108] H. Duncan Hall; C. C. Wrigley; and J. D. Scott, *Studies of Overseas Supply* (London: Her Majesty's Stationery Office, 1956), 20, 67; and memorandum of conversation between Purvis, Monnet, Weir, Salter, and Brand, 9 October 1940, CAB 115/751.

of fluctuating American political resistance: "He always attempted to take the wave at the crest and to put on the maximum pressure when there was least resistance. There were times when it was purely a waste of effort to fight against the stream."[109] This tactical management of British procurement requests cannot be explained by any change in British strategic requirements from the United States in this period, as there was none. Instead it indicates the intimate influence of American political considerations on the British procurement machinery that was supposedly responsible for advising Lothian and Whitehall in isolation on purely military supply needs.

By September 1940 the Monnet/Purvis axis had succeeded in expanding the spring 1940 Allied aircraft purchasing plan into an even larger aircraft procurement program. The objectives of this program were explicitly diplomatic, designed to entangle the United States economically in British fortunes:

> American finance must also be expected to rally to this industrial expansion, once it had satisfied itself that the danger of the United Kingdom being overwhelmed, and of the war being over in 1940, had passed away. No United States government would dare to call a halt to this great expenditure, once it was fairly on the way, and to assume responsibility for the ensuing economic slump.[110]

By the end of 1940, Purvis was enthusiastically exploiting statistical projections of self-defined deficiencies to "shock" his audience in the administration into meeting British plans, while advising Lothian to "dramatize" British appeals for aid.[111] Funding these programs outran British capacity, and the dilemma could only be resolved by Lend-Lease. If Lothian's approach had once been termed "blackmail," this had now become the accepted basis for British procurement plans in the United States. But it moved the focus of American supply even further away from the emergency programs of 1940 and their asserted immediate criticality; this was a strategy of long-term capital investment in economic mobilization, not immediate survival.[112] Lothian's comment on the two-

---

[109] Purvis, memorandum, 29 September 1940, CAB 115/751.
[110] 244th War Cabinet Conclusions, Minute 1 Confidential Annexe, 6 September 1940, CAB 65/15.
[111] W. K. Hancock and M. M. Gowing, *The British War Economy* (London: His Majesty's Stationery Office, 1949), 232.
[112] Hall, Wrigley, and Scott, *Studies of Overseas Supply*, 91.

year delay before new aircraft factories could begin full production was both accurate and significant.

Lothian's ultimate diplomatic objective was to secure U.S. involvement on the side of the Allies, but he was well aware of the political constraints on the Roosevelt administration. He was also aware of the severely limited military potential of the U.S. Army and Air Corps in 1940. He realized that the United States had "no effective army and no modern air force" at the same time that he advised London of the need to recognize the "immense" moral effect of American belligerency, quite distinct from the valuable supplemental assistance any available military supplies could provide the Allies.[113]

Lothian was therefore fully conscious of the limited direct and tangible military utility of the United States, as either a source of immediate supply or a participating combatant; but he also displayed a keen appreciation of the difference between the moral and material impact of U.S. involvement in the war. This sense of psychological significance and future potential can usefully be applied to explain his representation of 'criticality' in the supply diplomacy of 1940. Historians have been superficially aware of the apparent contradiction between the rhetorical significance associated with American aid, which arose from the assertion of criticality in Lothian's method, and its actual impact, which that rhetoric has obscured.[114]

The need for an American alliance decisively influenced British diplomacy, but it was soon apparent that assertions of criticality driven by military needs associated with the American supply measures of 1940 were transitory, and primarily associated with the fall of France in the period of May-June 1940. Much of the driving force for the representation of American aid as being critical to British resistance in the period that followed came from Lothian, and existed in a diplomatic rather than military context. The diplomacy which followed from July to Lothian's death in December 1940 took place against a background where American aid had not materialized, the British capacity to resist without it had been demonstrated, and British strategic appreciations of the value of immediately available American aid had changed. This left the British in this second phase struggling to reconcile the political and diplomatic

---

[113] Lothian to Foreign Office, Telegram No. 922, 6 June 1940, and Telegram No. 932, 7 June 1940, FO 371/24239.

[114] A. J. P. Taylor, *English History 1914-1945* (Oxford: Clarendon Press, 1992), 513, 565; and Reynolds, *The Creation of the Anglo-American Alliance*, 167.

significance attached to American supplies originating from the first phase with their evidently marginal military value. Simultaneously, they had to continue the assertions of criticality derived from the previous phase of supply diplomacy in order to facilitate steps toward a larger goal: the full economic collaboration required for eventual victory, and not just simple British survival. The life-or-death characterizations of American supply aid which persisted in this second phase were contradicted by both Lothian's and Churchill's private statements at the time.

This apparent contradiction can be resolved by understanding the supply measures of 1940 as stages in what Churchill during the base lease negotiations termed "a process" toward a greater objective: full Anglo-American strategic, economic and military collaboration.[115] An understanding of the transitory and tactical nature of the key Anglo-American supply measures in addressing American public opinion in 1940 is required, rather than the continuing assumption of their strategic military criticality which was asserted by contemporary British diplomacy, and by Lothian in particular.

Alex Danchev has identified the qualities required for a British ambassador to Washington in a description verging upon a caricature of Lothian: "It is tempting to suggest that the recipe for ambassadorial success in Washington is an amateur diplomatist of intellectual bent, compromising temperament, proconsular virtue, and strong religious belief."[116] In Lothian's case, these qualities did not all necessarily translate into clear advantages. His strong religious belief in Christian Science has had little attributed to it beyond his early death on 12 December 1940 after refusing medical treatment.[117] His compromising temperament had to shed an initial identification with appeasement and the notoriety of the 'Cliveden Set' before it could become a virtue, and the expression of his intellectual bent through his interwar association with federalism required posthumous development.[118] If Lothian did have proconsular virtue, it was expressed

---

[115] Whitham, "On Dealing with Gangsters," 619.

[116] Alex Danchev, *Oliver Franks: Founding Father* (Oxford: Clarendon Press, 1983), 110-111.

[117] Roberts, *"The Holy Fox,"* 272. Lothian was not above using religious references in his speeches, as when he paraphrased the declaration of conscience attributed to Martin Luther at the Diet of Worms. Lothian, NBC broadcast, 22 July 1940, *The American Speeches of Lord Lothian*, 115.

[118] Rhodri Jeffreys-Jones, "Lord Lothian: Ambassador 'To a People,'" in *The Larger Idea: Lord Lothian and the Problem of National Sovereignty*, ed. John Turner (London: Historians Press, 1988), 87-88; Norman Rose, *The Cliveden Set: Portrait of an Exclusive Fraternity* (continued)

less through any innate magisterial authority than through his influence as a facilitator; where he deliberately exceeded his authority it was through the selective indiscretion that formed a key part of his method.[119]

The influencing of American public opinion through his personal diplomacy in the crisis of 1940 represented a considerable success for British statecraft. Halifax, no easy victim to hyperbole, was later to describe Lothian's role in the crisis of 1940 as "the climax of his life," and his ambassadorial career as "one of the outstanding achievements of British diplomatic history."[120] This appraisal has been reflected by later historians and even critical observers have largely agreed with it.[121] After his death the strategic importance of his ambassadorial career received implicit acknowledgement when J. R. M. Butler, the editor of the Grand Strategy series of the British official wartime histories, was selected as his biographer. The complete revision in Lothian's reputation from dilettante phrasemonger to diplomatic and strategic success story sprang from the achievements of his method of personal diplomacy in the Anglo-American supply relationship.

The full extent of Lothian's method lay beyond the diversity of the groupings he was able to connect. The decisive element in his personal diplomacy was the nature of the message he preached as much as the audiences he could access to do so. By asserting the critical importance of immediate American aid to British survival, and establishing that survival as essential to American interests, Lothian's method overcame the crippling political and legislative opposition to Anglo-American strategic collaboration. Lothian exaggerated the importance of military supply measures such as the *Town*-class destroyers or the P-40 fighters for diplomatic reasons. On the economic front, for political reasons he conflated the problem of funding British procurement in the United States with the entirety of the British economy. In the process he placed the public representation of Anglo-American supply dealings at the center of the evolving Anglo-American relationship. But this cannot obscure the fact that

---

(London: Jonathan Cape, 2000), 45-47; and Lionel Curtis, *World War: Its Cause and Cure* (London: Oxford University Press, 1945), xi.

[119] At least once, though, Lothian's appearance led *Time* magazine to make a comparison between him and a Roman magistrate. "Lord Lothian's Job," *Time*, 8 July 1940.

[120] Halifax, Preface, *The American Speeches of Lord Lothian*, ix; and Reynolds, *The Creation of the Anglo-American Alliance*, 155.

[121] Reynolds, "Lothian, Roosevelt, Churchill and the Origins of Lend-Lease," 93-107; and Jeffreys-Jones, "Lord Lothian: Ambassador 'To A People,'" 77-92.

the actual impact of American supply on the British war effort in 1940 was not decisive, in contradistinction to the rhetoric employed at the time.

As contemporary characterizations of Lend-Lease and the almost identical summaries of later historiography indicate, Churchill's chiding of Lothian's indiscretion and Kimball's qualifications have not been heeded. The contemporary evidence of the expectational gap associated with American supply has not been comprehensively addressed, nor have the consequent implications for the history of the Anglo-American relationship been absorbed. The rhetoric inspired by Lothian's method has thus been left, largely without substantive challenge, to define contemporary characterizations of the Anglo-American supply relationship and the understanding of subsequent historiography.

The development of British procurement policy in America under Lothian's method in 1940 not only indicates that diplomacy and procurement were interdependent, but also demonstrates that the requirements of influencing American public opinion directly informed supply diplomacy. The expectational gap that arose between the assertions of Lothian's method of diplomacy and the historical reality of the impact of American supply to the British war effort was of little concern to journalists. It would have been of little concern even to Lothian, who was more concerned with the representation of American supply measures to the American public than he was with their actual military value. But the gap between the military and diplomatic value of American supply to Britain demands examination by historians if the evolution of the modern Anglo-American relationship is to be accurately understood.

CHAPTER SEVEN

LORD LOTHIAN AND THE PROBLEM OF RELATIVE DECLINE

DAVID P. BILLINGTON, JR.

Philip Henry Kerr (1882-1940), eleventh Marquess of Lothian, was a writer and sometime British public official who tried to build a more liberal world order anchored by the advanced English-speaking nations. As Britain's ambassador to the United States from September 1939 until his death in December 1940, he laid much of the groundwork for the Anglo-American alliance of the Second World War and after. During the 1930s, though, he was a leading private advocate of appeasing Nazi Germany. He also belonged to a circle whose influence in British imperial and foreign policy from 1909 to 1939 was and still is a matter of controversy.[1]

Philip Kerr came of age in 1900, as Britain entered a more acute stage in its relative decline as a great power. His subsequent life divided into two periods, each of which raises a question. In the first period, from 1905 to 1921, Kerr played a supporting role in political activity led by more senior figures, first as part of a circle of young men who were protégés of Lord Milner, and then from December 1916 as an aide and adviser to Prime Minister David Lloyd George. With Milner's support, Kerr and his friends launched a movement in 1909 to persuade the self-governing British Dominions to form a common electorate with the United Kingdom. When

---

[1] The authorized biography of Lothian is J. R. M. Butler, *Lord Lothian (Philip Kerr) 1882-1940* (London: Macmillan, 1960). The authoritative account of Lothian's service as ambassador to the United States is David Reynolds, *Lord Lothian and Anglo-American Relations, 1939-1940* (Philadelphia: Transactions of the American Philosophical Society, 1983). More recent studies include Andrea Bosco, *Lord Lothian: Un pioniere del federalismo 1882-1940* (Milano: Jaca, 1989); Stefan Schieren, *Vom Weltreich zum Weltstaat: Philip Kerrs (Lord Lothian) Weg vom Imperialisten zum Internationalisten* (London: Lothian Foundation Press, 1996); and David P. Billington, Jr., *Lothian: Philip Kerr and the Quest for World Order* (Westport, CT: Praeger, 2006). See also the essays in John Turner, ed., *The Larger Idea: Lord Lothian and the Problem of National Sovereignty* (London: Historians Press, 1989). For critical views of Lothian and his circle, see A. L. Rowse, *Appeasement: A Study in Political Decline 1933-1939* (New York: W. W. Norton, 1961); and Norman Rose, *The Cliveden Set: Portrait of an Exclusive Fraternity* (London: Jonathan Cape, 2000).

P. Roberts (ed.), Lord Lothian and Anglo-American Relations, 1900-1940, 201-228.

Kerr realized by 1917 that this goal was unattainable, he hoped for a continuation of the wartime partnership between Great Britain and the United States. This prospect also failed when the U. S. Senate rejected American membership in the League of Nations in 1919. The question about this period is whether Kerr and his friends could have devised a more successful strategy to secure Great Britain in a more dangerous world.

For most of the second period, from 1921 until 1940, Kerr (Lord Lothian after 1930) tried to promote closer Anglo-American ties to anchor the liberal world, and he argued that these arrangements would need to evolve into a democratic world state. Although he did not live to see it, the advanced English-speaking nations came together with other allies during and after the Second World War in an alliance system anchored by the United States. These nations, however, rejected Lothian's call to federate just as they repudiated his pre-war support for appeasement. The question from the latter half of his life is one that concerns the world since then: whether liberal nations need the goal of a community integrated and inclusive enough to function as a government of the world.

VICTORIAN BACKGROUND

In 1815, the United Kingdom emerged the victor in a world war, and for the next half century its industrial head start made Great Britain the world's leading modern economy. Following Britain, western Europe began to develop more liberal and industrial societies, while central and eastern Europe languished in an autocratic bloc dominated by Austria and Russia. The latter two states had a falling out, though, and a series of wars and uprisings from 1859 to 1870 broke Austrian hegemony, bringing independence to new parts of the continent. Like the 1990s for America, the 1860s vindicated much of what Britain had stood for in the preceding four decades. But afterward, Great Britain entered a long relative decline as the rest of the world industrialized. Germany and Russia began their rise as global challengers, as did (in a less threatening way) the United States. Internally within Britain, changing electoral demographics helped evoke a new concern for the condition of the British underclass.

Two movements in 1870s Britain responded to these changes. The first was domestic in focus. At Oxford University, the philosopher Thomas Hill Green argued that liberal individualism denied a basis for the common good and permitted large numbers of citizens to suffer through no fault of their own.[2] Inspired by Green's teaching, one of his students, Arnold Toynbee (uncle of the historian Arnold J. Toynbee), recruited students to join him in doing social service work in the slums of London. After Toynbee's death in 1883, his friends created Toynbee Hall, the first of many 'settlement houses' in London and other British cities, in which students served during or after their time at university to teach and perform other kinds of social work. Settlement houses spread to the United States, Canada, and Australia in the 1880s and 1890s.[3]

The other movement, given a boost in the 1880s by the historian John Robert Seeley of Cambridge University, called for Britain to federate with its settler colonies, which were now internally self-governing and on a path to peaceful independence. The federalist aim was to reconcile democracy with the conservation of British strength. Most federalists called for representation of the settler colonies either in the London Parliament or (with Britain) in a new federal government of the empire. Unlike the settlement houses, though, imperial federalism did not catch on. A majority of the voters in a federal electorate would have been British for some time to come, and Canada and Australia proved no more interested in British taxation with representation than the American colonies had earlier been to such taxation without it. Interest in Britain was also muted.[4] Great Britain in the 1880s and 1890s instead occupied new parts of Africa and Asia, as if its world power were growing rather than receding.

The 1895 Venezuelan boundary dispute with the United States, the Boer War of 1899-1902, and German naval building after 1898 finally drove home British vulnerability. Britain settled its differences with America, signed a new alliance with Japan in 1902, reached understandings

---

[2] For the thought and influence of T. H. Green, see Andrew Vincent and Raymond Plant, *Philosophy, Politics and Citizenship: The Life and Thought of the British Idealists* (Oxford: Basil Blackwell, 1984).

[3] On Toynbee and the founding of Toynbee Hall, see Asa Briggs and Ann Macartney, *Toynbee Hall: The First One Hundred Years* (London: Routledge and Kegan Paul, 1984), 1-10. See also Standish Meacham, *Toynbee Hall and Social Reform 1880-1914: The Search for Community* (New Haven, CT: Yale University Press, 1987); and for the movement's spread to the United States, Allen F. Davis, *Spearheads for Reform: The Social Settlements and the Progressive Movement, 1890-1914* (New York: Oxford University Press, 1967).

[4] See John Robert Seeley, *The Expansion of England*, ed. and with an introduction by John Gross (Chicago: University of Chicago Press, 1971). Seeley's book originally appeared in 1883. On the imperial federalist movement, see J. E. Tyler, *The Struggle for Imperial Unity (1868-1895)* (London: Longmans Green, 1938); and more broadly, Duncan Bell, *The Idea of Greater Britain: Empire and the Future of World Order, 1860-1900* (Princeton, NJ: Princeton University Press, 2007).

with France and Russia, and launched a domestic debate on how to renew the nation's capacities as a military and industrial power.[5] Liberals and Unionists (the latter name used by Conservatives from 1895 to 1922) agreed to build a larger fleet. But the two parties divided over economic and social policy; and party tensions soon deepened over constitutional reform and Irish demands for autonomy.

THE ROUND TABLE CRUSADE

Philip Kerr was born near the apex of British society. His father, Lord Ralph Kerr, a younger son of the seventh Marquess of Lothian, retired from the army in 1898 as a major-general. His mother, Lady Anne Fitzalan-Howard, was a daughter of the fifteenth Duke of Norfolk. A Roman Catholic, Philip attended the Oratory, a Catholic school near Birmingham, and went up to Oxford, where he earned a first-class (honors) degree in modern history in 1904. His father then obtained a position for him in the administration of postwar South Africa, where he joined a group of other young Oxford men serving as aides to Lord Milner, the British high commissioner.[6]

Alfred Milner (1854-1925) remains one of the most enigmatic figures of late nineteenth- and early twentieth-century Britain. An influential presence who never held elective office, he was perhaps the most fanatical advocate of an imperial federal electorate after 1900, yet he detested democratic politics and preferred to work behind the scenes. Milner was born in Germany to British parents of modest means, attended Oxford on scholarship from 1872 to 1876, and joined Arnold Toynbee in social service work in the slums of London. A visiting Canadian, George Parkin, converted him to the cause of imperial federation. After graduation, Milner studied law, worked briefly in journalism, and then began a meteoric rise in the civil service that included a stint in Egypt, which Britain occupied in 1882. The Unionist colonial secretary, Joseph Chamberlain, appointed him to South Africa in 1897, where Milner's hard line policy helped bring on war with the Boers. Although created a

---

[5] For the pressure on Britain at this time, see Paul M. Kennedy, *The Rise of the Anglo-German Naval Antagonism, 1860-1914* (London: Allen and Unwin, 1980); and Aaron L. Friedberg, *The Weary Titan: Britain and the Experience of Relative Decline, 1895-1905* (Princeton, NJ: Princeton University Press, 1988). See also Geoffrey R. Searle, *The Quest for National Efficiency: A Study in British Politics and Political Thought, 1899-1914* (Oxford: Basil Blackwell, 1967).

[6] For Kerr's family and early life, see Butler, *Lord Lothian*, 1-4.

Viscount after the war, he returned home in 1905 to face censure over the treatment of Chinese laborers imported to restart the Transvaal mines. Finding politics distasteful, he turned down an offer to lead the Unionist party after its defeat in 1906.[7]

From private life, however, Milner devoted himself to causes aimed at making Britain a stronger competitor in the world. The most important of these would be a new effort to federate the empire, for which he would need the young men he had left in South Africa under his successor, Lord Selborne. Walter Nimocks has described how, with the approval of Milner and Selborne, these young men launched a movement in 1907 to persuade the white settler minority to agree to a union of the four South African colonies. Britons and Boers agreed, mainly because the idea meant self-governing Dominion status on terms that kept the country under their control. But Kerr and his friends saw the union as largely the result of their effort to orchestrate public opinion, and the group resolved next to unite all of the Dominions with Britain. On their return to England in 1909-1910, the young men launched a wider movement with funds arranged by Milner.[8]

The Round Table movement that resulted has received substantial scholarly attention in the last half century.[9] Future scholarship may provide insight into certain themes and individuals associated with the movement that have yet to be explored.[10] One such theme, to be considered here, is the

---

[7] The best study of Lord Milner is still A. M. Gollin, *Proconsul in Politics: A Study of Lord Milner in Opposition and in Power* (New York: Macmillan, 1964). For his years in South Africa, see pp. 29-49, and on his censure, pp. 53-100. For his refusal of the Unionist leadership, see pp. 111-117.

[8] See Walter Nimocks, *Milner's Young Men: The "Kindergarten" in Edwardian Imperial Affairs* (Durham, NC: University of North Carolina Press, 1968), 17-122. See also Kenneth Ingham, "Philip Kerr and the Unification of South Africa," in Turner, ed., *The Larger Idea*, 20-32.

[9] Several of the group settled in South Africa but also remained active in the new movement. See John E. Kendle, *The Round Table Movement and Imperial Union* (Toronto: University of Toronto Press, 1975); and Deborah Lavin, *From Empire to International Commonwealth: A Biography of Lionel Curtis* (Oxford: Clarendon Press, 1995). See also the essays in Andrea Bosco and Alex May, eds., *The Round Table, The Empire/Commonwealth and British Foreign Policy* (London: Lothian Foundation Press, 1997). For a study of one dominion, see Leonie Foster, *High Hopes: The Men and Motives of the Australian Round Table* (Melbourne: Melbourne University Press, 1986).

[10] Studies of the Round Table Moot have left foreign policy in the interwar period mainly to individual biographies, such as those of Curtis and Kerr/Lothian. The views and influence of other Moot members and of the group as a whole need further examination. There are also (continued)

extent to which the movement had the potential to be a more effective response to British relative decline. The Round Table movement had a social vision and political philosophy that needs to be assessed along with its notion of external reform involving the empire, and its ability to link different parts of the English-speaking world to exchange views could be evaluated apart from the particular view that the founders tried to promote.

In keeping with Milner's inclination, his young men agreed that a new campaign should operate at first out of public view, reaching elites before it appealed to a mass electorate. Lionel Curtis and Philip Kerr worked full-time on the project and took the leading roles. Curtis created local groups in Canada, South Africa, Australia, and New Zealand to which he recruited young men from banking, business, the law, and academic life to discuss the future of the empire. The Round Table groups, as they were called, also exchanged news through a new journal of imperial and international affairs, *The Round Table*, that Kerr edited.[11] The Dominion groups began to debate a memorandum on the imperial situation that Curtis wrote and circulated, urging federal union as the equitable way to share the burden of a common defense. In a series of articles for *The Round Table*, Kerr argued that only through closer ties could the self-governing parts of the empire be secure against rival great powers. The founders in London formed an editorial and policy-making committee that they nicknamed the "Moot," which Lord Milner and (on his return) Lord Selborne also attended.[12]

Although focused on professional groups, the Moot also saw working people at home as part of their audience. Several of Milner's young men had served in Toynbee Hall and other settlement houses before going to South Africa, and in 1910, Milner became chairman of the

---

larger narratives having to do with imperial and social reform, suggested below, that could usefully explore continuities with the late nineteenth and mid-twentieth centuries.

[11] For the launching of the movement, see John Kendle, *The Round Table Movement*, 46-129; and Lavin, *From Empire to International Commonwealth*, 105-132. In addition to the Dominion groups, a small number of people in the United Kingdom also subscribed to *The Round Table* and participated in the movement's deliberations.

[12] The so-called "Green Memorandum" by Curtis is in Box 156, Lionel Curtis Papers, Bodleian Library, Oxford. For Kerr's early articles, see "Foreign Affairs: Anglo-German Rivalry," *The Round Table* 1:1 (November 1910), 7-40; "The Anglo-Japanese Alliance," *The Round Table* 1:2 (February 1911), 105-149; and "The New Problem of Imperial Defence," *The Round Table* 1:3 (May 1911), 231-262. Until 1966, *Round Table* articles were unsigned. For Kerr's authorship, see Butler, *Lord Lothian*, 323-325.

supervisory board of Toynbee Hall.[13] The Moot donated copies of *The Round Table* to the Workers Educational Association (WEA), a movement founded at Toynbee Hall in 1903 that brought university-level classes to working men and women around the country. The Moot encouraged local Round Table groups to create or support WEA branches in their Dominions.[14] Involvement with working-class education did not draw Milner or the Moot back into social service, nor did any workers belong to the Moot or to the Round Table movement. But in addressing the same arguments to professionals and to workers, and in thus seeing a need for both groups to deliberate on the same intellectual level, the Round Table founders tried to make their campaign more inclusive.

The Round Table goal reflected the political philosophy of Thomas Hill Green. Kerr and his friends called for an ideal of democratic citizenship defined in terms of individual rights coupled with a sense of duty to the community, which they contrasted to autocratic subordination and self-seeking individualism. The group called its idea of citizenship the "principle of the commonwealth" and the innovation of the Round Table Moot was to extend the idea from domestic society to the empire as a whole. To be true to it, in their view, the British Empire needed to give its citizens at home and in the self-governing colonies equal participation in a government of the whole. The citizens in turn owed this government their primary allegiance.[15]

---

[13] Two members, Patrick Duncan and Richard Feetham, had served in Toynbee Hall, and Curtis served in a mission sponsored by his public school, Haileybury. See their entries in the *Oxford Dictionary of National Biography* (Oxford: Oxford University Press, 2004). For Milner, see Gollin, *Proconsul in Politics*, 154.

[14] With public and privately raised funds, the WEA paid tutors to give small classes to working men and women in university subjects. These did not earn degree credit but required written work to a university standard. See Mary Stocks, *The Workers Educational Association: The First Fifty Years* (London: George Allen and Unwin, 1953); and Roger Fieldhouse, *The Workers Educational Association: Aims and Achievements 1902-1977* (Syracuse, NY: Syracuse University, 1977). For Round Table endorsement of the movement, see "Education and the Working Class," *The Round Table* 4:14 (March 1914), 255-279. For later Round Table donations to the WEA, see the circulation note, September 1930, Box 127, Robert Henry Brand Papers, Bodleian Library, Oxford. For Round Table encouragement of WEA work in the Dominions, see Lionel Curtis to Richard Feetham, 17 April 1914, cited in Kendle, *The Round Table Movement*, 182. See also Edward Kylie, "The Workers Educational Association," *University Magazine* [Montreal] 12:4 (December 1913), 665-672; and Foster, *High Hopes*, 55-56.

[15] For the "principle of the commonwealth," see Kendle, *The Round Table Movement*, 171-174. For statements of the principle, see "The Ethics of Empire," *The Round Table* 3:11 (continued)

Four difficulties, however, beset the Round Table movement. The first was the absence of the United States of America. Kerr and his friends wanted to achieve a federal union patterned after the American one.[16] But in the early twentieth century, the four Dominions only added about a quarter to the population and industry of the United Kingdom. The Moot expected the Dominions to grow rapidly and eventually dominate an imperial federation. In the early years, though, only partnership with America would have given an Anglo-Dominion group the weight to prevail against its likely adversaries. Closer ties may have been a possibility that Kerr tried to gauge on a visit to the United States in 1912, where he met former President Theodore Roosevelt on Long Island and some younger progressives in the federal capital, Washington. But Roosevelt lost his third-party campaign for president that autumn, and the younger Americans do not seem to have had an interest in foreign affairs.[17]

Another difficulty arose from the Moot's decision to remain neutral on contentious economic matters, such as trade policy. In 1903, Joseph Chamberlain had left the Unionist government to campaign for imperial preference, a system of tariffs by which Britain and the Dominions would prefer each other's trade to that of other countries. The Liberals won the election of 1906 in part by campaigning to prevent such "food taxes" against imported American grain. Although Milner favored preference, to sidestep the controversy he and the Moot limited the Round Table aim to

---

(June 1913), 484-501; and [Philip Kerr], "The Principle of Peace," *The Round Table* 6:3 (June 1916), 391-429.

[16] The British businessman Frederick Scott Oliver called on Kerr's generation to federate the British Empire in the way that Hamilton and American federalists had united the American states in the 1780s. See F. S. Oliver, *Alexander Hamilton: An Essay on American Union* (London: A. Constable, 1906). Oliver's book helped inspire Kerr and his friends to unite South Africa and aim for a union of the entire self-governing empire. See Nimocks, *Milner's Young Men*, 125-129. Oliver joined the Moot in its early years.

[17] There seems to be no record of the content of Kerr's discussions with Americans in 1912. See Billington, *Lothian*, 24-25. Kerr met with Theodore Roosevelt in Oyster Bay, New York. For Roosevelt's attitude to Britain, see Max Beloff, "Theodore Roosevelt and the British Empire," in *The Great Powers: Essays in Twentieth Century Politics* (London: Allen and Unwin, 1959), 215-232. Kerr also met the circle of younger progressives in Washington around Robert Grosvenor Valentine. A former settlement house volunteer, Valentine served as President William Howard Taft's Commissioner of Indian Affairs from 1909 until the fall of 1912, when he resigned to support Roosevelt's third-party presidential campaign. See Valentine's entry in the *National Cyclopaedia of American Biography* (New York: J. T. White, 1898-).

imperial political union.[18] A tariff would have also antagonized the United States, although this danger does not seem to have been a factor in the Round Table position. But the Moot's neutrality on trade alienated pro-tariff Unionists and, more deeply, expressed a sense that the British economy could be taken for granted.[19]

The dependent empire posed a third problem. A movement to federate the empire would have had to resolve the position of British dependencies, especially India, whose 300 million people formed three-quarters of the empire's population. In a memorandum to the Moot, Kerr argued for limited representation of India in an imperial federation, but Milner and the others wanted to confine a union to Britain and the white Dominions.[20] The Moot resolved in 1912 to leave India out of a federation but otherwise to grant it full autonomy someday as a Dominion.[21] This was a radical idea for anyone in Britain to advocate before 1914. But Kerr and his friends could not envision Dominion status for India anytime soon and they did not press for immediate reform.

Finally, and most seriously of all, the Dominions themselves resisted closer constitutional ties to the United Kingdom. Through *The Round Table* and the local groups, Dominion members learned about the wider world and began to realize that their countries would need to take more responsibility for their foreign relations and defense. But they disagreed over whether the threat to the empire in the Atlantic took priority.[22] More deeply, the London group's insistence on either closer union or breakup misjudged sentiment in the Dominions, which at the time wanted neither. As a result, the movement stalled in 1912. The Moot's methods also did not help matters. Although Curtis recruited the Dominion

---

[18] For the Round Table position on tariffs, see "The Unionists and the Food Taxes," *The Round Table* 3:10 (March 1913), 232-276.

[19] Leopold Amery believed that its neutrality on tariff reform isolated the Moot from needed political support. See L. S. Amery, *My Political Life*, 3 vols. (London: Hutchinson, 1953-1955), Vol. 1, *England Before the Storm, 1896-1914*, 270. The writer Richard Jebb attacked the Round Table goal of political union and called instead for a military and economic alliance with the Dominions as independent nations in his book, *The Britannic Question: A Survey of Alternatives* (London: Longmans, 1913).

[20] Lionel Curtis argued for a federation of the self-governing empire. For Round Table deliberations on India, see DeWitt Clinton Ellinwood, "The Round Table and India, 1909-1920," *Journal of Commonwealth Political Studies* 9:3 (November 1971), 183-209, especially 186-189.

[21] [Philip Kerr], "India and the Empire," *The Round Table* 2:8 (September 1912), 587-626.

[22] Australia and New Zealand objected to the concentration of the British fleet in home waters to meet the German naval challenge. See "Naval Policy and the Pacific Question," *The Round Table* 4:15 (June 1914), 391-462.

groups on the premise that the movement was open-ended in its aim, some subscribers correctly saw the process of debating a call for union as an attempt to guide local opinion toward a predetermined end.[23]

Controversy over Ireland then pulled the Moot disastrously into United Kingdom politics. In June 1912 the Liberal government headed by Prime Minister Herbert Henry Asquith introduced an Irish home rule bill that Ulster Protestants pledged to resist by force. Opposing Irish separation, Milner circulated a petition in Great Britain in the spring of 1914 whose signers also pledged forcibly to resist the British government, if home rule came to Ireland as a whole before a referendum was held on the measure in the United Kingdom as a whole. Kerr had gone on leave in early 1913 to recover from a nervous breakdown and did not participate in the Irish controversy.[24] But some Moot members joined Milner, while others tried to head off a confrontation by pressing for a four-way devolution of power to England, Scotland, Ireland, and Wales.[25] The Liberal government depended for its majority on Irish Catholic members of parliament, however, and the government pressed ahead with a separate Irish bill. With funds secretly raised by Milner, Ulster Protestants smuggled German rifles into Ireland in

---

[23] For the dissenting views in the Dominion groups, see the volume of responses to the Green Memorandum collected in *Round Table Studies*, Box 156, Lionel Curtis Papers. The Canadian dissent is on pp. 399-436 and the Australian is on pp. 480-483. See also Christopher R. J. Rickerd, "Canada, the Round Table, and Imperial Federation," and Alex May, "The London 'Moot,' Dominion Nationalism, and Imperial Federation," in Bosco and May, eds., *The Round Table: The Empire/Commonwealth and British Foreign Policy*, 191-221, 223-233; and Leonie Foster, "The Australian Round Table, the Moot, and Australian Nationalism," *The Round Table* 72:288 (October 1983), 473-484. For the views of two Canadians suspicious of Round Table motives, see Rodolphe Lemieux to George M. Wrong, 29 August 1913, B2003-0005/003 (Lemieux), and John W. Dafoe to George M. Wrong, 16 October 1916, B2003-0005/002 (Dafoe), George M. Wrong Papers, University of Toronto Archives, Toronto. For the growing sense of separate nationhood in the Dominions, see John Eddy and Deryck Schreuder, eds., *The Rise of Colonial Nationalism: Australia, New Zealand, Canada, and South Africa First Assert Their Nationalities 1880-1914* (Sydney: Allen and Unwin, 1988).

[24] On Milner's activity in 1912-1914, see Gollin, *Proconsul in Politics*, 172-222; and Billington, *Lothian*, 30-37. Milner named his petition and movement the "British Covenant." For Kerr's breakdown, see Butler, *Lord Lothian*, 49-55.

[25] Amery took an executive role and Lionel Hichens joined the general council of the British Covenant movement. For its leadership, see Walter Long, *Memories* (New York: E. P. Dutton, [1923]), 200-205. Curtis and other Moot members tried to persuade Unionist and Liberal leaders to agree to a four-way devolution of power to England, Scotland, Ireland, and Wales. See Kendle, *The Round Table Movement*, 130-155. Four-way devolution would have denied a separate status to Ireland that the Moot saw as a step toward independence.

April 1914.[26] Milner's original goal of building a stronger imperial state, primarily to defend against Germany, thus ended in preparations for a revolt at home using German arms to overthrow the British state. The outbreak of the First World War in August may have prevented an armed uprising in the United Kingdom. The Asquith government suspended the Irish bill until hostilities ended.

THE FIRST WORLD WAR AND AFTER

With the outbreak of war, Kerr resumed his editorship of *The Round Table*, and in a series of new articles he depicted the war as a struggle of liberty against tyranny.[27] Mounting casualties on the western front eventually enabled Unionists and dissident Liberals led by David Lloyd George to topple Asquith in December 1916. Lord Milner joined a new five-member War Cabinet and installed several of his younger men on the staffs of that body and the prime minister's own office. Kerr left his editorship to join the latter and became Lloyd George's principal assistant for foreign and imperial affairs. Kerr kept the Prime Minister informed of events and also drafted war aims statements and gave advice.[28] Instead, however, of enabling Kerr and his friends to fulfill their goals, proximity to power only ratified their defeat.

The War Cabinet brought the German submarine menace under control by moving vital supply ships in convoys, but a new offensive on the

---

[26] For Milner's role in funding the Ulster Volunteers, see A. T. Q. Stewart, *The Ulster Crisis* (London: Faber, 1967), 130-140. The Moot as a group began to express doubts about the wisdom of threatening civil war in "The Irish Crisis," *The Round Table* 4:14 (March 1914), 201-230. It appears, however, that Curtis and the others were prepared to cast their lot with Milner if civil conflict broke out. See Lavin, *From Empire to International Commonwealth*, 120-124.

[27] See [Philip Kerr], "The War in Europe," *The Round Table* 4:16 (September 1914), 591-615; "The Foundations of Peace," *The Round Table* 5:19 (June 1915), 589-625; "The End of War," *The Round Table* 5:20 (September 1915), 772-796; and "The War for Public Right," *The Round Table* 6:22 (March 1916), 193-231.

[28] For the coming to power of Milner, see P. A. Lockwood, "Milner's Entry into the War Cabinet, December 1916," *Historical Journal* 7:1 (March 1964), 120-134. For the work of the Prime Minister's secretaries, see John Turner, *Lloyd George's Secretariat* (Cambridge: Cambridge University Press, 1980). For Kerr's service, see John Turner and Michael Dockrill, "Philip Kerr at 10 Downing Street, 1916-1921," in Turner, ed., *The Larger Idea*, 33-61. On Kerr's wartime activity, see also Billington, *Lothian*, 45-54.

western front in the summer and fall gained little new ground.[29] In April 1917, Milner and his men bowed to necessity when Dominion leaders secured, in Resolution IX of the Imperial War Conference, language affirming their *de facto* independence at war's end.[30] Kerr and his friends helped craft a reform of Indian government that became law in 1919, giving some power at the provincial level to a small Indian electorate.[31] Kerr also served as a contact for the Zionist leader Chaim Weizmann and helped win War Cabinet backing for a Jewish home in Palestine.[32] The India reform did not go far enough to meet Indian demands, however, and British promises to Arabs could not be reconciled with those to Jews. With the public nearing exhaustion in 1917-1918, Philip Kerr urged the Prime Minister to lay increasing stress on the war as a moral struggle.[33] But Kerr carried out a secret mission to Switzerland in March 1918 to explore an expedient peace with Austria-Hungary, which the latter declined.[34]

Kerr attended the Paris peace conference in 1919 with the British delegation, where he proposed to Lloyd George that nations form a

---

[29] See John Terraine, *Business in Great Waters: The U-Boat Wars 1916-1945* (London: Leo Cooper, 1989), 3-84; and David French, *The Strategy of the Lloyd George Coalition, 1916-1918* (Oxford: Clarendon Press, 1995), 94-123.

[30] For the resolution on the Dominions, see *Parliamentary Papers (Commons)*, 1917-18, Vol. 23, Cmd. 8566, "Imperial War Conference, 1917," 5. For the Round Table's acquiescence, see "New Developments in the Constitution of the Empire," *The Round Table* 7:27 (June 1917), 441-459. The Moot had tried over the preceding year to launch a public movement for federation by publishing their case as a short book by Lionel Curtis, *The Problem of the Commonwealth* (New York: Macmillan, 1916). The Canadian Round Table leaders objected and the Moot agreed to decide after the war whether the Round Table groups should continue for discussion only or to seek political change. See Kendle, *The Round Table Movement*, 181-223.

[31] For Kerr's role in India reform during the war, see again Ellinwood, "The Round Table and India, 1909-1920," 183-209, especially 190-202.

[32] On the role of Kerr and others in the British pledge of a Jewish home in Palestine, see Leonard Stein, *The Balfour Declaration* (New York: Simon and Schuster, 1961), 314-322, 344-349. See also Chaim Weizmann to Kerr, 16 September and 7 October 1917, GD 40/17/42/96-99, 102-105, Papers of the Eleventh Marquess of Lothian, National Archives of Scotland, Edinburgh [hereafter Lothian Papers].

[33] For Kerr's advice to stress the moral character of the war, see Kerr, "Notes for speech on peace," no date but indexed 26 June 1917, copy, GD 40/17/640, Lothian Papers. Lloyd George stressed this theme in a speech in Glasgow, reported in *The Times*, 30 June 1917, p. 7, col. 6. See also Kerr's advice for the Prime Minister's speech before the Trades Union Congress on 5 January 1918, in Kerr to Prime Minister, 30 December 1917, enclosing memorandum, F/89/1/12, Lloyd George Papers, House of Lords Record Office, London.

[34] For Kerr's mission to Switzerland, see Kerr, "Report on Mission to Switzerland," 19 March 1918, F/160/1/13, Lloyd George Papers. See also French, *The Strategy of the Lloyd George Coalition 1916-1918*, 168-170.

permanent conference after the war to consult one another with no binding obligations. In the peace treaty with Germany, however, U.S. President Woodrow Wilson wanted and obtained clauses to found a League of Nations with powers to enforce peace.[35] In February, Kerr helped block an attempt by Winston Churchill to commit Britain to military intervention in revolutionary Russia on the anti-Bolshevik side. But with Lloyd George's backing, Kerr privately encouraged an unsuccessful American peace feeler to Lenin that the Prime Minister had to deny when it leaked out in April.[36] Kerr drafted the Fontainebleau memorandum in March, in which Lloyd George urged more moderate terms on Germany. In June, however, Kerr wrote the covering letter to the reply of the Allies to the objections of the German delegation to the peace treaty, in which Kerr condemned Germany for the war and defended harsher terms.[37] He watched in the autumn as the U.S. Senate rejected the treaty with Germany, mainly over Wilson's League, ending Kerr's hope of a postwar partnership of the British Empire with the United States.[38]

Although unwilling to plunge into Russia, Kerr urged Lloyd George to cling to a postwar imperial position that was no more tenable. Kerr's response to the postwar Catholic insurgency in Ireland was to compare it to the Confederate secession, and he resisted Irish separation

---

[35] Kerr gave his views on postwar international organization in memoranda to Lloyd George, GD 40/17/54/31-35, Lothian Papers. See also George Egerton, "Imperialism, Atlanticism, and Internationalism: Philip Kerr and the League of Nations Question, 1916-1920," *Annals of the Lothian Foundation* 1 (1991), 95-122.

[36] On Kerr's role in policy toward Russia, see Billington, *Lothian*, 58-59; and the chapter in this volume by Keith Neilson.

[37] For the Fontainebleau memorandum, see *Parliamentary Papers (Commons)*, 1922, Vol. 23, Cmd. 1614, "Memorandum circulated by the Prime Minister on March 25th, 1919." For Kerr's authorship, see Lloyd George to Kerr, 25 March 1919, enclosing draft with amendments, GD 40/17/61/90-122, Lothian Papers. For the covering letter, see President Clemenceau to Count Brockdorf-Rantzau, 16 June 1919, *Parliamentary Papers (Commons)*, 1919, Vol. 53, Cmd. 258, "Reply to the Observations of the German Delegation on the Conditions of Peace," 2-11. For Kerr's authorship of the letter, see H. W. V. Temperley, *A History of the Peace Conference of Paris*, 6 vols. (London: Hodder & Stoughton, 1920-1924), 1:271.

[38] For Kerr's hope of Anglo-American partnership, see Kerr to Curtis, 15 October 1918, reprinted in *Annals of the Lothian Foundation* 1 (1991), 383-386. See also [Lionel Curtis], "Windows of Freedom," *The Round Table* 9:33 (December 1918), 1-47. For British reaction to the U.S. Senate's rejection of the treaty in November 1919, see [Philip Kerr], "The British Empire, the League of Nations, and the United States," *The Round Table* 10:38 (March 1920), 251-253; and George W. Egerton, "Britain and the 'Great Betrayal': Anglo-American Relations and the Struggle for United States Ratification of the Treaty of Versailles, 1919-1920," *The Historical Journal* 21:4 (December 1978), 885-911.

almost to the end.[39] Unable to see any reason to give Turkey moderate peace terms after the wartime deaths of Armenians, Kerr backed the hard line favored by Lloyd George but not by the British Foreign Office. Kerr's last important service to the prime minister was to be a secret intermediary to the Greeks, urging them to continue a disastrous war with Turkish nationalists in 1920 while Lloyd George maintained in public and to his own foreign secretary that he favored peace.[40]

After another nervous breakdown in the autumn of 1920, Kerr resigned the following spring, ending a decade that had brought him, as he later observed, "almost as close to the centre of world affairs as it was possible for a man to be."[41] In 1910, he and his friends had concluded that, to survive in a world of growing rivals, Britain had to form a more centralized imperial state. But the movement they launched to reform the empire ran aground, and in 1914 their mentor, Lord Milner, almost led an insurrection against the British government. Milner and his men vaulted to the top of that government two years later, only to discover that even supreme power had its limits.

Could Philip Kerr and his friends have devised a better strategy in 1909 for British survival? The Dominions rallied to Britain's side in both world wars without having to be federated, and the Moot's vision of a secure commonwealth was inadequate in the absence of American support. A Round Table movement with a more limited and above-board purpose might, however, have had more success, if not before the First World War, then immediately after it.

---

[39] See Kerr to Lloyd George, 2 September 1920, GD 40/17/1280, Lothian Papers. For his view of postwar Ireland, see Kerr to Edward Lascelles, 24 December 1920, copy, GD 40/17/214/124-125, Lothian Papers. See also [Philip Kerr], "The Irish Crisis," *The Round Table* 8:31 (June 1918), 496-525; Gary Peatling, "The Last Defense of the Union? The Round Table and Ireland, 1910-1925," in Bosco and May, eds., *The Round Table, The Empire/Commonwealth and British Foreign Policy*, 283-305; and the chapter in this volume by Melanie Sayers.
[40] Kerr to Prime Minister, 7 April 1920, enclosing memorandum, F/90/1/4, Lloyd George Papers. For Kerr's role as a secret intermediary, see Lord Curzon, "Memorandum on some aspects of my tenure of the Foreign Office," November 1924, Curzon Papers, Mss. Eur. F112/319, Asia, Pacific, and Africa Collections, British Library, London. See also Karl G. Larew, "Great Britain and the Greco-Turkish War," *The Historian* 35:2 (February 1973), 256-270.
[41] Kerr, "The Mechanical Reason for War," in Lionel Curtis and Philip Kerr, *The Prevention of War* (New Haven, CT: Yale University Press, 1923), 8.

The late 1890s and early 1900s were a time of improving Anglo-American relations.[42] A private Round Table movement that included the United States as well as the Dominions might have organized in the years before 1914 to exchange news and discuss world problems without a political agenda. American and Dominion elites might then have developed a more common outlook on the world (and greater clarity about matters in which their needs and interests diverged) without being forced to make divisive constitutional or foreign policy choices. It is doubtful that such a movement could have brought the United States into the First World War sooner; but after America's entry, the movement might have debated a postwar form of world organization resembling the consultative gatherings that Britain had held at intervals with its self-governing colonies since 1887. An idea similar to Kerr's 1919 proposal for a permanent postwar conference might then have received more careful consideration on the American side, and if part of the peace treaty, might have met with Senate approval.[43]

The Round Table movement faded after 1919, although the Moot continued to publish *The Round Table* in the interwar years with the help of a few surviving members in the Dominions.[44] Lord Milner retired in 1921 and died four years later, still convinced that imperial federation was the highest end toward which Britain and the Dominions could aspire.[45] Philip Kerr realized that his country would need to belong to a larger world community that included the United States of America.

---

[42] See Bradford Perkins, *The Great Rapprochement: England and the United States, 1895-1914* (New York: Atheneum, 1968).

[43] George Egerton notes what the world lost in not following Kerr's alternative, in "Imperialism, Atlanticism, and Internationalism: Philip Kerr and the League of Nations Question, 1916-1920," *Annals of the Lothian Foundation* 1 (1991), 119. On the colonial meetings, see John Edward Kendle, *The Colonial and Imperial Conferences, 1887-1911: A Study in Imperial Organization* (London: Longmans, 1967). A majority in the U.S. Senate would have accepted more moderate terms. See Herbert F. Margulies, *The Mild Reservationists and the League of Nations Controversy in the Senate* (Columbia: University of Missouri Press, 1989).

[44] For the aftermath of the Round Table movement, see Kendle, *The Round Table Movement*, 260-300. Most of the groups disbanded, leaving a handful of members to supply a chronicle article from each Dominion for the journal and to discuss occasional memoranda on Commonwealth matters. These groups eventually dissolved. The Moot has continued, however, with new members drawn from the Commonwealth and the United States. The Moot has a website at: http://www.moot.org.uk/ (retrieved January 2009).

[45] For Milner's "Credo" of Anglo-Saxonism, published after his death, see Gollin, *Proconsul in Politics*, 128-132.

THE POLITICAL PILGRIM

The two late Victorian responses to British decline took new form in the three decades after 1920. Many settlement workers realized after 1900 that their local efforts were not enough to relieve poverty, and in later life these people achieved broader social reforms, designing the American social security system in 1935 and the British welfare state of the late 1940s.[46] Imperial federalism ceased after 1920 but Round Table alumni, in conjunction with returning members of the American delegation to the Paris Peace Conference, created a network of new institutes to study and influence international relations. The two flagships of this network were the Royal Institute of International Affairs in London, known as Chatham House, and the Council on Foreign Relations in New York. Where the original settlement houses had tried to educate and uplift the poor, the new institutes functioned as settlement houses to the powerful and tried to educate elites to take responsibility for a wider liberal-democratic civilization. The Council on Foreign Relations helped plan the foreign policy of the United States after the Second World War. Where the welfare states of the 1930s and 1940s aimed to strengthen domestic inclusion, the post-1945 Western alliance system tried to strengthen cohesion between the recovering liberal powers.[47]

During the interwar years, however, the post-1945 world was barely imaginable. The Round Table movement had only linked and modified the two kinds of late Victorian activism in a limited and tentative way. With the Round Table failure, welfare reform and internationalism returned to their largely separate worlds to await the crises of the 1930s and 1940s that finally brought them to realization. During the interwar years, Philip Kerr lectured on occasion at Toynbee Hall and participated in

---

[46] For the role of former settlement workers in the creation of the American and British welfare states, see George Martin, *Madam Secretary: Frances Perkins* (Boston: Houghton Mifflin, 1976), 58-64, 341-356; and José Harris, *William Beveridge: A Biography* (Oxford: Clarendon Press, 1997), 74-97, 365-450.

[47] On the institutes, see Stephen King-Hall, *Chatham House: A Brief Account of the Origins, Purposes, and Methods of the Royal Institute of International Affairs* (London: Oxford University Press, 1937); and Whitney H. Shepardson, *Early History of the Council on Foreign Relations* (Stamford, CT: Overbrook Press, 1960). For the influence of the latter on U.S. foreign policy, see Robert D. Schulzinger, *The Wise Men of Foreign Affairs: The History of the Council on Foreign Relations* (New York: Columbia University Press, 1984). The Canadian, Australian, and New Zealand Institutes of International Affairs were founded in 1928, 1933, and 1934 respectively.

discussions at Chatham House.[48] But his bridging of the two worlds was unusual and his involvement with such institutions was incidental to a more individual mission to address what he believed to be the deeper needs of his country and his time.

Kerr spent part of the early 1920s in the United States, living with American families of the Christian Science church, to which he had converted in 1914. His new faith gave him a sense of belonging to the Protestant tradition with which he identified the growth of liberty and democratic government. Although it took no position on matters of policy, in its doctrine that evil and suffering were states of mind, Christian Science encouraged in Kerr the belief that he could heal not only his own body through faithful effort but also seemingly hard differences in the world. He felt himself now to be on a more personal quest, as an anonymous column that he began to write in 1925 for the *Christian Science Monitor*, "Diary of a Political Pilgrim," made clear.[49]

Kerr began to realize during the war that a tension between liberty and tyranny was not, as he had originally thought, the deeper problem of world order. In lectures to a summer institute at Williams College in Massachusetts in 1922, he declared that the true cause of war was the division of the world into sovereign nation-states. Peace would be achieved only with a democratic world government similar to the American Union. Until then, the United States and the British Commonwealth needed to work together to keep the peace. Although he believed in the need for Britain and America to anchor the liberal world, Kerr was unusual in seeing Anglo-American cooperation as a means to the end of a world state and not

---

[48] For Kerr's association with Toynbee Hall in the 1920s, see Briggs and Macartney, *Toynbee Hall*, 106, 109. In 1928-1930, Kerr chaired a working group at Chatham House that tried to improve Anglo-American relations with a counterpart group in the Council on Foreign Relations. See Priscilla Roberts, "Underpinning the Anglo-American Alliance: The Council on Foreign Relations and Britain between the Wars," in *Twentieth Century Anglo-American Relations*, ed. Jonathan Hollowell (Basingstoke: Palgrave, 2001), 25-43.

[49] For Kerr's conversion to Christian Science, see Butler, *Lord Lothian*, 85-101; and Christopher Sykes, *Nancy: The Life of Lady Astor* (New York: Harper and Row, 1972), 138-144. For Kerr's view of his faith as a healing influence in the world, see The Marquess of Lothian, "Christian Science, Public Affairs, and the Christian Science Monitor," *The Christian Science Journal* 52:10 (1935), 508-511. On Kerr's authorship of his column, see Erwin D. Canham, *Commitment to Freedom: The Story of the Christian Science Monitor* (Boston: Houghton Mifflin, 1958), 204.

simply as a way to preserve the dominance of the advanced English-speaking nations.[50]

Kerr became secretary to the Rhodes Trustees in 1925. In this capacity, he administered the Rhodes Scholarships, which aimed to educate future leaders in the English-speaking world.[51] Kerr helped support the delicate task of a reform, led by Americans, to make nominations from the United States more selective. His Rhodes work continued afterwards to take him annually to the United States, where he developed contacts all over the country and gave talks on world affairs.[52] Kerr tried privately to mediate the Anglo-American naval dispute of 1927-1929. Although neither government took up his own ideas, in articles and private meetings he helped each side understand the other's official position and he earned American gratitude.[53]

Kerr's interest in cooperation did not extend to closer ties with the continent of Europe. He opposed any commitments to eastern Europe beyond those associated with British membership in the League of Nations, and he only reluctantly agreed to endorse the British pledge at Locarno in

---

[50] For his wartime view, see [Philip Kerr], "The End of War," *The Round Table* 5:20 (September 1915), 772-796. For his lectures at Williams College, see Philip Kerr, "The Mechanical Reason for War," "The Psychological Reason for War," and "The Only Road to International Peace," in Curtis and Kerr, *The Prevention of War*, 7-74.

[51] On Kerr's appointment and service as Rhodes secretary, see Anthony Kenny, "The Rhodes Trust and its Administration," in *The History of the Rhodes Trust 1902-1999*, ed. Anthony Kenny (Oxford: Clarendon Press, 2001), 25-39. Lord Milner joined the Rhodes Trustees on his return from South Africa and Rhodes funds helped underwrite the Round Table movement until about 1920. After the war, Moot members cycled in and out of the Rhodes Trust. Geoffrey Dawson succeeded George Parkin as secretary to the Trustees in 1919. Sir Edward Grigg replaced Philip Kerr as secretary to Lloyd George in 1921 and replaced Dawson as Rhodes secretary in 1922, when Dawson resumed his editorship of *The Times* (begun in 1912 and interrupted in 1919). Upon Grigg's appointment as Governor of Kenya in 1925, Kerr became Rhodes secretary. See the entries for these men in the *Oxford Dictionary of National Biography*.

[52] On the American reform, see David Alexander, "The American Scholarships," in Kenny, ed., *The History of the Rhodes Trust 1902-1999*, 127-140; and Billington, *Lothian*, 80-85. For an itinerary of his speaking engagements on a typical trip, see Philip Kerr, "Report to the Trustees on Visit to Canada and the United States in 1927," 24 January 1928, file 2657, Rhodes Trust Files, Rhodes House, Oxford.

[53] On Kerr's private efforts to mediate Anglo-American tensions, see Billington, *Lothian*, 91-97. For American appreciation of Kerr's role, see Christian A. Herter to Kerr, 5 April 1928, GD 40/17/228/244, and Frank B. Kellogg to Kerr, 19 June 1928, GD 40/17/231/565/567, Lothian Papers. Kellogg served as U.S. secretary of state in 1925-1929; Herter was secretary of state in 1959-1961. For the centrality of Anglo-American relations in Kerr's life and thought, see Priscilla Roberts, "Lord Lothian and the Atlantic World," *The Historian* 66:1 (April 2004), 97-127.

1925 to defend the mutual borders of France, Belgium, and Germany. Alarmed by the resolve of the French to collect postwar reparations, he came to believe that restoring Germany to military parity with France was a prerequisite for lasting peace. The war, he believed, had been fought not to establish the dominance of one group of nations over another, but to defeat a temporary act of aggression. For one side to maintain permanent domination of the other was unconscionable.[54] Kerr never asked if the Germans had abandoned the goal of avenging their wartime defeat; he saw only French determination to keep the Germans down.

As part of his Rhodes work, Kerr also traveled to South Africa, where he was troubled by the erosion of black African rights under the Union that he and his friends had helped to create two decades earlier. Conservatives in Britain pressed in the 1920s for the creation of a new white settler Dominion in the British territories of Kenya, Tanganyika, and Uganda to the north. Kerr believed that white settlement of Africa was advantageous to the development of the continent and he did not challenge white minority rule in South Africa. But in 1927 he urged London to represent Africans as well as settlers on legislative councils in the British colonies north of the Zambezi River. His suggestion made no headway but neither did plans for a new white Dominion.[55]

Kerr tried to find a middle way through economic problems at home. He saw the tariffs that Conservatives continued to seek and the nationalization favored by the new Labour Party as attempts to save declining technologies from necessary modernization. In a private exchange with John Maynard Keynes, who was beginning to argue that private economic activity could be managed in new ways by government policy, Kerr argued instead that the private sector itself needed to change, with labor and capital working as partners rather than as adversaries. An idea similar to Kerr's took hold in Scandinavia (independently of his ideas).

---

[54] For Kerr's skeptical view of Europe, see [Philip Kerr], "Europe, the Covenant and the Protocol," *The Round Table* 15:58 (March 1925), 219-241. Kerr shared the hostile British reaction to the French occupation of the Ruhr, described in David Williamson, "Great Britain and the Ruhr Crisis, 1923-1924," *British Journal of International Studies* 3:1 (April 1977), 70-91.

[55] On Kerr's anxiety over race relations in South Africa, see Kerr to Patrick Duncan, 13 April 1926, copy, GD 40/17/222/130-131, Lothian Papers. He gave his thoughts about British Africa to the Rhodes Trustees in Kerr, "The African Highlands," 25 February 1927, copy, GD 40/17/83/4-23, Lothian Papers. Copy in Box "Dr. Rendall's and Other Reports," Rhodes Trust Files. Kerr published his views in [Philip Kerr], "The New Problem of Africa," *The Round Table* 17:67 (June 1927), 447-472.

But in the English-speaking world, where labor and management were less organized, Keynes had greater appeal.[56]

After becoming eleventh Marquess of Lothian in March 1930, Philip Kerr's surname changed to Lothian, inheriting a title with substantial wealthgave him new social prominence. He remained Rhodes secretary until 1939 and continued to write articles for *The Round Table*. He also wrote letters and opinion pieces for several newspapers, including *The Times*, to which he had privileged access through its editor Geoffrey Dawson, a fellow Round Table Moot member.[57] In his writings on public affairs, Lothian continued to urge a moderate course for British policy at home, in the empire, and abroad. Unfortunately, the 1930s were anything but a moderate time.

Lothian joined other Liberals in calling for new spending on public infrastructure to address the deepening Depression after 1929. While also urging the modernization of private industry, he saw no problem in adding labor-saving capacity at a time of high unemployment. In 1933, he argued that nationalism was the obstacle to economic recovery. He did not recognize the extent to which economic nationalism was a response to saturated markets rather than the initial cause of the collapse.[58]

Lothian's major concern in the early 1930s, though, was India. The British government began a review of the 1919 India Act in 1927, and after conferences with Indians in 1930-1931, the government proposed that India receive greater self-rule at the provincial level and limited autonomy at the center. As under-secretary of state for India, an appointment he accepted in 1931, Lord Lothian chaired a committee of British and Indian notables that toured India in 1932 to devise a wider franchise. The panel recommended giving forty percent of men and ten percent of women the vote in provincial elections, leaving the smaller 1919 electorate of ten percent men and one percent women to choose a central legislature. Lothian supported the

---

[56] For Kerr's views on the British economy and industrial relations, see Kerr, *The Industrial Dilemma*, The New Way Series, No. 14 (London: Daily News, 1926). For his exchange with Keynes, see Kerr to John Maynard Keynes, 25 August 1927, copy, Keynes to Kerr, 31 August 1927, and Kerr to Keynes, 2 September 1927, copy, GD 40/17/229/309-310, 320, and 330-333, Lothian Papers.

[57] For Lothian's inheritance, see Butler, *Lord Lothian*, 144-158. He succeeded to the title upon the death of a cousin. For Geoffrey Robinson (Dawson after 1917), see again his entry in the *Oxford Dictionary of National Biography*.

[58] See David Lloyd George; The Marquess of Lothian; and B. Seebohm Rowntree, *How to Tackle Unemployment* (London: Press Printers Ltd., 1930); and The Marquess of Lothian, *Liberalism in the Modern World* (London: Lovat Dickson, 1933).

reservation of legislative seats for the principal minorities in each province.[59]

The proposals disappointed many Indians, including members of Lothian's committee, while at home Winston Churchill attacked the provisions as a step toward dissolution of the British Empire.[60] But in the parliamentary debate that followed in London, Lothian played a crucial role retaining the support of Indian moderates, without whom the Conservative government could not have passed the India Act of 1935. Although no one foresaw the end of British rule in India that came in 1947, in correspondence with leading Indians Lothian privately defended the 1935 Act as an irreversible step toward Dominion status. After the 1931 Statute of Westminster, such status meant independence.[61]

After 1933, Lothian's attention focused on the increasingly dangerous international situation. The new administration of Franklin D. Roosevelt in the United States dashed Lothian's hope that America might cancel Allied war debts, and Britain's default in 1934 led the U.S. Congress to prohibit future loans for war purchases.[62] To avoid antagonizing the United States and Canada, Britain had allowed its prewar alliance with Japan to lapse in 1922. In 1934 Lothian and the Moot helped publicize an attempt by the British Foreign Office to explore new ties to Japan, forcing the British government to back down to avoid incurring the hostility of Washington.[63] In a private meeting with President Roosevelt, however,

---

[59] For Lothian's work on 1930s India reform, see Gerard Douds, "Lothian and the Indian Federation," in Turner, ed., *The Larger Idea*, 62-76. For the work of Lothian's committee and the subsequent decision on Indian representation, see *Parliamentary Papers (Commons)*, 1931-32, Vol. 8, Cmd. 4086, "Report of the Indian Franchise Committee," and Cmd. 4147, "Communal Decision."

[60] For the dissents by Indian members of Lothian's committee, see *ibid.*, Cmd. 4086, 197-199, 206-220, 221-246. Dawson lauded the committee's report in *The Times*, 3 May 1932, p. 15, col. 2. For Churchill's criticism of Lothian and Dawson, see his speech to the Carlton Club on 25 May 1932, in Martin Gilbert, *Winston S. Churchill* (1966-1988), Vol. 5, Companion Volume, Part II, 434-436.

[61] See Lothian to M. R. Jayakar, 14 September 1934, copy, GD 40/17/174/326-330; Sir Tej Bahadur Sapru to Lothian, 3 April 1934, GD 40/17/174/273-275; and Lothian to Sapru, 16 November 1934, copy, GD 40/17/286/673-677, Lothian Papers.

[62] For his hopes, see [Lord Lothian], "The Opportunity at Washington," *The Round Table* 23:90 (March 1933), 270-285.

[63] See D. C. Watt, "Britain, the United States and Japan in 1934," in *Personalities and Policies: Studies in the Formulation of British Foreign Policy in the Twentieth Century* (Westport, CT: Greenwood Press, 1965), 83-99.

Lothian was unable to interest him in a more formal Anglo-American partnership to contain Japan.[64]

The coming to power of Adolf Hitler in Germany in 1933 alarmed Lothian.[65] But he blamed the Nazi takeover of Germany primarily on its postwar treatment by the Allies, and believed that ending the restrictions on German military power would moderate the extremism of the new regime.[66] In January 1935, Lothian visited Hitler in Berlin and returned proclaiming the Führer's peaceful intentions, and he approved the German annexation of the Rhineland in March 1936.[67] In 1914, to uphold Ulster's right to remain British, Lord Milner had obtained German arms to threaten the British state; in the 1930s, to restore what he believed to be their right to national equality, Lothian endorsed German efforts to rearm themselves and remilitarize their borders.

Although Lothian's appeasement rested on wishful thinking, he tried to give it a strategic aspect. He had come to believe in the 1920s that France and Germany would never be at peace until they came to an understanding as equals. To this idea he added an American angle. The United States wanted no part of any future war in Europe but Lothian believed that America might be open to a maritime alliance with Great Britain, if the latter limited its commitment in Europe to the defense of Belgium and France. He appears to have been unique in making influence on the United States a motive for trying to conciliate Nazi Germany. The United States showed no interest, however, in jettisoning its isolation, and Lothian did not explain how Britain could stay out of a war between Germany and an eastern neighbor that drew France into the conflict. He

---

[64] See Lothian, "Interview with the President," 11 October 1934, copy, GD 40/17/285/576-579, Lothian Papers. Lothian's meeting on October 10 is noted in the White House Stenographer's Diary, Franklin D. Roosevelt Presidential Library, Hyde Park, NY.

[65] See [Lord Lothian], "The Recoil from Freedom," *The Round Table* 23:91 (June 1933), 477-496.

[66] See Lothian, letter to *The Times*, 15 November 1933, p. 10, col. 4. See also [Lord Lothian], "The Future of the League," *The Round Table* 24:94 (December 1933), 1-13.

[67] For the transcript of Lothian's interview with Hitler, see Butler, *Lord Lothian*, 330-337. The original is in GD 40/17/201/73-84, Lothian Papers. For Lothian's public statements on his return, see his articles in *The Times*, 31 January and 1 February 1935, appearing both days on p. 15, col. 6. In an address the following year to the Anglo-German Fellowship in London, Lothian approved Hitler's reoccupation of the Rhineland and his other violations of the Treaty of Versailles, although he criticized the Nazi regime for its domestic conduct. See "Anglo-German Fellowship Dinner," 14 July 1936, GD 40/17/317/32-38, Lothian Papers.

discounted the threat to neighboring countries that a rearmed Germany would pose if Hitler was not content to coexist with them.[68]

The deeper motive for Lothian's appeasement, though, was not strategic but moral. In attempting to moderate Germany, he took the Round Table logic of his youth to a grim conclusion. The "principle of the commonwealth" that underpinned his earlier imperial federalism held that individual liberty and obligation to a community were each necessary to the other. The problem with this idea as a basis for world order was that it could work only with peoples who felt a common sense of belonging. None of the peoples to whom Lothian offered greater equality in a British or Anglo-American world system wished to make the reciprocal commitments that Lothian expected in return. Philip Kerr and his friends gave self-government to the white Afrikaners in South Africa without truly winning them over to the British Empire. Canada and the other Dominions resisted federation with the United Kingdom, and Catholic Ireland fought a war for its independence. The United States rejected partnership after the First World War and India sought more complete self-government. Finally, Nazi Germany accepted British concessions only to turn against liberal civilization.

Lothian's failure was, first, to confuse the idea of community itself with the imperial and then liberal-world communities that he successively advocated, and then more disastrously, to apply the same policy to Hitler as to other nations. In so doing, he also affirmed an earlier unilateralism. In his youth, Kerr argued that Britain had a duty to bring change to the less developed world, if necessary by force.[69] In trying to conciliate local nationalism, he seemed to repudiate such imperialism. But in a deeper sense he continued to believe that his own country's actions were the relevant factors in how other countries changed. The resistance to Lothian's notions of community did not vitiate the principle of a more integrated world based on equality and consent. But in the 1930s, democratic principles were in grave danger and needed first to be defended.

---

[68] See [Philip Kerr], "Europe, the Covenant and the Protocol," *The Round Table* 15:58 (March 1925), 219-241; and [Lord Lothian], "The Foundation for Disarmament," *The Round Table* 23:89 (December 1932), 1-20. For his hope of drawing the United States out of isolation, see [Lord Lothian], "World Crisis," *The Round Table* 26:103 (June 1936), 443-460; and The Marquess of Lothian, "The World Crisis of 1936," *Foreign Affairs* 15:1 (October 1936), 124-140.

[69] See P. H. Kerr, "Political Relations between Advanced and Backward Peoples," in A. J. Grant *et al.*, *An Introduction to the Study of International Relations* (London: Macmillan, 1916), 141-182.

Lothian visited Hitler again in May 1937 and found the Führer evasive about his intentions.[70] Over the following year, Lothian began to speak less of making amends and more of containment.[71] He approved the Munich agreement in September 1938 but the Nazi pogrom against the Jews in November finally shattered his belief that appeasement was possible.[72] On a second visit to Roosevelt in January 1939, he urged the president to take up Britain's burden of defending civilization, only to evoke a brusque response. But in the spring Roosevelt approved Lothian's appointment as the next British ambassador to the United States.[73] The new ambassador arrived in Washington at the start of September, just as the Second World War broke out.

Congress amended U.S. neutrality laws so that Britain could purchase munitions on a cash-and-carry basis. The Destroyers-Bases deal in the summer of 1940, at the height of a presidential election in which both candidates pledged to stay out of the war, was a tribute to Lothian's diplomacy, as was the groundwork he laid for the Lend-Lease program before he died at his embassy in December 1940. Just as his service under Lloyd George revealed the limits of Round Table power, so did his tenure in Washington reveal the limits of his personal influence. In public speeches and private meetings after the fall of France, Lothian could not persuade Americans to enter the war as a belligerent power. But his diplomacy helped Churchill and Roosevelt at a critical time, and the Anglo-American partnership that finally came a year after his death vindicated his nearly lifelong campaign to achieve it.[74]

---

[70] For the transcript of his second meeting with Hitler, see Butler, *Lord Lothian*, 337-345. The original, and interviews with Hermann Goering and Hjalmar Schacht, are in GD 40/17/204/294-317, Lothian Papers.

[71] See [Lord Lothian], "The Commonwealth and the Dictatorships," *The Round Table* 27:111 (June 1938), 435-452.

[72] For his relief over Munich, see Lothian to Lady Cecil Kerr (his sister), 30 September 1938, GD 40/17/470/6, Lothian Papers. For his abandonment of appeasement, see Lothian, "Britain Awake!," *The Observer*, 20 November 1938, p. 16, col. 5.

[73] On his second meeting with Roosevelt, on 2 January 1939, see the White House Diary for that date and Roosevelt to Roger B. Merriman, 15 February 1939, copy, in file "Great Britain," Box 32, President's Safe File, Franklin D. Roosevelt Papers, Franklin D. Roosevelt Presidential Library, Hyde Park, NY. For the president's assent to Lothian's appointment as ambassador, see David Reynolds, "FDR and the British: A Postscript," *Proceedings of the Massachusetts Historical Society*, Vol. 90 (1978), 106-110.

[74] On Lothian's embassy, see Reynolds, *Lord Lothian and Anglo-American Relations, 1939-40*, and the chapters in this volume by Greg Kennedy, J. Simon Rofe, and Gavin Bailey. For Lothian's private efforts to influence Americans, see Billington, *Lothian*, 144-154.

After 1921, Philip Kerr worked for a stronger form of English-speaking preponderance to replace the British maritime hegemony of the nineteenth century. But he also believed that an Anglo-American partnership someday had to evolve into an inclusive world state. To preserve an imperium of the few over the many, Lothian argued in 1934 in support of India reform, would sooner or later undermine liberty at home.[75] He also observed, in a 1935 criticism of the peace movement, that democratic liberty and the rule of law could not stop at national boundaries without forever being hostage to the balance of power between nations.[76]

The world in his time resisted being shaped to a universal purpose. Philip Kerr and the Round Table fellowship could not orchestrate world events, as they had set out in their youth to do (and came closer than most to doing). In the 1930s, the British concessions that Lothian backed may have prevented a more intense clash with Indian nationalism but helped precipitate an even greater conflict in Europe. The question about his legacy is whether he was also mistaken to believe that liberal civilization needed a federative purpose. America's foreign relations since 1945 may be seen in a different light if the United States could have done more to build an integrated world community able to sustain itself without a single dominant national power.

LESSONS FOR THE UNITED STATES?

Unlike the British Empire, which Kerr and his friends tried to refashion into the nucleus of a universal state, the United States of America began in a declaration of universal principles, and by 1900 the country had become the world's most powerful industrial nation. But America did not seek to absorb the world into its union. After 1945, the United States became the center of a maritime sphere of liberal welfare states linked by new peacetime alliances. With the end of the Soviet threat in 1991 and the subsequent development of Asia, though, the United States began a relative decline that is unlikely to be reversed if the rest of the world continues to modernize.[77]

---

[75] See his warning in *Parliamentary Debates (Lords)*, 5th Series, Vol. 95, 12 December 1934, cols. 295-296.

[76] See The Marquess of Lothian, *Pacifism is Not Enough, Nor Patriotism Either* (Oxford: Clarendon Press, 1935).

[77] For a forecast of U.S. relative decline, see *Global Trends 2025: A Transformed World* (Washington, DC: National Intelligence Council, 2008). For a more optimistic view, see Fareed Zakaria, *The Post-American World* (New York: W. W. Norton, 2008). The analysis (continued)

Could America have averted this prospect by taking a different path earlier in the twentieth century? In March 1939, an American Rhodes Scholar, Clarence Streit, published *Union Now*, a book calling for the democracies of the North Atlantic to federate. With the help of Lionel Curtis and Philip Lothian, Streit launched a federalist movement in the last desperate months before the Second World War.[78] When the effort failed, the movement dwindled. But several of its American adherents helped forge the North Atlantic Treaty Organization (NATO) after the war.[79] In 1949 some backed a limited federal union of the NATO member states.[80] Unlike the British Empire of 1909, a North Atlantic federation after the Second World War would have had the strength to meet external

---

in Paul Kennedy, *The Rise and Fall of the Great Powers: Economic Change and Military Conflict from 1500 to 2000* (New York: Random House, 1987), may outlast the criticism that greeted its publication.

[78] See Clarence Streit, *Union Now: A Proposal for a Federal Union of the Democracies of the North Atlantic* (New York: Harper and Brothers, 1939). Streit included all of the British Dominions in his proposed union. Materials relating to his movement may be found in the Clarence Kirshman Streit Papers, Manuscripts Division, Library of Congress, Washington, DC. For the Moot's endorsement, see "Union Now," *The Round Table* 29:115 (June 1939), 476-488. Streit's Federal Union movement should not be confused with a separate British-based movement of the same name to unite only the democracies of western Europe that Lothian and Curtis also simultaneously backed. For this effort, see Sir Charles Kimber, "Federal Union," in *Britain and the Threat to Stability in Europe, 1918-1947*, eds. Peter Caterall with C. J. Morris (London: Leicester University Press, 1993), 105-111. Materials in GD 40/17/377-389, Lothian Papers, and Boxes 14-16, Curtis Papers, document the efforts of Lothian and Curtis to recruit dignitaries in the United Kingdom to both movements. The Archbishop of Canterbury approved Streit's book in a letter to Lord Lothian, 26 April 1939, GD 40/17/380/182, Lothian Papers. William Beveridge mentioned his joining the federal European movement in *Power and Influence: An Autobiography* (London: Hodder and Stoughton, 1953), 266-267.

[79] The Americans Theodore Achilles, John D. Hickerson, and Will Clayton supported the Streit movement in 1939. As State Department officials in the late 1940s, they helped bring about the NATO alliance. See Ellen Clayton Garwood, *Will Clayton: A Short Biography* (Austin: University of Texas Press, 1958), 34-35; Ira Straus to David P. Billington, Jr., 12 March 1986; and Wilson D. Miscamble, *George F. Kennan and the Making of American Foreign Policy, 1947-1950* (Princeton, NJ: Princeton University Press, 1992), 113-140. The earlier federalism of these individuals was not the same as the world federalism of the late 1940s that sought to unite communist countries and democracies.

[80] See the Atlantic Union Committee Papers, Manuscripts Division, Library of Congress, Washington, DC. The committee formed in 1949 under the leadership of former Justice Owen Roberts of the U.S. Supreme Court as an offshoot of Clarence Streit's Federal Union organization. Its goals were a common defense and foreign policy, a common currency and trade policy, and a common citizenship. The two vice presidents were Robert P. Patterson, President Harry S. Truman's Secretary of War (1945-1947), and Will Clayton of the State Department.

challenges, and it might have opened itself to new countries and grown into a true world state. A North Atlantic union would, however, have faced challenges similar to those that would have confronted an Anglo-Dominion union a half-century earlier, including the need to agree on how to meet a powerful adversary, how to define military obligations elsewhere, whether to give taxing powers to the union, and how to resolve the needs of unrepresented peoples for full inclusion or independence.

Just as Britain and the Dominions were able to fight two world wars without needing to federate, so were America and its allies able to meet their security needs after 1945, through the Marshall Plan and NATO, without having to form a political union. Europe began a process of coming together as a region but its nation-states did not give up the most important attributes of their sovereignty. As they move further into the twenty-first century, though, the United States and its Cold War allies may come to resemble Britain and its Dominions after the 1870s, if the former resemble the latter in consisting of a relatively declining liberal superpower with self-governing dependencies that together lack the strength to prevent a more strongly multipolar world from emerging.

The United States may yet bring its traditional allies and other countries into a new kind of partnership, with the long-term goal of turning a multipolar world into one of stronger cooperation. In contrast to the Round Table movement, the United States could propose more limited forms of new cooperation instead of seeking radical change. America's allies and other nations might welcome an American offer to share decision-making in novel ways in exchange for new shared commitments. Debates over new ties will be more successful if they engage a broader public opinion from the start and if economic life is not taken for granted.

The obstacles to a more integrated world are nevertheless obvious and formidable. Cooperation between nations is more developed today than a century ago, but nations continue to guard their sovereignty and rising countries may see no need to accommodate relatively declining ones. If the democratic world resists any step toward closer union, and if the great powers cannot develop a larger and stronger community for security as well as trade, the future will depend on whether a multipolar world in the twenty-first century can avoid repeating the mistakes of 1914 to 1945.

It may be argued that the consequences of relative decline are less dangerous for America today than they were for Britain. Relative decline is a relative concept: the United Kingdom is more powerful now in absolute terms than it was at its zenith in the nineteenth century, and America is relatively more powerful today than Britain was in the 1870s. Whether a nation is endangered by its relative position also depends on the intensity of competition between nations. In the first forty-five years of the twentieth century, there was no limit to violence between states and as a result a declining Britain was in grave danger. Since then, nuclear weapons have inhibited states that possess them from risking all-out conflict.

Conditions could change in the twenty-first century, though, if inhibitions on the use of extreme force lessen, or if new technologies supersede the weapons and defenses that have kept the peace since the Second World War. The degree of continuity in international relations since the nineteenth century still casts a long shadow. America after 1945 tried to learn from British experience what not to do in response to a more dangerous world. What needs to be done is a more difficult and more important question.

CONCLUSION:

THE FINAL STAGE

PRISCILLA ROBERTS

The period when Lord Lothian served as British ambassador to the United States has drawn more attention from historians than any other, a bias apparent in this volume, three of whose chapters are devoted primarily to Lothian's time heading the Washington embassy. The verdicts they pass on the last stage of Lothian's varied career are for the most part favorable, albeit with some caveats. Undoubtedly, Lothian's last two years represented a surprisingly spectacular end to a life that, at least to the outside view, had until then failed to fulfil its early promise.

This did not mean that Lothian's performance was pitch perfect. However well his lengthy trips to and wide experience in the United States might have seemed to prepare him for his new responsibilities, Lothian's judgment often left something to be desired. To begin with, his own assessment of American attitudes toward the growing international crisis was initially far too optimistic. In spring 1939, before his appointment was announced, John Buchan (Lord Tweedsmuir), the governor general of Canada, told his brother:

> Philip Lothian, who was here last week, and has been all over the States in the last two months, said the change in opinion there was perfectly amazing. In his opinion the President would carry the people with him if he announced that the American fleet would join the British fleet in policing the seas of the world if there were any attempt at brigandage. That would be the surest way to secure peace, for the long peace of the nineteenth century was due to the omnipotence of the British navy.[1]

At this time Lothian handed Secretary of State Cordell Hull a memorandum suggesting that, if Great Britain and France manifested "a firm intention and preparedness to defend themselves," in the interests of avoiding war the United States conceivably might respond "not only by supplying the Western Democracies with the implements and materials of defense but by

---

[1] Buchan to J. Walter Buchan, 2 February 1939, ACC 11627/83, Tweedsmuir Papers, National Library of Scotland, Edinburgh.

P. Roberts (ed.), Lord Lothian and Anglo-American Relations, 1900-1940, 229-245.

making it clear that she would not tolerate their being forcibly squeezed or attacked."[2]

Such blithe over-confidence was decidedly premature, and Lothian soon revised it. In an episode that quickly became notorious around the Foreign Office, on 2 January 1939 he met Roosevelt and demonstrated what the irritated American president later termed a "'We who are about to die, salute thee' attitude." According to Roosevelt:

> Lothian ... started the conversation by saying he had completely abandoned his former belief that Hitler could be dealt with as a semi-reasonable human being, and went on to say that the British for a thousand years had been the guardians of Anglo-Saxon civilization—that the sceptre or the sword or something like that had dropped from their palsied fingers—that the U.S.A. must snatch it up—that F.D.R. alone could save the world—etc., etc.

By his own account, which may well have been somewhat exaggerated, Roosevelt "got mad clear through" and retorted "that just so long as he or Britishers like him took that attitude of complete despair, the British would not be worth saving anyway."[3] Lothian perhaps took this hint. In articles written immediately after his visit, Lothian stated that Americans still wished to remain aloof from any potential war, but that since Munich "the United States has felt in its bones that if a world war between the democracies and the totalitarian States breaks out" it would inevitably be "drawn into the struggle, partly by its sympathies, partly because such a war would almost certainly affect its own vital interests." The United States would nonetheless, he thought, act independently in protecting such interests, although he believed that, in the event of the Fascist powers threatening British naval supremacy, the United States "would decide to maintain, in a new form appropriate to her own needs, the control of the seas by the democracies as being by far the most safe, cheapest, and most certain road to her own security and the method most likely to save her

---

[2] Lothian, memorandum on Neutrality, misdated 1938(?), Reel 47, Cordell Hull Papers, Manuscripts Division, Library of Congress, Washington, DC; see also drafts of this manuscript, 7 February 1939, Box 40, Norman H. Davis Papers, Manuscripts Division, Library of Congress, Washington, DC.

[3] Roosevelt to Roger B. Merriman, 15 February 1939, quoted in David Reynolds, *Lord Lothian and Anglo-American Relations, 1939-1940* (Philadelphia: Transactions of the American Philosophical Society, 1983), 7; apart from the account of this episode in Reynolds, 6-8, see also David P. Billington, Jr., *Lothian: Philip Kerr and the Quest for World Order* (Westport, CT: Praeger, 2006), 135-136; and David Cannadine, *In Churchill's Shadow: Confronting the Past in Modern Britain* (New York: Oxford University Press, 2003), ch. 8.

from being drawn into world war." He warned, moreover, that the United States would not "underwrite" the British or French Empires, or take over burdens she considered to belong to the democracies and, echoing Roosevelt, stated: "The more independent and vigorous and powerful we are in resisting blackmail, or squeeze, or threats the more likely is the United States to rally in support."[4]

Lothian's vision of an ideal world order remained unchanged. He still believed that, as he told his long-time friend, South African Prime Minister Jan Smuts: "In the long run ... everything depends upon the United States abandoning its philosophy of neutrality." In his view, "the only foundation for world peace was close co-operation between the British Commonwealth and the United States for the restoration of the nineteenth century British system operated not by Britain alone but the whole English-speaking world." This would, he felt, provide a "nucleus" for a League of Nations backed by "overwhelming superiority of power behind the law." The dominant powers in this organization should "be able both to maintain overwhelming superiority in armaments behind the League system and to limit the armaments of individual nations." Readying himself to depart for Washington, Lothian confessed it was his "dream that in the United States I may be able to help promote such an end."[5]

When Lothian finally arrived at his post, the sanguine outlook he had expressed to Buchan was no longer in evidence, and he repeatedly told correspondents:

> The United States is beginning to feel that as things are going, it will eventually be forced into the war. She won't go in of her own accord, but she is in no sense Pacifist and will intervene when her own vital interests are menaced, that is, when she is far too late, after the time has passed when she can do something effective to prevent the spread of the conflict and when the cost to herself will be enormous. In other words, she is going to behave very much as we did during the last five years.[6]

In these circumstances, especially given Americans' own prevalent attitude of detachment from international affairs during the 1930s, Lothian's past efforts to reach some *modus vivendi* with Hitler and Mussolini, endeavors

---

[4] Lothian, "America after 'Munich'" I, *The Observer* (19 February 1939), and "America after 'Munich'" II, *The Observer* (26 February 1939).
[5] Lothian to Smuts, 6 June 1939, quoted in J. R. M. Butler, *Lord Lothian (Philip Kerr) 1882-1940* (London: Macmillan, 1960), 233-235.
[6] Lothian to Sidney Braithwaite, 29 April 1940, GD 40/17/399/175-76, Papers of the Eleventh Marquess of Lothian [hereafter Lothian Papers], National Archives of Scotland, Edinburgh.

at least partially impelled by his consciousness of British weakness and his longstanding belief that British interests lay primarily with the Empire and the United States, not on the continent, did not greatly impair his ambassadorial effectiveness. As the Second World War approached his Anglophile American friends were, indeed, as divided as British policymakers. Some, such as the banker Thomas W. Lamont, his fellow Morgan partner, Russell C. Leffingwell, long-term U.S. naval negotiator Norman H. Davis, and the lawyer Frederic R. Coudert, shared the pro-appeasement outlook of Lothian and the Astors, supporting the Munich agreement, not because they liked or admired Hitler, but in the belief that a European war would be disastrous for the British Empire's viability, and that the survival of Czech and other Central European states was not a cause worth fighting for.[7] Others, such as Hamilton Fish Armstrong, a leading Council on Foreign Relations figure, Allen W. Dulles, and Henry L. Stimson, contended that Britain and, indeed, the United States, should resolutely oppose the Fascist powers, and were allied with such British opponents of Lothian as John Wheeler-Bennett and Robert Vansittart.[8] With few exceptions, however, Council on Foreign Relations members generally united in support for American rearmament, opposition to the neutrality legislation of the later 1930s, and a deep conviction that, should war eventuate, the United States should range itself decisively with the Allies and do everything possible to facilitate an Allied victory over the Fascist powers.[9] Despite his occasional twitting of Lothian over his past

---

[7] Priscilla Roberts, "The American 'Eastern Establishment' and the First World War: The Emergence of a Foreign Policy Tradition" (Ph.D. dissertation, Cambridge University, 1981), 577; Comments by Frederic Coudert in digest of talk by Graham Hutton, 3 January 1939, Records of Meetings, Council on Foreign Relations Papers, Mudd Manuscripts Library, Princeton University, Princeton, NJ; Davis to Lothian, 21 February, 11 June 1935, 31 March 1939, Box 40, Norman H. Davis Papers, Manuscripts Division, Library of Congress, Washington, DC; and Edward M. Lamont, *The Ambassador from Wall Street: The Story of Thomas W. Lamont, J. P. Morgan's Chief Executive* (Lanham, MD: Madison Books, 1994), 427, 436-438.

[8] Priscilla Roberts, "'The Council Has Been Your Creation': Hamilton Fish Armstrong, Paradigm of the American Foreign Policy Establishment?," *Journal of American Studies* 35:1 (April 2001), 73-77; Peter Grose, *Gentleman Spy: The Life of Allen Dulles* (Boston: Houghton Mifflin, 1994), ch. 6; Godfrey Hodgson, *The Colonel: The Life and Wars of Henry Stimson, 1867-1950* (New York: Knopf, 1990), 215-220; and Henry L. Stimson with McGeorge Bundy, *On Active Service in Peace and War* (New York: Harper, 1947), 313-320.

[9] Roberts, "American 'Eastern Establishment,'" 576-581; Lamont, *Ambassador from Wall Street*, 444-447; Robert D. Schulzinger, *The Wise Men of Foreign Affairs: The History of the Council on Foreign Relations* (New York: Columbia University Press, 1984), ch. 3; and (continued)

support for appeasement, Roosevelt himself, who in 1938 had cabled Chamberlain "Good Man" when the latter set off for Munich, had little cause to be hypercritical. While Lothian's past might cause him some embarrassment, as when the pro-German American propagandist George Sylvester Viereck published a pamphlet, *Lord Lothian versus Lord Lothian*, highlighting inconsistencies between Lothian's previous and current utterances, at least it gave him vital insight into American reluctance to oppose Germany.[10]

When his appointment as ambassador was announced, in the interests of diplomatic impartiality Lothian had been forced to sever his connection with Clarence Streit's Union Now movement and the Federal Union organization. Several chapters in this volume also describe how friends and Foreign Office functionaries alike counseled him to moderate his rhetoric advocating the establishment of some rather nebulous form of international world organization, since this might compromise his ambassadorial effectiveness.[11] Lothian never, however, abandoned his over-riding faith in Anglo-American cooperation, telling the Labour politician Hugh Dalton on a brief visit to Britain in autumn 1940 of a plan for "a standing council in Washington representing all the states of pan-America and the British Commonwealth," which would coordinate their political, economic and strategic collaboration in every field both during and after the war. Attending a meeting of the Moot at Cliveden, Lothian enthusiastically discussed with his Round Table associates this proposal for a "Pan-American-British Empire Conference" or "Amphictionic Council for the British Commonwealth and the United States," which according to him originated with Roosevelt.[12] Many of Lothian's ambassadorial speeches carefully expounded his perennial theme, that in the past

---

Peter Grose, *Continuing the Inquiry: The Council on Foreign Relations from 1921 to 1996* (New York: Council on Foreign Relations, 1996), 18-22.

[10] On *Lord Lothian versus Lord Lothian*, see Sir John Wheeler-Bennett, *Special Relationships: America in Peace and War* (London: Macmillan, 1975), 76; and Thomas E. Mahl, *Desperate Deception: British Covert Operations in the United States, 1939-44* (London: Brassey's, 1998), 103-104.

[11] See also Butler, *Lord Lothian*, 243; Billington, *Lothian*, 137; and Ira Straus, "Lothian and the Anglo-American Problematic," in *The Larger Idea: Lord Lothian and the Problem of National Sovereignty*, ed. John Turner (London: Historians Press, 1988), 135.

[12] Hugh Dalton, diary entry, 24 October 1940, in *The Second World War Diary of Hugh Dalton*, ed. Ben Pimlott (London: Cape, 1986), 93; Memorandum, "Lord Lothian's Last Talk at Cliveden," [1940], Reel 7, Lord Altrincham (Edward Grigg) Papers, Bodleian Library, Oxford University; Reynolds, *Lord Lothian*, 40; and John Kendle, *The Round Table Movement and Imperial Union* (Toronto: University of Toronto Press, 1975), 295.

American security and the Monroe Doctrine had depended upon the British fleet, but the country could no longer rely upon such free protection. (He became so closely identified with this view, which together with his demand for postwar Anglo-American cooperation was also propounded during the Second World War by his close friend, the influential journalist Walter Lippmann, that in British governmental circles it was later termed the "Lothian thesis.")[13]

As ambassador, Lothian's support for both Anglo-American unity and ultimate world federalism would enable him to appeal to Atlanticists and universalists alike. Dalton thought him "the sort of man Americans like; very quick to take local colour ... and very fond of 'large ideas', particularly in a vague and unfinished form."[14] In 1939 and 1940, for example, Lothian corresponded amicably on international organization with the lawyer John Foster Dulles, who opposed U.S. intervention in the international conflict. Both men had attended a July 1937 international conference at Oxford on "Church, Community, and State," where Lothian gave a major address, and Dulles' ideas on Germany, Italy, and Japan as non-satisfied states deserving of concessions rather paralleled his own earlier stance toward Germany.[15] As Lothian's great friend Thomas W. Lamont, a dedicated Atlanticist Anglophile and partner in the leading investment bank, J. P. Morgan and Company, whose New York house Lothian used as a base during visits to that city, slightly cynically told Nancy Astor:

> Don't worry about Philip's speeches. They are excellent and much better designed for American than for English consumption. You know we Americans ... have a streak of Evangelism in our make-up, and Philip's talk

---

[13] This theme was sounded frequently in the speeches reprinted in Royal Institute of International Affairs, *The American Speeches of Lord Lothian* (London: Oxford University Press, 1941). On the "Lothian thesis," see Susan A. Brewer, *To Win the Peace: British Propaganda in the United States during World War II* (Ithaca, NY: Cornell University Press, 1997), 98, 190-191. For Lippmann's wartime views, see esp. Walter Lippmann, *U.S. Foreign Policy: Shield of the Republic* (Boston: Little, Brown, 1943); and Lippmann, *U.S. War Aims* (Boston: Little, Brown, 1944).

[14] Dalton, diary entry, 24 October 1940, in Pimlott, ed., *Second World War Diary of Hugh Dalton*, 93.

[15] Lothian to Dulles, 4 July, 8, 16 September, 26 December 1939, Dulles to Lothian, 1, 16 September, 31 October 1939, 3 January 1940, Reel 4, John Foster Dulles Papers, Mudd Manuscripts Library, Princeton University, Princeton, NJ; Billington, *Lothian*, 131. On Dulles' views on international affairs prior to Pearl Harbor, see Ronald W. Pruessen, *John Foster Dulles: The Road to Power* (New York: Free Press, 1982), chs. 8-9.

about a possible world state appeals to a lot of people. He may be star-gazing a bit, but it does no harm.[16]

And as in the First World War, Lothian predicated any such outcome on an Allied victory, telling another close friend: "If we are to get federation, not only must the Allies win, but the democracies must be willing to pool their sovereignties."[17]

Some rather inconclusive evidence exists that in June 1939, in June 1940, and toward the end of that year, Lothian showed interest in a negotiated peace settlement with Germany, abandoning much of Europe to German rule. In each case except possibly the last, when British intelligence may well have acted without his knowledge in an effort to discover future German strategic plans, Lothian apparently acted with Foreign Office sanction, and may simply have been attempting to buy time for a beleaguered Britain through prevaricating negotiations.[18] Whatever his motivation, as Warren Kimball and David Reynolds have pointed out, neither in June 1940, when Britain's ability to survive a German onslaught was by no means clear, nor later, did he permit any such private peace feelers to affect the posture of obdurate British determination to continue fighting to the end that he and other British leaders—in part at his urging—presented to American officialdom.[19]

Lothian's time in Washington has already attracted extensive study, including Reynolds' excellent account of Lothian's triumphs and shortcomings as ambassador, the thoughtful assessments of his two biographers, and Nicholas Cull's outstanding study of British propaganda in the United States before Pearl Harbor. Somewhat ironically given Lothian's dogged insistence that the British were merely providing "information" on the war, the latter gives him particular credit for his

---

[16] Lamont to Nancy Astor, 10 March 1940, File 82-6, Thomas W. Lamont Papers, Baker Library, Harvard Business School, Boston, MA.

[17] Lothian to Frank Aydelotte, 22 March 1940, GD 40/17/398/411, Lothian Papers.

[18] [Adam von Trott zu Solz], "Fact-Finding Visit to Britain (June 1-8, 1939)," in *Documents on German Foreign Policy 1918-1945*, Series D, Vol. 6 (London: Her Majesty's Stationery Office, 1956), 674-684; Butler, *Lord Lothian*, 228-233; A. L. Rowse, *Appeasement: A Study in Political Decline* (New York: Norton, 1963), 91-100; Reynolds, *Lord Lothian*, 22-23 and n. 78; Laurence Thompson, *1940: Year of Legend, Year of History* (London: Collins, 1966), 160-161; John Costello, *Ten Days to Destiny: The Secret Story of the Hess Peace Initiative and British Efforts to Strike a Deal with Hitler* (New York: Morrow, 1991), 346-351, 399-403; Andrew Roberts, *"The Holy Fox": A Biography of Lord Halifax* (London: Weidenfeld and Nicolson, 1991), 250; and Billington, *Lothian*, 138, 154-159.

[19] Reynolds, *Lord Lothian*, 22-23 and n. 78; and Warren F. Kimball, *The Most Unsordid Act: Lend-Lease, 1939-1941* (Baltimore: Johns Hopkins University Press, 1969), 24 n. 24.

contributions in this field.[20] These are now supplemented by several chapters in this volume, by Greg Kennedy, J. Simon Rofe, and Gavin Bailey. Kennedy focuses on Lothian's attempts from 1934 onward to promote Anglo-American cooperation on Far Eastern policy. Ironically, Lothian's amateur efforts in this direction during the mid-1930s helped to convince many in the Foreign Office that he was an indiscreet and uncontrollable maverick whose public pronouncements on sensitive topics, such as Anglo-Japanese cooperation, might well exacerbate rather than assuage delicate tensions in Anglo-American relations. During Lothian's early months in Washington, top State Department and Foreign Office diplomats also united in suspecting that Lothian's reporting of American attitudes toward Japan and the Far East was unreliable and tinged with wishful thinking. By late 1940, however, his skills and judgment had improved, allowing him to overcome this initial distrust, and to offer advice on hard choices in British Far Eastern policy in the confidence that Americans would appreciate the difficult dilemmas facing an overstretched Britain.

Lothian's attitude stemmed in part from the fact that he believed his tactics of seeking to win over both American elites and the general public with low-key factual accounts of Britain's situation, supplemented by statements that the United States must make its own decision how to respond to British requests for aid, had been effective in eliciting American sympathy and support. Rofe joins Cull in praising Lothian's handling of his twin American constituencies, administration officials and politicians in Washington and the broader public and news media. He also praises Lothian's ability to interpret the shifting situation in the United States to less knowledgeable government officials back in Britain, and to win their support for initiatives to tap American resources of munitions, money, and supplies that were considerably bolder than most in Whitehall initially favored. Kennedy, too, argues that where Far Eastern issues were concerned, by late 1940 Lothian had become a valued intermediary between officials in Washington and London, as both sides now had far greater trust in his ability to interpret each to the other.

Undoubtedly, Lothian's long experience of the United States and multifarious contacts with Americans gave him decided advantages in his assignment. Although Lothian diplomatically—in every sense of the word—eschewed formal involvement with such pro-Allied organizations as

---

[20] Nicholas John Cull, *Selling War: The British Propaganda Campaign against American "Neutrality" in World War II* (New York: Oxford University Press, 1995).

the Century Group and the Committee to Defend America by Aiding the Allies (CDAA), his close connections with many intimately involved in these organizations, among them the American Rhodes secretary Frank Aydelotte, former Rhodes scholar Whitney H. Shepardson, Hamilton Armstrong of the Council on Foreign Relations, Lamont, and Norman H. Davis and Frank L. Polk, both of whom he had known since the First World War, in practice meant that they consulted and informed him unofficially of their activities, and on occasion he furnished them with confidential British information. Lothian's efforts to enhance the influence of Rhodes scholars bore fruit during his time as ambassador, when many of the most committed American interventionists and Century Group members, Aydelotte, Shepardson, and Francis P. Miller of the Council on Foreign Relations among them, were past Rhodes scholars.[21]

Lothian's admiring subordinates, Frank Thistlethwaite and Wheeler-Bennett, both noted the range and variety of his American contacts, and his skill in handling the American media. As Wheeler-Bennett remarked, Americans generally liked the "democratic, easygoing, informal and ever-accessible Lord Lothian."[22] Raymond E. Lee, naval attaché at the American embassy in London, commented: "[T]he fact that he had written for the newspapers and could therefore parade himself as a journalist ... immediately put him on a first-rate basis with the newspaper fraternity in Washington, and he exploited it to the utmost."[23] Likewise, his contacts with the profoundly pro-Allied proprietors and editors of the press of the East Coast and beyond, including Herbert Elliston of the *Christian Science Monitor*, Eugene Meyer of the *Washington Post*, Arthur Hays Sulzberger of the *New York Times*, Helen Ogden Reid of the *New York Herald Tribune*, H. Freeman Matthews of the *Richmond Times-Dispatch*, and the Binghams of the *Louisville Times-Dispatch*, ensured extensive and usually friendly coverage of his speeches and other utterances, in which Lothian repeatedly stressed the theme that United States security ultimately depended upon the British fleet, an approach quickly taken up by the Century Group and the

---

[21] In 1940 Lee suspected Lothian was "trying to work out something in the way of influencing the United States through the many Rhodes scholars who have been passed back to us from Oxford." Raymond E. Lee, diary entry, 3 November 1940, in *The London Journal of General Raymond E. Lee 1940-1941*, ed. James Leutze (Boston: Little, Brown, 1971), 120.

[22] Wheeler-Bennett, *Special Relationships*, 72-73, quotation from 118; and Frank Thistlethwaite, *Our War 1938-45* (Cambridge: Frank Thistlethwaite, 1997), 46-50.

[23] Lee, diary entry, 13 December 1940, in Leutze, ed., *London Journals of General Raymond E. Lee*, 174.

CDAA. Despite a tendency to shoot from the hip, which occasionally compromised British negotiations with the United States, Lothian's final speech, delivered on his behalf the day before his death, in which he pleaded for additional American aid, likewise helped to lay the groundwork for Lend-Lease.

Gavin Bailey, in a nuanced appreciation of "Lothian's method" of presenting Britain's case to the United States, highlights what might be considered a shortcoming in his approach, one that would have a major impact on future historiography on U.S. assistance to Britain during World War II. Following tactics that future U.S. Secretary of State Dean Acheson, when helping to sell the Truman Doctrine program of aid to Greece and Turkey in 1947, described as making the situation "clearer than the truth," Lothian tended to exaggerate the 'criticality' of the material and financial support he was requesting from the United States in terms of its significance to Britain's continued ability to wage war. The Destroyers-Bases deal of mid-1940 was therefore presented as providing Britain with military equipment that was vital to Britain's ability to survive that summer, when in practice the supplies involved arrived too late to make any difference and were often, moreover, inferior in quality to British-produced armaments. Nor was the British financial condition in late 1940 as parlous as Lothian made it seem in his presentation of the subject to the American press and officialdom; the crisis was one of depleted foreign exchange reserves rather than the total exhaustion of British assets. Subsequent historiography has generally followed the Lothian line, hailing the Destroyers-Bases deal and Lend-Lease as U.S. initiatives that were vital to British survival, when in reality Britain was holding its own against Germany by late 1940, but could not win victory in the war without American aid. In practice, the greatest immediate impact of these programs was perhaps psychological: they were tangible proof that, even while still supposedly neutral, on the international stage the United States was already ranking itself unequivocally with Britain and its few remaining allies against Hitler's Germany. As such, both represented a huge boost to British morale.

The exaggeration of their immediate practical significance was not, of course, simply the result of Lothian's immediate presentation of these measures. David Reynolds and John Ramsden have perceptively described how former wartime prime minister Winston Churchill, determined to forge and maintain a close Anglo-American relationship during the early Cold War years, depicted a grand alliance characterized by harmony and intimate cooperation between Britain and the United States, in which American assistance made the critical difference to British survival.[24] Differences between the two countries were minimized and the salience of U.S. involvement in world affairs highlighted, as British leaders sought to ensure that the United States remained a military and economic partner against the perceived Soviet threat. As Lothian's most recent biographer, David Billington, perceptively states in the final chapter of this volume, Lothian's posture toward the United States throughout his life represented a response to a sense of British decline, as he sought to bolster the British Empire's standing in the world by strengthening not just ties among the Dominions and Britain but also his own country's links to the United States. He was always conscious that Britain was playing from a position of weakness, not strength, and that in terms of potential international power the United States far outweighed Britain.

In terms of Lothian's significance for the future, one intriguing coda is the question of his influence on one young American man. In late 1939 the American ambassador Joseph P. Kennedy, by then in less than fragrant odor with both British and American officialdom for his defeatism on the war, requested that Lothian meet with his young son, an appointment the busy Lothian duly arranged during a vacation at Kennedy's house in Palm Beach, Florida.[25] Six months later the youthful John F. Kennedy, who had just published his first book, *Why England Slept*, a volume Lothian took the time to read, thanked the ambassador for his time, telling him: "It was our talk that day last January that started me out on the job, and I am most appreciative of your kindness to me at that time."[26] So far no further record of that interview has been located. Lothian was almost invariably at his best with young people, who found him both stimulating and sympathetic, and it may not be too fanciful to trace his influence in the following passage:

---

[24] John Ramsden, *Man of the Century: Winston Churchill and His Legend Since 1945* (New York: Columbia University Press, 2003); and David Reynolds, *In Command of History: Churchill Fighting and Writing the Second World War* (New York: Random House, 2005).

[25] Joseph P. Kennedy to Lothian, 27 December 1939, Lothian to Kennedy, 27 December 1939, GD 40/17/402/16-17, Lothian Papers.

[26] John F. Kennedy to Lothian, 12 August 1940, GD 40/17/402/23, Lothian Papers. The young academic John Wheeler-Bennett, whose assistance Lothian requested in the British embassy, supervised Kennedy's Harvard senior thesis, which developed into this book. Wheeler-Bennett, *Special Relationships*, 34-35. On Lothian's role, see also Nigel Hamilton, *J.F.K.: Reckless Youth* (New York: Random House, 1992), 306-307; and Will Swift, *The Kennedys Amidst the Gathering Storm: A Thousand Days in London, 1938-1940* (New York: HarperCollins, 2008), 227.

[I]f the decision [of the war] goes to the British, we must be prepared to take our part in setting up a world order that will prevent the rise of a militaristic dictatorship. We withdrew from Europe in 1920 and refused to do anything to preserve the democracy we had helped to save. We thought that it made no difference to us what happened in Europe. We are beginning to realize that it does ....

If we had not been surrounded by oceans three and five thousand miles wide, we might ourselves be caving in at some Munich of the Western World.

Despite some misgivings on his father's part, Kennedy's book took a relatively sympathetic view of England's failure to rearm, blaming it as much upon British national psychology and public opinion as on British leaders. After arguing that "many of the very factors intrinsic in democracy resulted in England's falling further and further behind" the dictatorships, Kennedy ended with a clarion call for a massive, speedy and immediate United States defense build-up, a theme Kennedy would repeat in his 1960 presidential campaign.[27] One can only speculate what, if anything, his future emphasis on both military strength and the desirability of negotiating when possible with opponents owed to his early encounter with Lothian.

For thirty years, Philip Lothian adhered to one remarkably consistent perspective on Anglo-American relations, based upon Mahanist naval strategic teachings and British imperial needs, bolstered by appeals to shared values and ideology. Lothian's propaganda efforts during and well before the Second World War did much to popularize what would become the Realist foreign policy tradition enshrining this fundamental perspective. Exponents of this outlook, among them the popular theologian Reinhold Niebuhr and the German Jewish refugees Hans J. Morgenthau and Henry Kissinger, would emphasize the importance of preserving international stability and an international balance of power favorable to U.S. security interests, even as they sought to reconcile this quest with what they saw as

---

[27] John F. Kennedy, *Why England Slept* (New York: W. Funk, 1940), quotation from 230-231. For Joseph P. Kennedy's caveats, see Joseph P. Kennedy to John F. Kennedy, 20 May 1940, in *Hostage to Fortune: The Letters of Joseph P. Kennedy*, ed. Amanda Smith (New York: Viking, 2001), 433-435. Interestingly, Kennedy later named as one of his favorite books the autobiography of another of Milner's young men, John Buchan's *Memory Hold-the-Door* (London: Hodder and Stoughton, 1940), a work he apparently relished not just for its portrait of Buchan's friend, the brilliant, aloof, and doomed Raymond Asquith, killed in the First World War, who became one of his personal role models, but also for its depiction of the close-knit Kindergarten, brilliant and youthful "practical idealists" whose ability and dedication to public service seemed to anticipate the spirit of his own administration.

the need to maintain a basic level of moral authority in foreign affairs.[28] Ironically, the effort of fighting the war would destroy the British Empire whose preservation had been one of Lothian's great preoccupations, making Britain at best a junior partner in that Anglo-American alliance he had long sought to promote, even as it propelled Western Europe toward the federalism he had rather vaguely suggested. The ending of the British Empire was implicit in Lothian's finest hour, and in his own terms perhaps justified his desire of the 1930s to avoid war by all means possible, even by conciliating highly unsavory dictators and abandoning much of Eastern Europe to them.

In England's hour of desperate need, when Britain's power to repel and eventually defeat Hitler depended on its ability to win over the United States, Lothian's decades of American contacts proved their worth and his peculiar mix of talents came into full play, triumphantly vindicating both his otherwise somewhat anticlimactic career and his friend Lord Halifax's controversial gamble in appointing him. His background in journalism and publicity, albeit of a somewhat rarefied and intellectual nature, and his long-term ties to and knowledge of the United States proved their worth. Even Lothian's willingness to take independent action on public issues and steer his own course regardless of consequences, a characteristic that probably resulted from his elite social background and that had for over twenty years made him the bane of the Foreign Office and won him a reputation as a slightly loose cannon, came in useful during his time as ambassador, giving him the confidence to push London for new initiatives and stubbornly and relentlessly argue the case for these. No longer a slightly eccentric voice crying in the wilderness, he watched his visions of Anglo-American collaboration begin their transformation into reality. If Lothian sometimes paid less than adequate attention to the specifics of negotiations, this was because in his mind the development of Anglo-

---

[28] On the Realist tradition, see Michael W. Smith, *History and International Relations* (New York: Routledge, 1999); Michael Joseph Smith, *Realist Thought from Weber to Kissinger* (Baton Rouge: Louisiana State University Press, 1990); Joel H. Rosenthal, *Righteous Realists: Political Realism, Responsible Power, and American Culture in the Nuclear Age* (Baton Rouge: Louisiana State University Press, 1991); Séan Molloy, *The Hidden History of Realism: A Genealogy of Power Politics* (New York: Palgrave Macmillan, 2006); Christoph Frei, *Hans J. Morgenthau: An Intellectual Biography* (Baton Rouge: Louisiana State University Press, 2001); Greg J. Russell, *Hans J. Morgenthau and the Ethics of American Statecraft* (Baton Rouge: Louisiana State University Press, 1990); Eyal Naveh, *Reinhold Niebuhr and Non-Utopian Liberalism: Beyond Illusion and Despair* (Brighton, UK: Sussex Academic Press, 2002); and Martin Halliwell, *The Constant Dialogue: Reinhold Niebuhr and American Political Culture* (Lanham, MD: Rowman and Littlefield, 2005).

American understanding took precedence over minor details. Churchill noted how, under the stress of crisis, the agreeable lightweight had become "an earnest, deeply-stirred man ... primed with every aspect and detail of the American attitude," a personality whose advice even, as Reynolds, Bailey, and Rofe convincingly demonstrate, persuaded Churchill to be far more frank with Roosevelt than he had originally intended.[29]

Yet Lothian, however attractive, was hardly the "democrat" his posthumous admirers depicted. An easygoing and approachable style and relaxed public persona elegantly disguised a decidedly elitist outlook. To paraphrase the impact of another British aristocrat on Margery Allingham's Magersfontein Lugg, Americans were impressed by the combination of his manner, which was matey, and his title, which was not. Throughout his career Lothian indubitably and invariably sought to influence those who possessed either direct power or the ability to sway public opinion, and it seems clear that as ambassador he still followed such strategies. Admittedly, while in Washington Lothian also conducted a campaign to woo the general public and convince ordinary Americans that Britain was fighting a battle whose implications the United States could not ignore, since ultimately it affected American national security. As German bombers raided British cities, he also advised the British government to work closely with sympathetic American journalists reporting back to their own people, and accord them as much as possible in the way of facilities and unfettered access to stories. However much Lothian may have claimed that these tactics represented no more than the provision of information, in reality they were carefully designed to win over not just broad public opinion, but the journalists and media proprietors and other influential Americans who were in a position to shape official thinking and the presentation of news.

By no means, moreover, was Lothian simply Beatrice Webb's "ultra-refined aristocratic dreamer, with sentimentally revolutionary views, [who] spends what little time and thought he has over from secretarial work for the Prime Minister in devising phrases and formulas to express standards of perfection."[30] The hostile Oscar Gass of the American Treasury, who feared that Lothian "will be a big success in the United States" and "as influential an ambassador as has ever been sent us by Great

---

[29] Winston Churchill, *The Second World War*, 6 vols. (London: Cassell, 1948-1954), 2:490; and Reynolds, *Lord Lothian*, 43-48.

[30] Beatrice Webb, diary entry, 3 June 1917, in *Beatrice Webb's Diaries 1912-1924*, ed. Margaret I. Cole (London: Longmans, Green, 1952), 85.

Britain," was more accurate in uncharitably suggesting that Lothian would use "equalitarian," even "Socialist" and "left-wing" rhetoric and "outdo the State Department in the rhetorical force of his sermons," but that, after uttering a "high-sounding prelude in favor of world federation," he would pursue nationalistic British goals and seek "to create the background for American support of Great Britain should the latter ultimately be forced into a war in defense of her imperial interests."[31] Fuelled by pro-Soviet sympathies, Gass rather perceptively identified the manner in which, to quote the historian D. C. Watt, Lothian's rhetoric habitually embodied "that curious combination of power-political principles and Wilsonian morality which ruled international politics between the wars."[32] He sought justification from God and right, not the big battalions and might alone. For Lothian such methods may often have represented the best strategy to win broad support in both the United States and Britain for his objectives, but his habitual use of them suggests some underlying temperamental need for moral validation of even the most self-interested course of action. One can only speculate whether the contradictions between his stated principles and actual practice in any way impelled Lothian's journey from a morally rigorous and introspective Catholicism to an apparently rather personalized and mystical version of Christian Science which, he claimed, freed him from "false beliefs" about himself.[33]

Keith Neilson, in his chapter on Russia, finds an "atypical ... cynicism" in Lothian's attitude in 1921 toward British moves in the direction of granting more indirect rule to the "native inhabitants" of Egypt, when he concluded that, "if they [the Egyptians] fail, nothing will do us more good among foreign countries and in India than a practical demonstration that we are still indispensable."[34] But was this really such an uncharacteristic attitude for Kerr to take? And was he ever quite the earnestly high minded idealist that his blond good looks and pronounced interest in religion inclined onlookers to believe him? Melanie Sayers, in her chapter in this volume on Lothian and Ireland, makes it clear that Lothian invariably placed what he considered to be British interests in

---

[31] Oscar Gass to Harry Dexter White, 1 May 1939, Vol. 187, Diaries of Henry Morgenthau, Jr., Franklin D. Roosevelt Presidential Library, Hyde Park, NY.

[32] D. C. Watt, *Personalities and Policies: Studies in the Formulation of British Policy in the Twentieth Century* (London: Longmans, 1965), 173-174.

[33] Kerr to Woodrow Wilson, 22 May 1922, Reel 120, Woodrow Wilson Papers, Manuscripts Division, Library of Congress, Washington, DC; on his religious beliefs, see also Butler, *Lord Lothian*, 85-101; and Billington, *Lothian*, 75-80.

[34] Kerr to Winston Churchill (not sent), 28 February 1921, GD 40/17/207, Lothian Papers.

Ireland before his desire to conciliate U.S. opinion on the subject. As Greg Kennedy points out, underpinning Lothian's belief in Anglo-American cooperation there was always a hard-headed appreciation that, in terms of *realpolitik*, an overextended British empire had few alternatives except to ally itself with the United States.

Echoing Oscar Gass, in 1940 a former Rhodes Scholar, who had graduated from Oxford in 1932, confessed that his

> own attitude, while not strictly isolationist, is one of suspicion of England's endeavors to draw us into the war. My years at Oxford gave me first, a profound admiration for the British genius for government and politics, one of the principal features of which is the hard-headed ability never to do anything except in self-interest but at the same time to make it appear that in so doing they are assuming a "white man's burden"; and second, the knowledge that the English regard all Americans as rather crude and inferior people who owe them somewhat the same attitude of respect and servitude that their own lower classes properly adopt.[35]

Another Rhodes scholar who had studied at Oxford one year later and was pro-British and anti-German on the war nonetheless stated that: "England doesn't really give a hoot for democracy, was willing to see it perish in Spain and Czechoslovakia, [and] only fought when her own imperial interests were threatened."[36] Both men almost certainly encountered Lothian, who was secretary to the Rhodes Trust throughout their time at Oxford. One can only speculate whether either had him particularly in mind when uttering these comments.

Lothian's apparently liberal outlook could not entirely disguise a certain cold-blooded respect for power at every level, whether in the domestic political sphere or in international relations. At times, when dealing with India, Africa, Russia, and race relations, this outlook probably made Lothian willing to compromise and accept realities that ran counter to some of his fundamental preferences. On other occasions, as with Hitler's Germany, in an effort to safeguard his own country's security, he was willing to make concessions that many found morally reprehensible. Lothian could demonstrate a sardonic detachment when contemplating the messier aspects of politics. In 1933, former British Colonial Secretary Leo

---

[35] Reported in *The American Oxonian* 27(1940), as quoted in Thomas J. Schaeper and Kathleen Schaeper, *Rhodes Scholars, Oxford, and the Creation of an American Elite* (New York: Berghahn Books, 1998), 126.
[36] Reported in *The American Oxonian* 28 (1941), *ibid.*, 126.

Amery reported a conversation with Lothian, then engrossed in moves to give India a greater degree of self-rule, in which Lothian

> was rather interesting on the point that once the Federal Government is started the control at the centre will be in the hands of the Princes who will not only command a third of the members in the Legislature but have no difficulty whatever in buying up others. His whole picture in fact was one of a thoroughly corrupt but otherwise peaceful and monarchical India.[37]

Lothian's placid acquiescence in this prospect, which he apparently found quite acceptable, suggests he may not have been quite the unalloyed liberal democrat portrayed by his subsequent admirers.

In this world, however, as numerous American officials have since discovered, those who use high-flown idealistic rhetoric to justify self-interested national objectives are liable to attract opprobrium and charges of hypocrisy. Charm—for which the Kerr family, Lothian included, was famous[38]—if anything compounds the offense. While often ready to accept unpalatable hard facts and make concessions to these as appropriate, on the personal, political, and international level, Lothian gravitated relentlessly to power. In his own life Lothian, despite or perhaps by means of his protracted bouts of ill-health and nervous exhaustion and lengthy years of religious doubts, demonstrated a certain cool determination in evading the demands of his family, patrons, and friends that he marry suitably, produce an heir to the title he would eventually inherit, and follow a conventional career path toward the glittering prizes of politics and society, finding instead a comfortable niche that allowed him to pursue his own slightly idiosyncratic congeries of interests while traveling extensively in the United States and the British Dominions. The fragile, high-minded intellectual paragon proved remarkably adept in identifying and pursuing a lifestyle he found extremely congenial. Lothian was equally ruthless in his espousal of what he perceived as British national interests, and in extremis was prepared to sacrifice almost all other considerations to safeguard Britain's position. The discrepancy between Lothian's idealistic style, his proclamation of boldly universal internationalist goals, and the tough-minded promotion of narrowly British interests his actual policies enshrined, may well go far to account for the disproportionate controversy this fundamentally second-rank figure generated during his lifetime and long after his death.

---

[37] Leo Amery, diary entry, 16 June 1933, in *The Empire at Bay: The Leo Amery Diaries 1929-1945*, eds. John Barnes and David Nicholson (London: Hutchinson, 1988), 296.
[38] Butler, *Lord Lothian*, 238.

BIBLIOGRAPHY

ARCHIVAL SOURCES

Atlantic Union Committee Papers. Manuscripts Division, Library of Congress, Washington, DC.

Arthur H. Balfour Papers. Add MSS 49797. British Library, London.

Robert H. Brand Papers. Bodleian Library, Oxford University, Oxford.

British Admiralty Papers. ADM 116. The National Archives of the United Kingdom, Kew, London.

British Air Ministry Papers. AIR 19, AIR 20, AIR 27, AIR 88. The National Archives of the United Kingdom, Kew, London.

British Cabinet Papers. CAB 23, CAB 65, CAB 66, CAB 85, CAB 115. The National Archives of the United Kingdom, Kew, London.

British Foreign Office Papers. FO 371, FO 608, FO 794, FO 800. The National Archives of the United Kingdom, Kew, London.

British Prime Minister's Files. PREM 3. The National Archives of the United Kingdom, Kew, London.

John Buchan (First Lord Tweedsmuir) Papers. ACC 11627. National Library of Scotland, Edinburgh, Scotland.

R. G. Casey Diaries. National Library of Australia, Canberra, Australia.

1st Baron Chatfield Papers. Royal Maritime Museum Library, Greenwich, London.

Winston S. Churchill Papers. Churchill Archive Centre, Churchill College, Cambridge.

Council on Foreign Relations Records, 1921-1951. Microfilm ed. Mudd Manuscripts Library, Princeton University, Princeton, NJ.

Paul D. Cravath Papers. Record Group 56, General Records of the Department of the Treasury. U.S. National Archives II, College Park, MD.

Crawford Family Papers. ACC 9769. The National Library of Scotland, Edinburgh, Scotland.

Lionel Curtis Papers. Bodleian Library, Oxford University, Oxford.

George Nathaniel Curzon Papers. MSS Eur F112/212A. Oriental and India Office Collection, British Library, London.

Norman H. Davis Papers. Manuscripts Division, Library of Congress, Washington, DC.

John Foster Dulles Papers. Microfilm ed. Mudd Manuscripts Library, Princeton University, Princeton, NJ.

Felix Frankfurter Papers. Microfilm ed. Manuscripts Division, Library of Congress, Washington, DC.

Edward Grigg (Lord Altrincham) Papers. Microfilm ed. Bodleian Library, Oxford University, Oxford.

Edward M. House Papers. Manuscripts and Archives, Sterling Library, Yale University, New Haven, CT.

Cordell Hull Papers. Microfilm ed. Manuscripts Division, Library of Congress, Washington, DC.

Frank B. Kellogg Papers. Microfilm ed. Manuscripts Division, Library of Congress, Washington, DC.

Philip Kerr (Eleventh Marquess of Lothian) Papers. GD40/17. National Archives of Scotland, Edinburgh, Scotland.

William Lyon Mackenzie King Diaries. National Archives of Canada, Ottawa, Canada.

Thomas W. Lamont Papers. Baker Library, Harvard Business School, Boston, MA.

David Lloyd George Papers. House of Lords Record Office, London.

Jay Pierrepont Moffat Papers. Houghton Library, Harvard University, Cambridge, MA.

Henry J. Morgenthau, Jr., Diaries. Franklin D. Roosevelt Presidential Library, Hyde Park, NY.

Dwight W. Morrow Papers. Amherst College Library, Amherst, MA.

Rhodes Trust Files. Rhodes House, Oxford.

Franklin D. Roosevelt Papers. Franklin D. Roosevelt Presidential Library, Hyde Park, NY.

Theodore Roosevelt Papers. Microfilm ed. Manuscripts Division, Library of Congress, Washington, DC.

Round Table Papers. Bodleian Library, Oxford University, Oxford.

Royal Institute of International Affairs Archives. Chatham House, London.

Whitney D. Shepardson Papers. Franklin D. Roosevelt Presidential Library, Hyde Park, NY.

Henry L. Stimson Diaries and Papers. Microfilm ed. Manuscripts and Archives, Sterling Library, Yale University, New Haven, CT.

Willard D. Straight Papers. Microfilm ed. Cornell University Library, Ithaca, NY.

Clarence Kirshman Streit Papers. Manuscripts Division, Library of Congress, Washington, DC.

Woodrow Wilson Papers. Microfilm ed. Manuscripts Division, Library of Congress, Washington, DC.

George M. Wrong Papers. University of Toronto Archives, Toronto, Canada.

PRINTED SOURCES

Documents on German Foreign Policy 1918-1945. Series D, Vol. 6. London: Her Majesty's Stationery Office, 1956.

New York Times.

The Observer.

The Round Table. Vols. 1-31 (1910-1940).

The Times (London).

Acheson, Dean. *Fragments of My Fleece*. New York: Norton, 1971.

Alanbrooke, Lord. *War Diaries, 1939-1945: Field Marshal Lord Alanbrooke*. Eds. Alex Danchev and Daniel Todman. Berkeley: University of California Press, 2001.

Amery, L. S. *My Political Life*. 3 vols. London: Hutchinson, 1953-1955.

Amery, Leo. *The Leo Amery Diaries*, Vol. I: *1886-1929*. Eds. John Barnes and David Nicholson. London: Hutchinson, 1980.

Amery, Leo. *The Empire at Bay: The Leo Amery Diaries 1929-1945.* Eds. John Barnes and David Nicholson. London: Hutchinson, 1988.

Astor, Michael. *Tribal Feeling*. London: Murray, 1963.

Astor, Nancy. *My Two Countries*. London: Heinemann, 1923.

Beer, G. L. *The English-Speaking Peoples, their Future and Joint International Obligations*. New York: Macmillan, 1917.

Beveridge, William. *Power and Influence: An Autobiography*. London: Hodder and Stoughton, 1953.

Blum, John. Ed. *From the Morgenthau Diaries: Years of Urgency 1938-1941*. Boston: Houghton Mifflin, 1965.

Bosco, Andrea. Ed. *Two Musketeers for the Empire: The Lionel Curtis-Philip Kerr (Lord Lothian) Correspondene 1909-1940*. London: Lothian Foundation Press, 1997.

Bullitt, Orville H. Ed. *For the President Personal and Secret: Correspondence between Franklin D. Roosevelt and William C. Bullitt*. Boston: Houghton Mifflin, 1972.

Cadogan, Alexander. *The Diaries of Sir Alexander Cadogan O.M. 1938-1945*. Ed. David Dilks. London: Cassell, 1971.

Carroll, F. M. Ed. *The American Commission on Irish Independence 1919: The Diary, Correspondence and Report*. Dublin: Irish Manuscripts Commission, 1985.

Casey, R. G. *A Delicate Mission: The Washington Diaries of R. G. Casey, 1940-42*. Ed. Carl Bridge. Canberra: Australian National Library, 2008.

Churchill, Winston. *The Second World War*. 6 vols. London: Cassell, 1948-1954.

Colville, John. *The Fringes of Power: Downing Street Diaries*, Vol. I: *September 1939-October 1941*. London: Sceptre, 1986.

Cunningham of Hyndhope, Viscount. *A Sailor's Odyssey: The Autobiography of Viscount Cunningham of Hyndhope*. London: Hutchinson, 1951.

Curtis, Lionel. *The Problem of the Commonwealth*. New York: Macmillan, 1916.

Curtis, Lionel. *World War: Its Cause and Cure*. London: Oxford University Press, 1945.

Dalton, Hugh. *The Second World War Diary of Hugh Dalton*. Ed. Ben Pimlott. London: Jonathan Cape, 1986.

Dodd, William E., Jr., and Martha Dodd. Eds. *Ambassador Dodd's Diary 1933-1938*. London: Victor Gollancz, 1941.

Dulles, Allen W. "The Threat of Anglo-American Naval Rivalry." *Foreign Affairs* 7:2 (January 1929): 173-182.

Grant, A. J., *et al. An Introduction to the Study of International Relations*. London: Macmillan, 1916.

Great Britain. *Parliamentary Papers (Commons)*. 1917-1940.

Great Britain. *Parliamentary Debates (Lords)*. 1934.

Hancock, W. H., and Jean Van Der Poel. Eds. *Selections from the Smuts Papers*, Vol. III: *June 1910-November 1918*. Cambridge: Cambridge University Press, 1966.

Harvey, Oliver. *The Diplomatic Diaries of Oliver Harvey 1937-1940*. Ed. John Harvey. London: Collins, 1970.

Hendrick, Burton J. *The Life and Letters of Walter Hines Page*. 3 vols. Garden City, NY: Doubleday, Page & Co., 1922.

Howland, Charles P. "Navies and Peace: An American View." *Foreign Affairs* 8:1 (October 1929): 30-40.

Ismay, Lord. *The Memoirs of General the Lord Ismay*. London: Heinemann, 1960.

Jebb, Richard. *The Britannic Question: A Survey of Alternatives*. London: Longmans, 1913.

Jones, Thomas. *A Diary with Letters 1931-1950*. London: Oxford University Press, 1954.

Jones, Thomas. *Whitehall Diary*. Ed. Keith Middlemas. 3 vols. London: Oxford University Press, 1969-1971.

Kennedy, A. L. *The Times and Appeasement: The Journals of A. L. Kennedy, 1932-1939*. Cambridge: Cambridge University Press for the Royal Historical Society, 2000.

Kennedy, John F. *Why England Slept*. New York: W. Funk, 1940.

Kennedy, Joseph P. *Hostage to Fortune: The Letters of Joseph P. Kennedy*. Ed. Amanda Smith. New York: Viking, 2001.

Kerr, Philip, *et al. Approaches to World Problems*. New Haven, CT: Yale University Press, 1924.

Kerr, Philip. "Navies and Peace: A British View." *Foreign Affairs* 8:1 (October 1929): 20-29.

Kerr, Philip. *The Industrial Dilemma*. London: Daily News, 1926.

Kerr, Philip. "The Outlawry of War." *International Affairs* 7:5 (November 1928): 361-388.

Kerr, Philip. "What the British Empire Really Stands For." Address to Toronto Round Table Club, 30 July 1912. Toronto: n.p., 1917.

Kerr, Philip, and Lionel Curtis. *The Prevention of War*. New Haven, CT: Yale University Press, 1923.

Kimball, Warren F. Ed. *Churchill & Roosevelt: The Complete Correspondence*. 3 vols. Princeton, NJ: Princeton University Press, 1984.

Kipling, Rudyard. *The Letters of Rudyard Kipling*, Vol. 4: *1911-19*. Ed. Thomas Pinney. Iowa City: University of Iowa Press, 1999.

Lee, Raymond E. *The London Journals of General Raymond E. Lee 1940-1941*. Ed. James Leutze. Boston: Little, Brown, 1971.

Lippmann, Walter. *Public Philosopher: Selected Letters of Walter Lippmann*. Ed. John Morton Blum. New York: Ticknor & Fields, 1984.

Lippmann, Walter. *U.S. Foreign Policy: Shield of the Republic*. Boston: Little, Brown, 1943.

Lippmann, Walter. *U.S. War Aims*. Boston: Little, Brown, 1944.

Lloyd George, David; the Marquess of Lothian; and B. Seebohm Rowntree. *How to Tackle Unemployment*. London: Press Printers Ltd., 1930.

Long, Breckinridge. *The War Diary of Breckinridge Long: Selections from the Years 1939-44*. Ed. Fred L. Israel. Lincoln: University of Nebraska Press, 1966.

Long, Walter. *Memories*. New York: E. P. Dutton, 1923.

Lothian, Marquess of. "Christian Science, Public Affairs, and the Christian Science Monitor." *The Christian Science Journal* 52:10 (1935): 508-511.

Lothian, Marquess of. "Democracy and World Order." *The Observer* (5 March 1939).

Lothian, Marquess of. *Liberalism in the Modern World*. London: Lovat Dickson, 1933.

Lothian, Marquess of. "New League or No League." *International Conciliation* 325 (December 1936): 589-604.

Lothian, Marquess of. *Pacifism is Not Enough, Nor Patriotism Either*. Oxford: Clarendon Press, 1935.

Lothian, Marquess of. *Pacifism is not enough: Collected Lectures and Speeches of Lord Lothian (Philip Kerr)*. Eds. John Pinder and Andrea Bosco. London: Lothian Foundation, 1990.

Lothian, Marquess of. *The American Speeches of Lord Lothian*. Ed. Royal Institute of International Affairs. London: Oxford University Press, 1941.

Lothian, Marquess of. "The World Crisis of 1936." *Foreign Affairs* 15:1 (October 1936): 124-140.

Mahan, Alfred T. *Lessons of the War with Spain*. Boston, MA: Little, Brown, 1899.

Mahan, Alfred T. *The Interest of America in International Conditions*. Boston, MA: Little, Brown, 1910.

Mahan, Alfred T. *The Interest of America in Sea Power, Present and Future*. Boston, MA: Little, Brown, 1897.

Martin, Hugh. *Ireland in Insurrection: An Englishman's Record of Fact*. London: Daniel O'Connor, 1921.

Moffat, J. Pierrepont. *The Moffat Papers: Selections from the Diplomatic Journals of Jay Pierrepont Moffat, 1919-1943*. Ed. Nancy Harvison Hooker. Cambridge, MA: Harvard University Press, 1956.

Nicolson, Harold. *Harold Nicolson: Diaries and Letters 1939-1945*. Ed. Nigel Nicolson. London: Collins, 1967.

Scott, C. P. *The Political Diaries of C. P. Scott*. Ed. Trevor Wilson. Ithaca, NY: Cornell University Press, 1970.

Stevenson, Frances. *Lloyd George: A Diary*. Ed. A. J. P. Taylor. London: Hutchinson, 1971.

Stimson, Henry L., with McGeorge Bundy. *On Active Service in Peace and War*. New York: Harper, 1947.

Streit, Clarence. *Union Now: A Proposal for a Federal Union of the Democracies of the North Atlantic*. New York: Harper and Brothers, 1939.

Sylvester, A. J. *Life with Lloyd George: The Diary of A. J. Sylvester, 1931-45*. Ed. Colin Cross. London: Macmillan, 1975.

Thistlethwaite, Frank. *Our War 1938-45*. Cambridge: Frank Thistlethwaite, 1997.

Tree, Ronald. *When the Moon Was High: Memoirs of Peace and War, 1897-1942*. London: Macmillan, 1975.

U.S. Congress. *Congressional Record*.

U.S. Department of State. *Foreign Relations of the United States: Diplomatic Papers 1939*: Vol. II, *General, the British Commonwealth and Europe*. Washington, DC: Government Printing Office, 1956.

U.S. Department of State. *Foreign Relations of the United States 1940*: Vol. I, *General*. Washington, DC: Government Printing Office, 1959.

U.S. Department of State. *Foreign Relations of the United States 1940*: Vol. III, *The British Commonwealth, the Soviet Union, Near East, and Africa*. Washington, DC: Government Printing Office, 1958.

U.S. Department of State. *Foreign Relations of the United States 1940*: Vol. IV, *The Far East*. Washington, DC: Government Printing Office, 1955.

Vandenberg, Arthur H. *The Private Papers of Senator Vandenberg*. Eds. Arthur H. Vandenberg, Jr., with Joe Alex Morris. Boston: Houghton Mifflin, 1953.

Vansittart, Robert. *The Mist Procession: The Autobiography of Lord Vansittart*. London: Hutchinson, 1988.

Viereck, George Sylvester. *Lord Lothian versus Lord Lothian: Excerpts from the Speeches and Writings of the British Ambassador to the United States*. Scotch Plains, NJ: Flanders Hall, 1940.

Webb, Beatrice. *Beatrice Webb's Diaries 1912-1924*. Ed. Margaret I. Cole. London: Longmans, Green, 1952.

Wheeler-Bennett, Sir John. *Special Relationships: America in Peace and War*. London: Macmillan, 1975.

Wilson, Woodrow. *The Papers of Woodrow Wilson*. Vol. 40. Ed. Arthur S. Link. Princeton, NJ: Princeton University Press, 1982.

SECONDARY WORKS

Ambrosius, Lloyd E. "Wilson, the Republicans, and French Security after World War I." *Journal of American History* 59:2 (September 1972): 341-352.

Anderson, Stuart. *Race and Rapprochement: Anglo-Saxonism and Anglo-American Relations, 1895-1904*. East Brunswick, NJ: Fairleigh Dickinson, University Press, 1981.

Andrew, Chris. *Secret Service: The Making of the British Intelligence Community*. London: Heinemann, 1985.

Annals of the Lothian Foundation 1 (1991).

Aydelotte, Frank. *The American Rhodes Scholarships: A Review of the First Forty Years*. Princeton, NJ: Princeton University Press, 1946.

Bailey, Gavin. "The Narrow Margin of Criticality: The Question of the Supply of 100-Octane Fuel in the Battle of Britain." *English Historical Review* 123:501 (April 2008): 394-411.

Barnett, Correlli. *The Audit of War: The Illusion and Reality of Britain as a Great Nation*. London: Macmillan, 1986.

Barnhart, Michael A. *Japan Prepares for Total War: The Search for Economic Security, 1919-1941*. Ithaca, NY: Cornell University Press, 1987.

Bell, Duncan. *The Idea of Greater Britain: Empire and the Future of World Order, 1860-1900*. Princeton, NJ: Princeton University Press, 2007.

Beloff, Max. *The Great Powers: Essays in Twentieth Century Politics*. London: Allen and Unwin, 1959.

Beloff, Max. *Imperial Sunset: Britain's Liberal Empire, 1897-1921*. 2nd ed. London: Macmillan, 1987.

Bennett, G. H. *British Foreign Policy during the Curzon Period, 1919-24*. London: St. Martin's Press, 1995.

Berridge, Geoff. *Diplomacy: Theory and Practice*. 3rd ed. Basingstoke: Palgrave, 2005.

Beschloss, Michael R. *Kennedy and Roosevelt: The Uneasy Alliance*. New York: Norton, 1980.

Billington, David P., Jr. *Lothian: Philip Kerr and the Quest for World Order*. Westport, CT: Praeger, 2006.

Blair, Clay. *Hitler's U-Boat War: The Hunters 1939-1942*. London: Weidenfeld and Nicolson, 2000.

Bosco, Andrea. *Lord Lothian: Un Pioniere del federalismo, 1882-1940*. Milan, Italy: Jaca Books, 1996.

Bosco, Andrea. "Lothian, Curtis, Kimber and the Federal Union Movement (1938-40)." *Journal of Contemporary History* 23:3 (July 1988): 462-502.

Bosco, Andrea, and Alex May. Eds. *The Round Table, the Empire/Commonwealth and British Foreign Policy*. London: Lothian Foundation Press, 1997.

Bosco, Andrea, and Cornelia Navari. Eds. *Chatham House and British Foreign Policy 1919-1945: The Royal Institute of International Affairs during the Inter-War Period*. London: Lothian Foundation Press, 1994.

Bothwell, Robert. *Loring Christie: The Failure of Bureaucratic Imperialism*. New York: Garland, 1988.

Braisted, William R. *The United States Navy in the Pacific, 1909-1922*. Austin: University of Texas Press, 1971.

Brand, Robert H. "Philip Kerr: Some Personal Memories." *The Round Table*. 50:199 (June 1960): 234-243.

Brand, Robert H. "Kerr, Philip Henry." *Dictionary of National Biography 1931-1940*. London: Oxford University Press, 1949. Pp. 507-510.

Brewer, Susan A. *To Win the Peace: British Propaganda in the United States during World War II*. Ithaca, NY: Cornell University Press, 1997.

Bridge, Carl. "Casey and the Americans: Australian War Propaganda in the United States 1940-1941." *Working Papers in Australian Studies*, No. 30. London: Australian Studies Centre, Institute of Commonwealth Studies, 1988.

Briggs, Asa, and Ann Macartney. *Toynbee Hall: The First One Hundred Years*. London: Routledge and Kegan Paul, 1984.

Butler, J. R. M. *Grand Strategy*, Vol. II: *September 1939-June 1941*. London: Her Majesty's Stationery Office, 1957.

Butler, J. R. M. *Lord Lothian (Philip Kerr) 1882-1940*. London: Macmillan, 1960.

Canham, Erwin D. *Commitment to Freedom: The Story of the Christian Science Monitor*. Boston: Houghton Mifflin, 1958.

Cannadine, David. *In Churchill's Shadow: Confronting the Past in Modern Britain*. New York: Oxford University Press, 2003.

Carroll, Francis M. *American Opinion and the Irish Question, 1910-23: A Study in Opinion and Policy*. Dublin: Gill and Macmillan, 1978.

Cecil, Hugh, and Mirabel Cecil. *Imperial Marriage: An Edwardian War and Peace*. London: John Murray, 2002.

Clark, Dennis. *Irish Blood: Northern Ireland and the American Conscience*. Port Washington, NY: Kennikat Press, 1977.

Clark, Ronald W. *Tizard*. London: Methuen, 1965.

Cole, Wayne S. *Roosevelt and the Isolationists 1932-45*. Lincoln: University of Nebraska Press, 1983.

Cooper, John Milton, Jr. *Walter Hines Page: The Southerner as American, 1855-1918*. Chapel Hill: University of North Carolina Press, 1977.

Costello, John. *Ten Days to Destiny: The Secret Story of the Hess Initiative and British Efforts to Strike a Deal with Hitler*. New York: Morrow, 1991.

Crowl, Philip T. "Alfred Thayer Mahan: The Naval Historian." In *Makers of Modern Strategy from Machiavelli to the Nuclear Age*. Ed. Peter Paret. Princeton, NJ: Princeton University Press, 1986. Pp. 444-477.

Cull, Nicholas J. "Selling Peace: The Origins, Promotion and Fate of the Anglo-American New Order During World War II." *Diplomacy and Statecraft* 7:1 (March 1996): 1-28.

Cull, Nicholas John. *Selling War: The British Propaganda Campaign Against American "Neutrality" in World War II*. New York: Oxford University Press, 1995.

Dallek, Robert. *Franklin Roosevelt and American Foreign Policy, 1932-1945*. New York: Oxford University Press, 1995.

Danchev, Alex. *Oliver Franks: Founding Father*. Oxford: Clarendon Press, 1983.

Davis, Allen F. *Spearheads for Reform: The Social Settlements and the Progressive Movement, 1890-1914*. New York: Oxford University Press, 1967.

Dimbleby, David, and David Reynolds. *An Ocean Apart: The Relationship Between Britain and America in the Twentieth Century*. New York: Random House, 1988.

Dingman, Roger. *Power in the Pacific: The Origins of Naval Arms Limitation, 1914-1922*. Chicago: University of Chicago Press, 1976.

Dobson, Alan P. *US Wartime Aid to Britain, 1940-1946*. London: Croom, Helm, 1986.

Duff, John B. "The Versailles Treaty and the Irish-Americans." *Journal of American History* 55:3 (December 1968): 582-598.

Duus, P.; R. H. Myers; and M. R. Peattie. Eds. *The Japanese Informal Empire in China, 1895-1937*. Princeton, NJ: Princeton University Press, 1991.

Eddy, John, and Deryck Schreuder. Eds. *The Rise of Colonial Nationalism: Australia, New Zealand, Canada, and South Africa First Assert Their Nationalities 1880-1914*. Sydney: Allen and Unwin, 1988.

Egerton, George W. "Britain and the 'Great Betrayal': Anglo-American Relations and the Struggle for United States Ratification of the Treaty of Versailles, 1919-1920." *The Historical Journal* 21:4 (December 1978): 885-911.

Egerton, George W. "Conservative Internationalism: British Approaches to International Organization and the Creation of the League of Nations." *Diplomacy and Statecraft* 5:1 (March 1994): 1-20.

Egerton, George W. *Great Britain and the Creation of the League of Nations: Strategy, Politics, and International Organization, 1914-1919*. Chapel Hill: University of North Carolina Press, 1978.

Egerton, George W. "Imperialism, Atlanticism, and Internationalism: Philip Kerr and the League of Nations Question, 1916-1920." *Annals of the Lothian Foundation* 1 (1991): 95-122.

Ellinwood, DeWitt Clinton. "The Round Table and India, 1909-1920." *Journal of Commonwealth and Political Studies* 9:3 (November 1971): 183-209.

Elton, Godfrey. Ed. *The First Fifty Years of the Rhodes Trust and the Rhodes Scholarships 1903-1953*. Oxford: Basil Blackwell, 1955.

Fieldhouse, Roger. *The Workers Educational Association: Aims and Achievements 1902-1977*. Syracuse, NY: Syracuse University Press, 1977.

Fisher, John. *Curzon and British Imperialism in the Middle East 1916-19*. London and Portland, OR: Frank Cass, 1999.

Forcey, Charles. *The Crossroads of Liberalism: Croly, Weyl, Lippmann and the Progressive Era, 1900-1925*. New York: Oxford University Press, 1961.

Foster, Leonie. *High Hopes: The Men and Motives of the Australian Round Table*. Melbourne: Melbourne University Press, 1986.

Foster, Leonie. "The Australian Round Table, the Moot, and Australian Nationalism." *The Round Table* 72:288 (October 1983): 473-484.

Fox, James. *The Langhorne Sisters*. London: Granta, 1998.

Frei, Christoph. *Hans J. Morgenthau: An Intellectual Biography*. Baton Rouge: Louisiana State University Press, 2001.

French, David. *The Strategy of the Lloyd George Coalition, 1916-1918*. Oxford: Clarendon Press, 1995.

Friedberg, Aaron L. *The Weary Titan: Britain and the Experience of Relative Decline, 1895-1905*. Princeton, NJ: Princeton University Press, 1988.

Fry, Michael G. *Illusions of Security: North Atlantic Diplomacy, 1918-22*. Toronto: University of Toronto Press, 1972.

Garwood, Ellen Clayton. *Will Clayton: A Short Biography*. Austin: University of Texas Press, 1958.

Gilbert, Martin S. *Winston S. Churchill*, Vol. IV: *The Stricken World 1916-1922*. Boston, MA: Houghton Mifflin, 1975.

Gilbert, Martin S. *Winston S. Churchill*, Vol. V: *Companion Part 2: Documents: The Wilderness Years 1929-1935*. Boston: Houghton Mifflin, 1981.

Gilbert, Martin S. *Finest Hour: Winston S. Churchill 1939-1941*. London: Heinemann, 1991.

Gilbert, Martin, and Richard Gott. *The Appeasers*. 2nd ed. London: Weidenfeld and Nicolson, 1967.

Gilmour, Ian. "Termagant." *London Review of Books* (19 October 2000): 12.

Goldman, Emily O. *Sunken Treaties: Arms Control between the Wars*. University Park: Pennsylvania State University Press, 1994.

Goldstein, Erik. *Winning the Peace: British Diplomatic Strategy, Peace Planning, and the Paris Peace Conference, 1916-1920*. Oxford: Clarendon Press, 1991.

Goldstein, Erik, and John Maurer. Eds. *The Washington Conference, 1921-22: Naval Rivalry, East Asian Stability and the Road to Pearl Harbor*. New York: Routledge, 1993.

Gollin, A. M. *Proconsul in Politics: A Study of Lord Milner in Opposition and in Power*. New York: Macmillan, 1964.

Grayson, Richard S. *Liberals, International Relations and Appeasement*. London: Frank Cass, 2001.

Gregory, Ross. *Walter Hines Page: Ambassador to the Court of St. James's*. Lexington: University of Kentucky Press, 1970.

Grigg, John. *Lloyd George: War Leader*. London: Allen Lane, 2002.

Grose, Peter. *Continuing the Inquiry: The Council on Foreign Relations from 1921 to 1996*. New York: Council on Foreign Relations, 1996.

Grose, Peter. *Gentleman Spy: The Life of Allen Dulles*. Boston: Houghton Mifflin, 1994.

Guderzo, Giulio. Ed. *Lord Lothian: Una vita per la pace*. Pavia, Italy: University of Pavia, 1986.

Hagan, Kenneth J. "Alfred Thayer Mahan: Turning America Back to the Sea." In *Makers of Modern Diplomacy: From Benjamin Franklin to Henry Kissinger*. Eds. Frank J. Merli and Theodore A. Wilson. New York: Scribner, 1974. Pp. 279-303.

Hague, Arnold. *Destroyers for Great Britain: A History of the 50 Town Class Ships Transferred from the United States to Great Britain in 1940*. 2nd rev. ed. London: Greenhill Books, 1990.

Hall, Christopher. *Britain, America and Arms Control, 1921-37*. New York: St. Martin's Press, 1987.

Hall, H. Duncan. *North American Supply*. London: Her Majesty's Stationery Office, 1955.

Hall, H. Duncan; C. C. Wrigley; and J. D. Scott. *Sources of Overseas Supply*. London: Her Majesty's Stationery Office, 1956.

Halliwell, Martin. *The Constant Dialogue: Reinhold Niebuhr and American Political Culture*. Lanham, MD: Rowman and Littlefield, 2005.

Hamilton, Nigel. *J. F. K.: Reckless Youth*. New York: Random House, 1992.

Hancock, W. K., and M. M. Gowing. *The British War Economy*. London: His Majesty's Stationery Office, 1949.

Harbaugh, William H. *Lawyer's Lawyer: The Life of John W. Davis*. New York: Oxford University Press, 1973.

Harris, José. *William Beveridge: A Biography*. Oxford: Clarendon Press, 1997.

Healy, David S. *US Expansionism: The Imperialist Urge in the 1890s*. Madison: University of Wisconsin Press, 1970.

Henderson, Sir Nicholas. "The Washington Embassy: Navigating the Waters of the Potomac." *Diplomacy and Statecraft* 1:1 (March 1990): 40-48.

Higham, John. *Strangers in the Land: Patterns of American Nativism 1860-1925*. 2nd ed. New Brunswick, NJ: Rutgers University Press, 1977.

Hodgson, Godfrey. *The Colonel: The Life and Wars of Henry Stimson, 1867-1950*. New York: Knopf, 1990.

Hofstadter, Richard. *The Age of Reform: From Bryan to F.D.R*. New York: Vintage, 1956.

Hofstadter, Richard. *Social Darwinism in American Thought*. Revised ed. Boston, MA: Beacon Press, 1955.

Hogan, Michael J. *Informal Entente: The Private Structure of Cooperation in Anglo-American Diplomacy, 1918-1928*. Columbia: University of Missouri Press, 1977.

Holland, Jack. *The American Connection: U.S. Guns, Money, and Influence in Northern Ireland*. Dublin: Poolbeg, 1989.

Hopkins, Michael F.; Saul Kelly; and John W. Young. Eds. *The Washington Embassy: British Ambassadors to the United States, 1939-77*. Houndsmills, Basingstoke, and New York: Palgrave Macmillan, 2009.

Horsman, Reginald. *Race and Manifest Destiny: The Origins of American Racial Anglo-Saxonism*. Cambridge, MA: Harvard University Press, 1981.

Howarth, Stephen, and Derek Law. Eds. *The Battle of the Atlantic 1939-1945: The 50th Anniversary International Naval Conference*. London: Greenhill, 1994.

Hubback, David. *No Ordinary Press Baron: A Life of Walter Layton*. London: Weidenfeld and Nicolson, 1985.

Hunt, Michael H. *Ideology and US Foreign Policy*. New Haven, CT: Yale University Press, 1986.

Jeffery, Keith. *The British army and the crisis of empire 1918-22*. Manchester: Manchester University Press, 1984.

Jeffreys-Jones, Rhodri. *American Espionage: From Secret Service to CIA*. New York: Free Press, 1977.

Jeffreys-Jones, Rhodri. "Lord Lothian and American Democracy: An Illusion in Pursuit of an Illusion." *Canadian Review of American Studies* 17:4 (Winter 1986): 411-422.

Jeffreys-Jones, Rhodri. "The Inestimable Advantage of Not Being English: Lord Lothian's American Ambassadorship, 1939-1940." *Scottish Historical Review* 63:1 (April 1984): 105-110.

Kaufman, Burton I. *Efficiency and Expansion: Foreign Trade Organization in the Wilson Administration, 1913-1921*. Westport, CT: Greenwood, 1974.

Kendle, John Edward. *The Colonial and Imperial Conferences, 1887-1911: A Study in Imperial Organization*. London: Longmans, 1967.

Kendle, John. *The Round Table Movement and Imperial Union*. Toronto: University of Toronto Press, 1975.

Kennedy, David M. *Over Here: The First World War and American Society*. New York: Oxford University Press, 1980.

Kennedy, Greg. "1935: A Snapshot of British Imperial Defence in the Far East." In *Far Flung Lines: Studies in Imperial Defence in Honour of Donald Mackenzie Schurman*. Eds. Greg Kennedy and Keith Neilson. London: Frank Cass, 1997. Pp. 190-215.

Kennedy, Greg. *Anglo-American Strategic Relations, 1933-1939: Imperial Crossroads*. London: Frank Cass, 2002.

Kennedy, Michael. *Ireland and the League of Nations, 1919-1946: International Relations, Diplomacy and Politics*. Dublin: Irish Academic Press, 1996.

Kennedy, Paul M. *The Rise and Fall of the Great Powers: Economic Change and Military Conflict from 1500 to 2000*. London: Fontana, 1989.

Kennedy, Paul M. *The Rise of the Anglo-German Naval Antagonism, 1860-1914*. London: Allen and Unwin, 1980.

Kennedy, Ross A. *Woodrow Wilson, World War I, and America's Strategy for Peace and Security*. Kent, OH: Kent State University Press, 2009.

Kenny, Anthony. Ed. *The History of the Rhodes Trust 1902-1999*. Oxford: Oxford University Press, 2001.

Kimball, Warren F. "'Beggar My Neighbour': America and the British Interim Finance Crisis, 1940-41." *Journal of Economic History* 29:4 (December 1969): 758-772.

Kimball, Warren F. *The Most Unsordid Act: Lend-Lease, 1939-41*. Baltimore, MD: Johns Hopkins University Press, 1969.

Kimball, Warren F., and Bruce Bartlett. "Roosevelt and Prewar Commitments to Canada: The Tyler Kent Affair." *Diplomatic History* 5:4 (Fall 1981): 291-312.

Kimber, Sir Charles. "Federal Union." In *Britain and the Threat to Stability in Europe, 1918-1947*. Eds. Peter Caterall with C. J. Morris. London: Leicester University Press, 1993.

King, Desmond. *Making Americans: Immigration, Race, and the Origins of the Diverse Democracy*. Cambridge, MA: Harvard University Press, 2000.

King-Hall, Stephen. *Chatham House: A Brief Account of the Origins, Purposes, and Methods of the Royal Institute of International Affairs*. London: Oxford University Press, 1937.

Knock, Thomas J. *To End All Wars: Woodrow Wilson and the Quest for a New World Order*. New York: Oxford University Press, 1992.

Kottman, Richard N. *Reciprocity and the North Atlantic Triangle, 1932-1938*. Ithaca, NY: Cornell University Press, 1968.

Kylie, Edward. "The Workers Educational Association." *University Magazine* [Montreal] 12:4 (December 1913): 665-672.

Lamont, Edward W. *The Ambassador from Wall Street: The Story of Thomas W. Lamont, J. P. Morgan's Chief Executive*. Lanham, MD: Madison Books, 1994.

Larew, Karl G. "Great Britain and the Greco-Turkish War." *The Historian* 35:2 (February 1973): 256-270.

Lash, Joseph P. *Roosevelt and Churchill 1939-1941: The Partnership That Saved the West*. London: Andre Deutsch, 1977.

Lavin, Deborah. *From Empire to Commonwealth: A Biography of Lionel Curtis*. Oxford: Clarendon Press, 1995.

Leffler, Melvyn P. *The Elusive Quest: America's Pursuit of European Stability and French Security, 1919-1933*. Chapel Hill: University of North Carolina Press, 1979.

Lentin, A. *Lloyd George, Woodrow Wilson and the Guilt of Germany: An Essay in the Pre-History of Appeasement*. Baton Rouge: Louisiana State University Press, 1984.

Levy, David W. *Herbert Croly of The New Republic: The Life and Thought of an American Progressive*. Princeton, NJ: Princeton University Press, 1985.

Lockwood, P. A. "Milner's Entry into the War Cabinet, December 1916." *Historical Journal* 7:1 (March 1964): 120-134.

MacDougall, Walter A. *France's Rhineland Diplomacy, 1914-1924: The Last Bid for a Balance of Power in Europe*. Princeton, NJ: Princeton University Press, 1978.

Mahl, Thomas E. *Desperate Deception: British Covert Operations in the United States, 1939-44*. London: Brassey's, 1998.

Maiolo, Joseph A. *The Royal Navy and Nazi Germany, 1933-39: A Study in Appeasement and the Origins of the Second World War*. London: Macmillan, 2002.

Margulies, Herbert F. *The Mild Reservationists and the League of Nations Controversy in the Senate*. Columbia: University of Missouri Press, 1989.

Martin, George. *Madam Secretary: Frances Perkins*. Boston: Houghton Mifflin, 1976.

Matthew, H. C. G., and Brian Harrison. Eds. *Oxford Dictionary of National Biography: From the Earliest Times to the Year 2000*. 60 vols. Oxford: Oxford University Press, 2004.

May, Alexander C. "The Round Table, 1910-1966." D. Phil. thesis, Oxford University, 1995.

McDonald, J. Kenneth. "The Washington Conference and the Naval Balance of Power, 1921-22." In *Maritime Strategy and the Balance of Power: Britain and America in the Twentieth Century*. Eds. John B. Hattendorf and Robert S. Jordan. Basingstoke: Macmillan, 1989. Pp. 189-213.

Meacham, Standish. *Toynbee Hall and Social Reform 1880-1914: The Search for Community*. New Haven, CT: Yale University Press, 1987.

Middlebrook, Martin. *Convoy: The Battle of Convoys SC122 and HX229*. London: Allen Lane, 1976.

Miscamble, Wilson D. *George F. Kennan and the Making of American Foreign Policy, 1947-1950*. Princeton, NJ: Princeton University Press, 1992.

Molloy, Séan. *The Hidden History of Realism: A Genealogy of Power Politics*. New York: Palgrave Macmillan, 2006.

Murfett, Malcolm H. "Look Back in Anger: The Western Powers and the Washington Conference of 1921-1922." In *Arms Limitation and Disarmament: Restraints on War, 1899-1939*. Ed. B. J. C. McKercher. Westport, CT: Praeger, 1992. Pp. 83-104.

National Intelligence Council. *Global Trends 2025: A Transformed World*. Washington, DC: National Intelligence Council, 2008.

Naveh, Eyal. *Reinhold Niebuhr and Non-Utopian Liberalism: Beyond Illusion and Despair*. Brighton, UK: Sussex Academic Press, 2002.

Neilson, Keith. *Britain and the Last Tsar: British Policy and Russia, 1894-1917*. Oxford: Clarendon Press, 1995.

Neilson, Keith. *Britain, Soviet Russia and the Collapse of the Versailles Order, 1919-1939*. Cambridge: Cambridge University Press, 2005.

Neilson, Keith. "Defence and Diplomacy: The British Foreign Office and Singapore, 1939-1940." *Twentieth Century British History* 14:2 (June 2003): 138-164.

Neilson, Keith. "Perception and Posture in Anglo-American Relations: The Legacy of the Simon-Stimson Affair, 1932-1941." *The International History Review* 29:2 (June 2007): 313-337.

Neilson, Keith. "'That elusive entity British policy in Russia': The Impact of Russia on British Policy at the Paris Peace Conference." In *The Paris Peace Conference, 1919: Peace without Victory?* Eds. Michael Dockrill and John Fisher. Basingstoke and New York: Palgrave, 2001. Pp. 67-102.

Neilson, Keith. "'Unbroken Thread': Japan, Maritime power and British Imperial Defence, 1920-32." In *British Naval Strategy East of Suez, 1900-2000*. Ed. Greg Kennedy. London and New York: Frank Cass, 2005. Pp. 25-32.

Neilson, Keith, and T. G. Otte. *The Permanent Under-Secretary for Foreign Affairs, 1854-1946*. New York and London: Routledge, 2009.

Nelson, Keith L. *Victors Divided: America and the Allies in Germany, 1918-1923*. Berkeley and Los Angeles: University of California Press, 1975.

Nimocks, Walter. *Milner's Young Men: The 'Kindergarten' in Edwardian Imperial Affairs*. London: Hodder and Stoughton, 1970.

Nish, Ian H. *Alliance in Decline: A Study in Anglo-Japanese Relations 1908-23*. London: Athlone Press, 1972.

Nish, Ian H. *Japanese Foreign Policy in the Interwar Period*. Westport, CT: Praeger, 2002.

O'Halpin, Eunan. "British Intelligence in Ireland, 1914-1921." In *The Missing Dimension: Governments and Intelligence Communities in the Twentieth Century*. Eds. Christopher Andrew and David Dilks. London: Macmillan, 1984. Pp. 55-77.

Oliver, F. S. *Alexander Hamilton: An Essay on American Union*. London: A. Constable, 1906.

Padfield, Peter. *War Beneath the Sea: Submarine Conflict 1939-1945*. London: John Wiley, 1995.

Parmar, Inderjeet. "Anglo-American Elites in the Interwar Years: Idealism and Power in the Intellectual Roots of Chatham House and the Council on Foreign Relations." *International Relations* 16:1 (April 2002): 53-75.

Parmar, Inderjeet. "Chatham House and the Anglo-American Alliance." *Diplomacy and Statecraft* 3:1 (March 1992): 23-47.

Parmar, Inderjeet. *Special Interests, the State, and the Anglo-American Alliance, 1939-1945*. London: Frank Cass, 1995.

Parmar, Inderjeet. *Think Tanks and Power in Foreign Policy: A Comparative Study of the Role and Influence of the Council on Foreign Relations and the Royal Institute of International Affairs, 1939-1945*. Basingstoke: Palgrave Macmillan, 2004.

Parrini, Carl P. *Heir to Empire: United States Economic Diplomacy, 1916-1923*. Pittsburgh, PA: Pittsburgh University Press, 1969.

Patterson, Kathryn Segal. "The Decline of Dominance: India and the Careers of Lionel Curtis, Philip Lothian, and Reginald Coupland." Ph.D. dissertation, Bryn Mawr College, 1989.

Perkins, Bradford. *The Great Rapprochement: Britain and the United States, 1895-1914*. New York: Atheneum, 1968.

Pruessen, Ronald W. *John Foster Dulles: The Road to Power*. New York: Free Press, 1982.

Puleston, W. D. *Mahan: The Life and Works of Captain Alfred Thayer Mahan.* New Haven, CT: Yale University Press, 1939.

Quigley, Carroll. *The Anglo-American Establishment: From Rhodes to Cliveden.* New York: Books in Focus, 1981.

Ramsden, John. *Man of the Century: Winston Churchill and His Legend Since 1945.* New York: Columbia University Press, 2003.

Reitzel, William. "Mahan on Use of the Sea." In *War, Strategy, and Maritime Power.* Ed. B. Mitchell Simpson III. New Brunswick, NJ: Rutgers University Press, 1977. Pp. 95-107.

Reynolds, David. "FDR and the British: A Postscript." *Massachusetts Historical Society Proceedings* 90 (1978): 106-110.

Reynolds, David. *In Command of History: Churchill Fighting and Writing the Second World War.* New York: Random House, 2005.

Reynolds, David. *Lord Lothian and Anglo-American Relations, 1939-1940.* Philadelphia, PA: Transactions of the American Philosophical Society, 1983.

Reynolds, David. *The Creation of the Anglo-American Alliance, 1937-41: A Study in Competitive Co-operation.* Chapel Hill: University of North Carolina Press, 1982.

Rhodes, Benjamin D. "The British Royal Visit of 1939 and the 'Psychological Approach' to the United States." *Diplomatic History* 2:2 (Spring 1978): 197-211.

Roberts, Andrew. *"The Holy Fox": The Life of Lord Halifax.* London: Weidenfeld and Nicolson, 1991.

Roberts, Priscilla. "Lord Lothian and the Atlantic World." *The Historian* 66:1 (March 2004): 97-127.

Roberts, Priscilla. "The American 'Eastern Establishment' and World War I: The Emergence of a Foreign Policy Tradition." Ph.D. dissertation, Cambridge University, 1981.

Roberts, Priscilla. "The Anglo-American Theme: American Visions of an Atlantic Alliance, 1914-1933." *Diplomatic History* 21:3 (Summer 1997): 333-364.

Roberts, Priscilla. "'The Council Has Been Your Creation': Hamilton Fish Armstrong, Paradigm of the American Foreign Policy Establishment." *Journal of American Studies* 35:1 (April 2001): 65-94.

Roberts, Priscilla. "Underpinning the Anglo-American Alliance: The Council on Foreign Relations and Britain between the Wars." In *Twentieth-Century Anglo-American Relations.* Ed. Jonathan Hollowell. London: Palgrave, 2001. Pp. 25-43.

Roberts, Priscilla. "Willard D. Straight and the Diplomacy of International Finance During the First World War." *Business History* 40:3 (July 1998): 16-47.

Roberts, Priscilla. "Willard Straight, World War I, and 'Internationalism of All Sorts': The Inconsistencies of an American Liberal Interventionist." *Australian Journal of Politics and History* 44:4 (December 1998): 493-511.

Roberts, Priscilla. "World War I and Anglo-American Relations: The Role of Philip Lothian and *The Round Table.*" *The Round Table* 95:383 (January 2006): 113-139.

Rofe, J. Simon. *Franklin D. Roosevelt's Foreign Policy and the Welles Mission.* New York: Palgrave, 2007.

Rofe, J. Simon. "Prescription and Remedy: Lothian's Influence upon Anglo-American Relations during the Phony War." *The Round Table* 96:389 (April 2007): 155-175.

Rose, Norman. *The Cliveden Set: Portrait of an Exclusive Fraternity.* London: Jonathan Cape, 2000.

Rosenthal, Joel H. *Righteous Realists: Political Realism, Responsible Power, and American Culture in the Nuclear Age.* Baton Rouge: Louisiana State University Press, 1991.

Roskill, Stephen. *Hankey: Man of Secrets.* 3 vols. London: Collins, 1970-1974.

Roskill, Stephen W. *Naval Policy Between the Wars*, Vol. I: *The Period of Anglo-American Antagonism, 1919-1929.* London: Collins, 1968.

Roskill, Stephen W. *Naval Policy Between the Wars*, Vol. II: *The Period of Reluctant Rearmament, 1930-1939.* London: Collins, 1976.

Roskill, Stephen. *The War at Sea 1939-45*, Vol. I: *The Defensive.* London: Her Majesty's Stationery Office, 1976.

Rothwell, V. H. *British War Aims and Peace Diplomacy 1914-1918.* London: Oxford University Press, 1971.

Rowland, Peter. *Lloyd George.* London: Barrie and Jenkins, 1975.

Rowse, A. L. *Appeasement: A Study in Political Decline.* New York: Norton, 1963.

Russell, Greg J. *Hans J. Morgenthau and the Ethics of American Statecraft.* Baton Rouge: Louisiana State University Press, 1990.

Schaeper, Thomas J., and Kathleen Schaeper. *Rhodes Scholars, Oxford, and the Creation of an American Elite.* New York: Berghahn Books, 1998.

Schieren, Stefan. *Vom Weltreich zum Weltstaat: Philip Kerrs (Lord Lothian) Weg vom Imperialisten zum Internationalisten, 1905-1925.* London: Lothian Foundation, 1996.

Schulzinger, Robert D. *The Wise Men of Foreign Affairs: The History of the Council on Foreign Relations.* New York: Columbia University Press, 1984.

Seager, Robert, II. *Alfred Thayer Mahan: The Man and His Letters.* Annapolis, MD: Naval Institute Press, 1977.

Seaman, John T., Jr. *A Citizen of the World: The Life of James Bryce.* London and New York: I. B. Tauris, 2006.

Searle, Geoffrey R. *The Quest for National Efficiency: A Study in British Politics and Political Thought, 1899-1914.* Oxford: Basil Blackwell, 1967.

Seeley, John Robert. *The Expansion of England.* Ed. John Gross. Chicago: Chicago University Press, 1971. Reprint of 1883 book.

Seidemann, David. *The New Republic: A Voice of Modern Liberalism.* New York: Praeger, 1986.

Semmel, Bernard. *Liberalism & Naval Strategy: Ideology, Interest, and Sea Power during the Pax Britannica.* Boston, MA: Allen and Unwin, 1986.

Sharp, Alan J. "The Foreign Office in Eclipse 1919-22." *History* 61:202 (June 1976): 198-218.

Shepardson, Whitney H. *The Early History of the Council on Foreign Relations.* Stamford, CT: Overbrook Press, 1960.

Smith, Michael Joseph. *Realist Thought from Weber to Kissinger.* Baton Rouge: Louisiana State University Press, 1990.

Smith, Michael W. *History and International Relations.* New York: Routledge, 1999.

Steel, Ronald. *Walter Lippmann and the American Century.* Boston: Little, Brown, 1980.

Stein, Leonard. *The Balfour Declaration.* New York: Simon and Schuster, 1961.

Steiner, Zara. *The Lights That Failed: European International History, 1919-1933.* Oxford: Oxford University Press, 2005.

Stewart, A. T. Q. *The Ulster Crisis.* London: Faber, 1967.

Stocks, Mary. *The Workers Educational Association: The First Fifty Years.* London: George Allen and Unwin, 1953.

Stone, Ralph. "The Irreconcilables' Alternatives to the League of Nations." *Mid-America* 49:3 (July 1967): 163-173.

Stone, Ralph. *The Irreconcilables: The Fight Against the League of Nations.* New York: Norton, 1973.

Sumida, Jon Tetsuo. *Inventing Grand Strategy and Teaching Command: The Classic Works of Alfred Thayer Mahan.* Washington, DC, and Baltimore, MD: Woodrow Wilson Center Press and Johns Hopkins University Press, 1997.

Swaine, Robert T. *The Cravath Firm and Its Predecessors, 1819-1938.* 2 vols. New York: n.p., 1946-1948.

Swift, Will. *The Kennedys Amidst the Gathering Storm: A Thousand Days in London, 1938-1940.* New York: HarperCollins, 2008.

Sykes, Christopher. *Nancy: The Life of Lady Astor.* New York: Harper and Row, 1972.

Symonds, Richard. *Oxford and Empire: The Last Lost Cause?* Basingstoke: Macmillan, 1986.

Taylor, A. J. P. *English History 1914-1945.* Oxford: Clarendon Press, 1992.

Temperley, H. W. V. *A History of the Peace Conference of Paris.* 6 vols. London: Hodder and Stoughton, 1920-1924.

Terraine, John. *Business in Great Waters: The U-Boat Wars 1916-1945*. London: Leo Cooper, 1989.

Thompson, John A. *Reformers and War: American progressive publicists and the First World War*. Cambridge: Cambridge University Press, 1987.

Thompson, Laurence. *1940: Year of Legend, Year of History*. London: Collins, 1996.

Thorne, Christopher. *Allies of a Kind: The United States, Britain, and the War Against Japan, 1941-1945*. Oxford: Oxford University Press, 1979.

Tilchin, William N. *Theodore Roosevelt and the British Empire: A Study in Presidential Statecraft*. New York: St. Martin's Press, 1997.

Tillman, Seth P. *Anglo-American Relations at the Paris Peace Conference of 1919*. Princeton, NJ: Princeton University Press, 1961.

Turner, John. *Lloyd George's Secretariat*. Cambridge: Cambridge University Press, 1980.

Turner, John. Ed. *The Larger Idea: Lord Lothian and the Problem of National Sovereignty*. London: Historians Press, 1988.

Tyler, J. E. *The Struggle for Imperial Unity (1868-1895)*. London: Longmans Green, 1938.

Ullman, Richard H. *Anglo-Soviet Relations, 1917-1921*, Vol. II: *Britain and the Russian Civil War*. Princeton, NJ: Princeton University Press, 1968.

van der Pijl, Kees. *The Making of an Atlantic Ruling Class*. London: Verso, 1984.

Vincent, Andrew, and Raymond Plant. *Philosophy, Politics and Citizenship: The Life and Thought of the British Idealists*. Oxford: Basil Blackwell 1984.

Ward, Alan J. *Ireland and Anglo-American Relations, 1899-1921*. London: Weidenfeld and Nicolson, 1969.

Water, Christopher. "Casey: Four Decades in the Making of Australian Foreign Policy." *Australian Journal of Politics and History* 51:3 (September 2005): 380-388.

Watt, D. C. *Personalities and Policies: Studies in the Formulation of British Policy in the Twentieth Century*. London: Longmans, 1965.

Watt, D. C. *Succeeding John Bull: America in Britain's Place, 1900-1975*. Cambridge: Cambridge University Press, 1984.

West, Trevor. *Horace Plunkett: Co-operation and Politics, an Irish Biography*. Washington, DC: Catholic University of America Press, 1986.

Wheeler-Bennett, John W. *King George VI: His Life and Reign*. London: Macmillan, 1958.

Whitham, Charlie. "On Dealing with Gangsters: The Limits of British 'Generosity' in the Lease of Bases to the United States, 1940-41." *Diplomacy and Statecraft* 7:3 (November 1996): 589-630.

Williamson, David. "Great Britain and the Ruhr Crisis, 1923-1924." *British Journal of International Studies* 3:1 (April 1977): 70-91.

Wilson, Andrew J. *Irish America and the Ulster Conflict, 1968-1995.* Washington, DC: Catholic University of America Press, 1995.

Yearwood, Peter J. "'Real Securities against New Wars': Official British Thinking and the Origins of the League of Nations, 1914-19." *Diplomacy and Statecraft* 9:3 (November 1998): 83-109.

Young, Robert J. *In Command of France: French Policy and Military Planning, 1933-1940.* Cambridge, MA: Harvard University Press, 1978.

Zakaria, Fareed. *The Post-American World.* New York: W. W. Norton, 2008.

Ziegler, Philip. *Legacy: Cecil Rhodes, the Rhodes Trust and Rhodes Scholarships.* New Haven, CT: Yale University Press, 2008.

Zimmermann, Warren. *First Great Triumph: How Five Americans Made Their Country into a World Power.* New York: Farrar, Straus and Giroux, 2002.

ELECTRONIC SOURCES

The British Embassy website. http://britainusa.com/.

The Moot website. http://www.moot.org.uk/.

Time Magazine online. http://www.time.com.

INDEX

History of International Relations Diplomacy and Intelligence

Editor: Katherine A.S. Sibley

14 Kimberly Jensen and Erika Kuhlman (eds.), *Women and Transnational Activism in Historical Perspective*. 2010. (edited volume)
> hardback, ISBN 978-90-8979-037-8
> paperback, ISBN 978-90-8979-038-5

13 Priscilla Roberts (ed.), *Lord Lothian and Anglo-American Relations, 1900-1940*. 2010. (edited volume)
> hardback, ISBN 978-90-8979-034-7
> paperback, ISBN 978-90-8979-033-0

12 John W. Young and Raj Roy (eds.), *Ambassador to Sixties London: The Diaries of David Bruce, 1961-1969*. 2010. (source publication)
> hardback, ISBN 978-90-8979-013-2
> paperback, ISBN 978-90-8979-030-9

11 Nigel J. Brailey, *Imperial Amnesia: Britain, France and "the Question of Siam"*. 2010. (monograph)
> hardback, ISBN 978-90-8979-014-9
> paperback, ISBN 978-90-8979-026-2

10 Bruce Russell, *Prize Courts and U-boats: International Law at Sea and Economic Warfare during the First World War*. 2010. (monograph)
> hardback, ISBN 978-90-8979-011-8
> paperback, ISBN 978-90-8979-025-5

9 Tor Egil Førland, *Cold Economic Warfare: CoCom and the Forging of Strategic Export Controls, 1948-1954*. 2010. (monograph)
> hardback, ISBN 978-90-8979-012-5
> paperback, ISBN 978-90-8979-024-8

8 Gregory Russell, *The Statecraft of Theodore Roosevelt: The Duties of Nations and World Order*. 2009. (monograph)
> hardback, ISBN 978-90-04-17445-0
> paperback, ISBN 978-90-8979-023-1

7 Michael Salter, *US Intelligence, the Holocaust and the Nuremberg Trials*. 2009. (monograph)
> 2 volumes, hardback, ISBN 978-90-04-17277-7

6 Simon Davis, *Contested Space: Anglo-American Relations in the Persian Gulf, 1939-1947*. 2009. (monograph)
> hardback, ISBN 978-90-04-17130-5

5 Sean Greenwood, *Titan at the Foreign Office: Gladwyn Jebb and the Shaping of the Modern World*. 2008. (monograph)
> hardback, ISBN 978 90 04 16970 8

History of International Relations Diplomacy and Intelligence

Editor: Katherine A.S. Sibley

---

4 Louis Sicking, *Colonial Borderlands. France and the Netherlands in the Atlantic in the 19th century*. 2008. (monograph)

hardback, ISBN 978-90-04-16960-9

3 Andrew Stewart & Christopher Baxter (eds.), *Diplomats at War. British and Commonwealth Diplomacy in Wartime*. 2008. (edited volume)

hardback, ISBN 978-90-04-16897-8

2 Thomas Richard Davies, *The Possibilities of Transnational Activism and Its Limits: The Campaign for Disarmament between the Two World Wars*. 2008. (monograph)

hardback, ISBN 978-90-04-16258-7

1 Geoff Berridge, *Gerald Fitzmaurice (1865-1939), Chief Dragoman of the British Embassy in Turkey*. 2007. (monograph)

hardback, ISBN 978-90-04-16035-4

REPUBLIC OF LETTERS PUBLISHING – DORDRECHT
WWW.ROLPUB.COM/IRDI

9 789089 790330